THE TRANSFORMATION OF THE CLASSICAL HERITAGE

Peter Brown, General Editor

THE MAKING OF A HERETIC

VIRGINIA BURRUS

THE MAKING
OF A HERETIC

Gender, Authority, and the Priscillianist Controversy

UNIVERSITY OF CALIFORNIA PRESS
Berkeley · Los Angeles · London

University of California Press
Berkeley and Los Angeles, California

University of California Press, Ltd.
London, England

© 1995 by
The Regents of the University of California

Burrus, Virginia.
    The making of a heretic : gender, authority, and the
    Priscillianist controversy / Virginia Burrus
        p.   cm.—(Transformation of the classical heritage ; 24)
    Includes bibliographical references and index.
    ISBN 0-520-08997-9 (alk. paper)
    1. Priscillianism.   2. Priscillian, Bishop of Avila, ca. 350–385.   3. Women
in Christianity—Spain—History—Early church, ca. 30–600.
I. Title. II. Series.
BT1465.B87   1995
273'.4—dc20   94-33270
                                                                           CIP

Printed in the United States of America
9 8 7 6 5 4 3 2 1

Τάδε ἔμαθον ἔγωγε ὑπὸ τῶν σοφίας μετεχόντων,
αστείων, θεοδιδάκτων, κατὰ πάντα σοφῶν τε.
Τούτων κατ' ἴχνος ἦλθον ἐγώ βαίνων ὁμοδόξως.

These things I learned from those partaking in wisdom,
refined, divinely taught, wise in all things.
I came in their footsteps, walking in like opinion.

Arius, *Thalia*

For my teacher Rebecca

CONTENTS

PREFACE

A text, "once issued, can never be recalled," Sulpicius Severus wisely observed, and I am tempted, if not to abstain altogether from publishing this monograph, at least to defer doing so. By holding on to these pages a bit longer, I might not so much tell a different or better tale as give a better account of why the tale is worth telling in the first place. With Jerome, I have continued to ask, "Why speak of Priscillian, who was condemned by the secular sword and by the whole world?" In the course of the long gestation of this project, new answers have emerged for me, without entirely displacing previous responses.

Despite my confessed hesitance, I am also unquestionably relieved to be delivered of the burden of this work. The comparison of texts to children, of writing to labor, is by no means novel—it was already a rhetorical commonplace in late antiquity. The metaphor may, however, claim particular suitability in this case. The account of the Priscillianist controversy was conceived simultaneously with my first child, James, and written in the form of a doctoral dissertation during his infancy. The dissertation manuscript then travelled with me from West Coast to East, at which point I was again pregnant; and the journey also led to my own birth as a professional scholar, entering upon a first academic appointment. The revising of the dissertation into something recognizable as a book took place during the infancy of my second child, Mary, and, as it seems to me now, may represent not simply the maturing of an old work but also the overlaying of a second, new work upon the first.

For better or for worse, this text does not articulate a single, monologic perspective: one voice, for example, situates itself in the trajectory of social history; another explores the history of theology; still another drifts toward the analysis of discursive practices sometimes associated with the "cultural poetics" of the "new historicism." Aware that I have not succeeded altogether in harmonizing the multiple voices, I nevertheless hope to have struck a few resonant chords. I hope, too, that I have managed to tell a good story, without producing a deceptively tidy account.

This book is the offspring of a feminist scholar, but to what extent is it a feminist text? Tracing the threads from which late-ancient constructions of gender were woven, I quickly found myself entangled in altogether unexpected issues: finally, this study is "about," not women or gender, but rather the controversy over Priscillian. If gender and authority are prominent among the issues at stake in the disputes surrounding Priscillian and his followers, the documented preoccupation with these two issues points, I suggest, to three factors that crucially shaped the late-fourth-century Priscillianist controversy: the late-ancient construction of orthodoxy and heresy; the divergence between public and private perspectives on Christian community; and the conflict between accommodating and alienated stances toward the world. I not only attempt to address certain gaps and weaknesses in current Priscillianist scholarship by suggesting new interpretive frameworks; I also modify the dominant source theory first proposed by E.-Ch. Babut in 1909. Finally, too, I offer different or more detailed interpretations of recently discovered or previously neglected texts, such as the *Acts of the Council of Saragossa*, Priscillian's *Apology*, the *Acts of the Council of Toledo*, and a recently discovered letter from Consentius to Augustine.

It has not been my intention to examine all the texts dealing with Priscillianism or to offer an exhaustive account of the movement and its detractors; here the works of Benedikt Vollman and Henry Chadwick will probably remain standard for some time. Nor, obviously, does this study investigate similar controversies in the late-ancient Christian world, although it may be of relevance to them to the extent that the phenomena I describe, including both the strategies of labeling and the conflicts over gender, authority, and understandings of Christian community, were broadly characteristic of late-ancient Christianity. Elizabeth Clark's *The Origenist Controversy*, a study of the "cultural construction" of another late-fourth-century Christian debate, which appeared as I revised this manuscript for publication, illumines many areas of overlap among the contemporary disputes about Priscillianism, Origenism, and Pelagianism, while also persuading us to attend more closely to the nuances of these anthropological, ecclesiological, and cosmological controversies, so often overshadowed as a result of the privileged status traditionally granted the "high" trinitarian and christological debates of the fourth and fifth centuries.

First and foremost among the various midwiving communities that have sustained my work is my Bay Area dissertation committee, made up of Rebecca Lyman, Marty Stortz, Susanna Elm, and Robert Gregg; I am particularly grateful to Rebecca, who has been a faithful friend, an infinitely tactful and tolerant mentor, and an unsurpassed partner in scholarly conversation for a decade now, as we have shared our passion for late-ancient Christianity and sought to unravel the tangled constructions of orthodoxy and heresy. Special thanks are also owed to Ray Van Dam of the University of Michigan, who very generously agreed to long-distance mentorship of a feminist church history student from the Graduate Theological Union in Berkeley; his critical, thorough, and frequently skeptical responses to the dissertation saved me from various errors of mistranslation and interpretive misjudgment. Finally, I must acknowledge my daily companions in the San Francisco flat where I wrote the initial drafts of this text, including Soraya Merlos and two very little boys, one of them my son. Soraya not only made it possible for me to work on the dissertation without the constant distraction of childcare; she also taught me much about the disciplined, prayerful, Bible-centered spirituality of the small Christian communities that gather in the private space of somebody's living room or garage—and occasionally (in the densely packed living conditions of San Francisco's Mission District) provoke the neighbors' hostility with overimpassioned hymn singing or other disturbing displays of religious zeal.

On the East Coast, new study circles emerged to provide the context for revisions. I am grateful to colleagues and graduate students at Drew University who read parts of the manuscript, to the Theological School there for its financial support of my research, and to Peter Brown, a most welcoming neighbor at nearby Princeton. Extralocal networks have likewise continued to enrich my work: Harry Maier, Patricia Cox Miller, Mark Vessey, and Dan Williams all offered extremely helpful readings of portions of the manuscript; and I have also received extraordinarily respectful and provocative critiques from the University of California Press and its readers, including not only the series editor, Peter Brown, but also Liz Clark and Philip Rousseau. Finally, my husband, Bob Kelly, has accompanied me on this journey from dissertation to book, from studenthood to professorship, from West to East Coast; for this least "Priscillianist" of my sustaining relationships, I give thanks.

INTRODUCTION

"Why Is Contemporary Scholarship So Enamored of Ancient Heretics?"
So runs the title of a paper presented at Oxford's 1979 Eighth International
Conference on Patristic Studies.[1] Subsequent years have only intensified
this academic infatuation: extending sympathy to the ultimate losers in the
debates of the past, Patristic scholars have continued to be drawn to revisionist interpretations of ancient theological controversies. From one perspective, the recent fascination with controversy merely echoes the polemical preoccupations of the ancient texts, which inhabit a rhetorical
universe shaped by the pressures of an intensely competitive society. But
with the waves of postmodernist cultural theory beginning to lap at the
edges even of the highly conservative fields of ancient history and historical theology, other answers to the question of the current lure of the heretical also suggest themselves. A heightened interest in the subaltern and
the subversive flourishes in pockets of inquiry dispersed throughout the
academy, as scholars seek to uncover the strategies by which men and
women have historically resisted the social and discursive disciplines, the
"regimes of truth," of which orthodoxies are formed. As the clarity of the
monologic becomes suspect, a new appreciation emerges for the complexity of the dialogic, the many-voiced speech of the historical texts.

For scholars of ancient Christianity seeking to develop a postmodern
hermeneutic, gnosticism remains a rich resource,[2] both in the seeming
exuberance of its early resistance to the emergent Christian orthodoxy and
in the unusual fact of the accessibility of those "other" voices once again
made audible through the mid-twentieth-century rediscovery of the Nag

Hammadi corpus.[3] At the same time, the multifaceted evolution of orthodoxy and heresy in the Constantinian churches has begun to exert its own
fascination in the "heresy-enamored" pockets of Patristic scholarship, giving shape to a distinctive and equally compelling narrative that plays itself
out in both local and empirewide arenas. When volumes on Donatism,
Arianism, Nestorianism, and, most recently, Origenism have captured the
scholarly imagination, there is space for another look at Priscillianism.
Wedged into the westernmost corner of the empire and seeming initially
to represent just one more idiosyncratic local variant of Manichaeism,
Priscillian's geographically and theologically marginal heresy nevertheless demands attention based on its leader's unprecedented execution and
the intriguing fluidity of the movement's ambiguous texts, accessible since
their 1885 rediscovery in Germany. Stemming from Priscillian's own circle,
the so-called Würzburg tractates, like their Nag Hammadi counterparts,
offer an insider's view of a heresy, revealing the subtle strategies by which
a religious movement both resisted and coopted the late-ancient discourse
of orthodoxy in a time of particular social and cultural flux.

Like the gnostics, Priscillian had long been known from the reports of
hostile sources, and these continue to shape our understanding of him,
providing an unavoidable first context for the interpretation of Priscillianist works.[4] According to Sulpicius Severus' *Chronicle*, the most important of the sources, Priscillian began his career as a lay teacher with particular influence among women. His ascetic disciplines and supposedly
gnosticizing doctrines produced controversy and division within the
churches of Spain, and in 380 his practices and teachings were attacked by
a small group of Spanish and Aquitanian bishops gathered at Saragossa.
Soon thereafter Priscillian was consecrated bishop of Avila by other bishops friendly to his cause, but he and his two strongest episcopal supporters were subsequently forced to leave their sees in order to defend themselves against charges of heresy and an illegitimate episcopacy. Priscillian
and his colleague Instantius were eventually reinstated, only to be summoned thereafter to appear as defendants before an episcopal council at
Bordeaux. When Instantius was deposed by the council, Priscillian appealed his own case to the emperor. This appeal did not have the hoped
result: charges of heresy were augmented with accusations of sorcery and
sexual immorality, and circa 386 Priscillian and several of his associates,
including the Aquitanian noblewoman Euchrotia, were executed at Trier
by order of the emperor Magnus Maximus himself.[5] The ascetic's violent
end gave rise to continuing conflict. At the beginning of the fifth century,
the Gallic churches were still divided over the role played by the bishops
who had testified against Priscillian, and a core of supporters in the Gali-

cian province of northwestern Spain continued to honor Priscillian as a martyr for decades, if not longer,[6] while others agreed in condemning him as a heretic. Indeed, the charges against Priscillian were further elaborated after his death, at least partly in an effort to justify his brutal execution. Severus and other fifth-century sources depict the Spanish teacher variously as a gnostic seducer, a Manichaean astrologer, a Sabellian, a Samosatene, and the founder of a new heresy of "Priscillianism."[7]

In the course of the past century, the long-available sources on Priscillian have been brought into dialogue with the texts found at Würzburg: three apologetic works, seven Lenten homilies, and one prayer, produced within the circle of late-fourth-century Spanish heretics and probably written by Priscillian himself.[8] The second of the Würzburg tractates, a letter to Bishop Damasus of Rome, confirms the basic reliability of Severus' account of events from shortly before the Council of Saragossa to Priscillian's first departure from Spain, during which time the letter was composed. However, in other respects the tractates disrupt the heresiological tradition transmitted by Severus and others: the anticipated indications of blatant gnostic, Manichaean, or monarchian errors are elusive, if not altogether absent. The tractates reveal the thoughts of an ascetic exegete whose "road" (iter)[9] or "discipline of life" (vivendi . . . disciplinam)[10] is mapped by the traditional baptismal creed[11] and supported by the witness of the canonical scriptures. Priscillian does indeed defend the use of apocryphal writings, some of which he acknowledges to have been corrupted by heretical editors. However, his defense is based solidly on the authority of the canonical scriptures: he urges that the canonical text itself both impels the Christian scholar beyond canonical boundaries and enables the scholar to separate the wheat from the tares of heretical interpolation.[12] Similarly, Priscillian's exegesis of canonical texts does support a mitigated dualism on both anthropological and cosmological fronts. Yet in spite of his ambiguous assessment of temporal and embodied existence, Priscillian distinguishes his understanding of the material cosmos sharply from that of the Manichaeans,[13] insisting not only on the ultimate goodness of the material and temporal creation[14] but also on the potential holiness of the human body as a dwelling place suitable for God.[15] Finally, in a period in which trinitarian orthodoxy eluded even the most acute and well-informed Greek-speaking theologians, the high christology and strong monotheism implicit in Priscillian's repeated references to the "God Christ" do not seem to constitute any significant divergence from the western Nicene mainstream.[16]

Even this brief account should suggest some of the new paths of investigation opened up by the Würzburg tractates. The Priscillianist texts

have first of all challenged the heresiological claim that the opposition to
Priscillian derived primarily from his propagation of doctrines widely acknowledged by his contemporaries to be heretical. Church historians have
long tended to doctrinalize religious controversy narrowly by utilizing
predefined categories of theological deviance to identify the villains in the
Christian story. Predictably, then, some scholars have attempted to sal-
vage the portrait of Priscillian as a gnostic, a Manichaean, or a monarchian, claiming either that the tractates are not reliable evidence for Priscillian's secret heretical teachings or that there are hints of heretical beliefs
even in the tractates.[17] Nevertheless, there is a growing consensus that
these categories fail to capture the unorthodoxy of Priscillian's thought, as
measured by the doctrinal standards and religious sensibilities of his own
time. It consequently becomes necessary to look beyond conventional labels of theological deviance in order to understand the roots of the conflict
that brought about the condemnation and execution of Priscillian. Indeed,
one of the fascinations of the study of this controversy is that it nudges
scholarship off the narrow and well-trodden paths of doctrinal classifica-
tion, disrupting the false clarity offered by the categories of orthodoxy and
heresy—or, for that matter, by their modern sociological counterparts,
church and sect. Only by abandoning these paths, it seems, can we com-
prehend more fully the roots of the deep fear and mistrust that Priscillian,
and later "Priscillianism," inspired.

If the Würzburg tractates allow a clearer view of Priscillian, they also
reveal much about his opposition. By providing a more accurate impression of Priscillian's thought, the tractates help to clarify the source of his
opponents' outrage. Equally important, these documents allow a glimpse
into the evolving mechanisms of late-ancient orthodoxy. Used with caution—for Priscillian himself is not always reliable—the tractates offer a
standard of comparison against which the rhetorical strategies of Priscillian's detractors can be more clearly understood and appreciated. And insofar as they preserve a contemporary and firsthand account of the early
years of the controversy, the tractates expand our knowledge of the accusations Priscillian's opponents actually leveled against him. It becomes
possible to explore in some detail the process by which various labels of
deviance were crafted and invoked in order to define and strengthen late-
fourth-century constructs of orthodoxy.

"Why do I speak about Priscillian, who has been condemned by the
secular sword and by the whole world?"[18] Jerome's rhetorical question
gives expression to the interest that motivates this study and finally impels
it well beyond the Priscillianist tractates themselves. Why and how did
Christians of late antiquity "speak about Priscillian" both in the years

prior to his execution and in the decades following his death? The following pages trace the strategies of labeling deployed in the controversy surrounding Priscillian, locating these within the broader history of Christian heresiology. At the same time, looking beyond the particular offenses highlighted in the heresiological sources, this study seeks to identify and analyze the broader underlying cosmological and social conflicts negotiated through the "talk" about Priscillian. Disputes about authority and gender roles frequently surface in the ancient sources documenting the Priscillianist controversy. These, I suggest, point to larger anthropological, ecclesiological, and cosmological debates centering around fundamental questions about the nature of the Christian community and the relation of that community to the surrounding world.

Priscillian and his followers seem to have displayed little interest in distinguishing women's roles from those of men, and this very disregard scandalized their opponents. Additionally, the Priscillianist Christians were quick to recognize the informal authority of the exceptional ascetic, exegete, or teacher, while their detractors were more keenly attuned to the official authority wielded by bishops and clergy. These diverging attitudes toward gender and authority provide clues to the issues at the heart of the Priscillianist controversy: namely, the fundamental differences of perspective on the nature and location of the Christian community and its relation to the extra-ecclesial world. Was the church a "political" community in which relationships between individuals were sharply delineated by the hierarchical ranks of office and gender? Or was it a "familiar" social body in which relationships were ordered by the more fluid hierarchies of birth, material resources, experience, education, or personal gifts of insight or eloquence? Should the Christian community accommodate itself to the surrounding culture and society? Or was that community compelled to protest the corrupting influence of the secular arena with its dominant public hierarchies of office and gender? Correspondingly, were Christians fundamentally in harmony with the divinely created cosmos, or were they called to wage battle with the evil forces of a fallen world?

Members of the same late-fourth-century Spanish congregations seem to have answered these questions very differently, and their divergent outlooks derived in part from an ambivalent Christian heritage. The irrepressible authority of the prophet, visionary, confessor, and teacher had long sought an uneasy resting place along the edges of an emergent hierarchy of ecclesiastical office. Moreover, even in times of peace, Christian literature continued to interweave repeated invocations of the radical disjunction of the martyr's death with the strains of an assimilating apologetic. Affirmations of the goodness of the created order were juxtaposed with profound expressions of the distance separating the fallen material cosmos from its heavenly counterpart—conflicting sensibilities only occasionally brought together coherently within the conceptual framework of a theological genius like Origen. For at least two centuries, accusations of heresy had been used to clarify unsettling ambiguities and conflicts arising out of the varying interpretations of a complex tradition, and the orthodoxy that had emerged was appropriately malleable, constantly reshaped in response to pressures that shifted with time and place.

If the Spanish dispute had its roots in earlier Christian tradition, it also had a peculiarly late antique cast. In a period of social flux, divergent secular social models affected the church both indirectly, by a kind of cultural osmosis, and more directly through the influence of newly converted upper-class men and women who were accustomed to exercising authority within the secular realm. At the same time, on the cosmological front, late-ancient Christians responded variously to dual pressures of transcendence and anti-determinism as they confronted theological problems that seemed to emerge with new clarity in a society reorganizing itself around a simplified and radicalized contrast between the very powerful and the powerless.[19] Tracing these fourth-century influences and pressures, it is possible to identify two strands running through the documents of the Priscillianist controversy: first, the divergence between public and private perspectives and, second, the divergence between culturally accommodating and culturally alienated strategies of social and theological self-definition. One notes finally that the negotiation of the dispute between Priscillian and his opponents took place in the context of an imperial patronage of Christianity that lent new urgency to the old questions of orthodoxy and heresy; the fourth-century constructions of orthodoxy and heresy form the third connective strand of this interpretation.

Mapping the Christian Community: The Shifting Boundaries of Public and Private Spheres

The terms "public" and "private" have the advantage of a certain familiarity and intuitive comprehensibility. Thus, the general editor Georges Duby, in his foreword to the first volume of the *History of Private Life*, can avoid lengthy definitions of the private by simply appealing to the "obvious fact" that "at all times and in all places a clear, commonsensical distinction has been made between the public—that which is open to the community and subject to the authority of its magistrates—and the private."[20] Indeed, as terms of "ordinary discourse" evoking "unreflectively held notions and concepts" that shape day-to-day lives,[21] "public" and "private" may not appear in need of interpretation at all. But it is doubtful whether the dichotomous categories with which so many operate are in fact either as universal or as transparently "commonsensical" as is sometimes claimed. Indeed, I would suggest that the public-private distinction is most fruitfully applied to the study of the Priscillianist controversy precisely because it is an artifact of the very Mediterranean cultures that shaped the terms of the late-ancient controversy. Having received its classic articulation in the works of Athenian philosophers, it became part of the cultural *koine* of hellenistic Greece and of Rome, whence it has seeped so deeply into Western consciousness that the dichotomous construct seems to reflect some "obvious" aspect of all social life. The public-private distinction remains useful as an analytical tool that resonates not only with our own habits of thought but also with the self-understanding of the late-ancient cultures with which we are concerned. But at the same time it is itself a cultural construct, which must be contextualized and interpreted in its particularity.[22]

Briefly summarized, the classical elaboration of the public-private distinction rests on the assertion that human society is typically organized into households and political states, social units that can be distinguished by group, function, physical space, and hierarchical relationship to one another. "The household is the community established by nature for all daily needs," writes Aristotle; it includes free men and women, children, slaves, and additional property required for the production of food, clothing, and other necessities of life. The political state, composed of all free male heads of households, provides an overarching structure that both unifies and subordinates these individual households, while serving as the locus of higher culture. Whereas the household supplies basic needs for living, the political state exists "for the sake of living *well*" and thereby constitutes the final cause and goal of all human social organization. It is in this sense that the human being—or more accurately, *man*—can be defined as "a political animal."[23]

The seemingly neutral and descriptive terms of this formulation should not obscure the fact that such a conceptualization of the public-private dichotomy crystallized within a very particular and highly charged context—namely, the fragile democratic polity of classical Athens. Articulated from a public, male perspective, the classical public-private distinction undergirded a political ideology that strained to defend the privileged status of public life by restricting public access to a limited group of male citizens, while at the same time weakening the pull of the private sphere on those men. As part of a publicly centered discourse, the public-private dichotomy inevitably constructed the private sphere as the realm of the "other," defined in relation to a public, political "self."

The political theorist Jean Bethke Elshtain suggests that "politics is in part an elaborate defense against the tug of the private, against the lure of the familial, against evocations of female power."[24] Her statement illumines certain dynamics of ancient Greek texts, which frequently depict the quintessentially "familiar" and nurturing sphere of the household as paradoxically alien and threatening. Various rhetorical strategies of control and defense were pursued in relation to a private sphere thus construed. One strategy was to depict the private sphere as a microcosm of the political sphere, thereby transferring the explicitly articulated hierarchical relations of the political arena to the private sphere.[25] Such an approach reflected the universalizing impulses of male theorists for whom public life was the only life worth living. Additionally, it constituted an attempt to exert control over an arena in which social relationships could seem disturbingly fluid and vaguely defined in comparison with the articulate social structures of the public sphere. For the domestically centered private sphere did not always closely resemble a miniature patriarchal state. Rather, it constituted a social arena in which distinctions of gender and office carried relatively little weight in and of themselves; authority was calculated instead by a complex and flexible equation in which class, age, wealth, education, personal talent, and influence accrued within the networks of kinship and patronage relationships all factored significantly.

A second common strategy pursued by Greek political theorists was to represent the private sphere as a woman's world, downplaying any male connection.[26] This rhetorical ploy served to feminize and devalue domestic pursuits as trivial and "basic" in the interests of cultivating male loyalty to the state, while also addressing fears of women's power by symbolically compartmentalizing and diminishing its scope. Again, the gap between rhetoric and social experience here appears to widen, for however dim our view of the private sphere may be, it nevertheless seems clear that the household constituted an arena of shared male and female interest and participation.[27] There were, then, dual and somewhat contradictory distorting tendencies toward both the politicization and the feminization of the private sphere in the public discourse of classical antiquity, tendencies that persisted into late antiquity and beyond. The common thread was the insistence on the subordination of the private to the public sphere and of the female to the male, a theoretical move that established the fundamental hierarchies on which the internal ordering of the public sphere was grounded. Thus the subordination of women to men was closely linked to, and indeed provided the foundation for, the construction of the public hierarchy of office.

This complex classical conceptualization of public and private proved remarkably tenacious. At the same time, the public-private dichotomy was significantly transformed, in rhetorical function at least, when transferred from the speeches of Athenian citizens to the rhetoric of the Latin-speaking provincials of the late Roman empire. By the fourth century of the common era, certain aspects of "private life" were receiving considerably more attention than in classical times,[28] whereas the "public sphere" had contracted into the machinery of a highly centralized and autocratic government, leaving a vast ambiguous social territory stretching between the household and the state. Criss-crossed by the networks of patronage and friendship, this expanse of late-antique social life, however hard to see from the perspective of the idealized public-private distinction, was nonetheless the central stage on which urban landowners, retired imperial officials, Christian ascetics, and bishops jostled for position.[29] The paradoxically liminal centrality of this social space gave particular weight to the implicit negotiations that ensued when speakers and writers invoked the categories of household and state, or private and public spheres. For invoke them they did, and with a rhetorical effect often seemingly enhanced rather than undercut by the imperfect correspondence between the classical formulation of the public-private dichotomy and the actual structures of late-ancient social life.

One pattern of late-antique appeal to the public-private distinction can be discerned in the rhetorical habits of the fourth-century western aristocrats who routinely wrote of their desire to avoid politics in preference for the life of *otium*, or leisure. This literary convention has often been interpreted as an indication of the moral decadence of the aristocracy; however, it is probably more helpfully read as a sign of the degree to which aristocratic identity and activity had come to be centered on private life, focused above all on the meticulous administration of relationships of patronage or friendship.[30] Such an emphasis by the elite on private life reflected in part the real exclusion of the traditional senatorial aristocracy from the governance of the empire, which under a ruler such as Valentinian I (364–75) was overwhelmingly dominated by a nonaristocratic imperial bureaucracy.[31] However, the rhetorical contrast of *otium* with *officium*, or political office, also created a misleading formal distinction, which masked the large overlap of public and private concerns and the continuing political influence of the aristocracy.[32] From the time of Gratian (375–83), the aristocracy regained significant influence over even the imperial court, and by the fifth century the western aristocrats had again become the primary bearers of Roman tradition by virtue of an authority grounded, not primarily in political office, but rather in the more enduring private resources of landed wealth and patronage. In this sense, notes John Matthews, "the government of the western empire seems progressively in these years [of the late fourth and early fifth centuries] to fall from public into private hands."[33]

If elite writers of the late fourth century consistently appealed to the public-private distinction in a political situation in which distinctions between the public and the private were not, in fact, easily made, the pressing question becomes how this public-private rhetoric functioned. Indeed, published expressions of reluctance to take up public office often seem to invoke the public-private dichotomy only to further the entanglement of supposedly distinct spheres: ancient authors publicly praise the private life of *otium* precisely in order to demonstrate their peculiar fitness for political office. A privately centered sense of identity, however real and "sincere," functioned paradoxically to enhance the public status and career of one who thereby eluded accusations of a grasping or overweening ambition while presenting himself as superior to less restrained rivals.[34]

We here reach a point of significant contact with the Priscillianist controversy. My proposal is that Priscillian and his supporters, like other members of the western aristocracy to which some of them belonged, grounded their identities and their understandings of community and authority in the private sphere. They did not, however, thereby abandon their claims to status in the public sphere. Indeed, when Priscillian chooses to represent himself as a private person, it is in a rhetorical context shaped by the need to demonstrate his fitness for the office of bishop. At the beginning of his *Apology*, probably written shortly before his ordination to the episcopacy, Priscillian alludes to his former position in the world—a position "not obscure," he assures his readers—only in order to emphasize his rejection of such public "glory"; this renunciation is, however, clearly to be parlayed into still higher status in the Christian community.[35] In the closing lines of this same document, Priscillian hints that his opponents are to be seen as ambitious and grasping in their envious and slanderous attacks, by implied contrast with his own controlled and disinterested behavior. Intriguingly, at this very point he turns the tables and portrays his rivals—the bishops Hydatius and Ithacius—as men who are inappropriately mired in the private sphere, "pursuing domestic enmities [*domesticas inimicitias*] under the name of religious matters."[36] This momentary negative privatizing of his opponents foreshadows Priscillian's subsequent readiness to defend his own claim to the episcopal office,[37] while still consistently preferring to present himself in the private role of ascetic scholar and exegete.

A rather different strategy was pursued by Priscillian's opponents, who argued that it was precisely Priscillian's "privacy"—including his purported predilection for meeting in household space—that demonstrated the illegitimacy of his public role and indeed unmasked his true identity as a heretic or sorcerer. Here again a glance at patterns of social exchange and rhetorical practice outside the ecclesiastical context may prove suggestive for our understanding of how appeals to the public-private distinction functioned in late-ancient Christian polemics. Peter Brown maps the high incidence of sorcery accusations brought by members of the late-fourth-century imperial bureaucracy against "the holders of ambiguous positions of personal power . . . based largely on skills, such as rhetoric, which, in turn, associated the man of skill with the ill-defined, inherited prestige of the traditional aristocracies."[38] Imperial officials, functioning as members of a highly fractured elite, seem to have attacked rivals outside the bureaucracy by drawing the boundaries of the public sphere in such a way as to delegitimate the social influence exercised by traditionally educated elites. The Antiochene rhetorician Libanius, for example, could be discredited by being represented as a private individual who influenced events in the public sphere only by the illegitimate wresting of power involved in invoking the "magic" of words; by this means, the rhetorician was accused of sorcery.[39] Brown suggests that such sorcery accusations "reach[ed] a peak at a time of maximum uncertainty and conflict in the 'new' society of the mid-fourth century" and subsided when stability was reestablished in subsequent centuries.[40] They can thus be read as indicators of levels of social and political instability.

The tense rivalry between the fourth-century bishop Hydatius and the ascetic scholar Priscillian echoes the uneasy competition of the imperial bureaucrat with the pagan rhetorician and aristocrat. Within the fourth-century church, as within secular society, both "systems of power"[41] were momentarily held in balance during a period of transition and uncertainty, as church and empire struggled to absorb the impact of the fundamental political, social, spiritual, and cultural shifts traditionally associated with the reigns of Diocletian and Constantine. Confronted by the "disturbing intangibles"[42] of private-sphere authority and the more informally negotiated relationships characteristic of the Priscillianist Christians, the opponents of Priscillian—much like the imperial officials studied by Brown—claimed to have detected an imbalance in the relationship of public and private, thereby justifying the need to reestablish the dominance of the public sphere by asserting their own authority. Their attacks on Priscillian followed conventions of polemical rhetoric, which in turn reflected the underlying biases and anxieties shaping public attitudes toward the private sphere. They portrayed the Priscillianist Christians as anarchic or rebellious, members of a subversive and immoral secret society who not only disdained the authority of public office but also ignored the fundamental hierarchy of genders. In this manner, Priscillian's opponents implicitly transferred the structures and values of the political sphere to the realm of private life, and by these standards judged the Priscillianists lacking. Depicting Priscillian as a seducer of women, they furthermore exploited threatening images of women's power, while at the same time trivializing the ascetic movement as "effeminate."

Ultimately, such arguments were successful in defining the followers of Priscillian as dangerous deviants. This success in part reflects the effectiveness of the more aggressive rhetorical strategy pursued by Priscillian's opponents; moreover, the polemical campaign drew strength from a faint yet significant correspondence between actual social dynamics and the stereotypes of subversion. Eventually, the progressive overlapping of spheres traced by Matthews in the secular arena contributed to the resolution of the western ecclesiastical conflict in a manner perhaps more in line with the blurred representation of public and private implicitly favored by Priscillian. But the late fourth century was a period of ecclesiastical history characterized more by an awareness of problematic disjunction than by an acknowledgement of the convergence of public and private structures of authority, and a particular rhetoric of opposition was to prevail before the subsequent reassimilation of public and private forms of authority could take place.

The Christian Community and the "World": Strategies of Accommodation and Alienation

If many fourth-century western aristocrats perceived their lives to be centered in the private sphere, some of these same aristocrats were not merely ambivalent about but even outright hostile to political life. That is, the rhetoric of reluctance might take the form of a rhetoric of stark refusal to take up public office, a refusal often literally enough intended. This expressed rejection of political life has been read as an embittered response to the involuntary political marginalization of the traditional aristocracy.[43] But in many cases such language may be interpreted more neutrally as an indication of a shift in the relations of local elites to the imperial administration: by presenting themselves as having chosen a privatized role in relation to the imperial administration, provincial notables created flexibility on one front while simultaneously protecting a constancy of power and influence on another, more local front.[44]

More important for our purposes, however, is still another, overlapping function of these late-ancient expressions of political alienation. For the rejection of *officium* in favor of *otium* did not merely support a more localized political involvement; it also bespoke the possibility of what might be designated a more "transcendent" political involvement. Carried to its extreme, the expressed preference for private life might lead to a severing of even those ties of patronage and friendship that linked a person indirectly to the political sphere. And such a drastic paring of relationships and social advantages could in turn result in a paradoxical enhancement of social status and the creation of new social networks, constituting the attainment of a public authority appropriately "ascetic," insofar as it represented the fruits of a disciplined renunciation of the social ties and physical anxieties that were understood to inhibit free speech and the resistance of tyranny. The truly ascetic leader, whose qualities were distilled in the ancient image of the philosopher, "could address the great directly, in terms of a code of decorum and self-restraint that he himself exemplified to the highest degree, because he was uncompromised by political attachments."[45] If this image was for the most part just that— "mainly an image"[46]— by late antiquity, it nevertheless stood as an ideal of a role that might on occasion be seen reflected, with varying degrees of clarity, in the stance of a philosopher, a rhetorician, a bishop, or a monk.[47]

The identification of such productive undercurrents of alienation contributes to our understanding of how late-antique Gallic nobles such as Paulinus of Nola and Sulpicius Severus could have abandoned promising political careers in order to embrace lives of Christian asceticism, or how the Spaniard Prudentius could dismiss as "folly" his own two provincial governorships and court appointment.[48] A culturally sustained capacity for political disillusionment left such men not depleted but rather energized for the pursuit of alternative careers within the Christian community, and they were particularly drawn to ascetic movements like that of Priscillian. The routine, even ritual, acts of negation and separation that were fundamental to the ascetic life resonated with their experience of self-chosen political alienation and provided the means to express a new, paradoxically privatized political authority. Thus, in the churches of the late-fourth-century west, these aristocrats discovered—and likewise contributed to—an emerging sense of Christian identity that was, like their secular identity, not only private but also anti-public. Indeed, for many privately identified Christians, the experience of alienation from the structures and concerns of the public sphere proved crucial for the social and theological self-definition of the church. Men and women like Priscillian were quick to perceive themselves as separate from or even in opposition to the institutions of secular authority—although at the same time they unhesitatingly made use of social networks to influence officials. They also demonstrated considerably less interest than their opponents in the authority of ecclesiastical office or the rituals reinforcing that authority. But it was in their theology that they most freely expressed their sense of self-chosen alienation, drawing upon particular dualistic strains in the cosmological heritage of Christianity in order to articulate an embattled hostility toward the controlling demonic forces that they perceived to dominate their age, and from which they could hope to win liberation only through the power of the fully transcendent Christ.

Significantly, the Priscillianists' alienated cosmology and their ascetic lifestyle struck their opponents as dangerously heretical. Views of the relationship of the Christian community to the larger world it inhabited thus constituted a second major point of divergence between Priscillian and his opponents. While Priscillian's opponents seem to have been generally optimistic about the convergence of Christian and secular society and culture, Priscillian and his followers were driven by a sense of alienation that expressed itself in their asceticism, in their cosmology, and in their relationship to both secular and ecclesiastical political structures.

It is crucial to acknowledge that the ascetic renunciations of such alienated Christians were very differently experienced by men and women. For men, the pursuit of Christian ascesis entailed the rejection of public life and therefore of the hierarchies of office and gender; in this respect, their opponents were not far off the mark when they insinuated that male ascetics were feminized by their rejection of the most basic cultural expressions of male identity. For women, on the other hand, asceticism involved not so much a rejection of public life—from which they were always in theory excluded—as a rejection of the dominant ordering principles of the public sphere—for example, the restriction of women to the private sphere or the intrusion of patriarchal structures of male dominance into the private sphere. A masculinization of the role of the women took place insofar as women resisted subordination and privatization.[49] For both sexes, asceticism initially involved radical withdrawal from the public sphere; ultimately, however, it threatened to subvert the very distinction between public and private and to destabilize the gender roles and relations supporting that distinction. Thus it is that Priscillian's detractors emphasize the untidy mingling of men and women within the movement, symbolized above all in imagined expressions of unbounded sexuality.

Naming the "Other": The Discourse of Orthodoxy in Late-Fourth-Century Spain

A third and final factor may be figured into the interpretation of the Priscillianist controversy, and that is how the categories of "orthodoxy" and "heresy" controlled the expression and resolution of the social and cosmological conflicts at the heart of the controversy. Brief mention has been made of the function of sorcery accusations in the fourth century, a case that suggests by analogy that heresy charges, like labels of deviance more generally, would have functioned in Christian antiquity as a means of clarifying doctrines, practices, or social relationships in periods of transitional ambiguity. But more needs to be said about the precise constellation of beliefs and social practices that clustered around the concepts of orthodoxy and heresy, defining the content and function of this peculiarly Christian articulation of normativeness and deviance.

The conceptual foundations of the categories of orthodoxy and heresy were laid during the second-century gnostic controversy in the polemical writings of Justin and Irenaeus.[50] Several aspects of the creative and enduring contribution of these first self-consciously orthodox Christian thinkers are here noteworthy. Of primary importance is Justin's doctrinalization of religious controversy through his borrowing of the classic concept of philosophical "succession" from the tradition of hellenistic historiography, also utilized within early rabbinic Judaism. Justin likewise contributed to the demonization of religious dissent: placing the teachers of divergent "heresies" or "schools of thought" within a mythical framework drawn from apocalyptic Judaism, he associated them with the false prophets, who in turn embodied the archetypal apostasy of Satan and the fallen angels.[51] Irenaeus refined Justin's scheme by drawing tighter parallels and contrasts between the single, unchanging, divine succession of truth and the multiple, shifting, demonic successions of error. He also nuanced the portrait of the heretic, who was no longer viewed simply as alien but now acknowledged explicitly as an internal or intimate enemy who either betrayed or dissimulated a shared faith.[52] This Irenaean refinement of the concept of heresy helps explain the ease with which the label of heresy could be applied to control or expel even influential "insiders" like Priscillian: the claim to have uncovered secret doctrinal deviance hidden behind false appearances of conformity was practically irrefutable.

The fourth-century Arian controversy, which coincided with the advent of the imperial patronage of Christianity, did not fundamentally alter these foundations but did place the inherited concepts of orthodoxy and heresy in a context that intensified both the oppositional dynamic of the polarity and its significance for Christian identity. The alliance of Christianity with empire resulted in an innovative technology of orthodoxy, as emperors not only facilitated the convening of councils but also used their secular authority to influence and enforce the disciplinary decisions and credal formulations of those councils. It appeared for the first time possible to achieve unity and even uniformity within the church, but in reality those goals remained more elusive than ever, for the high stakes of imperial rewards and punishments intensified rivalry and bitterness: theologically articulated enmities proliferated alongside new alliances. Meanwhile, the churches became increasingly concerned with the issue of Christian self-identity, as they confronted the rapid and sometimes very incomplete conversion of former pagans, as well as inherited internal differences, which were made more visible and problematic by the new political process. This concern with Christian self-identity heightened interest in defining a single catholic orthodoxy and, correspondingly, heresy was problematized through the multiplication and elaboration of heresiological categories, which functioned as negative boundary markers for orthodoxy. Finally, the polarity of orthodoxy and heresy received a gender "charge" in the face of both the new politicization (and consequent masculinization) of the church's self-image and the need to combat the disturbing emergence of alienated movements that undermined the traditional hierarchy of genders and were therefore perceived as not only rebellious but also effeminate.[53]

Spain had a distinctive role to play in the fourth-century struggle to define a monolithic orthodoxy, and indeed it seems possible to speak of an identifiably Spanish ethos of orthodoxy emerging in the period prior to the outbreak of the Priscillianist controversy. In most of the west, the theological issues at stake in the Arian controversy were crudely grasped, at best; nevertheless, an instinctive preference for the more unitive theology of the Nicene party, combined with adamant support for the controversial Alexandrian bishop Athanasius, led to the formation of an intensely loyal pro-Nicene faction. Loyalty evolved into near fanaticism in the context of the emperor Constantius' attempt to force the westerners to repudiate the troublesome Athanasius and accept credal compromise at the councils of Arles (353) and Milan (355).[54] The most extreme wing of the western pro-Nicene party was led by the Sardinian bishop Lucifer of Calaris, one of several westerners exiled for his refusal to cooperate with Constantius' efforts to enforce ecclesial unity. After Lucifer's death circa 370, the Spaniard Gregory of Elvira was considered the preeminent representative of the "Luciferian" faction,[55] whose purist adherents complained that "the church had become a brothel."[56] But Gregory was not the first Spanish advocate of an intensely pro-Nicene orthodoxy. When in 357 Ossius, the aged bishop of Cordoba, finally capitulated to imperial pressure and signed the so-called "Arian" Second Creed of Sirmium, not only he but also all who continued to communicate with him were excommunicated by more rigorist fellow bishops in Spain.[57] A letter sent to the emperor Theodosius by two Luciferian presbyters reports several instances of divine miracles punishing lenient or Arianizing bishops in Spain. Florentius of Merida was said to have been hurled down and seized with fits of trembling when he twice attempted to seat himself on his episcopal throne; the third time, he was struck dead. The letter notes somewhat menacingly that Florentius suffered this fate, not because he subscribed to any impiety, but merely since he had knowingly communicated with those who did.[58]

The convergence of zeal for orthodoxy with anti-imperial sentiments influenced Spanish Christian culture long after the death of Constantius and the accession first of more religiously neutral and finally of actively pro-Nicene emperors. Indeed, the idealized role of the "martyr for orthodoxy" seems to have shaped the self-understanding even of the Spanish emperors Magnus Maximus (383–88), under whom Priscillian was executed, and Theodosius (379–95), generally regarded as the architect of imperial orthodoxy.[59] Here the tradition of orthodox witness was aligned with the most public of figures, but its impact on more private expressions of Christianity is evidenced, not only in the works of Priscillian himself,[60] but also in the self-consciously orthodox writings of the late-fourth-century Spanish poet Prudentius, who composed a series of hymns in praise of martyrs, which have recently been identified as "devotional reading-matter for a cultured audience outside a church context."[61] Thus, in fourth-century Spain, the discourse of orthodoxy within which the conflicts over community and cosmology in the Priscillianist controversy were articulated was highly charged indeed. In this context, it is not altogether surprising that the tension in the portrayal of the heretic as an intimate enemy was eventually resolved in favor of a more purely alien representation of deviance, as the labeling strategies used against Priscillian shifted their focus from heresy to Manichaeism and finally to sorcery.

Plan and Scope of This Work

Chronology and shifts in labeling strategies shape the organization of this exploration of the social and cosmological differences underlying the Priscillianist controversy. The first three chapters examine the chain of events that led from the earliest recorded opposition to Priscillian's movement at the Council of Saragossa (380) to the final condemnation and execution of Priscillian and his closest associates circa 386. An initial divergence of social and theological orientation within Spanish Christianity will be seen to have evolved quickly into violent conflict, as polemical discourse shifted from vague innuendo to explicit charges of heresy and Manichaeism, and finally to the still more damning accusation of sorcery, which resulted in Priscillian's death. That death itself may be interpreted as a victory of sorts for the more publicly oriented and culturally accommodating stream of Christianity. Later, Priscillian enjoyed an afterlife in polemical rhetoric, and here two distinct streams of tradition can be discerned.

Chapter 4 explores the early-fifth-century portrayal of Priscillian as the founder of an independent heretical sect, highlighting the use of the label of Priscillianism to define the boundaries of Spanish orthodoxy, and chapter 5 ranges further afield to consider the more subtle and abstract rhetorical function of the portrayal of Priscillian as a gnostic by the western ascetics Sulpicius Severus and Jerome in works spanning the years from 392 to 415. In both of these later traditions, alienated cosmologies and lifestyles were brought under control and privately centered expressions of Christianity were reshaped, further renegotiating and clarifying the earlier "victory" of an accommodating, public Christianity.

Excursus: A Selective Review of Priscillian in Twentieth-Century Scholarship

Investigations of the broader social and cosmological aspects of the Priscillianist controversy have been under way since the discovery of the tractates, and the present study rests on the insights of previous scholarship.[62] Of particular significance is E.-Ch. Babut's 1909 monograph *Priscillien et le priscillianisme*. Babut places the conflict surrounding Priscillian within the context of the divergence between ascetic and anti-ascetic currents in fourth-century western Christianity. As the "new gospel" of asceticism arrived from the east and swept the western provinces, there arose simultaneously a movement of reaction and protest against the ascetic "saints." This protest centered above all in the clergy, explains Babut, and was frequently expressed by means of accusations of Manichaeism.[63] "Mutual hostility could not fail to arise. The clergy considered themselves raised above the common run and brought closer to God by ordination, the monks by the practice of sanctity. Each of these two aristocracies, the one sacramental, the other purely moral, was inclined not to recognize any kind of excellence other than its own."[64] Babut goes on to argue that Priscillian should be viewed, not as the leader of his own movement, but rather as a member of a broader network of ascetic "fraternities" scattered throughout Gaul and Spain. The members of these fraternities were not concerned merely with their personal spiritual growth, Babut further suggests; they also pursued the broader goal of educating an ascetic clergy and thereby countering the growing trend toward the secularization of episcopal office.[65] The attempt to link Priscillian closely and directly with other western ascetics appears to have been poorly founded, as does the emphasis on the explicit clerical ambitions of Priscillian and his followers.[66] Nevertheless, Babut's basic positioning of the Priscillianist controversy in the context of the fourth-century ascetic movement and the related conflicts of authority is fundamental to any discussion of its social roots.

In an unpublished 1957 dissertation, Willy Schatz builds on the foundation laid by Babut.[67] Not content with a generalized discussion of the conflict between ascetics and anti-ascetic bishops,[68] Schatz attempts a more precise social analysis of the forces which gave rise to the fourth-century proliferation of ascetic splinter-movements. Ultimately, he identifies the underlying cause of division between the mainstream church and these ascetic sects as "the polarity between office and charisma."[69] Acknowledging that Priscillian and some of his ascetic associates were themselves bishops, Schatz nevertheless argues that their authority was essentially charismatic, remaining deeply embedded in an ascetic spirituality: "they based their priesthood, not primarily on office, but much more on their charismatic gift."[70] The conflict between office and charisma at the heart of the Priscillianist controversy was defined primarily from the point of view of those who identified themselves as officeholders. "Spiritual" Christians like the ascetic Priscillian did not typically perceive any inherent conflict or contradiction between official and charismatic authority.[71] Nor was it Priscillian who initiated the schism in Spain. Rather, the Spanish bishops made the first move to exclude Priscillian and his followers

from the Christian community. "The heresy is therefore at first actually
artificially created. And the purpose of this is equally clear: *with the consti-
tution of the 'sect'* the bishop gains the possibility of proceeding against the
ascetics in order to enforce their acknowledgement of his authority and
their incorporation into the hierarchically determined ecclesiastical order" (emphasis mine).[72] Schatz here emphasizes the bishops' initiative
in labeling Priscillian's movement heretical or sectarian and thereby enforcing either conformity or exclusion from the community. But he also
adds that Priscillian and his followers played a part in provoking such
opposition: first, they implicitly claimed a competing ecclesiastical authority on the basis of their ascetic calling, and second, they organized themselves into a separate group (*Eigenorganisation, Sonderorganisation*) whose
existence threatened the unity and integrity of the episcopally led urban
congregation.[73]

In the broader context of a work that traces the emergence of western
monasticism, Schatz presents Priscillian's brand of asceticism as an inter-
mediate stage on an evolutionary path leading from more primitive forms
of asceticism to the fully developed structures of monasticism.[74] This transitional positioning of the movement has certain strengths as a strategy for
interpreting Priscillianism. Schatz is surely right to point to the inadequacy of such traditional categories as either "primitive asceticism" or
"monasticism" for characterizing Priscillian's movement. In addition, he
highlights the apparent instability of the social organization of the early
Priscillianists and points to possible explanations for that instability in the
movement's failure to adapt to the increasing institutionalization of the
church. However, Schatz's transitional positioning of the movement risks
inconsistency or even anachronism. Stressing that Priscillian and his followers remained closely identified with the urban congregation, he explicitly characterizes their asceticism as "intra-congregational" (*innergemeind-
lich*).[75] Moreover, as we have seen, Schatz suggests that the impression of
the sectarian nature of Priscillian's movement derives primarily from the
polemical rhetoric of Priscillian's opponents. Here he seems to be moving
toward an analysis that criticizes the use of the categories "heresy" or
"sect" and at the same time illumines both the factors that motivated the
polemical invocation of these categories and the social and ideological
function of such labels in shaping subsequent events. However, as Schatz
discusses the ascetics' private meetings and their periodic withdrawal
from the urban congregation, he also refers repeatedly to the separatism
of the Priscillianist movement in language that implicitly invokes the
Weberian-Troeltschian polarities of "church" and "sect," as well as "office" and "charisma."[76] The result is a somewhat predictable portrait of

Priscillian's movement as a "charismatic sect" in conflict with an established hierarchical mainstream "church"—a depiction ironically close to the distorted portrait that Schatz himself characterizes as the rhetorical creation of Priscillian's opponents. Such subtle inconsistencies in Schatz's interpretations do not, however, undercut the value of his work, and Benedikt Vollman's 1964 review of Priscillianist sources and scholarship rightly highlights Schatz's significant contribution to the study of Priscillianism.[77] In a 1974 encyclopedia article that remains one of the most balanced and reliable surveys of Priscillian and his movement,[78] Vollman follows Schatz closely, while emphasizing even more strongly than his predecessor the tendencies toward separatism in the social organization of what he terms Priscillian's "school."

A Spanish study that placed the conflicts of authority evident in the Priscillianist controversy in a somewhat different interpretative framework, Abilio Barbero de Aguilera's significantly subtitled "El Priscilianismo: ¿Herejía o movimiento social?" was published in 1963, two years before Vollman's early monograph. Barbero de Aguilera opts for the second alternative, but he does so by suggesting, not that Priscillianist Christianity be viewed as a charismatic movement in conflict with a mainstream church, but rather that it be understood as the product of an indigenous, rural Spanish resistance to Roman domination represented by imperially coopted urban bishops.[79] Here he follows the lead of W. H. C. Frend's revisionist account of the Donatist movement in North Africa, and his provocative interpretation is subject to some of the same criticisms as Frend's, particularly insofar as he imposes an urban-rural distinction on material that most often resists such categorization.[80] In addition, his understanding of the politicized nature of the late fourth-century episcopacy seems to suffer from some of the same lack of nuance as does Schatz's Weberian representation of bishops as wielders of "official" or "rational" authority. At the same time, Barbero de Aguilera's work remains important, not only for its careful critique of the basis of the doctrinal charges brought against the Priscillianist Christians, but also for its attentiveness to the local dynamics that shaped the experience of Spanish Christians in the late fourth century.

Henry Chadwick's comprehensive 1976 monograph returns to the scholarly tradition of presenting Priscillian's movement as solidly sectarian, if not also heretical. In addition, Chadwick departs somewhat from the more apologetic line of interpretation represented by such scholars as Babut, Schatz, Vollman, and Barbero de Aguilera. Emphasizing the seemingly idiosyncratic and esoteric elements of Priscillian's teachings, Chadwick calls attention to what he describes as Priscillian's "frankly avowed interest in the occult." He suggests that Priscillian may have taken part in magic rituals and worn a magical amulet, that he attached "deep importance to number mysticism," and that his interest in demonology led him into "cabbalistic investigations into such occult mysteries" as were found in gnostic and Manichaean texts.[81] "The evidence suggests, in short, that while Priscillian was not a Manichaean, his doctrine is not, as has been suggested by W. Schatz and others, explicable simply in terms of ascetic influences from the Egyptian desert. He has a place in the long line of Christians who have sought for hidden mysteries in the Bible or in nature."[82]

Conflicts of authority are implicit both in Chadwick's discussion of Priscillian's teachings concerning prophecy and revelation and in his detailed account of the social and political processes that led to Priscillian's execution and to the subsequent polarization of Priscillianists and anti-Priscillianists in Spain and elsewhere.[83] However, he does not address issues of authority in either explicit or theoretical terms. Chadwick's emphasis remains on the supposedly esoteric nature of Priscillian's teachings, in which he seems to find the explanation for Priscillian's vulnerability to accusations of sorcery and Manichaeism. Many of his arguments are based in large part on circumstantial evidence indicating that certain magical or quasi-magical practices were common among Christians in late antiquity[84]—evidence that, if accepted, seems to undercut the explanatory value of Chadwick's portrayal of Priscillian as a "sorcerer's apprentice."[85] Nevertheless, insofar as Chadwick's careful analysis of the tractates represents an attempt to take Priscillian's thought seriously on its own terms, his refocusing of interest on Priscillian's cosmology constitutes a valuable contribution to the study of this controversy.[86]

One of the most recent and significant accounts of Priscillian and Priscillianism, Raymond Van Dam's *Leadership and Community in Late Antique Gaul*, explicitly rejects both Chadwick's particular depiction of Priscillian as an "occultist" and the more generally prevailing tendency to externalize Priscillian, variously, as sorcerer, heretic, sectarian, or rural revolutionary. At the same time, this study offers a fresh analysis of the conflicts of authority that have interested so many scholars. Van Dam suggests that the Priscillianist controversy "was an *internal* problem generated by the rivalries appearing when a religious organization for which books were central acquired educated men as members" (emphasis mine).[87] Building upon the insights of anthropological studies of charges of witchcraft, Van Dam proposes that labels of heresy and Manichaeism functioned to mediate rivalries in the small, face-to-face communities of late Roman antiquity.[88] He further suggests that the failure of the labeling process to resolve conflict locally and relatively peaceably in Priscillian's case points to the structural and ideological inadequacies of Christianity for integrating converts from the upper strata of Hispano- and Gallo-Roman society.[89] In particular, the Christian community found it difficult to assimilate well-educated men—among whom Van Dam numbers Priscillian and many of his associates—and wealthy unmarried women, such as Priscillian's supporter the widow Euchrotia.[90]

In the case of well-educated men, Van Dam suggests, the problem was essentially an imbalance in the supply and demand of leadership. The location of the imperial court in Gaul and the presence of thriving schools of rhetoric in Gaul and Spain generated a particularly large population of upwardly mobile, ambitious, well-trained men in this period. When these men became Christians, their ambitions were often transferred to the ecclesiastical arena, where they assumed a natural authority by virtue of their aristocratic culture and established skill and reputation as speakers and interpreters of books. On the one hand, the church accentuated the authority of such men, insofar as it placed high value on the role of the teacher and exegete. On the other hand, Van Dam observes, the church provided a limited number of options for these men within its relatively simple and rigid hierarchical institutional structure, since few could be recruited into the clergy, and fewer still might expect to become bishops. Learned men could, however, be patronized as teachers without formal rank; they could become monks; or they could simply live as laymen under the jurisdiction of bishop and clergy. Under these circumstances, rivalries and tensions naturally arose among laymen, teachers, monks, ambitious clergy, and bishops.[91]

Wealthy unmarried women constitute the second group that late-antique Christianity failed to accommodate. Here again Van Dam points to the purported ideological and institutional rigidity of the church as the primary factor inhibiting the assimilation of a crucial sector of the urban population. The traditional patriarchalism of Christianity became problematic, he suggests, when the fourth-century church found itself confronting a large number of independent women among the wealthy converts who were its potential patrons. For such women even the limited ecclesiastical roles available to educated men were lacking. "Like Roman society in general, Catholic Christianity was a 'man's world,'" Van Dam comments.[92] But while he rightly highlights the problematic of women's authority in fourth-century Christianity, Van Dam's analysis here raises as many questions as it answers. It is not clear why wealthy Roman women should have presented problems of accommodation for a church that mirrored the secular world that had shaped the identities and expectations of those women. In what respect was the problematic patriarchalism of the church distinct from the social and cultural environment to which these independent women were accustomed?

If Van Dam's analysis of gender roles is not completely satisfying, his tendency to depict late-fourth-century Christianity as rigid and inflexible also rings false at points. I would suggest that the uncontrolled escalation of charges of heresy in Priscillian's case did not primarily arise from institutional and ideological rigidity. Rather, it stemmed, first, from the lack of definition of social roles and beliefs in a period of rapid social and theological change and, second, from the difficulty of containing a local conflict in a society knit together by extralocal networks of patronage and friendship. Nevertheless, Van Dam's emphasis on ecclesiastical rigidity paradoxically opens the way for appreciating the fluidity of Christianity in a time of transition. For the rigidity that Van Dam describes is not the rigidity of a strongly entrenched institutional "church"; he invokes, rather, the image of an uncompromising "sect" unable or unwilling to assimilate the mainstream culture of the late Roman towns. By thus emphasizing the vulnerability and marginality of even mainstream Christianity in fourth-century Spain and Gaul, Van Dam challenges common depictions of western catholic orthodoxy and likewise calls for a reevaluation of the catholic church's relation to movements labeled heretical. This is a significant shift in Priscillianist scholarship.

Pursuing one set of implications of Van Dam's work, I begin by deliberately setting aside the Weberian-Troeltschian typology implicitly invoked in many twentieth-century studies, as well as the heresiological model that dominated earlier approaches to Priscillianism. In order to press beyond the insights of scholars such as Schatz, it is necessary to abandon the polarity of "orthodox church" and "heretical sect." In its place, we must seek new analytical frameworks that do not privilege Priscillian's opposition, but make it possible instead to view the Priscillianist and anti-Priscillianist factions as parallel, competing streams of Christianity that emerged simultaneously in response to the changed social, cultural, and theological landscape of the late fourth century. In this context, the invocation of labels of deviance may be understood, not as an indication of the inherent "heretical" or "sectarian" nature of Priscillian's movement, but as an available means whereby particular groups of Christians attempted to assert the dominance of their own theological and social models in situations of profound religious pluralism and ambiguity.

CHAPTER ONE

"A STRANGE MAN"

Opposition Emerges
at the Council of Saragossa

On October 4th in the year 380, twelve bishops gathered at Saragossa to discuss certain disturbing innovations in Christian lifestyle and worship. Their gathering provides the earliest evidence of the influence of the Spanish lay teacher Priscillian. The historical record of the Saragossan council is, however, perplexing. While the writings of Priscillian and the early-fifth-century historian Sulpicius Severus clearly indicate that the council was hostile to Priscillian, the *Acts of the Council of Saragossa* does not mention Priscillian by name. Priscillian denies that the bishops who gathered at Saragossa went so far as to condemn him or his associates by name; Severus, however, contradicts Priscillian on this point, reporting that the Council of Saragossa explicitly denounced four individuals—Priscillian, Elpidius, and the bishops Instantius and Salvianus. Were Priscillian and his associates condemned by name at the Council of Saragossa in a proceeding whose records no longer survive, even though this is explicitly denied by Priscillian? Probably not, but the contradictory testimony remains. Do some or all of the eight preserved judgments of that council directly oppose the practices of the unnamed Priscillian? Probably so, but the sources do not allow us to prove this, and any conclusions regarding Priscillian's circle are therefore necessarily tentative.

If there is much about the Council of Saragossa that must remain obscure, the *Acts of the Council of Saragossa* nevertheless supplies reliable and important evidence of the values and concerns of bishops hostile to Priscillian. By allowing us to define the nature of the opposition, if not always to see clearly who and what was opposed, the document provides a valuable key to interpreting the roots of the dispute, which do not seem to lie primarily in a disagreement over doctrine or even about asceticism per se. Hinting that their opponents are seditious and disorderly rebels, the Saragossan bishops locate their offense in failure to acknowledge the centrality of the public liturgy, the supreme authority of ecclesiastical office, and the necessity for the separation and subordination of women. The Saragossan council thereby attacks private-sphere representations of authority and gender, while at the same time attempting to construct and defend an alternative and equally innovative public model of Christian community. Patterned on the minutes published by both municipal councils and the Roman Senate itself, the *Acts of the Council of Saragossa* reinforces the close link between the judgments issued by the council and the emerging public definition of Christian community and episcopal authority.

This chapter begins with a preliminary examination of Priscillian's and Severus' descriptions of the episcopal gathering at Saragossa in order to place the council firmly within the context of the Priscillianist controversy. Attention then shifts to the chapter's primary focus, the *Acts of the Council of Saragossa*, which enable us both to explore the social roots of the early opposition to Priscillian and his circle and to examine the form that opposition took at a very early stage of the controversy. Negative stereotypes begin to emerge, but are not yet crystallized into labels, and vague threats hurled at unnamed targets seem designed to intimidate dissenters into conformity rather than to exclude them from the community. Priscillian does not yet appear as a heretic. He is not even explicitly portrayed as a rival. He remains at this point the unnamed representative of a perspective on Christian community and authority that is troublingly at odds with the emerging sense of identity of the bishops gathered at Saragossa.

Contextualizing the Council of Saragossa: The Evidence of Priscillian and Sulpicius Severus

The accounts of Priscillian and Sulpicius Severus provide an outline of the events that led to the convening of the Council of Saragossa. According to Priscillian's *Letter to Damasus* (c. 381), he and his companions had lived quiet lives dedicated to God for several years before the council:

> After we had been renewed by the regeneration of the living bath and had cast off the filthy darkness of worldly acts, we had given ourselves

wholly to God; for we read that whoever loves anyone more than God cannot be his disciple. At that time, while some of us had already been chosen for God in the churches and others of us labored with our lives so that we would be chosen, we pursued the quiet of catholic peace.[1]

Priscillian's implicit characterization of himself as a layperson with episcopal ambitions serves an apologetic function in the later context of the *Letter to Damasus*. Nevertheless, he is probably accurate in claiming that his early zeal for the ascetic life was shared by a group of Spanish Christians, which included some who were "already chosen for God" (*electi Deo*) in the clerical leadership of their communities.[2]

Severus' *Chronicle* (c. 403) supports Priscillian's picture of a network of Spanish ascetics that included both laypeople and clergy, and he supplies the names—Instantius and Salvianus—but not the sees of two of the bishops associated with Priscillian during the period before the council. Severus further reports that the first opposition to the ascetics came from Hyginus, bishop of Cordoba in the southern Spanish province of Baetica.[3] Hyginus is described as being "from the neighborhood" of Priscillian and his episcopal associates (*ex vicino*),[4] and we furthermore know from Jerome that Tiberianus, one of Priscillian's early lay supporters, was a Baetican[5]—two possible indications that Priscillian and his friends were initially active in Baetica. However, subsequent events suggest that the three were more likely from the nearby western province of Lusitania, and Severus' narrative quickly shifts the scene to that province.

Severus relates that Hyginus sent a report to Bishop Hydatius, whose Lusitanian see of Merida was well connected with Cordoba by road.[6] This communication—the content of which remains unspecified—produced a vehement reaction on Hydatius' part.[7] "Provoking Instantius and his companions without measure and more than was necessary, he put a torch to the nascent fire, so that he irritated the evil ones rather than suppressing them."[8] Many struggles followed, as Severus summarizes all too briefly, before an episcopal meeting was convened at Saragossa at which "even Aquitanian bishops were present."[9] The reasons for convening the council in the northeastern province of Tarraconensis are unknown. Saragossa was well connected by road with most parts of Spain but was at some distance from the areas where the conflict raged most fiercely, and this may have been seen as advantageous for a successful resolution of the conflict.[10] The desire to include bishops from Aquitaine may also have been a factor: there are indications of close links between Aquitaine and northern Spain in this period.[11]

Attendance at the council was relatively low, with only twelve bishops present, no more than ten of them from Spain, in comparison with the nineteen Spanish bishops and twenty-four Spanish presbyters who had gathered at the Council of Elvira (309) some seventy years earlier, or the nineteen Spanish bishops at the Council of Toledo twenty years later. The esteemed Aquitanian bishop Phoebadius of Agen heads the list of attendees in the council's *Acts*,[12] probably owing to his seniority in years of consecration;[13] Phoebadius may also have presided over the council, since such documents typically name the presider first. The name of another Aquitanian, Delphinus, bishop of the prominent see of Bordeaux, is listed second; he was later to number among Priscillian's staunch opponents, perhaps in part because of his consternation at the success of Priscillian's ascetic teachings in his own congregation.[14] Little or nothing is known of the next four bishops listed: Euticius, Ampelius, Augentius (probably of Toledo), and Lucius. Ithacius, bishop of Ossonuba in Lusitania, emerges after the council as a violent opponent of Priscillian and a close ally of Hydatius. Splendonius and Valerius (probably of Saragossa) are otherwise unknown.[15] Symposius later joined Hyginus in supporting Priscillian and his friends[16] and is probably identical with the Galician bishop Symphosius whom the Acts of the Council of Toledo (400) describe as having left the Council of Saragossa after the first day.[17] Carterius is perhaps the Spanish bishop criticized for his second marriage, and, if so, he is not likely to have been a friend of censorious ascetics.[18] Hydatius of Merida, who may have summoned, if not presided over, the council, is the last-named attendee.[19]

Priscillian's friends Instantius and Salvianus did not attend the council; nor did Hyginus of Cordoba, who by this point had ceased to oppose Priscillian, receiving him in communion both before and after the council.[20] Severus implies that the council was perceived to be hostile to Priscillian from the start,[21] and it is likely that Priscillian's closest supporters stayed away from a meeting that they viewed as prejudiced by the accusations of Hydatius. However, we have seen that Symposius, known to have supported Priscillian immediately after the council, did attend for at least one day. Other bishops present may have had more conciliatory goals and more moderate positions than either Hydatius or Priscillian's active supporters.

Whatever the initial intentions and inclinations of the attending bishops may have been, Hydatius exerted considerable effort to turn the council against Priscillian. Priscillian reports that the bishop of Merida came to the council prepared with a memorandum, which evidently presented a program of Christian lifestyle and worship aimed at correcting the supposed abuses of Priscillian and his circle. Priscillian's language is vague and dismissive, whether owing to ignorance as to the precise contents of the document or to awareness of his own vulnerability to its criticisms. "I know not what memorandum was given there by Hydatius," he writes to Damasus, "which laid out instruction as if for the life that should be led" (*quod velut agendae vitae poneret disciplinam*).[22]

Priscillian then goes on to defend the ascetic discipline that he himself advocates. He first describes it in seemingly unobjectionable terms as the elimination of "the wicked habits and unseemly standards of life that actually fight against the faith of the God Christ." He next urges that neither those who reject all family ties, education, possessions, and worldly honors nor those who strive to live a life dedicated to God without fully renouncing their ties to the world should be opposed in their pursuit of a true Christian life.[23] Priscillian's defense suggests that Hydatius' memorandum sought to establish a definition of ascetic practice that excluded his own way of life. Hydatius may also have accused Priscillian of denying the possibility of salvation for more worldly Christians. If so, such an accusation was probably unfair. Priscillian endorses the possibility of salvation for ascetic and non-ascetic Christians alike, as well as the need for mutual toleration, not only when under attack by Hydatius, but also in less defensive contexts;[24] moreover, his sermons clearly address not an ascetic elite but a diverse congregation.[25] It is possible that Hydatius' memorandum on Christian life served somehow as a basis for the council's judgments,[26] which are directed toward the same goal of reorienting and controlling ascetic practice.

Hydatius probably arrived armed with another document, or set of documents, aimed at damaging the reputation of Priscillian. According to Priscillian, Hydatius attacked Priscillian and his followers at the council for reading apocryphal scriptures, and he urged the bishops gathered at Saragossa to "let what ought to be condemned be condemned, what is unnecessary not be read."[27] Later, in a work explicitly defending the reading of extracanonical literature, Priscillian mockingly rephrases Hydatius' inflammatory cry: "Condemn what I do not know, condemn what I do not read, condemn what I do not seek by pursuit of sluggish leisure!"[28] At some point around the time of the council, Hydatius collected a few of the apocryphal scriptures purportedly read by Priscillian and his companions, and it was perhaps at the council itself that he "brought them forth from his own cupboard and introduced them with calumnious tales," as Priscillian relates.[29] Since the published judgments of the council contain no prohibition of the use of apocrypha, Hydatius must have been unable to convince his fellow bishops to endorse such a ruling. Priscillian's defensiveness indicates, however, that Hydatius was not altogether unsuccessful in his attempt to use the issue of apocryphal literature to prejudice others against Priscillian and his circle.

In spite of Hydatius' efforts to turn the council against Priscillian, the bishops at Saragossa do not appear to have been prepared to attack Priscillian or his associates directly. On this point, we have not only the silence of the council's *Acts* but also Priscillian's explicit and repeated denials: "At the episcopal assembly in Saragossa, no one of us was held as a defendant; no one was accused, no one convicted, no one condemned; no crime was charged against our name or vow or manner of life; no one had to be summoned, or was even anxious that he or she would be summoned."[30] Priscillian refers to a letter written by Damasus of Rome urging that no one be condemned without a hearing. At the council, this letter "prevailed against the wicked," Priscillian assures Damasus,[31] indicating that some had indeed desired his condemnation and had perhaps very nearly achieved that goal.

Later accounts seem to contradict Priscillian's persistent denials of conciliar condemnation: the *Acts of the Council of Toledo* (400) refers to a judgment being made at Saragossa against certain persons,[32] and Severus reports quite specifically that Instantius, Salvianus, Elpidius, and Priscillian were condemned by vote of the council.[33] It is highly unlikely that Priscillian would lie about his own condemnation in a letter to the Roman bishop if such a condemnation had actually been issued. But there was probably real ambiguity in the situation, and this ambiguity could have been exploited in different ways by authors in different circumstances. It may have been widely known in the Spanish congregations that the council had been convened in a spirit of hostility to Priscillian and his supporters. Their practices had been the topic of discussion and had been judged negatively by some of the bishops present. Moreover, Priscillian and his associates were almost certainly the explicit target of at least some of the council's rulings; this may, in fact, be the only meaning of the reference in the *Acts of the Council of Toledo*. It has also been suggested that Priscillian and the three other prominent leaders of the group named by Severus— Elpidius, Instantius, and Salvianus—may subsequently have been excommunicated on the basis of those rulings.[34] If so, Priscillian conveniently suppressed this information in his letter to Damasus, while Severus, writing many years later, simply merged two originally separate rulings: the general judgments issued by the council and the personal excommunications that may have been enacted by an enforcing bishop like Hydatius.

The Form of the Conciliar *Acta*

The *Transcript of the Judgments of the Bishops of the Saragossan Council, October 4, 380,* as the original document was entitled, has come down to us as part of a seventh-century canonical collection known as the *Hispana*.[35] A prefatory clause sets the scene of the council, identifying the consistory of Saragossa as the place of meeting and listing the names of the twelve episcopal participants. The account of the proceeding begins to unfold with the recording of the bishops' command that their judgments be read aloud. One of their number, Lucius, recites a series of eight judgments. After the reading of each judgment, the gathered bishops pronounce their approval in unison: "It is agreed"; "Let it be so."

Hamilton Hess has identified the *Acts of the Council of Saragossa* as belonging to a small group of conciliar documents that represent a "rudimentary stage of canonical preservation, being simply a stenographic record of the essential phases of the parliamentary process."[36] While these documents are admittedly not as detailed as other extant verbal transcriptions, their form nonetheless identifies them as procedural minutes, "either in abridgement or as the only minutes which were taken at the sittings in question."[37] According to Hess, the distinguishing characteristics of the form are:

> (1) the introductory phrase ". . . *Episcopus dixit*"; (2) the putting of the question: *si omnibus (hoc) placet*; and the vote: *placet, placere sibi* or other expressions of assent, usually introduced by *omni* or *universi dixerunt*; (3) the informal, discursive phraseology of each proposal.[38]

Behind these verbal patterns, we can glimpse elements of the procedure adopted by the Christian synods in imitation either of the Roman Senate or—more likely—of local town councils:[39] a speaker, usually but not always the presider, briefly set forth the problem (*relatio*); each council member offered his judgment (*sententia*); a "vote" was taken by reading the proposed judgments aloud until one received majority approval; and, finally, the majority judgment was officially recorded by the presider as the formal judgment of the council. Alternatively, a speaker might incorporate both problem and proposed judgment into a single proposal, which could be ratified immediately by acclamation without other judgments being offered; this streamlined procedure was commonly followed in the late empire.[40]

Hess distinguishes conciliar documents that take the form of procedural minutes from those modeled on the *liber sententiarum*, or published resolutions of the Senate.[41] He designates the latter the "*placuit* form," since its judgments are typically introduced by the clause "it was agreed that." The *placuit* documents abandon the direct discourse of the procedural minutes, and the phraseology of their judgments tends to be somewhat more concise and consistently patterned. Hess's analysis would indicate that the *Acts of the Council of Saragossa*, like other documents of its type, reflects the actual discussions of the council to a greater extent than do the majority of contemporary conciliar documents, which are in the *placuit* form. The casting of the Saragossan *Acts* in the form of direct discourse and the inclusion of the formulaic language of acclamation actually used in such assemblies suggests that the *Acts* derives directly from the procedural minutes of the council. In addition, the discursive, informal phraseology of the judgments appears to result from the relatively close adherence of the *Acts* to the wording of the original discussion.

The *Acts of the Council of Saragossa* departs, however, from the typical form of procedural minutes in at least one respect. The document is presented as a transcript of only the final moments of the council: the reading and approval of the council's previously recorded judgments. Thus, whereas typical minutes of a council's proceedings introduce each judgment with the name of the bishop who originally proposed the problem or opinion—"Bishop X *said*"—the Saragossan document substitutes the name of the council's secretary—"Bishop Lucius *read*." Curiously, the *Acts* nevertheless gives the illusion of representing an abridged form of the minutes of the council's entire proceedings. Whereas in the case of the final reading and approval of the council's minutes one would expect introductory and closing formulae to be found only at the end and beginning of the recitation, the *Acts* repeats both the introductory phrase—"Bishop Lucius read"—and the episcopal acclamation—"It is agreed"—before and after each judgment. It furthermore interweaves the acclamations with the judgments in such a way as to suggest that those acclamations are emerging out of the original discussion.[42] The unusual literary form of the document thus paradoxically combines the dramatic immediacy of procedural minutes with the anonymous unanimity of a recorded secondary approval of those minutes. The official authority that all conciliar acts implicitly claim is thereby heightened, while the roles of individual bishops are masked.

Samuel Laeuchli has suggested that even conciliar judgments like those of the earlier Spanish council of Elvira, published in the more formalized *placuit* form, preserve traces of the sequence of encounters and conflicts that produced those judgments. The conciliar documents reveal the Christian appropriation of the secular decision-making process, as Hess and others before him have shown; even more important for the analysis of an individual council, they also preserve the original, seemingly spontaneous, order in which topics were raised and discussed. This fact allows the reconstruction of the "flow" of the original meeting: by noting which topics were raised earliest and which recur most frequently, the highest priorities and concerns of the gathered bishops can be identified; by observing the juxtaposition of topics, the chain of associations that linked one to another can be reconstructed; by analyzing the use of more and less highly charged language, shifts in emotional intensity can be detected. In addition to calling attention to the order of judgments, Laeuchli highlights the significance of inconsistencies, first, in the language of the published judgments and, second, in the punishments threatened. These inconsistencies may reveal relative levels of agreement or conflict, indifference or anger, hesitancy or strength of authority.[43]

Because the judgments of the Council of Saragossa are relatively few in number (eight compared to the eighty-one drafted at Elvira), there is only limited basis for comparison among them. However, this limitation is balanced by the advantage of the Saragossan *Acts'* seemingly closer adherence to the original language of the discussion. A careful reading of the *Acts* allows one, not only to identify and analyze the council's major concerns and strategies of opposition, but also tentatively to reconstruct the dramatic event of the meeting itself, mapping probable shifts in levels of passion, agreement, and confidence in the bishops' discussions.

Strategy and Performance in the Conciliar *Acta*

> *I. All women who are of the catholic church and faithful are to be separated from the reading and meetings of strange men, but other [women] are to meet with those [women] who read in pursuit of either teaching or learning, because the Apostle commands this. By all the bishops it was said: Let those who do not observe this judgment of the council be anathema.*[44]

Following Roman legal tradition, the published judgments of church councils typically begin by naming the person or group of persons to whom the decision is directed.[45] In the first judgment of the Council of Saragossa, the naming of the target of "women" is given particular emphasis. With the intensifying qualifiers piled onto the named target, the bishops move immediately to delineate the boundary between insiders and outsiders and to communicate an implicit threat: those who transgress this ruling will be placed beyond the pale of catholic orthodoxy. The subsequent juxtaposition of "faithful catholic women" (*mulieres . . . ecclesiae catholicae et fideles*) with "strange men" (*virorum alienorum*) further heightens the emotional tenor of the judgment's language. Here the bishops raise the specter of women meeting familiarly with nonfamilial men and emphasize the impropriety of mixed-sex gatherings. With a single word—"strange"—the council is able to invoke deeply embedded conceptions of female virtue and honor in order to excite moral outrage at the implied

violation of women's essential privacy. At the same time, fear of the heretical "other" is manipulated through the suggestion that the boundaries
of a vulnerable community have been penetrated by hostile invaders.[46]

Although the bishops open with an implicit prohibition of mixed-sex
study groups, they quickly shift to a positive injunction.[47] The common
themes of women's activities and of reading provide a link between the
two parts of the judgment. The phrase "reading and meetings" (*lectione et
coetibus*), which highlights the activity central to the offensive mixed meetings,[48] is almost immediately followed by the reference to "those [women]
who read" (*ipsas legentes*) at proposed all-female meetings. The bishops'
message is therefore that women are not to attend study groups to read
with men, but should study in the company of literate women. The enthusiasm for reading that the bishops attempt to control seems to echo the
zeal of learned ascetics like Priscillian, who urges that Christians have a
"responsibility to read" and will be held accountable if they have not
"read all that has been prophesied about God" in both canonical and
extracanonical books.[49]

Having evoked the image of women mingling scandalously with unrelated men, the council here seeks not to prohibit but to redirect the female zeal for study.[50] It does so by constructing a separate and implicitly
subordinate female sphere within the publicly defined church, a sphere in
which the fictive privacy of those women who meet to read and study can
be maintained. This first judgment is one of only two that include an invocation of scriptural authority.[51] The council probably has in mind 1 Cor.
14:34—"women should keep silence in the churches"—and 1 Tim. 2:12—
"I permit no woman to teach or to have authority over men; she is to keep
silent." These scriptural references support the bishops' publicly defined
social order and underline the violations of hierarchy hinted at in the objections to mixed-sex study groups where women not only speak freely
but may even presume to teach men.

The judgment closes with the formulaic language of conciliar agreement, which in this case serves both to invoke episcopal authority and to
communicate the threat of punishment to potential offenders, now indi-
cated with an inclusive masculine grammatical form (*futuros qui . . .*).[52]
Here the bishops threaten excommunication without specifying whether
or how the offender may be received back into the community. The severity of this punishment reinforces the emotionally loaded language of this
first judgment: it appears that the topic of mixed study groups inspires
passionate opposition from at least some of the bishops present. But, at the
same time, the bishops at Saragossa seem either to disagree among themselves or to feel uncertain of support in the broader Christian commu-

nity.[53] They therefore choose their words carefully, couching even their initial prohibition in grammatically positive terms and then offering an approved alternative. Furthermore, they hesitate to put their authority to the test by specifying either penance or perpetual exclusion from the community.[54]

> II. One is not to fast on Sunday, for the sake of the day or belief or superstition; or, rather, those who persist in these opinions are not to be absent from the churches during Lent, nor to lurk in the hiding places of cells and mountains, but they are to keep the example and precept of the bishops, and they are not to meet on strange estates in order to hold meetings. By all the bishops it was said: Let the one who does this be anathema.[55]

The length and complexity of the second judgment suggest that its wording may have emerged out of a protracted discussion, and the passage offers a number of difficulties of interpretation.[56] The judgment can be divided into two main parts. The phrase "those who persist in these opinions" (qui in his suspicionibus perseverant) appears to link the two parts, referring back to the Sunday fasters whose activities are forbidden in the first clause and at the same time serving as the grammatical subject of the second series of clauses, which amend the initial prohibition.[57] The council first attempts to dissuade Christians from fasting on Sunday by prohibiting the practice and casting vague yet damaging aspersions on the motivations of the fasters.[58] The bishops then back off somewhat from their initial stark prohibition. Their primary concern is that the targeted Christians, whether or not they continue to fast on Sunday (during Lent only?),[59] should not withdraw from the episcopal congregation during Lent. The initial prohibition is accompanied by vague innuendoes, which may imply doctrinal unorthodoxy as well as social subversion; later, Augustine was to suggest that the supposed Priscillianist custom of fasting on Sunday associated them with the Manichaeans.[60] However, the longer and weightier second series of clauses focuses exclusively on the social implications of practices that fragment the community and deviate from the norms defined by the bishop. Underlining such concerns is the positive injunction to follow those Lenten observances exemplified and commanded by the bishop. As in the first judgment, the goal is not simply to prohibit but rather to redirect ascetic zeal, in this case by channeling it into practices that support rather than undermine the authority of the bishop and the publicly defined community he represents.

The council's preoccupation in this judgment with episcopal authority and the integrity of the episcopally led community is further emphasized by the strategies employed for stereotyping the opponents. Those who observe separate fasts and withdraw from the congregation during Lent are described in terms that evoke the image of the secret and seditious gatherings commonly associated with the Manichaeans or other religious or political sectarians. They are followers of a superstition (*superstitio*); they seek out hiding places (*latibula*); they come together for private meetings (*conventus*).[61] Such meetings furthermore take place on "strange estates" (*alienas villas*)[62]: like the women who mix with "strange" men, the Christians targeted in this judgment are perceived to participate in inappropriate and subversive relationships by frequenting the private homes of those with whom they have no legitimate social connection. Priscillian's *Tractates* include what appears to be a set of Lenten sermons, and it is clear that he—like many ascetically inclined Christians—placed great importance on the penitential season of Lent;[63] it is thus probable but not certain that he is among those whom the bishops here attack.

As in the first judgment, potential transgressors are threatened with anathematization. Again, the invocation of this relatively harsh threat suggests the likelihood that there were strong feelings among some of the bishops present, while at the same time either lack of unity or lack of confidence about enforcement deterred them from defining the punishment in more specific terms.

> III. *If someone is proved not to have consumed the grace of the Eucharist received in church, let that one be anathema in perpetuity. By all the bishops it was said: It is agreed.*[64]

Although this third judgment is brief and far simpler in structure than either of the first two, questions nevertheless remain as to what exactly is being proscribed. Are the targeted offenders crypto-Manichaeans who secretly abstain from the chalice? Or is the council perhaps opposing the apparently common and seemingly less alarming practice of reserving some part of the eucharistic elements for later consumption?[65] Manuel Sotomayor argues persuasively, based in part on a comparison with the thirteenth and fourteenth judgments of the Council of Toledo (400), that this judgment is directed against Christians who attend the eucharistic assembly but—for unclear and possibly varied reasons—do not partake of the elements at all.[66] The goal of the bishops gathered at Saragossa was thus to eliminate the ambiguous category of persons who seated themselves with the community yet did not fully "commune." The judgment attempts to draw clear boundaries between insiders and outsiders and, as in the second judgment, to oppose those who foster the creation of subgroups within the episcopally led Christian community.

The severity of the threatened punishment—perpetual anathema—is striking. The Manichaean associations of eucharistic abstention may account in part for the bishops' willingness to take such a strong position on this issue. Still more significant, however, is the centrality of the public act of eucharistic communion for the definition of the episcopally led Christian community.

> IV. *On the twenty-one days from December 17th to Epiphany, which is the 6th of January—on these continuous days, let no one be allowed to be absent from the church: they are not to be concealed in houses, nor to stay on estates, nor to head for the mountains, nor to walk with bare feet, but to flock to the church. Let whoever of the baptized who does not observe this be anathema in perpetuity. By all the bishops it was said: That one will be anathema.*[67]

The fourth judgment is closely parallel to the second in structure, wording, and content, and it seems to represent a continuation of the earlier discussion of seasonal retreats; the language of the fourth judgment, which gives the impression of being somewhat more carefully crafted, is probably modeled on that of the second. Evidently some Christians were observing practices of withdrawal during the pre-Epiphany season similar to the Lenten practices opposed in the second judgment. The bishops, in turn, advocate attendance at daily services during the three weeks before Epiphany: on these continuous days, they declare, Christians are to come together in church. The careful identification of the pre-Epiphany season implies, as the paucity of external evidence for such a practice confirms, that many Christians were unfamiliar with the custom of observing this Advent period of penitence.[68] The council here seems to propose novel congregational Advent observances in competition with the opposed ascetic practices.

The new element introduced in the fourth judgment is the opposition to the practice of walking barefoot. The parallel construction of the infinitive phrases, "to hide in houses" (*latere in domibus*), "to stay on estates" (*sedere ad villas*), "to head for the mountains" (*montes petere*), and "to walk with bare feet" (*nudis pedibus incedere*), suggests that these were alternative ascetic practices observed during the pre-Epiphany season. Within this series, the sedentary and indoor practices of staying in houses and on country estates are paired and contrasted with going to the mountains or walking barefoot. Walking barefoot, the judgment suggests, is a mobile and outdoor ascetic practice parallel to periodic withdrawal to the mountains; it may be associated with pilgrimages, or may simply represent an ascetic discipline valued in itself. Henry Chadwick has pointed out that the practice of going barefoot was also a point of contention among Christians in the northern Italian city of Brescia; those who defended it were able to argue their position based on both Old and New Testament passages.[69] The practice was not, however, necessarily controversial: Augustine reports no outrage against his friend Alypius, who walked barefoot in the cold months of Lent as part of his preparation for baptism in Ambrose's Milan.[70]

Chadwick has also argued alternatively that going barefoot may have had magical associations for the Christians who formulated this judgment. A number of ancient pagan rites, including rites to ensure agricultural productivity, required bare feet. And Priscillian was later to defend himself against the charge, put forth by Ithacius, of taking part in magic rituals involving the consecration of firstfruits and curses to the sun and moon.[71] Although there is no evidence that Ithacius mentioned bare feet in the context of his accusations of magic, Chadwick speculates that such a suspicion of magic may lie behind the council's prohibition of walking with bare feet.[72] If Chadwick is right—and this is difficult to prove or disprove— Ithacius did not succeed in persuading the other bishops to include explicit reference to magic in the language of the council's judgment.[73]

The fourth judgment, like the third, closes with the most severe of threats, permanent exclusion from the Christian community. There is a clear discrepancy between this penalty and the vaguer punishment prescribed by the otherwise closely parallel second judgment. This discrepancy probably derives more from a shift in the general level of interest or excitement at the meeting than from any rational perception of difference in the severity of the transgressions.[74] In the third and fourth judgments, the bishops most passionately defend the public gathering of the urban congregation for the worship of God.

> V. Those who through the instruction or judgment of a bishop have been separated from the church are not to be received by other bishops. If bishops do this knowingly, let them not have communion. By all the bishops it was said: Let whoever of the bishops does this not have communion.[75]

The fifth judgment addresses the need for episcopal solidarity in order to achieve the goals of the first four judgments. With the introduction of bishops as the named targets, the strident cry of "Anathema!" is replaced with the more neutral reference to communion withheld, and there is no explicit mention of the possibility of deposition. Nevertheless, the judgment represents an aggressive move to enforce episcopal compliance with the council's judgments.[76] While the problems created by episcopal disunity were by no means new, no previous council had dared withhold communion from bishops who failed to enforce the rulings of their colleagues.[77]

Severus appears to offer evidence that this judgment was in fact used against the supporters of Priscillian.[78]

> VI. If one of the clerics leaves his office of his own will on account of presumed luxury and vanity and wants to seem to be some sort of observer of the law in a monastic lifestyle, rather than a cleric, he must thus be driven away from the church; unless he makes amends by beseeching and begging many times, he is not to be received. By all the bishops it was said: Let it be so.[79]

It is not clear whether the offenders targeted in this judgment are actually rejecting their clerical status (*officium*) or are merely redefining their understandings of the lifestyle and duty (also *officium*) appropriate to that status. Regardless of the actual position of the monastic clergy here condemned, the Saragossan bishops clearly wish to set up a strong opposition between the rightful clergy and those living "in a monastic lifestyle" (*in monacho*). The monks follow "their own will" (*suo sponte*) and abandon their duty to their congregations; they pronounce judgment against the established church for its vanity of luxurious living; and they want to appear superior to the other clergy in their observance of the law. The bishops are outraged by the monks' arrogance, their audacious choice to cultivate their personal virtue and authority rather than to serve the bishop and his public congregation dutifully. Such a "presumption" is itself "vanity."[80]

The punishment threatened evokes powerful visual imagery: the monks are not to be "anathematized" or "excommunicated" but rather "driven out of the church" (*de ecclesia repellendum*). Conditions for reacceptance are specified, uniquely among the judgments of the Council of Saragossa. The offenders may be received back by the bishop if they have "beseeched and begged" him repeatedly (*rogando atque obsecrando*), thereby concretely symbolizing their acceptance of their subordination to the bishop and the needs of the congregation. While less severe than perpetual anathema, the penalty is nevertheless harsh, implying a lengthy penance and leaving the determination of the limits of that penance to the judgment of the excommunicating bishop.

> VII. One is not to take for oneself the name of teacher, except those persons to whom it has been granted, according to what has been written. By all the bishops it was said: It is agreed.[81]

The seventh and eighth judgments continue to address situations of tension arising from competition between various forms of leadership recognized in the Spanish churches. The seventh sets out specifically to restrict the authority of independent teachers. The mention of teachers recalls the first judgment, with its reference both to the "strange men" (*virorum alienorum*) who meet and read with others and to the literate women who gather with others to teach and learn.[82] Here, however, innuendoes of sexual impropriety are absent, and the opposition is more tentatively expressed. As in the previous judgment against monastic clergy, the bishops hint at an inappropriate presumption or assertion of self, which constitutes a form of insubordination. However, the vagueness of the language and the unwillingness of the bishops to threaten any punishment of potential offenders indicate that the Saragossan council was not confident of its ability to challenge the authority of independent teachers directly.[83]

Who might legitimately grant the authority implied in the title of teacher? The judgment implies that it is the bishop's right, but this is not explicitly claimed. The invocation of scripture is likewise vague and unpersuasive. If the reference is to Matt. 23.8, which restricts the title of teacher to Jesus, it seems to contradict the council's assertion that some Christians have been legitimately granted the title; other possibilities include James 3.1 ("Let not many become teachers . . .") or 1 Tim. 1.6-7 ("Certain persons . . . have wandered away into vain discussion, desiring to be teachers of the law"). The bishops know that the authority to teach is popularly recognized in certain individuals possessing particular education or insight or eloquence. "The work of the teacher," notes Priscillian himself, "is reading and preaching the gospel."[84] The bishops attempt not to oppose this authority altogether but rather to subordinate it more firmly to the bishop and the episcopally led congregation.[85]

> *VIII. Virgins who have dedicated themselves to God should not be veiled unless of proven age of forty years, which the priest shall confirm. By all the bishops it was said: It is agreed.*[86]

The council's new note of tentativeness persists in its eighth and final judgment, which also omits any threat of punishment. This judgment seeks to establish a distinction between two different categories of dedicated virgins: the veiled and the unveiled. This may be a novel distinction, since there are no earlier instances of differentiation between virgins who have merely taken a private vow and "consecrated" or "veiled" virgins.[87] The judgment restricts the category of the veiled to those who are at least forty years old and further specifies that this age limit is to be enforced by the bishop. The council's intention seems to reduce the visibility and status of young ascetic women in particular, and to exert some degree of episcopal control over ascetic women in general, by placing severe limits on the number publicly honored by the veil. The use of a minimum age requirement to limit women's access to special status in the church was not unprecedented; however, the establishment of a lower age limit as high as forty for veiled or consecrated virgins was uncommon at this time.[88] The assertion of episcopal control only in the area of confirmation of the age requirement is nevertheless remarkably restrained: it suggests that the bishops gathered at Saragossa could not lay claim to a right of consecration or ritual veiling of virgins.[89] The language of the judgment thus implies the existence, not of an institutionalized "order of virgins" whose membership requirements were being reasserted or redefined, but rather of informal and autonomous groups of ascetic women over whom the bishops were attempting to exert some minimal control. It is likely that the bishops could not realistically expect—and perhaps did not want— anything more than an acknowledgement of their symbolic authority over the virgins.

The origins of the ascetic practice of veiling are obscure, and the significance attributed to the custom varied even in late antiquity according to shifts in cultural context and perspective. In North Africa during the late second and early third centuries, for example, it was anomalous for a mature woman to appear in public with her head uncovered; the dedicated virgins seemingly embraced this anomaly, refusing to cover their heads in church in order to signify their unique position within the Christian community and to express their freedom from male authority.[90] On the other hand, in many western Christian communities of the fourth century, male writers compared the virgins' veil, not with a head covering signifying matronal status, but rather with the veil worn in Roman and Christian marriage ceremonies.[91] In this context, it was the wearing rather than the rejecting of the veil that expressed the Christian virgins' special condition:[92] permanent brides, poised for the duration of their lifetimes in a liminal state between childhood and marriage, they were adult women, yet under the authority of no husband, linked instead to Christ in a special, and theoretically inviolable, relationship. By refusing some dedicated virgins the right to wear the veil, the bishops at Saragossa would seem to be denying them a powerful symbol of status, independence, and spiritual authority.[93]

In general, fourth-century Christian men seem to have been well-nigh obsessed with cases (whether actual or merely anticipated) of virgins who broke their vow of sexual continence, and most modern scholars have been happy to assume that it was the high incidence of sexual transgression on the part of female virgins that led to the imposition of minimum age limits like the one established by this council.[94] By forty, the age of menopause,[95] a woman's passions and desirability were thought to have come to an end, along with her ability to disgrace herself publicly with pregnancy;[96] she was therefore less likely to dishonor her vow. Peter Brown points out, however, that it was not only the weak morals of the young girl but also her family's desire to use her to as "a pawn in the game of family alliances" that might threaten her vow; he suggests that in countries such as Spain, where the minimum age limit for virgins was high, virgins may typically have been from families of high social status, for whom their role in the transmission of wealth and lineage was crucial.[97] In a period characterized by a certain cautiousness in approaching sacramental acts—consider the common postponement of baptism—and in a culture that tended to view a woman as property that must be handed over by her "father" (in this case, the bishop) to her "betrothed" (Christ) perfectly intact,[98] extreme care to avoid the tarnishing of the virgin's consecrated vow is perhaps not surprising.

But a high incidence of sexual transgression on the part of virgins—whether owing to their own weakness of purpose or to the dynastic machinations of their families—is neither a necessary nor a sufficient "explanation" of the doubtless overdetermined efforts of the bishops at Saragossa to reduce the status and visibility of young virgins. In the context of late-ancient culture, an unmarried woman of marriageable age was always a potentially disturbing figure, whose anomalous status was measured on a number of different psycho-social registers. The implicit social challenge of the young virgin's rejection of a husband's authority resonated with the perceived threat of her unfettered sexual potency: witness, for example, the Spanish poet Prudentius' awe in the face of the twelve-year-old virgins of his own literary construction whose eroticized ferocity is tamed only by a death figured as marriage to Christ.[99] By postponing the honoring and recognition of virgins, the bishops may have sought to reduce the appeal of the virgin life. As for those women who nevertheless persisted in the pursuit of asceticism, they were encouraged to live out their vows in quiet privacy until they had reached a stage of life at which singleness was no longer interpreted as an assertion of will and sexual energies were understood to have subsided of their own accord. Only then could a public expression of the "virgins' " anomalous status be tolerated.

Conclusions

The *Acts of the Council of Saragossa* allows a partial reconstruction of the conciliar drama of which the document is but "the last verbalized stage."[100] By observing the pattern of the council's discussions, we can both identify the issues of greatest concern to the assembled bishops and uncover some of the strategies employed to combat their opposition. Such a reconstruction of the council's concerns and strategies can be applied directly to our understanding of the early stages of opposition to Priscillian. The works of Priscillian and Sulpicius Severus indicate that the council was convened in large part to counter the influence of Priscillian and his associates. In addition, at least three of its twelve participants—Hydatius, Ithacius, and Delphinus—left the council strong and active opponents of the Spanish ascetic, while only one—Symposius—is said to have supported him afterwards. We should not assume that all of the council's judgments were necessarily directed against Christians associated with Priscillian, but the *Acts of the Council of Saragossa* as a whole clearly reflects the attitudes of Christians who were disturbed by Priscillian's influence.

When they came together at Saragossa, the twelve bishops seem to have immediately positioned their discussion within the context of the public-private distinction in order to construct and defend a particular definition of Christian community. Their initial debate over women's participation in mixed-sex study groups cuts to the heart of the issue of communal location. Spanish Christians like Priscillian may have presented their meetings as the private gatherings of men and women joined in a shared—indeed, a familial—scholarly and ascetic pursuit. However, by interjecting the adjective "strange" into their description of the relations between those men and women, the bishops denied the legitimacy of such a reading of their activities. They insisted instead that all Christian gatherings took place in the public eye, a context in which women related to men not as familiars but as strangers. The mixed-sex study groups thereby acquired a taint of scandal, seeming to represent a violation of a fundamental principle of social order in the public sphere—the separation and subordination of women.

In their first judgment, the bishops did not prohibit small-group meetings but were content merely to urge that such meetings be segregated by sex. In their subsequent three judgments, however, the bishops tried actively to prevent practices that created a "centrifugal" pull away from the centralized public structures of the urban congregation and toward the decentered social organization typical of a sphere of social life in which individuals were connected by more complex networks of personal relationships.[101] The powerful social symbolism of food in defining the locus of community is evidenced in the bishops' concern with fasting and the Eucharist. The second judgment opens by prohibiting fasting practices that diverge from those of the episcopally led congregations and thereby challenge the unity of those congregations. The third explicitly confronts offenders who remain aloof from full participation in the congregational

Eucharist, while the second and fourth deal implicitly with the same topic by opposing seasonal absence from episcopally led worship. Symbolism of place as well as of food is highlighted in the second and fourth judgments, where withdrawal to private and rural spaces—houses, estates, mountains—is unfavorably contrasted with constant public presence in the urban churches where the bishops preside.

In the midst of these discussions focusing on the definition of Christian community, a shift in the emotional tenor of the meeting took place. The first two judgments formulated are recorded in complex, highly charged language, suggesting the lively, involved participation of a number of bishops. In both cases, the judgment's language, although inflammatory in some respects, also sounds a conciliatory note and suggests a willingness to compromise so long as the offenders comply with the basic demands for sex-segregation within study groups, on the one hand, and faithful church attendance during Lent, on the other. In both the first and second judgments, the bishops invoke the threat of the harsh punishment of anathema while remaining vague with regard to its conditions or duration. All of this suggests strong convictions on the part of at least some of the bishops, tempered either by disagreement at the council itself or by anticipated resistance in the Spanish communities.

In contrast to the first two judgments, both the third and fourth are relatively straightforward in wording and therefore appear to reflect less protracted discussions. And in both cases, the bishops boldly invoke the severest penalty available to them: perpetual anathema. Passions were still high, and the earlier ambivalence had dissipated. The bishops were now more united and confident in their opposition to liturgical and ascetic practices that challenged the centralized focus of the publicly defined Christian community. The order of the recorded judgments suggests that it was the discussion of abstention from the Eucharist that consolidated episcopal opposition, and that the excitement generated remained high during the discussion leading to the fourth judgment. The possible Manichaean associations of eucharistic abstention may explain this consolidation of the opposition, but it is equally likely that the centrality of the Eucharist for the public self-definition of the Christian community alone accounts for the strong terms of these two judgments.

Whereas the first four judgments are aimed at indefinite targets and focus on the public definition of the Christian community, the next four judgments target specific classes of persons and focus more narrowly on the public definition of authority in the Christian community. With this second set of judgments, the bishops attempted to assert control over groups that included the most powerful supporters of Priscillian and other ascetics. The fifth and sixth judgments are aimed at members of the ecclesiastical hierarchy: bishops who dissent from conciliar opinion and ascetic clergy who presume to criticize their more worldly colleagues. The punishments invoked, while less severe than those of the previous two judgments, are nevertheless harsh, especially in light of the high status of the targets. The threat of excommunication of offending bishops and clerics suggests a somewhat more cautious and controlled, yet still aggressive, attitude on the part of the assembled bishops.

The language of the seventh and eighth judgments reflects a further drop in the emotional intensity of the discussions: these judgments are moderate in tone and include no threat of punishment. The failure to threaten punishment may indicate that the bishops were either relatively confident or relatively indifferent to the challenge represented by lay teachers and female virgins, individuals with little or no public authority. Other evidence, however, seems to counter this appearance of confidence or indifference. The seventh judgment concerning teachers recalls the strongly worded first judgment, which attempts to control the interactions of men and women who read and teach, while the eighth contains a muted echo of the bishops' initial preoccupation with the symbolic implications of women's activities for communal definition: here again, the bishops seem to express disapproval of women's apparent anomalous public manifestation of authority. In this case, the council focuses on female virgins, whose rejection of marriage offers a further implicit challenge to the principle of women's subordination. Given that the seventh and eighth judgments thus tap into issues of demonstrated concern to the council, it is likely that the bishops' failure to threaten to punish offenders stemmed, not from confidence or indifference, but rather from their awareness of their limited ability to control the authority of lay teachers and ascetic women.

It should by now be apparent that the eight judgments promulgated by the small episcopal gathering at Saragossa were not the confident act of an entrenched majority; rather, they constituted an early step toward creating consensus on the public definition of the Christian community and its leadership. Throughout the conciliar *Acts*, there is evidence of tension between the bishops' drive to consolidate their public authority and their assessment of the limits of that authority. In spite of the *Acts'* generic claims to quasi-senatorial authority and the document's careful adaptation of the literary form to emphasize not only confidence but unanimity, the language of the conciliar judgments betrays signs that the bishops found it necessary at points to compromise, to conciliate, and to avoid putting their authority to the test. They doubtless anticipated resistance in some of the Spanish congregations. The suppression of the names of individual bishops in the conciliar *Acts* and the later reference to Symposius having left the council early suggest that the bishops also disagreed among themselves on some issues.

Although the Council of Saragossa's attempt to buttress public definitions of community and authority was an ambivalent or tentative first step, it was not without effect. Through the *Acts* of the council, the bishops successfully represented themselves as legitimate leaders contending in a heroic struggle with disorderly, insubordinate, subversive, or arrogantly ambitious opponents. The bishops' self-assertion was thus intimately intertwined with their dramatized opposition to ascetic Christians like Priscillian. That Priscillian and his most prominent associates were ultimately not only condemned by name but also executed, that his ascetic circle came to be consistently characterized as a movement of heretics, magicians, and loose women, and that association with Priscillian's name was eventually enough to mandate exclusion from the Christian community— these are all indications of the success of the effort begun at Saragossa.

· CHAPTER TWO ·

"MANICHAEAN"

Charge and Countercharge
in Priscillian's *Tractates*

In 380, the Council of Saragossa sought to control ascetic practice and to heighten the importance of the episcopally led liturgy for the identity of the Christian community. The council's *Acts* leave open the possibility that ascetics like Priscillian might remain part of the publicly defined congregations of Spain. However, the fundamental differences that split the Spanish churches could not be so easily resolved. Some six years after the Saragossan bishops dispersed,[1] two of their number testified for the prosecution in a civil trial at Trier that led to the executions of Priscillian, Felicissimus, Armenius, Euchrotia, and Latronianus. Between Saragossa and Trier, conciliar debate had given way to the uncompromising language of exclusionary labels, the brutal violence of mobs wielding sticks and stones, and the harsh finality of the imperial sword.

Sulpicius Severus' *Chronicle* is our primary source for reconstructing the chain of events of the years 380 to 386: the conflict in Merida immediately following the Council of Saragossa, Priscillian's ordination as bishop of Avila, the departure and subsequent return of Priscillian and two episcopal associates, the summoning of bishops Priscillian and Instantius to a council at Bordeaux, the civil trial of Priscillian at Trier, and the execution of Priscillian and several followers. In a chronological presentation shaped by the literary conventions and political interests of classical historiography, Severus focuses on the high reaches of the ecclesiastical and imperial hierarchies. His account highlights the significance of personal ambition and competition in driving the events of the Priscillianist controversy and enables us to trace with particular clarity the formation of networks of alliance and opposition between various bishops and imperial officials. We thereby observe the process by which a local dispute was transformed into an ecclesiastical controversy in which two emperors and the most influential bishops of the Latin-speaking world were ultimately forced to take part.[2]

Priscillian's works are much less complete in chronological scope and certainly less susceptible to chronological organization than Severus' historical account. However, for the stage of the controversy immediately following the Council of Saragossa, they provide valuable perspectives that are missing from Severus' narrative. As Raymond Van Dam has emphasized, it was not only the leaders who shaped the Priscillianist controversy but also "the desires and aspirations of the people who joined them."[3] While "the people" for the most part remain submerged in Severus' narrative, Priscillian's report on the conflict at Merida in his *Letter to Damasus* provides a glimpse of the social dynamics of the local communities that shaped both the leaders and the conflicts between those leaders.[4] In addition, Priscillian's *Apology* and his *Book on the Faith and the Apocrypha* shed still more light on the process of labeling by which the faction that supported Bishop Hydatius attempted to undercut Priscillian's authority and thereby to resolve the dispute.[5] At the same time, these apologetic works illumine Priscillian's view of the differing understandings of community and authority that seem to have been at the heart of the conflict at both Saragossa and Merida, giving new insight into Priscillian's self-understanding and his own strategies of rhetorical combat. Priscillian presents himself as an authoritative Christian teacher and interpreter of scripture who has been unjustly assailed by an uneducated and contentious bishop; the learned exegete complains that "untaught madness presses, ignorant insanity drives us out," and describes his opponents as "schismatics" who "pursue domestic enmities under the name of religion."[6] Priscillian's writings also, however, suggest that the controversy was not merely about authority but also involved significant differences in theological perspective that were closely entangled with the divergent understandings of authority. The sermons preserved in the Würzburg corpus complement the evidence of the *Apology*, providing a broader perspective on Priscillian's thought and thereby aiding us in situating the cosmological aspect of this controversy in the history of late fourth-century Christian thought.

The Priscillianist tractates stand at the center of inquiry and thereby provide this chapter's textual unity. In addition, the labeling strategies of Priscillian's opponents continue to organize the chronological investigation. The testimony of Priscillian, complemented by Severus and other hostile sources, indicates that a series of distinct, yet overlapping, labels was invoked in the period between the Council of Saragossa and Priscillian's death. Manichaeism, sorcery, and sexual immorality figured prominently among the negative associations that contributed to a growing public perception that Priscillian and his companions were dangerous and fundamentally alien to the Christian community. It was the accusation of Manichaeism that seems to have dominated the earliest phase of the conflict that developed following the Council of Saragossa, beginning with Hydatius' initial struggles to discredit a rival who was eroding his support both locally and abroad, and reaching the peak of effectiveness when Hydatius forced Priscillian to leave Spain under threat of deposition and exile. The label was persuasively applied in a context in which Priscillian's asceticism, his eclectic reading habits, his preoccupation with demonology and dualistic cosmology, and his predilection for small-group meetings lent plausibility to Hydatius' damaging suggestion that the "false bishop" was a Manichaean merely masquerading as an orthodox Christian. Furthermore, the charge of Manichaeism was particularly effective as part of a continuing rhetorical strategy to represent Priscillian's circle as private and therefore subversive, since the Manichaeans were commonly associated with secretive and seditious behavior. And, finally, the use of a label implying marginality even to the category of heresy itself had sinister implications. Priscillian's own writings reflect the marginal location of Manichaeism on the late ancient Christian map of the "other": situated somewhere between the more intimate enmity of the heretic and the absolutized alterity of the magician, the label of Manichaeism ultimately mediated the slide from charges of heresy to the more deadly accusation of sorcery.

This chapter traces the first act in the dramatic chain of events that led from Saragossa to the sword, using the writings of Priscillian as a window from which to gaze upon the scene of Spanish controversy in the period from Hydatius' return to Merida to Priscillian's forced departure from Avila—the period in which the label of Manichaeism seems to have been crucial to the representation of Priscillian as "heretical other." The first and largest task of the chapter is to reconstruct the disputes at Merida immediately following the Council of Saragossa, relying primarily on Priscillian's *Letter to Damasus* and his *Apology*, secondarily on the *Book on the Faith and the Apocrypha*. While the *Letter to Damasus* has been used in previous studies of the early controversy surrounding Priscillian, the

value of the *Apology* for the historical reconstruction the social and cosmological conflicts of this period has not yet been fully exploited; here, in
particular, fresh insights may be gained. In addition, Priscillian's sermons,
less directly influenced by apologetic concerns, will give a different angle
on the more controversial aspects of Priscillian's thought, which, far from
being simply subsumable under the category of Manichaeism, may be
seen to play a distinctive role in the history of the late-fourth-century resurgence and suppression of cosmological reflection and debate. With the
introduction of a more purely theological dimension to this controversy, a
new layer is added to the ongoing account of the social conflict and rhetorical strategies of mediation already begun with the initial reading of the
Acts of the Council of Saragossa.

Conflict at Merida and the Rescript against "Pseudobishops and Manichaeans": The *Letter to Damasus*

The second of the Würzburg tractates is a letter addressed to Damasus,
bishop of Rome, by a group of Spanish bishops who seek to be exonerated
from the charges of Manichaeism and "pseudo-episcopacy" by means of
which Hydatius of Merida has threatened them with exile. Severus supplies us with the names of the three Spanish bishops who travelled to
Rome to appeal for the support of Bishop Damasus: Priscillian, Instantius,
and Salvianus.[7] It seems certain that the letter discovered in the Würzburg
corpus represents a defense of the orthodoxy and episcopacy of these
three bishops. Priscillian is the most likely candidate for the actual authorship, since the defense of his own ordination plays a central role.[8] He takes
the opportunity in the letter not only to present his own orthodox profession of faith but also to give a narrative account of the conflict in Merida
that led to the forced departure of the three bishops. The *Letter to Damasus*
is thus an extremely valuable source for the reconstruction of the early
stages of the conflict between Priscillian's circle and Hydatius and his
supporters.

    Although the letter provides us with a firsthand report of events writ-
ten soon after those events occurred, the report is hardly unbiased. In tracing the process by which the label of Manichaeism was first made to
"stick" to Priscillian and his companions, we must therefore contend with
the ambiguities of an apologetic work that seeks to conceal as well as to
reveal. Although he cannot, like Severus,[9] simply omit reference to the
sensitive charge of Manichaeism, Priscillian has strong reasons to sup-
press certain aspects of the process that led to his being successfully la-

beled a Manichaean. In the *Letter to Damasus*, he attempts to hide the role he and his companions played in provoking the conflict that eventually resulted in their condemnation as Manichaeans. He also takes great pains to sever the continuity between events at the Council of Saragossa and those that took place soon afterwards at Merida. In both cases, Priscillian's rhetorical strategy obscures the context and significance of the imperial rescript. A critical examination of the relevant portions of the *Letter to Damasus* will therefore be necessary in order to untangle the chain of events leading from Saragossa to the imperial rescript.

Priscillian begins his account of the events following the Council of Saragossa by emphasizing, not only the orthodoxy and virtue, but also the peaceable intentions of his own circle. After the council, he and his companions wished merely to pursue their lives of simplicity and piety without disturbance, he claims.[10] They had remained in communion with Hydatius, and Hydatius had brought back no report against them from the Council of Saragossa. Nevertheless, Hydatius was subsequently driven by an irrational hostility, indeed a "madness," to disrupt the peace.[11] It was a local squabble that led to his unjustified and isolated resentment of Priscillian and his companions, Priscillian explains. But his account of that local squabble calls into question his initial characterization of Hydatius' antagonism as both unexpected and unprovoked.

Hydatius was denounced in his own church by one of his presbyters shortly after his return from the Council of Saragossa, Priscillian says. Subsequently, "certain people of our churches" circulated a *libellus* containing even more damaging attacks on Hydatius. As a result of these two sets of accusations, some of the Meridan clergy withdrew from Hydatius' communion until he could be cleared.[12] Earlier in the letter, Priscillian succinctly summarizes the causes of the controversy: "conflicts arose out of necessary reproof or envy of our way of life or the power of the most recent times."[13] "Necessary reproof" (*necessaria redargutione*) probably refers to these criticisms directed against Hydatius in the period immediately following the Council of Saragossa, if not also before; "envy of our way of life" (*aemulatione vitae*) seems to indicate Hydatius' opposition to Priscillian's asceticism; and the apocalyptic phrase "the power of the most recent times" (*novissimi temporis potestate*) must refer to the imperial intervention eventually solicited by Hydatius. Nowhere, however, does Priscillian indicate the nature of the charges brought against Hydatius, whether because he cannot expect Damasus to be sympathetic to those charges, or because he fears to reveal his own close involvement.[14] Their seriousness is nevertheless underlined by Priscillian's suggestion at the end of the letter that Hydatius still fears that the accusations will resurface.[15]

When the dispute arose, "we assembled," writes Priscillian.[16] Since, as we shall see, it is unlikely that Priscillian had already been ordained, the episcopal "we," strictly speaking, must refer only to Instantius and Salvianus, although Priscillian may also have been present at their meeting; here, as elsewhere in this account, Priscillian is deliberately obscuring the timing and circumstances of his ordination. Priscillian presents the bishops as neutral mediators, but both their alacrity in gathering and their subsequent actions suggest rather that they were themselves interested participants in the Meridan dispute.[17] Priscillian's friends not only met but also appealed to their episcopal allies Hyginus and Symposius; these in turn suggested that they call a council to reestablish peace in the churches.[18]

Symposius' response, which is cited by Priscillian, reveals that the Meridan conflict was not merely an isolated schism among local clergy, as Priscillian initially implies. First, it seems that a number of laypeople were among those in Merida who had criticized Hydatius and subsequently been excommunicated. Symposius offers the opinion that these Meridan laypeople could be received by other bishops on the witness of their orthodox profession of faith, "if Hydatius were suspected by them."[19] If the phrase "if Hydatius were suspected by them" indicates that charges brought against him had called into question Hydatius' status as bishop, Symposius is directly undermining Hydatius' authority in the face of the fifth judgment of the Council of Saragossa.[20] Second, it appears that there was a close connection between the Council of Saragossa and what transpired in Merida thereafter, although the exact nature of this connection can no longer be reconstructed. Symposius, who was present at the council, responds to questions about the council and assures Instantius, Salvianus, and their friends that no one was condemned at Saragossa.[21] Perhaps it was Hydatius' failure to secure an official condemnation of the ascetics in his congregation that had emboldened them to challenge him directly following the council. Under attack, Hydatius may have begun to make claims about the council's hostile stance toward the ascetics that alarmed Priscillian's supporters.

In spite of their colleagues' advice that a new council be convened, Instantius and Salvianus decided to proceed to Merida for a personal interview with Hydatius. They may sincerely have hoped to attain a peaceful resolution of the dispute, as Priscillian claims.[22] However, it is more likely that Priscillian's episcopal friends went to Merida with the intention of influencing—if not forcing—events in their own favor without submitting to the uncertainties and ambiguities of a conciliar process.[23] From

Priscillian's defensive language, it is clear that they were accused by their opponents of initiating disputes, of wrongdoing, and of insubordination. They may have wished to intimidate Hydatius into capitulation by a dramatic show of episcopal support for the dissident Meridan laity and clergy. Priscillian mentions that while in Merida, the bishops received a confession of faith from the Meridan laity, "which we could not reject because it was catholic." Whatever the real intentions of the episcopal delegation, peace was not the result of their visit. As the company of Instantius and Salvianus approached the presbytery of Merida, a hostile crowd barred their way and beat them with sticks. Priscillian's brief but vivid description of the scene hints at the deep division running through all levels of the local Christian community and the intense hostility that characterized both sides by this point.[24]

Upon returning from Merida, the visiting bishops hastened to write to "nearly all" their fellow bishops, Priscillian reports. They must have felt some urgent need to control the manner in which the story of the Meridan confrontation circulated. But evidently this was not the only urgent matter. Priscillian reports that in addition to their account of events at Merida, the bishops submitted to their colleagues the Meridan laity's profession of faith; "nor did we pass over in silence the fact that many of them were sought for the episcopacy after their profession." The reply to their letter, as cited by Priscillian, underlines the significance of this hitherto unmentioned reference to the proposed ordination of some of the Meridan laity. The unnamed episcopal respondent reiterates the need for a council to resolve the dispute at Merida and adds specifically that "the profession held should be believed, and just as the dedication of a bishop occurs in a bishop, so the choice of candidacy occurs in the people"—a cautiously worded confirmation of the potential eligibility of the dissident Meridan laity for ordination to the episcopacy.[25]

Priscillian himself was probably among the Meridan laity who were in conflict with their bishop and whose orthodoxy and eligibility for the episcopacy was of such great concern to Instantius and Salvianus and their supporters.[26] Priscillian's defense of the Meridan laity in the *Letter to Damasus* therefore represents a subtly contrived defense of his own episcopacy, for he himself acknowledges in the letter that "a bishop who as a layperson deserved formerly to be condemned can be deposed."[27] Without openly calling attention to challenges raised in reference to his own ordination or even referring explicitly to the circumstances of that ordination, he carefully documents the steps by which the Meridan laity were received as orthodox, in spite of their excommunication and condemnation by their own bishop following the fifth judgment of the Council of Saragossa. And Priscillian makes it clear that respected bishops judged those laypeople worthy of the episcopacy.

Sulpicius Severus reports that Instantius and Salvianus appointed Priscillian bishop of Avila sometime shortly after the Council of Saragossa and suggests that it was this act that led Hydatius and his ally Ithacius to "press more keenly" and approach the civil authorities for a decree banishing their opponents from the Spanish communities.[28] Priscillian's own account is less direct but also confirms the close link between his ordination and Hydatius' request for an imperial rescript. Immediately after recording the episcopal support for the potential ordination of some of the Meridan laity, Priscillian introduces the topic of the rescript: "Hence, being more afraid than was necessary, he produced requests falsely and, weaving a tale of the events, with our names concealed, he sought a rescript against pseudo-bishops and Manichaeans and of course obtained it, because everyone who heard of pseudo-bishops and Manichaeans hated them."[29] Priscillian must have been ordained shortly after the violent confrontation in Merida, and his ordination appears to have further destabilized the situation in Merida and the surrounding communities. By ordaining Priscillian to the episcopacy, Instantius and Salvianus not only removed him from the sphere of authority of a hostile bishop but also increased the number of their own episcopal supporters. Hydatius must have felt seriously threatened, and his fear may have been more justified than Priscillian admits.[30]

With the balance of power turned against him locally, Hydatius sought support further afield, appealing to "secular judges," as Severus puts it.[31] This was not such an unlikely step, although it came to be viewed with disapproval in the light of a later and rather different act of secular intervention in the controversy.[32] Heretics in general and Manichaeans in particular had been outlawed by imperial decree: their leaders were subject to fines or banishment, and their meeting places could be confiscated.[33] Priscillian reports that Hydatius succeeded in gaining the sympathies of Ambrose, in a context suggesting that this took place as Hydatius was seeking the rescript.[34] Severus' account first mentions Ambrose's opposition in relation to Priscillian's later visit to Milan;[35] however, it is possible that the bishop of Milan also played a role earlier in helping Hydatius obtain from Gratian either an order for the Spanish enforcement of standing laws against heretics or Manichaeans or, as both Priscillian and Sulpicius Severus seem to suggest, a new rescript specially tailored to the Spanish situation.[36] Perhaps Gratian's pronouncement authorized Hydatius to identify the guilty parties.[37] Priscillian reports that when the rescript was issued, Hydatius "rushed against all Christians, calling even Hyginus a heretic along with us."[38]

It must have been immediately clear to Priscillian and his companions that resistance to the enforcement of an imperial rescript would be of no avail on a local level. Sulpicius Severus and Priscillian agree that the bishops left their churches voluntarily, not waiting for a formal sentence of exile and deposition. "We entrusted our churches to God, and we have given you their letters of communion, conveyed with the signature of all the clergy and people," Priscillian writes to Damasus. Subsequently, Priscillian insists on his readiness to submit to public trial in language suggesting that he has been accused of avoiding just such a trial, an accusation that may not be far from the truth; it may, thus, be misleading to speak of either the "exile" or the "deposition" of the three bishops at this point.[39] In Severus' words, "the gnostics despaired of their own affairs, not daring to dispute the judgment, and those who were bishops appeared to leave voluntarily; fear dispersed others."[40] Priscillian, Instantius, and Salvianus then set out for Italy to seek the support of the bishops of Milan and Rome and to defend their case before the imperial court.[41]

Priscillian's letter to the bishop of Rome is a defense of his own orthodoxy and the orthodoxy of the other two bishops who had been threatened with exile. His proof of orthodoxy proceeds in part according to convention: he offers a catholic profession of faith and a condemnation of acknowledged heresies, focusing in this case above all on the Manichaeans. In addition, he includes a less conventional item in his apologetic letter—namely, a defense of the use of the apocrypha. Priscillian's use of the apocrypha appears to have constituted his greatest vulnerability to the accusations of Manichaeism, and the charge of reading heretical scriptures must have been extensively exploited by Hydatius. We have seen that he raised the issue of apocryphal literature at the Council of Saragossa, and the order in which Priscillian introduces his defense in the *Letter to Damasus* suggests that the use of the apocrypha was a major topic of discussion in the subsequent conflict at Merida as well.[42] Priscillian was the author of a separate treatise devoted to the defense of the use of the apocrypha, and this may have been composed during or shortly after the events at Merida.[43]

Priscillian is also very concerned in this letter to persuade Damasus that he was not condemned by the Council of Saragossa.[44] This was a crucial part of his defense before the bishop of Rome. He and his episcopal friends had never been judged heretical by an episcopal assembly or through any formal heresy process, which would have required the presence of the defendants, according to Damasus himself.[45] They had been condemned only by the irresponsible accusations of one bishop, whose own episcopal status had been questioned. Thus, Priscillian insists, in the eyes of the church, he and his associates were still orthodox and their episcopacy was valid. Gratian's rescript could not legitimately be used against them.

Priscillian's Defense

Among the Würzburg tractates is a second major apologetic work attributed to Priscillian or a close associate of his: the so-called *Apology*.[46] Unlike the *Letter to Damasus*, this document is difficult to place within the framework of the chronology of the Priscillianist controversy and includes little narrative material. It is, therefore, of less use in reconstructing the sequence of events that led to the ultimate execution of Priscillian and his followers. However, the *Apology* is of great help in interpreting the content of the accusations brought against Priscillian's circle in Spain in the early stages of the controversy. Whereas the *Letter to Damasus* glosses over the unsavory charges circulating in the Lusitanian communities, it is precisely the purpose of the *Apology* to respond in detail to a series of accusations brought against the Spanish ascetics. Whereas the *Letter to Damasus* is a carefully constructed appeal addressed to a powerful bishop distant from the heart of the conflict, the *Apology* was intended for an audience of local bishops. Whereas the tone of the *Letter to Damasus* is sober and controlled and its language replete with legal terminology, the *Apology* is a spirited and loosely organized work that interweaves exegesis with preacherly exhortation, and passionate anathemas with fervent professions of faith. If the *Letter to Damasus* provides the characters and basic plot for the early stages of the Priscillianist controversy, the *Apology* supplies the dialogue.

Determining the exact circumstances of composition of the *Apology* is difficult.[47] Scholars have argued that it was written by Priscillian or one of his companions before the Council of Saragossa,[48] at the request of some Spanish bishops immediately following the conflict at Merida,[49] as part of the defensive campaign following the rescript of Gratian, or for the Council of Bordeaux;[50] in other words, the document has been dated to almost every stage of the Priscillianist controversy and its authorship attributed to various members of Priscillian's circle. The most likely context for the *Apology* is, however, the conflict at Merida after the Council of Saragossa and before Priscillian's ordination, and the most likely author is Priscillian himself.[51] The treatise was therefore probably composed earlier than the *Letter to Damasus* and may be the work referred to at the end of that letter, where Priscillian appeals to "what we have written against the Manichaeans."[52] A date before the Council of Saragossa is possible but more difficult to support since, as we shall see, the *Apology* replies to charges of Manichaeism as well as charges of sorcery raised by Ithacius of Ossonuba, and there is no evidence that Ithacius was an active part of the opposition to the Priscillianist circle or that explicit charges of Manichaeism or sorcery were raised before the council. A later date is also possible, but much less likely than a date before Priscillian's ordination and Gratian's rescript, since the *Apology* seems to have been written by a layperson, makes no reference at all to the quasi-legal issues that are of such great concern in the *Letter to Damasus*, and is generally more confident and combative in tone.

Like the *Letter to Damasus*, the *Apology* is written on behalf of a group by an individual—presumably Priscillian—who seems naturally to assume the role of leader or spokesperson for the group. The author's sense of identity emerges most clearly in the introduction, where he offers his personal credentials. While protesting that "it is not proper to boast of what we have been," he nevertheless emphasizes his former social status and education: "We were not placed in such an obscure position in regard to the world or called so foolish that faith in Christ and the knowledge of belief could bring death to us rather than salvation."[53] Compare Severus' statement that Priscillian was wealthy, well-educated, and of noble birth.[54] In the *Apology*, these worldly credentials are transformed through their apparent rejection into the ascetic authority of one who has been converted in baptism to a "road" of life mapped out by the catholic creed and consisting of total surrender to Christ. Priscillian expresses a reluctance to respond to the bishops' request that he "go through each item" in defending his own orthodoxy: how could one with his credentials not "condemn the silly dogmas of the heretics"? This professed reluctance has a rhetorical function, but also appears to reflect a real ambivalence on the author's part. On the one hand, he clearly feels that his ascetic life and his past professions of orthodox belief, which are not secret but "established in the light of faith," grant him a certain authority and freedom. On the other hand, he acknowledges that scripture calls him to give witness whenever requested, both for the further perfecting of his own faith and for the sake of those who might sin through their mistaken opposition to him.[55]

In the end, Priscillian agrees to comply with the "most blessed bishops"; he indicates that they leave him little choice. Undertaking to condemn a series of errors of which he and his associates have been accused, Priscillian hopes thereby to persuade the bishops of the falseness of those accusations. Indeed, he announces that he will take the opportunity, not only to respond to the specific items with which he has been presented, but also to "speak more broadly" in professing his faith and opposing heresy.[56] The large number of errors condemned in the *Apology* supports the impression that Priscillian does indeed "speak more broadly": while many of these condemnations function as a direct defense against actual accusations, others are included to serve more complicated rhetorical purposes or arise out of interests unrelated to the controversy at hand. A brief overview of the document will provide a sense of its structure in relation to the apologetic purpose of Priscillian's condemnation of heresies, while also allowing us to identify and explore more fully those condemnations that seem most certain to reflect actual accusations against Priscillian and his circle.

Priscillian's introductory remarks include a condemnation of the "Binionites," those who divide Christ from God.[57] All the tractates place great stress on the unity of Christ and God, and Priscillian may well have created the Binionites—who appear only in his writings—as a fitting counterpart to his own highly unitive theology.[58] At any rate, he never suggests that he has been charged with this heresy. Priscillian next moves to the main body of his work, opening with four relatively brief condemnations of heresies that may likewise have little or nothing to do with the controversy between Priscillian's circle and their opponents: the Patripassian heresy, the Novatian heresy, the heresy of those who deny that Jesus Christ came in the flesh, and the Nicolaitans.[59] Priscillian's strong emphasis on the unity of God does, in fact, leave him somewhat vulnerable to the accusations of Patripassianism (an error Priscillian does not even seem to understand) and Docetism, and both of these were doctrinal errors associated with Manichaeism,[60] of which he was certainly accused. The possible charge of Novatianism—which Priscillian describes as a heresy characterized by multiple baptisms—may reflect disagreements between Priscillian's circle and their opponents on the subject of baptism.[61] Finally, the brief reference to the Nicolaitans may reflect charges of immorality being levied against Priscillian and his circle. Nevertheless, the connection between these four anathemas and the accusations actually brought against Priscillian and his associates is never made explicit and must therefore remain uncertain.[62]

Most of the weight of Priscillian's anathematizing efforts in the *Apology* falls on the next four errors condemned: worship of animals, worship of gentile gods, worship of demons, and Manichaeism. The errors of animal-, idol-, and demon-worship are treated at great length, and here finally Priscillian makes it clear that in each case the errors condemned represent actual accusations brought against his circle. The condemnation of the followers of Mani is more concise, but quite violent; in both respects it anticipates the condemnation of sorcery later in the work, where Priscillian again makes it quite clear that he is responding to an actual charge, even naming his accuser. Between the condemnations of Mani and of sorcery, Priscillian inserts a catalogue of ten heresies, including some (but not all) of the heresies already condemned, as well as several not previously mentioned; this list again does not seem to represent a response to actual charges against Priscillian but rather functions rhetorically to suggest the inclusiveness of Priscillian's condemnation of heresy, to deflect attention from the heresies of which Priscillian and his circle were actually being accused, and to separate all the foregoing condemnations from the discussion of the terrible accusation of sorcery that follows.

Priscillian's closing remarks include a positive profession of his own orthodox belief and a discussion of the criteria by which one distinguishes orthodoxy and heresy. Embedded in the statement of his own orthodoxy is a final condemnation of those who are led by an overly "carnal" interpretation of scripture to consider God masculo-feminine. These heretics also deny the Resurrection and take demons (Armaziel, Mariame, Joel, Balsamus, Barbilos) to be God. The subsequent discussion of how to distinguish orthodox and heretical teaching appears to engage one of Priscillian's favorite topics, as well as to respond to a point on which he has been attacked. Priscillian gives a brief treatment of his distinctive views concerning the canon, the apocrypha, prophecy, and revelation, in the course of which he condemns those who add a fifth gospel to the canon—an error of which he has also been accused.

This overview of the *Apology* suggests, then, that the condemnations that represent direct responses to actual accusations include the anathemas aimed against worshippers of animals, gentile gods, and demons, the condemnation of the followers of Mani, the anathematization of sorcerers, and the objection to the addition of a fifth gospel to the canon. The first and most lengthy of these is the condemnation of those who worship animals, which opens as follows: "Let the one be anathema who, upon reading about griffins, eagles, asses, elephants, serpents, and unnecessary beasts, has been captured by the emptiness of confused respect and constructed, as it were, a mystery of divine religion—though their works and abominableness of form are the nature of the demons, not the truth of the divine glories."[63] Priscillian here vehemently denounces exegetes who identify certain scriptural animals as symbols of God or the sacraments, implying that such exegetes thereby condone the worship of animals.[64] He insists that any scriptural mention of animals or fabulous beasts must instead be understood as a reference to demonic powers and moral vice:

"We have renounced what we have renounced in the devil, and that is what is called a wild animal."[65] The interpreter who fails to recognize this meaning confuses demons with God and evil with virtue and thereby condemns him or herself. "The prophets wanted all that was put in their visions to be read by all and, having been understood, to be avoided; and therefore the hearts of those who investigated those things and did not understand rightly what it was that they read have been given to the beast and their flesh will be devoured," Priscillian explains, citing the apocalyptic visions of bestial adversaries described in Daniel and Revelation.[66] Those who interpret scriptural beasts correctly, on the other hand, are enabled to attain the virtue of the true Christian and ascetic: "The one who understands the natures of beasts that have been described in parables may reject the things of this world and purify the character defects in him or herself."[67]

In defending his position, Priscillian is able to marshal an impressive, if also somewhat tedious, number of scriptural passages mentioning animals or fabulous beasts. He presents himself self-consciously as an authoritative interpreter of scripture who is called to the interpretive task by the canon itself, which urges him to "search the scriptures" (cf. John 5.39)[68] and to strive to understand the "turns of speech and the interpretation of parables" (cf. Wisd. of Sol. 8.8 and Ecclus. 39.2–3),[69] since "the law is spiritual" (cf. Rom. 7.14) and "all prophecy requires interpretation" (cf. 2 Peter 1.20).[70] If scripture calls him to his task, it is the God Christ who empowers him: "we have the God Christ in our minds as guide, through whom even if we should think otherwise, these things will also be revealed to us."[71] Priscillian is clearly satisfied that his long labor to interpret the scriptural references to animals has produced fruit, and his words reflect both confidence and inflexibility on a topic crucial to his exegetical defense of asceticism.

It is unlikely that either the idiosyncrasy or the intolerance of Priscillian's exegetical stance would have been enough to provoke an accusation of heresy, much less of animal-worship. The explanation for his accusers' hostile response lies, I suggest, in Priscillian's probable use of gnostic apocrypha to interpret canonical references to animals. His emphasis on his own authority as interpreter hints that the use of apocrypha may here be at stake, since it recalls similar language in his *Book on the Faith and the Apocrypha*, in which he twice cites John's exhortation to "search the scriptures" and concludes that the scriptures themselves command him to study even noncanonical texts in his search for knowledge of God.[72] Moreover, we shall see that elsewhere in the *Apology*, Priscillian identifies scriptural beasts both with the seven planetary gods and with demons called by the gnostic names Saclas, Nebroel, Samael, Belzebuth, Nasbodeus, and Belial.[73] A gnostic work like the *Apocryphon of John* would have suggested precisely such an identification: according to this work, the lustful chief archon Yaltabaoth, also known as Saclas or Samael, has the form of a lion-faced serpent; in addition, six of the seven planetary "powers" of Yaltabaoth take bestial shapes, bearing the faces of lion, donkey, hyena, serpent, dragon, monkey, and fire, respectively; and, finally, the two archons Yave and Eloim, produced through the adulterous union of the chief archon and Eve, have the faces of cat and bear.[74] Salvation in the gnostic text hinges on the recognition that the bestial archons are not gods but ignorant and despicable demons whose rule drags humanity down under the weight of temporality, immorality, and animal nature. If some such form of gnostic cosmology does indeed influence Priscillian's interpretation of the canonical scriptures, it is not surprising that he considers the question of the true identity of scriptural beasts to be crucial to salvation.

Priscillian's symbolic interpretation of scriptural animals in relation to a text like the *Apocryphon of John* by no means implies his acceptance of a distinctly gnostic cosmology and mythological schema. Nevertheless, his use of gnostic apocrypha must have caused some alarm and given rise to the accusation that Priscillian regarded the scriptural beasts as divine powers. When asked to respond to this accusation, Priscillian suggests that it is not he but his "schismatic" opponents who worship animals—or rather, who fail to reject what the animals clearly symbolize—when they refuse to acknowledge the demonic significance of scriptural beasts. "Let no one attribute to us the understanding of his or her own perversity," he admonishes.[75]

Having concluded his lengthy discussion of the proper interpretation of animals in scripture, Priscillian moves on to consider the "idolatrous images, Saturn, Venus, Mercury, Jupiter, Mars, and the other gods of the gentiles" that have been "produced" in the accusations of his opponents. Priscillian expresses astonishment that "even in these things the faithfulness of our profession is questioned." However, this protest is preceded by an elaborate set of qualifying clauses that refer to a time when Priscillian "lived indifferent to God and uninstructed in the faith through the scriptures," "took delight in dealings of mundane foolishness," and—significantly—was educated in works of classical literature that included allusions to the pagan gods. In this way Priscillian suggests, but does not explicitly state, that such readings took place only in the distant past, and he furthermore insists that even when he read these works, he "recognized that these things were against our faith" and both "disparaged the gods of the gentiles" and "laughed at the worldly foolishness and misfor-

tunes of those whose works we nevertheless read for the sake of education." Despite his disclaimers, Priscillian seems to be aware that his readings in pagan literature leave him vulnerable to accusations of idolatry,
and his language allows for the possibility that such readings were not
confined to his youth.[76]

It is probably no accident that Priscillian's initial mention of only five
gentile gods—Saturn, Venus, Mercury, Jupiter, Mars—deflects attention
from the astrological associations of the deities he denounces. In fact, he
is most acutely interested in two deities he does not immediately mention—the sun and moon—and in the seven gods who correspond to the
seven days of the week and the seven planetary spheres. Important to Priscillian's condemnation is the construction of an opposition between temporal existence, which is under the control of demons and the seven planetary gods, on the one hand, and the life of the ascetic Christian, who is
liberated by the immortal God Christ from these bonds of temporal existence, on the other. The following passage is excerpted from a lengthier
section in which Priscillian denounces each of the seven planetary gods in
turn, contrasting the bondage of the temporal deities with the freedom of
the eternal God Christ.

> Let those whose dwelling is the fire of Gehenna say that the sun is their
> god, and let those who do not want the God Christ to be their foundation
> confess themselves the sun's elements: for us, all things which are under
> the sun are futile and the presumption of a perverse wind, since we know
> that the sun will die with the world. Let those who, having been led about
> by every wind of doctrine, determine to observe the days and the seasons
> and the years and the months confess that the moon is god in their evil
> deeds; let those who have pleased themselves with the adulterous Mars
> and who in their addiction are bound by the fornications of the desire of
> the flesh, say that Mars is their god. . . . However, for us, the Christ Jesus
> is God, who when we had died from our sins, made us alive with him,
> forgiving all our sins and destroying the bond that was against us, that
> was opposed to the decrees, and abolished it, nailing it to the cross; he
> exposed the principalities and powers to ridicule confidently, triumphing
> over them in himself.[77]

As was the case with his passionate condemnation of animal worshippers,
it is difficult to imagine that Priscillian is insincere in this condemnation of
the worshippers of planetary deities. The very passion of his denunciation
offers a clue to the origin of the accusation that he himself worshipped the
planetary deities. Like animals, the seven planetary gods—and particularly the sun and moon—seem to have played a prominent role in Priscillian's scriptural support for asceticism. Through the life of Christian dis-

cipline, he argues, men and women are freed from the bonds of the temporal realm symbolized by the dominance of the beastly rulers of the planetary spheres. Priscillian's eclectic reading habits and his development of the negative symbolism of the planetary powers must have provided the basis for his opponents' claim that he considered the seven planetary gods divine.

Later detractors were to maintain that Priscillian, like Mani, indulged in elaborate astrological speculations. Orosius not only accused Priscillian of astrological speculation but also supported his accusation with a citation from a purported letter of Priscillian's.[78] This claim is neither proved nor disproved by Priscillian's *Apology* or by his other works. On one level, Priscillian simply takes for granted the cosmology of his day.[79] On another level, we have seen that he uses this cosmology symbolically to express the profound disjunction between the bonds of the temporal world and the free reign of the God Christ. But in the end, Priscillian challenges the validity of traditional cosmic piety altogether, emphasizing that sun and moon are in fact neither divine nor powerful, good nor evil, but are merely part of the order of God's creation, as their visible mutability clearly reveals. In the passage cited above and at two other places in his works, Priscillian invokes Ecclus. 17.31 to underline this point: "What is brighter than the sun? Yet its light will fail."[80] And in the *Tractate on Exodus*, Priscillian offers the examples of solar and lunar eclipses and of the monthly waxing and waning of the moon as evidence of the created nature of sun and moon: "All that shrinks or grows—sun of day, moon of night—is not the rule of our captivity, but the working order of nature."[81] These somewhat divergent and even contradictory tendencies within Priscillian's own works are typical of Christian attitudes toward astrology and do not in themselves place Priscillian outside the mainstream;[82] in addition, a certain productive inconsistency, or rather multiplicity, of interpretations is completely in keeping with Priscillian's flexible and multilayered exegetical method.

As we have seen, Priscillian's condemnation of idolatry identifies the sun, moon, and other gentile gods, not only with the idols prohibited in scripture, but also with the animals and demons already described in the previous section. The continuity provided by the equation of the pagan gods, scriptural beasts, and demons extends into the next section, in which Priscillian anathematizes "those who worship Saclas, Nebroel, Samael, Belzebuth, Nasbodeus, Belial, and all such, because they are demons, by the unfruitful sanctification of religious ceremonies, or who say that they should be worshipped. . . . For whatever shapes, forms, or names the devil changes himself into, we know that he can be nothing else but the devil . . . whether he is regarded as a beast . . . or a serpent or a dragon, we know that he is the devil."[83]

Evidently, some of Priscillian's opponents had requested that Priscillian respond to "the individual things that have been written" about creation in a certain apocryphal text, which Priscillian had probably been accused of reading.[84] This text seems to resemble portions of the *Apocryphon of John*[85]—which we have seen also contains striking bestial representations of the archons of the planetary spheres—and extant accounts of the Manichaean creation myth.[86] It includes the story of the chief archon Saclas' seduction of Eve and the subsequent birth of Cain and Lamech, and perhaps also the creation of Adam and Eve through the union of the archons Saclas and Nebroel.

In Priscillian's discussion of scriptural beasts, one glimpses how he may have used apocryphal scriptures as an aid to the interpretation of canonical texts. Here, on the other hand, he uses canonical texts in order to control his reading of an apocryphal text. Priscillian begins by affirming that those who worship demons are "rightly related to the earthly Adam" and rightly identified as the product of Eve's intercourse with the demon Saclas. Instead of rejecting the apocryphal creation story outright, Priscillian moves to offer an explicitly canonical interpretation. First, he identifies the unfaithful Eve of the apocryphal text with the allegorical representation of Israel as the unfaithful wife of God in the canonical prophets. Next, he complements the apocryphal account of Eve's adultery with the canonical affirmation that she will return to her rightful husband and God through childbearing. Finally, Priscillian avoids a literal interpretation of childbearing by further equating Eve with the mother church whose children are identified by their good works. Thus, in retelling the apocryphal creation story, Priscillian does not reject the dualism of the gnostic-Manichaean myth that pits the archons of the world against the heavenly pleroma and attributes the creation of humanity to a joint effort of heavenly agents and evil archons; but he gives that dualism a symbolic and predominately moral interpretation, affirming that "we are the creation of God in our good works." Furthermore, insists Priscillian, having been created by the God Christ, humanity was worthy to be his temple. He then invokes canonical scripture again in order to anathematize the one who denies the fleshly existence or the real suffering of the crucified Christ, thus rejecting the materialist or essentialist cosmological dualism commonly attributed to the Manichaeans.[87]

Priscillian's use of apocryphal scriptures is defended briefly in both the *Letter to Damasus* and the *Apology* and at length in his *Book on the Faith and the Apocrypha.* He points out that the canonical scriptures contain many allusions to extracanonical texts, and that some of these are explicitly given prophetic authority. In this manner, the canon is continually pointing beyond itself, Priscillian argues; it not only allows but mandates the reading of extracanonical works.[88] Many apocryphal works have, however, been interpolated by heretics, as is the case with passages reflecting a docetic christology: "The schismastics or heretics, falsifying scriptures and inserting their own unfruitful interpretation into the divine discourses, mix false lies with catholic truths."[89] Apocryphal texts must, therefore, be interpreted in relation to the canon—"Moses, the gospels, or the prophets."[90] While Priscillian acknowledges that certain texts "ought not be committed to inexperienced ears,"[91] he does not doubt the ability of a skilled exegete like himself to separate the wheat from the tares. Moreover, to fail to read the interpolated texts, according to Priscillian, is to play into the hands of the devil, who "introduced his own words among the holy for the very reason that, if it were not under a careful reaper, the grain would die with the tares and he would make the good perish with the very bad."[92]

Following his condemnation of the worshippers of demons, Priscillian offers a brief but harsh condemnation of the Manichaeans:

> Let the one who does not condemn Mani and his works, doctrines, and principles be anathema. If it could be done, we would punish their turpitudes in particular with the sword and send them to the lower world and whatever is worse than Gehenna and sleepless torment, where the fire is not quenched and the worm does not perish. Their evil deeds have been exposed by divine judgment, so that the impurity would not be concealed, as well as by secular judgments. For besides those things that they asserted by erring perceptions, they considered the sun and moon, governors of the whole world, to be gods, although it is written, "What is brighter than the sun, and it will fail?" They magnified the follies of their miserable sacrileges to such an extent that they said that they dedicated their minds, which were crushed by blindness, more piously whenever they bound them more execrably.[93]

The reference to the importance of the sun and moon in Manichaean cult and myth links this passage with Priscillian's earlier denunciation of sun- and moon-worshippers. However, his tone here is considerably harsher. By invoking the threat of the imperial sword, Priscillian distinguishes the Manichaeans from other heretics and associates them instead with the nefarious crimes of sorcerers.[94] He implicitly endorses the right of the secular courts to judge the Manichaeans, like sorcerers, although he elsewhere expresses the conviction that matters of religion should be judged by the church alone.[95] He recommends death for Manichaeans as well as sorcerers, despite the fact that no imperial law after Diocletian's rescript had threatened the Manichaeans with death, while sorcerers were typically threatened with capital punishment.[96] In the *Letter to Damasus*, Priscillian expresses still more clearly his conviction that the Manichaeans are completely alien to the Christian community, having passed beyond even the pale of heresy: "The Manichaeans are no longer heretics, but idolaters, sorcerers, and slaves of the sun and moon."[97]

The severe condemnation of Mani and his disciples—in which Priscillian never directly acknowledges that he is responding to an accusation—is followed by the summary catalogue of heresies discussed above.[98] Priscillian then launches into a response to the allegation of sorcery made by Bishop Ithacius. Ithacius' accusation is a "new saying," notes Priscillian, not only recent but of unprecedented gravity: something so terrible had never before been proposed "by any heretical author." While Priscillian's rhetorical sophistication should not be underestimated, there is a ring of sincerity in the horror expressed in his response to the charge of sorcery. His ears have been polluted by merely listening to Ithacius' charge, and Ithacius himself is worthy of condemnation—indeed, of punishment with the sword—simply for speaking of such things.[99]

The specific magical acts of which Ithacius accused Priscillian included consecrating the firstfruits of crops with magical enchantments and consecrating an ointment with curses to sun and moon, "with which it will fail."[100] Chadwick has suggested that this latter phrase refers to the unguent decreasing with a solar eclipse or the moon's waning through some sort of sympathetic magic. The curses were probably understood to have an apotropaic effect. In the passage immediately following his citation of Ithacius' accusation, Priscillian denounces those who believe that what is of rock, horn, or stone is a god, who are satisfied with rain from the devil, and who worship bestial demons.[101] Chadwick infers from this that the unguent of Ithacius' accusation was to be poured over a holy stone representing some god or demon—a well-documented practice—and that the purpose of the ritual was to ensure good weather for the crops.[102]

Chadwick's speculative proposal that Ithacius accused Priscillian specifically of taking part in fertility rituals related to securing good weather is plausible. But it is highly unlikely that Priscillian participated in such rituals, as he goes on to suggest. Chadwick bases this suggestion on the relative mildness of Ithacius' charge, the likelihood that ancient Christian bishops were occasionally called upon to attend such peasant rituals, and the fact that he finds other hints in the tractates that Priscillian dabbled in magical practices.[103] This last point is the most serious, but also the most poorly founded. Chadwick claims, for example, that Priscillian was proud of the possession of a magical amulet bearing the picture of a lion and the name of God inscribed in several languages. But he bases this claim on a dubious interpretation of an exegetical passage in which Priscillian interweaves the reference to a name inscribed on a white stone in Rev. 2.17 with the reference to the title "King of kings and Lord of lords" in 1 Tim. 6.15 in order to emphasize that Christ alone is God; Priscillian goes on from this point to illustrate the metaphorical character of scriptural descriptions of God as "lion" or "deer."[104] Nor is there any evidence that Priscillian held nocturnal meetings, or was even accused of doing so at this point, although Severus does record that Priscillian confessed several years later, perhaps under torture, to holding nocturnal meetings with women.[105] Although some bishops probably did attend or even preside over peasant rituals, Priscillian's polarized view of the fundamental opposition between the God Christ and the virtuous Christians, on the one hand, and the demons and their immoral worshippers, on the other, argues in favor of the sincerity of his horrified response to Ithacius' charge that he trafficked with demons.

As for Chadwick's argument that the seeming mildness of the accusation implies its accuracy, one could just as easily claim that Ithacius was constrained by his very lack of evidence. At a stage in which the conflict was still largely local and most of his audience knew Priscillian personally, it would be difficult for Ithacius to fabricate lies that had no basis whatsoever in Priscillian's teaching or practice or in current public perceptions of Priscillian. There are indications that Ithacius' charges of sorcery at this point were closely intertwined with the accusations of Manichaeism that were also circulating. As part of his condemnation of sorcery, Priscillian denounces those who believe that rain comes from the devil[106]—a common Manichaean notion.[107] There may also be some connection between Priscillian's use of Ecclus. 7.31 to demonstrate the falseness of Manichaean veneration for the sun and moon—"What is brighter than the sun? And it will fail" (*et hic deficiet*)[108]—and Ithacius' accusation that Priscillian teaches that an ointment should be consecrated to the sun and moon, "with which it will fail" (*cum quibus deficiet*).[109]

As noted above, Priscillian's final condemnations of errors occur in the concluding section of the *Apology*. Just as in his introductory remarks, he denounces the heresy that appears to him the most contemptible—the error of the "Binionites"—here, it seems, he again removes himself partially from the context of the accusations brought against him and gives his own opinion of what is most reprehensible in the apocryphal scriptures he has read. It is not the doctrine of demons or even of creation that Priscillian

finds most problematic in these writings, although that is evidently what
he has been asked to denounce. Rather, it is the false understanding of God
on which he here focuses. Seeming not to know to which heresy to attribute the apocryphal scriptures that he reads, Priscillian remarks vaguely
that the "unfortunate" err in ascribing to God a "masculo-feminine" nature based on an overly literal interpretation of Gen. 1.27–28. As is often
the case, a salvific reading of scripture is at the heart of the issue for Priscillian: "For them, therefore, may all that they read be a confusion; for us,
may it be reckoned as knowledge to understand what is written and to
know the power of the living word."[110]

The heretics further err in referring to Armaziel, Mariame, Joel, Balsamus, and Barbilos as God; there is only one God, insists Priscillian, and
that is the Christ Jesus, as scripture makes clear. Priscillian goes on to describe his own method for distinguishing truth and falsehood or orthodoxy and heresy in extracanonical writings: whoever condemns worldly
sins, prophesies or preaches about the God Christ, and teaches in agreement with the canonical scriptures and the catholic faith is to be honored;
whoever condones sin, denies that Jesus is God, or contradicts "Moses,
the gospels, or the prophets" is anathema. Given the importance of canon in his thought, Priscillian is appalled at the "odium" attributed to his
circle of "fabricating or confessing some fifth gospel beyond the fourth
gospel."[111]

If one now steps back to observe the different fragments in the *Apology's* mosaic of condemnations, a discernible pattern emerges. Priscillian
seems to have given an important place in his theology to demons em-
bodying the worldly vices rejected by the true—that is, ascetic—
Christian. The multiplicity of demons (who were, however, all ultimately
identifiable with the one devil) was opposed to the oneness of Christ God.
Their bondedness and fragmentation in the divisions of time was contrasted with the freedom and unity of the eternal God Christ. Priscillian
almost certainly used apocryphal scriptures and probably also pagan literature to undergird his explication of the demonic forces, although he
always interpreted all texts in light of the canonical scriptures. He presents
himself as a man who derives his authority from his inspired interpretation of books. His persistent preoccupation with demons and the breadth
of readings to which his quest for knowledge led him seem to have provided the excuse for accusations of Manichaeism and magic, both popularly connected with secret books as well as demons.

Priscillian evidently responded to an itemized list that contained the
following accusations: interpreting the animals of canonical scripture as
gnostic demons; identifying the sun and moon and planetary gods as di-

vine powers; and reading heretical apocrypha and endorsing their cosmology, including their distinctive presentations of the archons, creation, and the docetic Christ. Priscillian refutes each of these accusations and caps his refutations with a violent condemnation of Mani. The nature and position of this condemnation indicate that Priscillian is attempting somewhat delicately both to separate Mani from the controversial points already discussed, and to acknowledge that these points have become controversial in large part because of the claim that they imply that he is a Manichaean. The same delicacy is apparent in Priscillian's positioning of the accusation of magical practices relating to the sun and moon. The charges of sorcery and Manichaeism often went hand in hand, and it is evident that this is Priscillian's view: he condemns both Manichaeans and sorcerers with singular violence to execution by the sword. However, by inserting a summary catalogue of heresies before his condemnation of sorcery, he also attempts to separate the sorcery accusation from the previous charges, which culminate in the accusation of Manichaeism. Whereas he seems implicitly to acknowledge some grounds for discussion on the questions of interpretation of scriptural beasts and the sun and moon and the heretical interpolations in apocryphal scriptures, he is appalled at the fabrication of charges of sorcery that implicate him in actual dealings with the abhorred demons.

Cosmology and the Ascetic Body: Priscillian's Sermons

Hydatius' cry of "Manichaeism!" cannot be read as a straightforward description of Priscillian's beliefs or ecclesiastical loyalties; nor should Priscillian's elaborate protestations of his own anti-Manichaean orthodoxy be too lightly dismissed as mere defensive rhetoric. Nevertheless, the question may be raised: when all is said and done, was Priscillian not "really" a Manichaean, as evidenced above all by his cosmological speculations? The answer, I think, is no; yet still some further exploration of the relationship of Priscillian's thought to Manichaeism may prove fruitful, if properly contextualized. When we are able to see Manichaeism as only one solution to a set of cosmological and ascetical problems that pressed themselves more broadly upon the consciousness of late-fourth-century theologians, the spiritual and intellectual context shaped by these pressures becomes clearer. In other words, Manichaeism rightly draws our attention, not because it provided the direct source for Priscillian's thought, but rather because it is peculiarly revealing of the pressures to which Priscillian and other theologians of his time also responded.

The theological as well as political context of the late-fourth-century churches had been fundamentally shaped by the Arian controversy, which in turn had been influenced, not only by imperial patronage and the rise of the ascetic movement, but also by a profound religious "paradigm shift" involving both a perceived narrowing of human access to the divine and a polarization of divine and earthly power.[112] In a period in which an orthodox affirmation of absolute divine transcendence had finally been securely established, it became increasingly evident that the new trinitarian orthodoxy implied a radical disruption of pre-Nicene cosmological frameworks. What was the status of the created order, in the wake of the shift from a mediating Word to a fully transcendent Son? And where was the human being located in relation to the nearly unbridgeable chasm that now opened up between creation and the divine Creator? With the discarding of the fluid and connective Middle Platonic "ladder of being," the salvific communion of divinity and creation became imaginable only through the paradox of the Incarnation, not infrequently conceived of as an act of divine violence that threatened to shatter the integrity of the cosmos itself. Responding to the pressures of such cosmological questions, the late-third-century followers of Mani had already embraced the notion of a fractured cosmos, coherently enough also positing a parallel fracturing of transcendent power figured in the opposition of God and devil, or the principles of Light and Darkness. The Manichaeans had furthermore placed the human being precisely at the site of the cosmic fissure, insisting on the original and essential "divinity" of the human soul and the original and essential "earthliness" of the body in which that divine soul was imprisoned, and from which it must ultimately be liberated through the body's destruction. For most late-ancient thinkers, including Priscillian, this Manichaean solution represented a clear and precise boundary stone marking one point of departure from the realm of legitimate cosmological speculation: such a radical and essentialist dualism could not be tolerated. Indeed, from a Christian point of view, Manichaeism could be constructed as the negative mirror-image of an orthodoxy that affirmed creation. But the sharp dualism of the Manichaean thought-world also functioned more ambiguously, not merely repelling, but also tugging at the imaginations of fourth-century writers like Priscillian by resolving with chilling and compelling clarity the very cosmological questions that those Christian thinkers were likewise asking.[113]

The late fourth century appears, then, to have been a period of Christian intellectual history marked by a preoccupation with certain dualistically framed cosmological questions that emerged with renewed persistence as the trinitarian debates subsided. However, such a description is not yet sufficiently precise. Elizabeth Clark has rightly pointed out that "the broad cosmic vision" characteristic of the earlier gnostic debates, and above all of the thought of Origen, had shrunk considerably by the time of the Origenist controversy with which her study is concerned.[114] Clark's account of the debates surrounding the figure of Origen highlights the late-fourth-century resurgence of theodicy and "questions concerning the worth of the material world, human freedom in relation to divine benevolence, sin and forgiveness"; her study also points to the widespread interest among late-fourth-century Christian authors in combating astrological determinism.[115] Clark's work thus underlines the significance for late antiquity of issues traditionally framed in cosmological terms, while also reflecting the hesitancy of theologians of the period to address cosmology head-on. Indeed, I would sharpen the point still further: both the Origenist and Priscillianist controversies provide evidence that cosmology itself had come to be construed as a risky topic of discussion by the late fourth century. However urgent the implicit cosmological concerns of the period, they remained, paradoxically, for the most part submerged or redirected.[116] Clark attributes the late-fourth-century shrinkage of cosmological vision, first, to an increasingly rigid definition of theological orthodoxy and, second, to the relocation of previous cosmological issues within the narrower framework of the human person.[117] This last point is important, for the study of the Origenist controversy suggests that constructions of the human body came to carry most of the weight of theological concerns precisely within a late-fourth-century ecclesiastical context defined above all by eucharistic and ascetic praxis.[118] It is intriguing that Clark's identification of the "practical" issues that pressed to the fore in the debates of the Origenist controversy aligns so closely with the conflicting emphases on eucharistic and ascetic practices already noted in the *Acts of the Council of Saragossa*. But equally resonant with this analysis of the Priscillianist controversy is the suggestion that issues traditionally framed in broad cosmological terms are most often refracted through the prism of the human body in the writings of late-fourth-century theologians. We shall see that the human body figures centrally in the sermons preserved among the tractates of Priscillian, in which the body constitutes both the site of the proposed ascetic practices and the ambiguous vehicle of cosmological assertions. The worldview that emerges from the sermons is consistent with that of the *Apology*, where Priscillian must respond to attacks on his most explicitly cosmological teachings. Yet the sermons' strongly anthropocentric tendency to ground cosmology in the human person locates these works even more comfortably within the late-fourth-century context.

"The body that is corrupted makes the soul heavy, and the earthly habitation drags down the mind that thinks many things" (Wisd. of Sol. 9.15).[119] This passage, cited at three crucial points in Priscillian's sermons, attracts to itself many of the complexities and ambiguities of Priscillian's thought on the body and the cosmos. It therefore provides a convenient point of entry into the exegetical homilies of a theologian whose fluid and elaborately intertextual method of exposition does not easily lend itself to a systematic summary. First appearing in the so-called *Tractate on Genesis*, the passage is there cited in the context of an attack on false readings of the creation story, an attack intriguingly juxtaposed with Priscillian's response in the *Apology* to the charge that he himself taught falsely about creation under the influence of heretical apocrypha. Here it is Priscillian who complains that certain heretics judge the nature of the world to be evil, in direct contradiction to the canonical account. "Ascribing the making of their own body to the devil," they deny their corporality in such a way as to elude responsibility for their evil acts; they indulge their bodily desires, ignorantly "supposing that their corporeal sin is no concern to the divine disposition."[120] It is at this point that Priscillian invokes the authority of the Wisdom passage, suggesting that the heretics' error lies in a failure to understand the divinely established unity of the human person or to take seriously the implications of the embodiment of the soul. On this reading, the seemingly dualistic Wisdom passage actually resists a radically dualistic anthropology: it is precisely the capacity of the body to make the soul heavy, or the ability of the "earthly habitation" to drag the mind down, which indicates to Priscillian the close linkage of body and soul or mind.

Having thus rebuked those who denigrate the body and the earthly creation, Priscillian goes on to criticize "others" who fall into the seemingly opposed error of divinizing certain aspects of the cosmos: "Thinking that the sun and moon, lights established for the service of human beings, are gods, they assign the power of the elements to the principles of the world."[121] In fact, the "others" whom Priscillian here has in mind are probably the same Manichaeans he has just attacked. Utilizing a common rhetorical ploy, he has split his opposition into polarized extremes and thereby created an impression of multiple errors in relation to which his own position appears as a single moderate and mediating solution: his is not a mind that "thinks many things" but one that perceives the unity of truth. Yet beyond the rhetorical purposes of bifurcation, Priscillian also here introduces a second point of real dissonance between his teaching and Manichaean thought: for while the Manichaeans, who maintain that divine and earthly material mingle in the conflicted cosmos, can claim literally to see not only the devil but also God in every blade of grass, Priscillian insists on the relative inferiority of *all* materiality to an incorporeal and invisible God. He agrees with the Manichaeans that humanity is linked to and resonant with the order of the cosmos, but rejects the particulars of this Manichaean teaching when he insists on both the hierarchical superiority of the human being and the finitude of the cosmos. Scornful of those who give too much honor to the sun, Priscillian points out that they thereby reveal that they "do not know that all that is visible will perish in the end established by God." It is furthermore absurd to claim that human beings might serve some part of the cosmos, he observes, since the entire cosmos itself was divinely ordered for the salvation of human beings: "the darkness was illumined and the nature of creation was contrived so that the numerical divisions into seasons and days would offer a habitation for the human being laboring in the work of Christ." With his reference to the earthly "habitation" of the human being, Priscillian returns us again to the Wisdom passage, here offering a still more positive reading of the body-cosmos created by God as an appropriate workplace for humanity.[122]

A slightly different interpretation of the Wisdom passage emerges in the *Tractate on Exodus*. Here, the rhetorical context is no longer shaped primarily by the need to combat Manichaean teachings, and Priscillian emphasizes, not the close link between soul and body, but rather the problematic status of the body itself. Acknowledging that the "nature of the body" was made by the hand of God, he returns again to the Genesis account of creation, where he notes that however divine the "hand" that creates, it nevertheless grasps "mud," a detail suggesting the body's association with a problematic "earthly birth" and a fall into temporality that dulls the "divine birth" of human beings "with the traps of earthly habitation." Again, it is the mention of the "earthly habitation" that leads directly to Wisd. of Sol. 9.15: "The body that is corrupted weighs down the soul, and the earthly habitation presses down on the mind that thinks many things."[123] Contrasting metaphors of birth—divine versus earthly, virginal versus corrupt, baptismal versus physical—here and elsewhere underline the dualism of soul and body invoked in the Wisdom passage. Yet at the same time Priscillian's very preoccupation with birth—a highly corporeal metaphor—also resists any unambiguous devaluation of corporality, and indeed he immediately goes on to contrast the image of the "body that is corrupted" not with the soul—as we might expect, and as the Wisdom passage invites—but with the body whose nature is "purified [*castigata*] through the law of the Old Testament and offered to the tabernacle of God" in the New Testament.[124] This "purified" or "clarified" (*clarificatus*) body,[125] represented by both the unblemished sheep of the paschal offering—ostensibly the main topic of this sermon—and the flesh of

Christ affixed to the cross, "owes nothing now to the days and seasons," having died to sin and been resurrected in new life, as Paul teaches.[126] Salvation lies, then, not so much in the loosing of mind or soul from an imprisoning body as in the transformation of a dim earthly body to a dazzling heavenly body.[127] In spite of his rejection of the Manichaeans' material dualism, Priscillian may not, after all, be so far from a position that envisions the resolution of the cosmic conflict taking place in the obliteration of a material body of Darkness by a material body of Light. But here again, he shares still more with orthodox ascetics of the period than with the Manichaeans.

The third and perhaps most strongly dualistic reading of the Wisdom passage occurs in Priscillian's treatment of the first psalm, in a homily that sounds the psalm's warning to avoid "the counsel of the impious," "the way of the sinners," and the "seat of pestilence." Priscillian reminds his readers again why such "discipline of life" is necessary: the human being is the "dwelling place of Christ" and must "prepare a home worthy of such a dweller." Secular ambition, desire, and greed are particularly to be shunned. Discipline can be achieved, he insists, but only because we have been "reborn into salvation . . . of mercy not of nature," through baptismal rebirth escaping the natural "birth of the flesh" that confines humanity with the "vices of the evil world." In this context, the Wisdom passage recalls the dangers of the fleshly or earthly birth: "the body that is corrupted makes the soul heavy, and the earthly habitation drags down the mind that thinks many things." Priscillian goes on to identify the "earthly habitation" explicitly with greed, anger, and other sinful—but not necessarily physical—impulses; it represents "our subjugation, and its own corruption," serving as the site of diabolical attack and therefore as the source of its own undoing. The "earthly habitation" is the Pauline "flesh." But as both Isaiah and First Peter remind us, "all flesh is as grass": it withers.[128]

As this last reading of the Wisdom passage most dramatically illustrates, on one level Priscillian shares with the Manichaeans—and indeed, one could easily argue, with most theologians of his time—a profoundly dualistic framework of anthropological and cosmological thought. He implies that the body tends toward corruption and can therefore be saved only against its nature; and at several points he seems to envision the eschaton as involving not so much the salvation of bodies as the final liberation of minds from bodies, arguing in much the same vein as his Origenist contemporary Evagrius. If dualistic, Priscillian's cosmology is not, however, distinctly Manichaean; he works rather within a late-Platonic framework that rejects both essentialist dualisms and materialist conceptions of divinity. Whereas the Manichaeans radically oppose a material divinity with a material devil and thereby place the divine stuff of souls in conflict with the earthly stuff of flesh, Priscillian relegates all materiality to an earthly realm that, however fallen, is still the creation of God; materiality itself is thereby made more problematic, in comparison with the Manichaean view, while the category of earthliness becomes redeemable, if not yet redeemed.

But on another level, Priscillian's works raise the question of the value of even the categories of "dualism" and "Platonism" for locating Priscillian's thought, or indeed the thought of many of his contemporaries. For Priscillian, like both the Manichaeans and more orthodox ascetic Christians, seems to be distancing himself significantly from the traditional Platonic mind-body dualism, as he slides from language that opposes a mind to a body into language that compares a body to a body, language in which not only the terms of the dualism but even the dualism itself begins to dissolve.[129] In Priscillian's writings, "mind" and "body" are not so much divisions of the human being as alternative ciphers for the unified ascetic "self," which is pulled by conflicting impulses, and it is finally not the destruction of the body but its transformation that fascinates Priscillian. That a battle was being waged both within and outside the human person was not to be denied: for Priscillian, as for other ascetics of the period, the cosmic struggle provides the context for the microcosmic ascetic endeavor in which metaphors not only of strife but also of violence have their place. But Priscillian seems to suggest that in the final victory of the God Christ, the visible, earthly realm will not so much cease to exist as cease to resist, ultimately becoming fully transparent to the invisible divine truths: words will then unlock their hidden meaning, while purified bodies will fully reveal the nakedness of souls. That this salvific transformation is already beginning to take place in the moment of the text is one source of Priscillian's audacious confidence. Invoking the image of the dazzling heavenly body, he boldly urges his readers to prepare in themselves "the heaven *and earth* of the Lord" (emphasis added), "so that when the evening of ignorance dissolves . . . and when the darkness of the corruptible body has been purified and the light of the divine spirit has been placed in you, you may be called the day of the Lord! . . . Made the Sabbath of the Lord and keeping holiday from all acts of the world, you may owe nothing to the world but may rest in Christ."[130]

Just as Priscillian's anti-public rhetoric finally functions to dissolve distinctions between public and private, so too his anti-worldly dualism finally functions to dissolve distinctions between body and mind, earth and heaven. If he is not at home in this body or world, Priscillian—like many of his ascetic counterparts—is very much at home in the body and world that are already beginning to be.

Conclusions

Putting this examination of Priscillian's thought back into the social context elucidated in my preceding analysis of the Meridan conflict gives a more complete picture. It becomes more comprehensible both how and why Hydatius came to expel Priscillian and his supporters from the Lusitanian churches as Manichaeans and false bishops. The conflict in Merida between Hydatius and Priscillian takes the shape of a competition between an intellectually conservative bishop with a strong sense of the public authority of his own office and a learned ascetic teacher who prides himself on his ability to interpret texts that illumine the nature and seriousness of the Christian battle against worldly demons. In terms that seem to echo the teachings of Origen,[131] Priscillian suggests that the guidance of an expert exegete is required if one is to follow the tortuous scriptural path to salvation; and he raises serious doubts as to whether Bishop Hydatius, described as "lazy" and "untaught," can provide such guidance. Hydatius, in turn, suggests that Priscillian has already strayed from the salvific path of orthodoxy by indulging in extracanonical readings and heretical cosmological speculations undertaken in the secrecy of private meetings. For both men, texts are of central importance.

Far from dispelling fears of a subversive privacy, Priscillian's writings highlight the private construction of the authority of one who has given up worldly position in order to pursue the higher goals of study and reflection. His self-conscious identity as a man of great learning is nowhere clearer than in those works where he begins, following standard rhetorical technique, by seemingly distancing himself from the role of the scholar or rhetorician. The fragmentary introduction to Priscillian's *Book on the Faith and the Apocrypha*, for example, contains a dramatic condemnation of "book-learning," identified as "the author of scandal, the food of schism, the nourishment of heresy, the model of a crime committed"; yet Priscillian goes on to impress the reader with his own knowledge of written texts, confidently appealing for support to "the careful investigator of the scriptures," suggesting that he himself has not only investigated everything which is said in the canonical books but also gone on to peruse extracanonical texts, scornfully contrasting his opponents' lack of education with his own learning, and finally acknowledging in a more pastoral, if equally condescending, vein that not all have the experience to distinguish truth from falsehood in noncanonical texts.[132] Priscillian follows a similar rhetorical strategy of self-presentation in a work preserved outside the Würzburg corpus, the *Canons of the Letters of the Apostle Paul*. In the prologue to the Pauline *Canons*, Priscillian disowns the "cunning eloquence of the orator" and "syllogisms of slippery dialectic," only to assert that his own rhetoric exhibits the power of "pure truth," a truth that reflects the fruits of a "shrewd investigation into the divine scriptures," by which he may claim to have cracked open their hidden content, modestly presenting the entirety of Paul's thought distilled and systematized into ninety pithy canons to be used against "heretics."[133] For Priscillian, claiming of the authorial voice is an elaborate—and indeed endless—renunciation of public position, which is in turn paradoxically productive of the enhanced authority of the scholar who publicly advertises his own privacy.

Real differences in doctrine accompanied these conflicting strategies and competing claims to authority, not least because the theological stances of Hydatius and Priscillian provided the undergirding for their different claims to authority. Priscillian's opponents seem to have been most disturbed by his attempts to grapple exegetically with the oppressive forces of evil and immorality, which he identified symbolically in the figures of cosmic beasts, planetary powers, or demons; and it is no accident that it was precisely through his special expertise in the avoidance of the treacherous ways of the world that Priscillian legitimated his own role as ascetic teacher. In the figure of Priscillian, one observes how the emerging emphasis on demonology in late ancient Christian cosmology "transformed society itself as well as the nature of leadership, because men who were able to find demons and force them to reveal their true selves had tapped into a new source of authority."[134] "Beloved in God," Priscillian addresses his congregation in Avila, "we have been appointed to free your minds, which are besieged within the narrow paths of human weakness, sending you into new light, as it were, through the religious exhortation of our teaching."[135]

The conflict between Priscillian and Hydatius could not easily be resolved, since there was no clear consensus in the Spanish churches on the disputed issues of either doctrine or authority, and since both individuals had significant support in Merida and the outlying communities. In the absence of overwhelming popular support for one party, both resorted to the use of labels that were not precisely accurate but were at least generally agreed to be worthy of condemnation. Some attempt was made to attack Hydatius, whom Priscillian seems to refer to as a "schismatic," but Priscillian's account masks the content of the accusations. We are able to see more clearly the process of labeling as it affected Priscillian and his circle. By pointing to real differences in reading habits, which reflected differing sources and understandings of authority, and divergent attitudes toward the "world," which shaped cosmology as well as ascetic lifestyle, Hydatius was able to identify his rivals as detested Manichaeans.

Unable to resolve the conflict at home, both parties soon appealed to neighboring bishops. Hydatius was supported by Ithacius, who seems to have been primarily responsible for the emphasis on a second, closely related labeling strategy, the accusation of sorcery. Priscillian was supported by Instantius and Salvianus, who buttressed his position by consecrating him to the episcopacy, as well as by Elpidius,[136] Tiberianus,[137] Asarbus,[138] and other influential laypeople.[139] Such was the strength of both sides and the fierceness of the antagonism that the conflict would not be resolved until still broader circles of powerful men and women had been drawn into the web of alliance and opposition.

CHAPTER THREE

"SORCERER"

Alliances, Enmities, and the Death of Priscillian

Priscillian presents himself in the role of a learned teacher and bishop responding indignantly to the damaging accusations of certain "schismatics." A somewhat different portrait emerges from the works of his detractors, on which the history of the controversy after Priscillian's first departure from Avila largely depends: here we encounter head-on, not only Priscillian the Manichaean, but also Priscillian the sorcerer and sexual profligate, the pseudo-Christian whose very privacy connotes secrecy and duplicity. Simultaneous with this shift in the perspective or angle of vision comes an enlargement of its scope. In this chapter, the view expands beyond Spain and indeed beyond the orbit of Priscillian himself, reaching to encompass the other contexts that conditioned the responses of those members of the Gallic and Italian elites who were drawn into the controversy.

Severus is the primary guide for unraveling the strands of the social networks that lead into other nexuses of conflict in Bordeaux, Milan, and Rome. Rome truly represented the end of one journey for Priscillian, insofar as its influential bishop closed the doors on the possibility of a purely ecclesiastical resolution to the conflict. However, Bordeaux and Milan—sites significantly not merely visited but revisited—had a more ambiguous import for Priscillian. In both cities, the hostility of the local bishop—

a hostility almost necessitated by his assertively *public* construction of episcopal authority—was in tension with, and indeed held in check by, the support of other powerful members of the elite. Ultimately, it was the influence, not of the more aloof Gratian, but of the aggressively orthodox usurper Maximus that interjected the simplicity of autocratic power into these complicated urban contexts in such a way as to dissolve the tension in favor of Priscillian's episcopal enemies. Thus, the second journey to Bordeaux was redirected to the imperial capital of Trier, which produced a secular version of the solution already hinted at in the finality of Damasus of Rome's uncompromising refusal to "see" Priscillian.

Priscillian ended his life as the focus of a public gaze that rendered him paradoxically both private and obscure. The violence of the strategies by which Priscillian was thereby refashioned as the "other" stemmed in part from the relatively open accessibility of imperial power, the progressive intensification of enmities and resentments, and the alien context in which the conflict came to be played out. Even before Priscillian's episcopal consecration, Bishop Ithacius had begun to insinuate that Priscillian was not merely a Manichaean but, still worse, a dabbler in magic. Now, as the center of conflict shifted away from the local Spanish communities in which Priscillian and his associates must have been known personally by most Christians, this label of sorcery gained prominence in the accusations against Priscillian: it was as a sorcerer that Priscillian was executed at Trier. Attached to the labels of both Manichaeism and sorcery was the stereotype of the sexual profligate, and charges of sexual deviance eventually contributed significantly to the overall characterization of Priscillian as a demonic outsider who was so morally abhorrent and utterly alien to the Christian community that even his violent death could be justified.

It has already become clear that the sexualization of Priscillian also had another motivation and function as early as the Council of Saragossa. By hinting that ascetic teachers like Priscillian might have had illicit sexual relations with their female associates, Christians like Hydatius and Ithacius expressed their continuing discomfort with the relatively free social relations of women and men within Priscillian's circle. In other words, to talk about sex was also to talk about gender, and while this later stage of the controversy may appear to be centered more on issues of authority than on issues of gender, conceptions of gender and sexuality are once again intertwined with attitudes toward authority, and indeed are spectacularly showcased in Severus' account of the trial and sentencing of Priscillian and his companions.

Bordeaux

Severus' concise report supplies most of our information about the journey made by Priscillian, Instantius, and Salvianus following their departure from their Spanish churches. The three bishops apparently crossed the Pyrenees through the western passes and followed a route "through the interior of Aquitaine."[1] In Aquitaine they campaigned actively and successfully for support. They seem to have directed their course toward Agen and Bordeaux, perhaps hoping to obtain letters from bishops Phoebadius and Delphinus confirming that they had not been condemned at the Council of Saragossa. Along the way the travellers stopped at Eauze, where they made a favorable impression: Severus reports that Instantius, Salvianus, and Priscillian "with depraved speeches perverted the people of Eauze, who were indeed at that time good and devoted to religion."[2] This passage indicates that the Christians of Eauze had *not* formerly been supporters of Priscillian; there is no evidence that Priscillian had followers in Aquitaine before his departure from Avila.[3]

From Eauze the travellers continued on to Bordeaux, where they likewise met with a strong, although by no means universally favorable, response. Indeed, if the Spaniards had hoped for Delphinus' support, they were disappointed: according to Severus, Priscillian and his companions were driven out of town by the bishop himself.[4] This seemingly dramatic gesture of hostility invites comparison with the previous reception of the ascetic bishops in Merida; there, as we have seen, they were met by a crowd of Bishop Hydatius' supporters, who barred them from the presbytery and beat them with sticks. The situations at Merida and Bordeaux were by no means identical: Priscillian and his friends presumably approached the bishop of Bordeaux as supplicants, rather than as mediators or even accusers, as had been the case in Merida. However, Delphinus' action suggests that the presence of the Spanish bishops in Bordeaux, as in Merida, was perceived as a sufficiently serious threat to the unity of the local Christian community and to the authority of its bishop to require a public gesture of repudiation. Here again, we need not hypothesize some early "Priscillianist" influence in Bordeaux to explain either Delphinus' original motivation for attending the Council of Saragossa or his response to Priscillian's subsequent appearance in Bordeaux. Not only is such a hypothesis poorly supported by the sources; it also seems misleadingly to externalize the causes of Delphinus' defensiveness, which must finally also be explained in terms of the dynamics of the local community.

That Delphinus had some reason to fear lack of support from power-ful members of the local community is confirmed by Severus' report that certain well-placed Christians of the region readily patronized Priscillian's circle in spite of their bishop's strong repudiation of the Spaniards. Indeed, Euchrotia, widow of the well-known rhetorician Attius Tiro Delphidius, received the Spanish ascetics hospitably on her estate, where they re-mained for at least a brief period.[5] It was probably also at this point that a certain Urbica of Bordeaux became a supporter of Priscillian. A Priscilli-anist Urbica is known to us from an entry in Prosper's *Chronicle* (c. 433): "At Bordeaux a certain disciple of Priscillian by the name of Urbica was stoned to death by a mob on account of her obstinacy in impiety."[6]

This Urbica is probably to be identified with the aristocratic Pomponia Urbica who was related by marriage to the poet Ausonius and who is com-memorated by the same poet in his *Parentalia*.[7] Pomponia Urbica seems to have died in the mid 380s after a brief widowhood;[8] thus the date of her death, as well as her name and provenance, supports her identification with the Priscillianist Urbica. Moreover, Ausonius' portrayal of Pomponia Urbica reflects personal ambivalence and an apologetic intent, which could plausibly derive from Pomponia Urbica's embarrassing associa-tion with Priscillian and her unseemly death at the hands of an anti-Priscillianist mob in Bordeaux.

Ausonius opens his brief poem by praising his subject in stereotypical terms for her high birth and old-fashioned morals, emphasizing her iden-tity as the wife of the respected Julianus Censor. He acknowledges the strength of her innate qualities, but moves quickly to emphasize the influ-ence of her husband's teaching and example:

> Strong in inborn virtues and enriched also by those that her spouse, that
>   her father and mother taught—
> That Tanaquil, that the Pythagorean Theano possessed, and that
>   perished without copy in the death of her husband.[9]

The coupled allusions to Tanaquil and Theano, both known for their close partnerships with their husbands, are double-edged. Although each could be interpreted as a symbol of traditional Roman wifely virtue, contribut-ing to Ausonius' positive depiction of Pomponia Urbica as a devoted wife and virtuous woman, both Theano and Tanaquil were foreigners, one Greek, the other Etruscan, and both took on social and religious roles un-usual for a woman, one being a Pythagorean philosopher, the other an interpreter of omens and a powerful queen.[10] It is thus possible that, as one scholar has suggested, the "novelties of the Priscillianists" may be alluded to in the comparison of Pomponia Urbica to Theano, wife of Pythagoras and member of a sect known for its secrecy, asceticism, and tolerance of female participation.[11] The reference to Tanaquil, who was skilled in both divination and politics, may function similarly to evoke Pomponia Urbica's disturbing religious activities, as well as her notable courage and independence, particularly since Ausonius seems to use the figure of Tanaquil elsewhere to imply Priscillianist leanings.[12] Final support for the identification of Prosper's Priscillianist Urbica with Ausonius' Pomponia Urbica is found in Ausonius' emphasis on Pomponia Urbica's readiness for death.[13]

> And if fate had allowed you so to exchange, Censor would still live now
>   in this time of ours.
> But you were not tormented for long by widowhood, joining your
>   husband immediately through your desired death.[14]

In these lines, poetic reinterpretation seems to transform an unseemly martyr's death into a classical manifestation of wifely virtue.

Severus does not mention Urbica by name, whether out of ignorance of her story or because he, like Ausonius, had some reason to be embarrassed by her death. He does, however, report that Euchrotia and her daughter Procula joined Priscillian, Instantius, and Salvianus on their journey to Rome. He refers sarcastically to the "disgraceful and, to be sure, *modest* company, including wives and even unrelated women" who accompanied the bishops.[15] Although the group may have included married couples, it is more likely that Severus simply knew that Priscillian was criticized for travelling with Euchrotia and Procula; from this seed he grew his "company" of women, who included not only wives—which, he implies, might have been scandalous enough—but even "strange" or "unrelated" women (*alienis etiam feminis*). The bishops at Saragossa had used the same term—*alienus*—to object to the mingling of women with "strange" men in the Priscillianist study groups, thereby implying the scandal of both heresy and sexual promiscuity.[16]

Severus adds that it was the "common talk" that Euchrotia's daughter Procula had become pregnant through the "violation" (*stupro*) of Priscillian and used herbs to abort the pregnancy.[17] Ausonius seems to offer independent confirmation of the existence of such a rumor when he refers to the "mistake" (*errore*) of Delphidius' daughter.[18] The report probably stemmed originally from local outrage at Priscillian's having left Aquitaine with "strange" or "unrelated" women, particularly younger women. We are reminded that the bishops at Saragossa had been particularly concerned to limit and control young female ascetics.[19] The choice of older women like Euchrotia to lead an ascetic life was more easily accepted than were their daughters' vows of celibacy.[20] Indignation at the young girls' rejection of conventional social roles—above all, the duty to procreate—combined with heightened suspicions of sexual immorality in the young.[21]

The motivations of the Gallic women who accompanied the Spanish bishops on their journey are unknown. Perhaps Euchrotia hoped to use her money and influence to aid Priscillian's cause in Italy. Possibly she and the others were taking advantage of the opportunity to hear the famous bishop of Milan preach or to make a pilgrimage to the holy shrines in Rome.[22] Severus makes no further reference to Procula and mentions Euchrotia again only in the context of her execution at Trier. The understatement and ambiguity that characterize Severus' representation of Priscillian's elite female supporters evoke the multiple interpretive possibilities available to the late-ancient historian and his readers. The familiar and all-pervasive relationships of patronage and friendship might always be made suspect, becoming tinged with the conspiratorial and the effeminate by their hinted dislodgement from the public sphere of legitimate masculine governance.

Milan

The travellers apparently stopped in Milan after leaving Gaul.[23] Although Severus fails to mention a Milanese visit prior to their stay in Rome, his reliability is here compromised by complicated polemical motives: by suggesting that Priscillian and his companions appealed first to the Roman and Milanese bishops and only subsequently sought the support of the secular authorities at the imperial court, he intends to contrast them favorably with their opponents, who—like members of an opposing faction in his own time—rashly involved secular judges from the start.[24] Priscillian's letter to Damasus, in contrast with Severus' account, seems to posit at least a brief sojourn in Milan prior to the Roman visit, during which the letter was presumably composed, since it makes it clear that Priscillian and his companions had already made attempts to appeal their case at the imperial court.[25] Priscillian protests to Damasus that his opponents have prejudiced the quaestor, who, "although he said the requests were fair, was slow to respond."[26] Chadwick's suggestion that the quaestor mentioned by Priscillian might be identical with the Gregory who was praetorian prefect of the Gauls in 383 is intriguing, inasmuch as this same Gregory subsequently intervened in the conflict on behalf of Ithacius.[27] Another fragment of the social networks within which this controversy played itself out seems to emerge into view here.

Whether or not they also attempted to see Ambrose during this prob-able first stop in Milan, Priscillian and his companions must have con-cluded that his support was not going to be forthcoming. The Milanese bishop had been "completely deceived" by Hydatius' story, Priscillian writes to Damasus, and indeed he seems to imply that Ambrose had been instrumental in procuring the rescript directed against Priscillian and his circle.[28] Although Ambrose never mentions Priscillian by name in his ex-tant writings, Severus' report seems to confirm the bishop's early opposi-tion to Priscillian, which thus appears to be a crucial factor in the unfold-ing of the controversy—a factor that must be contextualized, not only in terms of the extralocal networks of alliance and opposition in which the aristocratic bishop of Milan was embedded, but also in terms of the dy-namics of the local Milanese community, whose pressures conditioned the bishop's relationships with other powerful men and women.[29] Fortunately, the Christian community of late-fourth-century Milan is significantly bet-ter known than that of contemporary Bordeaux, and here it is possible to discern still more clearly points of overlap or resonance between the Span-ish conflict and the conflicts in the local communities visited by Priscillian and his friends. Particularly striking is the manner in which the rhetorical and topographical manipulation of public and private space shaped the ecclesiastical politics of Milan and set the terms for the reception of Pris-cillian by that community and its bishop.

Perceptions of the Milanese Christian community and of Ambrose's position within that community have shifted significantly as the bishop's aura of invincible authority has begun to dissipate in recent scholarship; both the strength of the anti-Nicene community and the consequent vul-nerability of Ambrose's episcopacy in the late 370s and early 380s have sprung into sharp relief. Indeed, it now seems fairly clear that the first two books of Ambrose's early treatise *On the Faith*, probably written in the win-ter of 378–79, constitute an apologetic *libellus* responding to a pointed re-quest that Ambrose defend himself against damaging accusations of heresy.[30] In other words, the basic rhetorical context of this work is not unlike that of Priscillian's own *Apology*, demanded and produced some two years later. The request for self-defense in this case came directly from the emperor Gratian, mediating opposition both from local opponents of Ambrose and from the Homoian bishops of Illyricum with whom they were allied.[31] The situation was thus structurally parallel to the one that emerged in the Meridan conflict, although Gratian took both a more cau-tious and a more active mediatory role in relation to the bishop of Milan, a city obviously of central importance to the western emperor. Indeed, by the spring of 379, Ambrose had received a letter from Gratian indicating his favorable receipt of the defense and inviting a further development of Ambrose's arguments on the Holy Spirit.[32]

Gratian's signal of cautious support for the Milanese bishop came as a great relief to the beleaguered Ambrose; nevertheless, little progress had been made toward the resolution of the Milanese conflict. Before Ambrose could respond to the new imperial request, he found himself again facing attacks, which necessitated extending his apologetic *On the Faith* with three new books, probably sent to the emperor sometime during the autumn of 380 and therefore closely contemporaneous with the Council of Saragossa.[33]

It is significant that these last three books of *On the Faith*, like the first two, were addressed to the emperor during a period when he was resident at Sirmium and in conversation with the Homoian bishops of Illyricum, above all Palladius of Ratiaria, author of an attack on the initial books of Ambrose's *On the Faith*. Given the fragile position of the Nicene community in Milan, Ambrose perceived himself to be directly threatened by any show of sympathy for the rival party. He thus employed an aggressive rhetoric, whose intent was to erode a relatively tolerant imperial religious policy. In a period of military crisis, Ambrose suggested that any openness toward the theological enemy was a sign of either a traitor's betrayal or a coward's flight: if Gratian was not with him, the bishop insinuated, he was against Christ. Conflating his Homoian opponents with the Goths advancing on Italy, Ambrose moved boldly to construct an image of Gratian as the champion of orthodoxy. "This emperor has no slippery mind, but a firmly fixed faith," he proclaims at the end of book 2, seemingly contrasting Gratian with the pro-Homoian Valens, while praising him for his steady defense of Italy against "barbarian" attack. Sometime later, Ambrose takes up the same theme in book 3, here identifying his own position as bishop with Gratian's as emperor by noting that he had written the first two books hastily, "being like one on the eve of battle," but now writes at greater length, so as not to seem to have doubted and abandoned the defense of his earlier propositions—an implied challenge to Gratian not to prove himself "slippery" after all.[34]

If Gratian's relations with the Illyrian bishops were much on Ambrose's mind between 378 and 380, this concern was, as I have suggested, fueled by tensions within the local Christian community. Although Ambrose's unexpected election to the episcopacy in 374 came to be seen as a victory for the Nicene community of Milan, which had previously suffered almost twenty years under a bishop hostile to Nicea, the strength of the anti-Nicene party in this city was far from broken; nor was Ambrose's uncompromising allegiance to the Nicene cause a foregone conclusion at the time of his election.[35] The late 370s had brought the Homoian bishop Julian Valens from Illyricum to Milan, and through both the ordination of followers and the cementing of alliances with powerful figures like Ursinus, formerly a contender for the Roman episcopacy, Valens seems to have established a strong local network.[36] Indeed, in the period immediately following the arrival of the anti-Nicene empress Justina in late 378, the Homoian community was emboldened to request a basilica for its own use. Gratian's response was carefully neutral: "sequestering" the basilica so as to remove it from Nicene control, he may even have made it accessible to the Homoians.[37]

Access to public space has recently been identified as a highly significant factor in the Milanese conflict, which is bracketed chronologically by two attempts on the part of the Homoian party to move out of private meeting places through the acquisition of basilical space: the effort in the late 370s resulting in Gratian's ambiguous "sequestering" of the basilica, and a later attempt in 386 that ended in a more conclusive defeat for the Homoian party.[38] Indeed, Ambrose's success at solidifying his episcopal authority in Milan can literally be "mapped" upon the surface of a city that included, on the one hand, a growing number of prominent basilicas built and occupied with ever-greater confidence by the Nicene party and, on the other hand, a contrastingly privatized network of Homoian meeting places.[39] Crucial to the establishment of a strong Nicene episcopacy in Milan was Ambrose's ability not only to control access to public space but also to enhance its power of authorization through sacralizing rituals. During the conflict over the basilica in 386, for example, Ambrose is said to have introduced novel liturgical practices to the Nicene community gathered within the walls of the disputed public building, including "antiphons, hymns, and vigils."[40] Despite the previously noted parallels between Ambrose's and Priscillian's positions in relation to the emperor Gratian, these strategies of episcopal self-authorization align Ambrose rather with Hydatius and the other bishops who gathered at Saragossa in order to undercut the authority of a privately centered asceticism by constructing an alternative, more centralized congregational "discipline" that would enhance the authority of a publicly defined episcopacy.[41] As Harry Maier notes, that Ambrose "devoted so much energy to establishing orthodoxy in a public domain is an indication of the danger of an Arian community which stubbornly survived for over a decade in private space, and the degree to which sacred space was coming to function as a source of legitimation and authority in the last decades of the fourth century."[42]

The year 381 was a crucial turning point in the conflict between the Homoian and Nicene parties in Milan. In the early spring of that year,

Gratian was in Milan and finally returned the sequestered basilica to the Nicene party, thereby demonstrating, if somewhat belatedly, at least a measure of openness to Ambrose's rhetorical construction of the orthodox imperial role. With Gratian present, Ambrose now published the treatise on the Holy Spirit that the emperor had earlier requested, praising Gratian's recent, seemingly spontaneous decision to return the basilica as a sign of the working of the Spirit itself.[43] A still more significant event was the Council of Aquileia, which Gratian convoked in September of the same year, not as the balanced "general council" the emperor had originally envisioned, but rather as a local gathering packed with Ambrose's pro-Nicene allies, who moved quickly to interrogate and condemn several of the Homoian clergy of Illyricum as "Arians."[44] The deep shock and anger of the condemned Homoians is reflected in the fragments of Palladius' *Apology*—yet another apologetic *libellus* almost precisely contemporaneous with Priscillian's work.[45] While there is evidence that the Homoians continued to press Ambrose both in Milan and Illyricum, and that Gratian was still far less adamantly pro-Nicene than his bishop, the Council of Aquileia remained a significant victory for Ambrose and the pro-Nicene party of northern Italy.[46]

This brief survey of the history of Milanese Christianity in the years leading up to 381 provides some insight into the religio-political climate that shaped Ambrose's response to Priscillian. The rescript seems most easily datable to the period of Gratian's sojourn in Milan in the spring of 381 or the months immediately following, when Gratian was living in northern Italy, while Priscillian's subsequent visit to Italy must have taken place somewhat later, in 381 or perhaps 382.[47] During this same period, both Ambrose's actions and his rhetorical self-presentation suggest the bishop's dominant preoccupation with his emerging role as the western champion of an anti-Arian orthodoxy. It was a time marked for Ambrose both by optimism, in the light of Gratian's increasing willingness to support the pro-Nicene party in Milan, and by the caution of one who had to consolidate gains carefully in the face of continued opposition from the Milanese Homoians, as well as of enemies further afield, such as Palladius of Ratiaria. We can easily imagine, then, that both Ambrose's own vulnerability to charges of heresy and his self-conscious orthodoxy would have inhibited him from risking the potential embarrassment of association with a Spaniard accused of heresy. Indeed, the timing of Priscillian's visit could scarcely have been worse.

In addition, it appears unlikely that Ambrose would have recognized in Priscillian a natural ally, whatever their similar commitments to asceticism. Ambrose's perception of Priscillian was probably shaped not only by Hydatius' report but also by rumors transmitted through Gallic colleagues like Delphinus.[48] The heresiological catalogue of Ambrose's neighbor and pro-Nicene ally Filastrius of Brescia, generally dated to the early 380s, may well reflect what was "known" locally of the Priscillianists at this point.[49] Filastrius refers to certain heretics "in the Gauls, the Spains, and Aquitaine" who reject marriage and abstain from certain foods. Not sure who these heretics are, he calls them "abstinents, so to speak" and identifies them as followers of the gnostics and the Manichaeans and proponents of the doctrine that creation is the work of the devil. Apparently uncertain whether to classify the Gallo-Hispanic ascetics as Manichaeans or to place them in a category of their own, Filastrius elsewhere mentions Manichaeans "lurking in both Spain and Gaul."[50]

As a former imperial official who used language, ritual, and architecture to articulate a distinctly *public* orthodoxy in direct competition with a privatized rival bishop in Milan, Ambrose would have felt little sympathy for one introduced to him as a "pseudo-bishop" and associated with the subversive privacy and alienated asceticism of the Manichaeans.[51] Indeed, to accentuate the illegitimacy of the private, partly feminized networks that supported Priscillian would have far better suited the strategies of a bishop who, when she attempted to secure basilical meeting space for the Homoian Christians and their bishop, was later to compare a female patron—the empress Justina herself—to Jezebel and Herodias; "those temptations are more severe that arise through women," remarked Ambrose.[52]

Rome

After their initial failure to win support in Milan, the ascetic company turned to Damasus of Rome, Ambrose's most powerful colleague in the western episcopate, and a man who might be flattered by a strong appeal to his authority. Priscillian's *Letter to Damasus* was submitted to the Roman bishop—"you who are senior to all of us"—along with letters of communion from the clergy and laity of the churches of the three Spanish bishops. In the letter, as we have seen, Priscillian skillfully defends his orthodoxy and the legitimacy of his episcopacy, stressing that he has never been condemned by a council, and invoking the authority of a letter of Damasus "in which, in accordance with gospel laws, you had enjoined that nothing be decided against those absent and unheard." Priscillian emphasizes his preference for ecclesiastical rather than secular judgment in matters of faith and requests that Damasus call for the convening of an episcopal council at Rome. Alternatively, suggests Priscillian, Damasus might use his influence to persuade the Spanish bishops to convene a council in their own territory. At such a council, Hydatius would be forced to substantiate his accusations, and Priscillian and his companions would be heard and judged fairly. Priscillian adds that Hydatius need not fear that Priscillian and his supporters would press charges against him.[53]

Priscillian's attempt to clear himself fell on deaf ears—or rather, blind eyes. Severus notes briefly that Damasus refused to see the supplicants: Priscillian and his companions were "not even admitted into Damasus' sight."[54] It is possible that Damasus, like Ambrose, had already been persuaded by Hydatius' claim that the Spanish bishops were Manichaeans. On the other hand, he may have been considerably less adamant in his judgment of the Spanish controversy. Jerome, who was closely associated with the Roman bishop in the years immediately following Priscillian's visit, still had a remarkably neutral opinion of Priscillian in 392, when he wrote from Palestine that, although Priscillian was accused by some of gnosticism, others considered him orthodox.[55] Particularly if Jerome's comment at this point reflects views shared by Damasus a decade earlier,[56] the Roman bishop's refusal to see Priscillian may have been motivated not so much by strong opposition to the Spanish ascetics as by the political concerns of his own position. Again, the paucity of our knowledge of Priscillian's visit to Rome is balanced by the relatively rich documentation of the local context that would have conditioned Damasus' response to Priscillian.

In Rome, as in Milan, the Arian controversy had created deep fissures in a Christian community that had long been characterized by extraordinary diversity, including in the late fourth century identifiable groups of Manichaeans, Donatists, and Luciferians, at the very least.[57] Here too, conflicts increasingly took the form of struggles to claim the authority of the public sphere and, correspondingly, to represent the opposition as suspiciously privatized. Damasus' election following the death of Bishop Liberius had been secured only by a series of forceful acts of imperial intervention, which ended two years of bloody fighting between local ecclesiastical factions whose allegiances had crystallized around the remembered rivalry between Liberius and Felix, the latter appointed bishop of Rome during the period of Liberius' exile (355–58).[58] Indeed, Damasus had not been the only man consecrated bishop of Rome in 366, and although his opponent Ursinus had finally been expelled from Rome in 368, both the letter of a synodal gathering in Rome in 378 and Ambrose's request for Ursinus' exile from Milan in 381 suggest that he was still actively agitating around the time of Priscillian's Italian visit.[59] In this intensely competitive context, Damasus was unlikely to support Priscillian at the risk of alienating such a crucial ally, or offering an advantage to so serious a rival as Ambrose, no matter how benign Damasus' assessment of Priscillian's position may have been.[60] Nor could the Roman bishop afford to associate himself with a group of Spanish bishops whose asceticism and relationships with women left them vulnerable to the same privatized representation and accusations of sexual promiscuity with which Ursinus had attempted to discredit Damasus in 368, accusations that had seemingly resurfaced in the form of adultery charges as recently as 378.[61]

In the context of such factionalized heterogeneity, facilitated by complex networks of patronage, within which diverse competing movements flourished, Damasus—himself a most skillful broker of patronage relationships—had moved to consolidate a more centralized episcopal authority, which aggressively constructed itself as both public and orthodox over against opponents who were correspondingly hereticized and privatized.[62] As in the case of Ambrose, imperial support proved crucial to the solidification of Damasus' episcopal authority, and in 378 Gratian continued his father's policy of backing Damasus against Ursinus in Rome.[63] But imperial rescripts provided just one buttress for the structure of episcopal authority. In Rome, as in Milan, topography proves particularly revealing of a bishop's explicitly public articulation of ecclesiastical authority through the liturgical and architectural manipulation of space. Damasus is credited with having transformed the face of Rome in the period of its "second Christian establishment" through a building program that included the erection of at least three churches and the beginnings of one or two more, as part of a campaign to replace the private architectural forms of the old Roman "community centers"—the *domus ecclesiae* of the original *tituli*—with ostentatiously public basilicas.[64] Damasus' enhancement of the architectural space of the historic churches seems to have been matched by his development of the mobile liturgical practices that subsequently played a crucial role in linking Roman episcopal authority with the complex Roman Christian topography.[65]

The events surrounding Damasus' episcopal ordination further suggest that his manipulation of the existing topography was as important as his role as builder in the articulation of an explicitly public episcopal authority. When in 366 Ursinus was consecrated bishop in the Basilica of Julius, Damasus moved immediately to occupy Rome's cathedral, the sumptuous Lateran basilica—a product not of the "second" but of the "first Christian establishment" in Rome under Constantine.[66] It was in the Lateran that Damasus was consecrated soon thereafter, thus choosing to make his audacious bid for the episcopacy from a building whose very architecture, setting, and history provided a metaphor for the ambiguous and complex process by which the Christian community and its leadership was moving to claim the public sphere. An unmistakably public edifice, the church founded by Constantine yet rose startlingly and somewhat incongruously from the midst of an upper-class residential neighborhood at the edge of Rome, on the site of a private villa formerly owned by Constantine himself.[67] The particular juxtaposition of the public and private architecture of the Lateran and its setting seems to mirror visually the social rise of the episcopal "seat" from private into public space under Damasus' leadership, while also hinting at the possibility that the bishop's locus of authority remained, after all, just one more Christian *domus* among so many potential competitors in Rome; indeed, we have seen that his rivals' jibes at Damasus' "womanizing" emphasize precisely Damasus' *private* networks of influence. If it was Constantine's power that initially defined the Lateran's publicity, imperial power continued to provide not only a direct source but also the closest analogue for the aggressively public construal of the authority of a Roman bishop whose own building projects harked back to the classical style of the period of the first Augustus.[68]

This brief glimpse into the historical context of Damasus' episcopacy provides a meaningful context—if not an "explanation"—for the Roman bishop's refusal to give Priscillian a hearing. Like both Ambrose of Milan and Delphinus of Bordeaux, Damasus struggled to maintain his authority over a diverse and factious Christian community. Like Ambrose and perhaps also Delphinus, he moved to strengthen his position both by monopolizing control of the church's public space and by enhancing the authority of that space through the skillful manipulation of architecture, ritual, and rhetoric. Here his strategies aligned him more closely with Hydatius than with Priscillian. Priscillian's own more private and ascetic techniques of self-authorization had been effectively turned against him through the accusation of Manichaeism. "Not even admitted into Damasus' sight,"[69] he now found himself further damagingly privatized by being denied visibility on the public stage of the Roman church.

Milan, Spain, and Bordeaux Revisited

Leaving a Christian Rome whose doors had remained closed to them, Priscillian and his companions returned to Milan. This time, Gratian's capital proved friendlier. Whether through bribery, persuasive argument or clever political maneuvering around Ambrose to reach his adversaries at court, the Spanish bishops were able to win the support of the powerful Macedonius, *magister officiorum*.[70] Macedonius procured a rescript direct-

ing that the Spanish bishops be restored to their churches—an act of legislative incoherence not unusual for a government that exercised power
within the context of complicated networks of patronage relationships.[71]
Subsequent to the issuing of the new imperial rescript, "Instantius and
Priscillian returned to Spain (for Salvianus had died in the city), and then
without any strife they took back the churches over which they had
presided."[72]

Severus' report that Priscillian and Instantius experienced no opposition upon their return to their episcopal sees is remarkable and strength-
ens the suggestion that Priscillian had not technically been either deposed
or exiled, although threatened with both. Priscillian's claim that he and his
fellow bishops had the support of their churches and did not fear to argue
their case before a Spanish council seems, moreover, justified. The majority of the Spanish Christians must have remained either neutral or
supportive of Priscillian and his friends, despite—or perhaps partly because of—Hydatius' initial success in invoking imperial authority against
them.[73]

The period immediately following the return of Priscillian and Instantius from exile is perhaps the most obscure stage of the controversy. Severus makes no mention of any conflict between Hydatius and Priscillian
or Instantius following their return to Spain. Their dispute with Ithacius
continued, however, for reasons that Severus either did not know or does
not report. He merely remarks that Ithacius did not lack the spirit, although he did lack the power, to resist the return of the two bishops.
Whatever the origins of this second round of conflict, a chain of political
events similar to that following the earlier conflict at Merida was soon set
into motion, as each party again appealed to the imperial court for support. The proconsul Volventius, governor of Lusitania, attempted to arrest
Ithacius as a "disturber of the churches."[74] Ithacius was sufficiently
alarmed at the prospect of a trial in Lusitania that he fled to Gaul, where
he succeeded in gaining the ears of both Bishop Britannius of Trier and
the praetorian prefect, Gregory. The latter, after determining to look into
the affair personally, sent a report to the emperor Gratian—who was now
probably residing in Gaul—in an apparent effort to persuade him to intervene directly and thereby to enforce a more consistent imperial policy in
relation to the Spanish disturbance. Such direction and coherence on the
issue was not, however, forthcoming from this emperor. Although Gregory now issued an order for Priscillian's party to appear in Trier, Priscillian
and his companions again appealed to Macedonius, who arranged for the
case to be transferred back to Spain and sent officials to escort Ithacius to
the trial. Ithacius managed to elude arrest. Hearing rumors of Maximus
Magnus' rebellion in Britain, he decided to remain quiet until it became

clear who would win the battle for imperial power. By August of 383, matters were decided: Gratian was dead, and Maximus entered Trier as emperor.[75]

Yet another round of conflict then began. Ithacius, still in Trier, succeeded in bringing his interests to the new emperor's attention with "petitions full of ill-will and accusations directed against Priscillian and his associates."[76] Maximus, in marked contrast to Gratian, eagerly seized this opportunity to portray himself as a staunch defender of orthodoxy and thus to win the powerful support of the western episcopacy—as well as of the ardently pro-Nicene emperor Theodosius in the east.[77] Accordingly, he sent orders to the governors of Gaul and Spain to escort all the parties involved to Bordeaux, where an episcopal council would judge the dispute; and this time, the orders were carried out effectively.[78] It has been suggested that Maximus' response was crafted to appeal to the two major episcopal constituencies of his realm. First, he appeased the majority of the Spanish episcopacy by acknowledging Priscillian and Instantius as legitimate bishops whose orthodoxy could be judged only by a council of their episcopal colleagues. Second, he appeased the bishops who supported Ithacius, seemingly a majority in Gaul, by ordering that the council be convened not in Spain but in Bordeaux, territory that we have seen was potentially less friendly to Priscillian and his followers.[79]

The council, which probably took place in 384, proved unfriendly indeed. No official records survive, but Severus' account implies that the principal matter at hand was to decide whether or not Instantius and Priscillian were guilty of heresy—probably, more specifically, of Manichaeism. Instantius spoke first, and failed to persuade the gathered bishops, who judged him "unworthy of the episcopacy." Priscillian perceived that he would not get a sympathetic hearing from the council and chose to appeal to the emperor rather than submit to the judgment of the bishops present.[80] He may have hoped, as did the Donatists and Athanasius in analogous situations, that the emperor would convene a new, more impartial council to hear his case.[81] The bishops allowed the appeal to go through and the case to be taken from their hands.[82] Meanwhile, there were outbreaks of violence in Bordeaux if, as seems most likely, the stoning of Urbica occurred in connection with the council.[83]

Trier

Even if this had been a "simple" case of heresy, the emperor Maximus might have felt justified in investigating it himself on the basis of Priscillian's personal appeal and the council's acquiescence. The ambiguity of the accusation brought against Priscillian further facilitated the intervention of an emperor and, ultimately, the execution of a heretic in a case that seems in retrospect both shocking and ominous.[84] The charge of Manichaeism defied the neat boundaries separating "heresy" and "crime" and the respective jurisdictions of bishop and emperor. As we have seen, Priscillian felt strongly that matters of faith should be judged by bishops, yet he himself noted approvingly that the Manichaeans had been condemned by secular as well as divine judgments and urged that Manichaeans, like magicians, should be punished with the sword for their "turpitudes."[85]

This ambiguity inherent in the charge of Manichaeism was exploited by Ithacius' anti-Priscillianist propaganda in Gaul. Severus states specifically that Ithacius, like Hydatius earlier, attacked both ascetic practices and private reading as heretical or Manichaean: "His foolishness went so far that he labeled all—even holy men—who possessed a zeal for reading or were determined to struggle by fasting associates or disciples of Priscillian."[86] Even Martin of Tours was accused of Manichaeism on these grounds, and Severus protests the emptiness of the label. "For at that time judgments were based on appearances alone, since one was considered a heretic on account of pallor or dress rather than faith."[87]

Meanwhile, the charges of sorcery and sexual immorality, originally secondary to the charge of Manichaeism, gained prominence in Ithacius' rhetoric as he addressed a Gallic populace not personally familiar with Priscillian. Ithacius' earlier accusations of participation in fertility rites seem to have been elaborated considerably at this point, if the story of Priscillian's youthful study of sorcery, known and partially discounted by Severus, originated during Ithacius' Gallic sojourn.[88] Charges of sexual immorality would have been particularly effective with those Aquitanians already outraged by the ascetic conversions of women like Euchrotia and Procula, and perhaps it was only during Ithacius' residence in Gaul that the rumors of Priscillian's sexual relations with Procula were coupled with charges of abortion.[89] Priscillian "the magician" might well be thought to command a knowledge of abortifacient herbs, whose use was part of both the magician's and the physician's lore. And many Gallic Christians would readily believe that Priscillian the "Manichaean" secretly indulged in promiscuous sexual relations and condoned the use of contraception or abortion, while publicly exhorting Christians to live lives of continence.[90]

The triple charges of Manichaeism, sorcery, and sexual immorality are highlighted in Isidore's summary of Ithacius' *Apology*, which was probably written several years after Priscillian's execution, in the face of serious attacks on Ithacius' role in the civil process against Priscillian.[91] "Ithacius,

bishop of the Spains, famous in name and eloquence, wrote a certain book
in apologetic form in which he demonstrates the cursed dogmas of Priscillian and his arts of sorcery and his disgraceful acts of lechery, showing
that a certain Mark of Memphis, expert in the magic art, was the student
of Mani and teacher of Priscillian."[92] Although some details, such as the
introduction of the figure of Mark of Memphis, may have been added after
Priscillian's death, the summary of Ithacius' *Apology* confirms the general
impression of the nature of his anti-Priscillianist propaganda in Gaul in
the years prior to Priscillian's trial and execution.

The charge officially under investigation at Bordeaux and initially at
Trier as well was almost certainly Manichaeism, but accusations of sorcery
and sexual immorality must also have been in the air from the start of the
process at Trier. Severus reports that Martin of Tours, who was present in
Trier during the early stages of Maximus' investigation, immediately
feared that bloodshed would result from the civil process the emperor had
initiated:

> He did not cease to rebuke Ithacius, urging that he cease from his accu-
> sation, or to beg Maximus to refrain from shedding the blood of the un-
> fortunate ones; he said that it was enough and more than enough that,
> judged heretical by episcopal decision, they should be thrown out of the
> churches, and that it was a new and unheard of evil for a secular judge to
> judge an ecclesial case.[93]

As noted, no emperor since Diocletian had threatened to punish Manichaeism with death, whereas death was commonly the penalty for various
practices of sorcery. Martin must, then, have known or suspected that sorcery accusations would surface in the investigation at Trier, although he
himself insisted that the question about Priscillian was essentially a question of orthodoxy and heresy, appropriately judged by bishops. According
to Severus, his protests had some effect on Maximus. The emperor hesitated, neither canceling the civil investigation and convening a new council, as Martin seems to have urged, nor proceeding with the investigation.
Finally, Martin left Trier with a promise from Maximus that he would
shed no blood. Severus reports, however, that bishops by the names of
Magnus and Rufus "corrupted" Maximus after Martin had left.[94]

It was perhaps at this point that Ambrose visited Trier and, despite his
earlier coolness toward Priscillian, claimed to have angered Maximus by
holding himself aloof from "the bishops who were in consultation with
[Maximus] and were asking that certain persons, having admittedly
strayed from the faith, be put to death."[95] As in his initial convening of the
Council of Bordeaux, the emperor seems to have followed a policy of com-

promise. He allowed the trial to proceed but withdrew himself from direct participation, placing the new prefect Evodius in his place as judge. Ithacius also seems to have seen the wisdom in withdrawal, and he was replaced by the secular official Patricius, *fisci patronus*, as prosecutor.[96] The trial was probably redefined at this point explicitly as a trial for sorcery rather than heresy or Manichaeism.

Under questioning, and perhaps torture, Priscillian "did not deny that he had studied obscene doctrines, held nocturnal gatherings even of disgraceful women, and prayed naked."[97] All three of the confessions recorded by Severus could plausibly derive from some documented or at least probable activity of Priscillian; and at the same time, their vague yet suggestive wordings seemed to confirm the essentially false triple accusations of Manichaeism, sorcery, and sexual immorality. The ambiguous phrase "obscene doctrines" recalled the suspicions of unorthodoxy provoked by Priscillian's private and extracanonical reading and at the same time hinted at immoral behavior. "Nocturnal gatherings" could describe either ascetic vigils or magicians' rituals performed by the light of the moon, while the modifying phrase "of disgraceful women" evoked the sexual promiscuity commonly assumed to accompany the meetings of both magicians and Manichaeans.[98] Finally, the practice of "praying naked" may, as Henry Chadwick has suggested, relate to the council of Saragossa's prohibition against going with naked *feet* and derive from an ascetic practice that could also have been perceived to have magical significance;[99] when "naked feet" became simply "naked" and was conjoined with a confession to nocturnal meetings with women, the phrase again evoked graphic images of sexual immorality. The essential reliability of Severus' report that Priscillian was convicted by his own confessions is strengthened by Maximus' letter to Bishop Siricius of Rome, in which he records that certain "Manichaeans" have been convicted after confessing to deeds "so foul and disgusting" that he cannot repeat them without blushing and must instead refer the Roman bishop to the minutes of the trial.[100] In Rome in the late 380s, Augustine also heard about certain "Manichaeans" in Gaul who confessed to deviant sexual practices (which included eating semen, he implies); his informant may have derived his report from the minutes sent to Siricius.[101]

On the basis of his confessions, Priscillian was, then, convicted of *maleficium*, or sorcery. He was imprisoned, and Evodius referred the case to the emperor for the pronouncement of punishment. Maximus determined that Priscillian and his associates should be condemned to death, and Priscillian was subsequently executed by sword, along with two clergymen—Felicissimus and Armenius—and two laypeople—Euchrotia and the

Spanish poet Latronianus.[102] Euchrotia's death received particular notice from the outraged Gallic rhetorician Pacatus, who rails sarcastically against Maximus in his panegyric to Theodosius:

> Do I speak of the deaths of *men*, when I recall that he descended to the blood of *women* and raged in peace against the sex wars spare? But undoubtedly there were serious and odious reasons that the wife of a famous poet was seized with the criminal's hook for punishment. For the widowed woman's excessive piety and overly diligent worship of divinity was alleged and even proven![103]

The sentiments of Pacatus' friend Ausonius were probably similar, though rather differently expressed in the understated congratulation offered to his former colleague Delphidius for a timely death that had enabled him to escape the ignominy of his wife's punishment.[104]

Conclusions

The local conflict at Merida stands at the beginning of the construction of Priscillian as a heretic. In the early 380s, the Meridan Christians appear to have been deeply divided over their self-definition as a community. The public liturgy and the hierarchy of ecclesiastical office provided the focus of communal identity for some. These Christians looked to Bishop Hydatius to embody their public definition of community and authority and, like him, were scandalized by the insubordinate men and women who implicitly challenged his leadership. Others defined the Christian community as the private gathering of men and women dedicated to Christ; they located authority primarily in the learning, eloquence, and exemplary life of the well-read ascetic teacher who might most appropriately be chosen to fill the office of bishop. These Christians looked to individuals like Priscillian to embody the authority of superior culture, talent, and discipline and, like him, were scandalized by the ignorant and worldly Christians who denied the legitimacy of his leadership.

The questions raised in the early stages of the controversy surrounding Priscillian were not easily answered, and the two perspectives persisted side by side for some time, championed with equal strength and tenacity within the Meridan community. Two developments ensued as the community searched for resolution to its internal conflict. First, labels were invoked in order to create consensus by associating the opponents with easily vilified enemies: hence, in an attempt to discredit both Priscillian's learning and his asceticism, there arose the charge of Manichaeism and, some time later, the even more injurious accusation of sorcery. Second, the conflict moved beyond the boundaries of the local community, as both Hydatius and Priscillian sought to strengthen their own local prestige and credibility and weaken the position of their rivals by activating alliances with other leaders outside the community. This process of alliance and opposition between bishops and other elites proved difficult to limit or control, with the ultimate result that the Meridan dispute was settled by a usurping emperor who probably understood very little of the original source of disagreement.

As Priscillian sought the support of Christians in Aquitaine and Italy, his teachings as well as his personal influence seem to have tapped similar conflicts about the nature of community and authority among the Christians in those regions. There are indications that the local conflict may have run deep at Bordeaux. In 380, Delphinus was already concerned enough about the issues raised by Hydatius to cross the Pyrenees to attend the Council of Saragossa along with his neighbor Phoebadius. When Priscillian, Instantius, and Salvianus subsequently arrived in Bordeaux, he drove them out of town—a dramatic public act that may have been calculated to intimidate factions within his own community. Finally, we know that some of Priscillian's strongest support came from Euchrotia, a wealthy Christian woman of the well-educated circles of Bordeaux, who was eventually executed alongside Priscillian at Trier; some of the most virulent rumors were directed against her daughter Procula; and the most violent popular reaction against any of Priscillian's followers was directed against the well-born Urbica, who was stoned to death by a mob in Bordeaux. Clashes between the male-dominated public authority of office and the relatively ungendered private authority of education and aristocratic culture appear to have been central to the conflict in Bordeaux as in Spain.

In the more distant cities of Italy, the response to Priscillian seems to have been equally ambivalent, if less dramatically expressed. In Milan, Bishop Ambrose was unsupportive and the praetorian prefect, Gregory, prevaricated, while another powerful palatine official, the master of offices, Macedonius, finally procured for the Spanish bishops a rescript intended to prevent their persecution by Hydatius and his allies in Spain. In Rome, Priscillian seems to have had less success in winning support; Severus mentions only that the bishop refused to see him. In both Italian cities, as in Bordeaux, the opposition of bishops appears to reflect underlying conflicts in their own communities. I have suggested that Ambrose and Damasus responded negatively to Priscillian at least partly out of awareness of their own vulnerability to similar charges and their own strong—and ultimately successful—personal interests in consolidating an episcopacy that would subsume the authority of the ascetic and learned teacher under a publicly defined authority of office.

For reasons that now seem impossible to recover, Priscillian's primary opposition in Spain shifted from Hydatius to Ithacius upon his return from Italy. With the entry upon the scene of Maximus as emperor, the focus of the conflict between Priscillian and his opponents similarly moved away from Spain again, and at the same time the labeling strategies of his opponents also seem to have shifted subtly. No longer, as in Merida, was the dispute carried out in a face-to-face community where accusations bore at least some remote resemblance to reality. In Gaul, Priscillian was an outsider, and Ithacius and his other detractors were correspondingly freer in their construction of a condemning portrait. The charge of Manichaeism was maintained, along with the issues of authority, education, and ascetic life that it evoked, and Priscillian was further used as an excuse to direct the charge of Manichaeism against problematic Gallic leaders such as Martin of Tours. But other accusations, with still less basis in fact, were also elaborated—namely, the charges of sorcery and sexual immorality.

Discomfort with the role of women in Priscillian's circle lent particular power to conventional charges of sexual immorality. In Spain, as early as the Council of Saragossa, there had been rumblings of unease with the mingling of the sexes and the lack of hierarchical distinction between men and women among Priscillianists and other ascetic Christians. Severus is probably conveying the views of Aquitanian contemporaries of Priscillian when he expresses similar discomfort at the mingling of ascetic men and women in Euchrotia's household and in the company that journeyed from Aquitaine to Italy. His work, together with Prosper's brief mention of the stoning at Bordeaux, documents strong disapproval of the behavior of particular Aquitanian women of prominence: Euchrotia, Procula, Urbica. Similarly, through the indirect medium of literary allusion, Ausonius casts aspersions on "Tanaquils" suspected of Priscillianist leanings. The private authority of women of wealth and social influence here stands in juxtaposition, not only to a narrowly public definition of authority, but also to the ambivalent attitudes of men like Ausonius and Severus, whose own lives and strategies of self-authorization located them ambiguously in relation to the public and private spheres.

The invocation of the label of sorcerer added an edge of violence to the message already implicit in the label of Manichaeism: Priscillian was an outsider, a dangerous manipulator of demonic forces, one completely in opposition to the traditional virtues of Romans and Christians. When they succeeded in thus identifying Priscillian as a sorcerer, Ithacius and Hydatius did not merely achieve the death of a rival. They also constructed as private and subversive those models of community and leadership that competed with the particular public definition of church and office in which their own authority was embedded.

CHAPTER FOUR

"PRISCILLIANIST"

Heresy Inquisitions at Toledo and Tarragona

Priscillian and his associates were condemned, not as "Priscillianists," but as Manichaeans and sorcerers. If the dispute surrounding the Spanish ascetic had ended with his death, perhaps he would have been remembered merely as one more of the anonymous crypto-Manichaeans whom zealous western bishops claimed to have apprehended in the late fourth and early fifth centuries. However, the dramatic and controversial circumstances of Priscillian's execution ensured that the conflicts of his lifetime would not easily dissipate, nor would his memory quickly fade. In Gaul, disagreements concerning the behavior of the bishops who took part in the trial at Trier divided the Christian community for at least fifteen years. In Spain during the same period, Christians in the northwestern province of Galicia revered Priscillian as a martyr and continued to study his writings, while others vigorously opposed such practices.[1] One result of these enduring conflicts was that Priscillian's movement was transformed through the mythologizing forces of Christian heresiology into a new symbol of deviance, both defining and enforcing the evolving standards of orthodoxy.[2] "Priscillianism" emerged in the vocabulary of conciliar acts[3] and imperial legislation,[4] while Christian writers worked out diverse interpretations of the relation of Priscillianism to other heresies.[5]

The sources do not allow the construction of a continuous narrative of either the positive influence of Priscillian's teachings in the decades following his death or the evolving use and content of the negative label of

Priscillianism. However, they do provide glimpses into two dramatic moments in that history. The first is the Council of Toledo, which met twenty years after the Council of Saragossa and inquired into the orthodoxy of certain Galician bishops charged with being members of a "sect" of Priscillian. The second is the investigation of accusations of heresy or "Priscillianism" in Tarragona almost twenty years later still, under the destabilized sociopolitical conditions of the Germanic invasions of Spain. Scholars have used the texts recording these two heresy proceedings to reconstruct the history of a distinct Priscillianist Christianity in Spain.[6] But the sources describe the heresy of Priscillian in terms progressively more abstract and stylized, more distant from any real connection with the ascetic bishop executed at Trier. Indeed, a close reading suggests that the proceedings of the Council of Toledo provide only sketchy evidence for a localized Galician form of Christianity that honored Priscillian and his teachings, while the record of the investigation at Tarragona offers no reliable evidence of Priscillianist Christianity at all. The sources *do*, however, clearly attest to the establishment of a heresiological category of Priscillianism by which a publicly defined orthodoxy sought to discredit various forms of Christian community that remained rooted in the private sphere. Conflicts over the nature of Christian community and authority were still at the heart of these later controversies associated with Priscillian's name, and the evolution of the label of Priscillianism was part of the larger process of the evolution of ecclesiastical structures in Spain.

This chapter examines, first, the surviving minutes of the Council of Toledo (400)[7] and, second, Consentius' recently discovered report to Augustine on the heresy inquisition at Tarragona (c. 418).[8] In each of these cases, as in the controversies during Priscillian's own lifetime, conflicting attitudes toward authority and gender prove to be intimately related both to one another and to the shifting perception of the location of the boundaries of public and private spheres. The minutes of the Council of Toledo suggest a growing tendency to merge public and private authority and to subordinate the private to the public. Yet in 400 some Christian men and women still gathered in small groups for study or prayer and honored the authority of their learned teachers: the bishops at Toledo insist even more vehemently than their predecessors at Saragossa that women be restricted to the narrow confines of the family and that worship take place only under the auspices of the bishop or his clergy. At Toledo, as earlier at Saragossa, Bordeaux, and Trier, bishops raised accusations of heresy in order to challenge or control private authority. At Tarragona, in contrast, a layperson made the attack on the private authority of a member of the clergy, and—significantly—the attack ultimately failed. Although a disruption of the ties that linked bishops and other locally influential figures with the structures of imperial government may initially have destabilized the authority of these figures, the Spanish communities soon recentered themselves around their local leaders. Indeed, a degree of resolution of the conflicts of authority appears to have been achieved with a more complete fusing of public and private authority in the persons of learned and aristocratic bishops and presbyters. Conflicts concerning gender seem likewise to have moved toward resolution with the successful confinement of women to a more narrowly defined domestic sphere. The triumph of the public model of Christian community was thus accomplished through its absorption of much of what was formerly regarded as private, or at least nonpublic, a move resulting both in the restriction of women's activity and in the privatization of public authority itself.

The Council of Toledo (400)

Our knowledge of the first Council of Toledo derives from two edited selections from its minutes. The formal *Acts of the Council of Toledo* has been transmitted in the *Hispana* collection, which also preserves the records of the Council of Saragossa. The twenty published judgments recorded in the *Acts* reflect the council's concern with such matters as the process of ordination, requirements for eligibility for clerical office, relations within the ranks of the clergy, participation in the public liturgy of the Eucharist, the behavior of ascetic women, and the communal disciplining of sinners. The editor of the document—perhaps the person who selected these judgments for inclusion in the *Hispana*—notes that the nineteen bishops gathered at Toledo were "the ones who also in other acts directed a written decision against the followers of Priscillian and the heresy he had established."[9] These words reflect awareness of the council's investigations of the orthodoxy of certain Galician bishops, recorded elsewhere in the council's original minutes.[10] Fortunately, fragments of these minutes have also survived through a separate manuscript tradition,[11] and they allow us a remarkable glimpse into the trial of a group of bishops and presbyters accused of belonging to a "sect of Priscillian."

Investigation of the Orthodoxy of the Galician Bishops

The *Transcript of the Professions Held in the Council of Toledo against the Sect of Priscillian* was "excerpted from the full acts" by a redactor whose primary goal appears to have been the documentation of the orthodoxy of the bishops of a certain Galician city, probably Astorga.[12] This redactor compiled the document at a time when the bishops under suspicion were already dead, recording "the professions of the lord Symphosius and of the lord Dictinius, bishops of sacred memory, and of the lord Comasius of sacred memory, then presbyter." Presumably relying on the complete minutes, the redactor reports that the Council of Toledo met from the first through the third of September in the year 400. Subsequently, "various investigations" were held; and, finally, on the sixth of September, the anti-Priscillianist professions of Dictinius, Symphosius, and Comasius were heard.[13] On September seventh, these professions were repeated, and the assembled bishops delivered their final verdict concerning the various bishops and clergy who had been held under suspicion of Priscillianist leanings.[14]

The minutes record the accusing bishops' account of the events that had led to their own gathering at Toledo. In this context, the bishops refer to the earlier council at Saragossa "in which judgment was pronounced against certain ones." Symphosius was present at the Saragossan council only one day, and he later refused to listen to the judgment of that council, they note disapprovingly; this refusal had made it difficult for the bishops gathered at Toledo to listen to what Symphosius and his associates had said.[15] The implication that the Council of Saragossa—which was remembered, rightly or wrongly, for its judgments against Priscillian—marked the beginning of Symphosius' separation from the majority of the Spanish bishops is misleading, as becomes apparent in what follows.

The bishops invoke the authority of the now-dead bishops of Milan and Rome, Ambrose and Siricius "of sacred memory." They recall that "after that council," Ambrose wrote certain letters advising that the bishops under suspicion be restored to peace with their fellow bishops "if they condemned what they had falsely done and satisfied conditions that the letters contained in writing"; Siricius seemingly seconded Ambrose's counsel. The conditions are specified in the lines following, in which the bishops at Toledo lament the fact that Symphosius and his associates have failed to fulfill them: the Galicians were to omit Priscillian and his associates from the list of martyrs read aloud in the church; they were to read neither condemned apocrypha nor the writings of Priscillian; Dictinius was to remain a presbyter rather than be consecrated bishop; and Symphosius and his associates were to cease to ordain bishops, at least until the other conditions had been satisfied. Such conditions, together with the invocation of the authority not of Damasus but of Siricius, reveal that the bishops are using the phrase "after that council" loosely: in fact, they refer not to the period immediately following the Council of Saragossa, but rather to the years following Priscillian's death. The bishops at Toledo likewise mention that Symphosius and his associates proposed these conditions in Ambrose's presence.[16] One can infer, then, that the Galicians were criticized by other bishops in Spain sometime in the late 380s or early 390s. The attack seems to have been sufficiently serious that the Galicians travelled to Milan to appeal to Ambrose, who attempted to mediate a compromise between emergent episcopal factions in order to preserve the unity of the churches in Spain.

Evidently Symphosius and his fellow bishops were unable to satisfy the conditions they themselves had proposed. Although Symphosius claimed to have ceased reading Priscillian's name from the list of martyrs, it was revealed that he had not in fact done so. Furthermore, he was "forced" to ordain Dictinius as bishop, as well as to ordain other bishops to some of the surrounding sees, including the prestigious see of Braga.[17] Symphosius remained innocent only of the reading of apocrypha and Priscillian's works; and, there, the letters of his son and episcopal colleague Dictinius proved that he had "fallen."[18] Eventually, perhaps in 396,[19] Symphosius' and Dictinius' opponents' "great patience" ran dry, and they summoned the Galician bishops to give an account of themselves before a council of bishops at Toledo. Initially, the Galicians refused to attend.[20] But sometime later, in 400, with both Ambrose and Siricius dead, Symphosius and his allies felt the need to make their peace with the other Spanish bishops, and they agreed to be present at another council, known traditionally as the first Council of Toledo.

The editor of the anti-Priscillianist professions has preserved only those statements in which the Galicians most strongly separate themselves from Priscillian. The accused evidently comply with requests that they condemn certain heretical books and teachings attributed to Priscillian, "together with the author himself" (*cum ipso auctore*).[21] Dictinius, in addition, condemns his own writings in which he has claimed—in language that indeed seems to echo Priscillian's emphasis on the "divine birth" of humanity—that "the nature of God and humanity is one."[22] He makes much of the bishops' right to "correct" those who have erred and begs for such correction in his own case, so that he may be included in the kingdom of heaven.[23] His use of biblical citations likewise recalls Priscillian,[24] and he hedges a bit in his condemnation of Priscillian's teachings: "all which has been discovered against the faith I condemn with the author himself"; "all that Priscillian either wrongly taught or wrongly wrote I condemn with the author himself."[25] In the end he, like the presbyter Comasius, professes his allegiance to Symphosius: "I follow the opinion of my lord and my father and begetter and teacher. . . . Whatever he said, I say."[26] Symphosius himself seems even more anxious than the others to comply with the bishops' requests. He is particularly eager to clear himself of the charge of claiming, with Priscillian, that the Son is "unbegettable" (*innascibilis*),[27] a term whose monarchian or docetic associations the Toledan bishops exploit in order to demonstrate the unorthodoxy of Priscillian's teachings. "In accordance with what was read a little before on some parchment, in which it was said the Son is unbegettable, I condemn this doctrine, which claims either that there are two principles or that the Son is unbegettable, along with the very author who wrote it."[28] Symphosius asks for the piece of paper on which the charges have been written, so that he can condemn them word for word; his presbyter Comasius does likewise, reiterating that he follows the authority of his bishop.[29]

Not all the Galician bishops were as compliant as Symphosius and Dictinius, who were rewarded with reacceptance into communion conditional upon the approval of the bishops of Milan and Rome, as well as their continued compliance with the rulings of the council.[30] The clergy of bishop Herenias shouted out spontaneously that Priscillian was a catholic and a saint; Herenias agreed and added that Priscillian "suffered persecution by bishops." At this point three other bishops were emboldened to speak up in support of Priscillian's memory, and all four were deposed from the episcopacy by decree of the council; their testimony was furthermore declared unreliable. Galician bishops in communion with Symphosius who had failed to attend the council were given the chance to sign a statement issued by the council. Upon signing, they would be readmitted into communion, with their acceptance again conditional upon the approval of the bishops of Milan and Rome. If they refused to sign, the Galician bishops were to be expelled from their churches along with Herenias and his three episcopal cohorts.[31]

The bishops at Toledo close their verdict with a call for vigilance on the part of their fellow bishops, warning that those whom they have excommunicated are not to be allowed to gather in the homes of women, that condemned apocrypha are not to be read, and that Christians in communion with the bishops of Toledo are not to associate with those whom those bishops have excommunicated. In addition, the bishops specify that their fellow bishop Ortygius, who has been driven out of his churches, is to be returned to his see.[32] These closing lines, which at first seem strangely unrelated to the preceding investigations, suggest that the bishops gathered at Toledo perceived Galician Christianity as threatening not least because of its potentially unsettling effect on those bishops' authority in their own communities.

The fifth-century Galician bishop and chronicler Hydatius specifies that Ortygius was driven out by the Priscillianists because of his catholic faith.[33] Ortygius' case was probably exceptional and unlikely to have arisen outside Galicia. However, the Toledan bishops were ready to believe that even Symphosius had been unable to resist demands that he ordain Dictinius as bishop. In Dictinius, the people had chosen a leader who seems to have been noted for his study of the apocrypha and the writings of Priscillian[34] as well as for his own theological compositions. As already noted, Dictinius refers to his writings (*scriptis meis*) at the council, stating that they belong to the early days of his conversion; in their summary statement, the Toledan bishops refer to these writings as "letters" (*epistolis*).[35] Some twenty years after the Council of Toledo, when Dictinius was dead, one of his works, known as the *Libra*, which consisted in a discussion of twelve questions, was still read and discussed in Galicia and beyond.[36] Unfortunately, little is known about the content of the *Libra* or the circumstances of its composition, although Augustine claimed it included a defense of lying about religious beliefs.[37] In the mid fifth century, Bishop Turribius of Astorga complained to Leo of Rome that the Priscillianist "tractates" (*tractatus*) of Dictinius were still greatly respected and read by many.[38]

The people's insistence that Dictinius be consecrated bishop suggests that while authority was more firmly consolidated in the clergy than it had been some twenty years earlier—note again that all of the main actors in this drama are bishops or presbyters—an individual of exceptional learning, eloquence, or ascetic piety could still provide a significant challenge to the official hierarchy of the church. A weak sense of ecclesial hierarchy seems to have been particularly characteristic of the churches of Galicia, probably owing both to the relatively late establishment of Christianity in that province and to the distinctively rural cast to fourth-century Galician social organization.[39] Now, even more than in Priscillian's day, there was pressure in the broader Spanish community to resolve the tension between public and private sources and models of authority by incorporating the ascetic teacher into the official hierarchy. Nevertheless, some threat of competition remained, and the bishops gathered at Toledo were particularly anxious to prevent members of their own communities from receiving the excommunicated Galicians. They warned that any who did so would be considered guilty by association; indeed, they could expect to be burdened with even heavier penalties. The Toledan bishops feared that the Galicians would challenge their own public authority of office: they might encourage private meetings with women as well as men, and they might promote the study of apocryphal literature, two activities that supported the authority of learned teachers.[40] Thus anxieties about decentered forms of community life, destabilized gender roles, and privatized sources of authority continued to arise on the margins of even a strengthened ecclesiastical hierarchy. Divergent and shifting strategies of extralocal alliance further complicated the conflict. The Spanish bishops who gathered at Toledo attempted to ally themselves with the authority of Milan and Rome and opposed the Galician bishops in communion with Symphosius. Symphosius, for his part, succeeded at one point in gaining at least the qualified support of the Milanese bishop, and he had still greater success at swelling the ranks of his episcopal supporters with new ordinations in Galicia, in the case of Ortygius perhaps even replacing a hostile bishop with one sympathetic to his faction.[41]

The bishops at Toledo combated the threat represented by Galician Christianity not only by invoking the authority of the Italian bishops but also by utilizing the figure of Priscillian to insinuate accusations of heresy more locally.[42] The council insisted that the Galician clergy condemn the heretical content of Priscillian's teachings—of which Priscillian's designation of the Son as "unbegettable" (*innascibilis*) seems to have been their primary evidence—and that they "condemn the author himself." Priscillian himself was made to personify heresy, and denunciation of Priscillian became the touchstone of orthodoxy in the repetitious cadences of the council's acts. Priscillian's own writings were now condemned as heretical alongside the apocryphal scriptures. Images of a pernicious "sect of Priscillian" emerged to challenge the cult of Priscillian and the private authority of leaders like Dictinius.

The Judgments of the Council of Toledo

The formal judgments published in the *Acts of the Council of Toledo* pertain to matters more generally applicable to the church as a whole and reveal the broader concerns that were uppermost in the minds of the bishops gathered at Toledo. An analysis of these judgments both confirms and nuances impressions of the anxieties and disagreements relating to authority and gender that continued to trouble Spanish churches in the early fifth century.

The discussions that resulted in the council's twenty formal judgments probably took place on the three initial days of meeting, September 1–3, as is suggested by the minutes of the investigation of the Galician bishops.[43] The title of the conciliar *Acts* indicates that the judgments were presented and given final approval on September 7, at the close of the council, at the same time that the final verdict concerning the Galician bishops was delivered.[44] The *Acts* opens with a statement by the presider, Patruinus, bishop of Merida, that different customs regarding ordination have produced schism in the church; he urges that the ordinances of Nicea henceforth be followed by all.[45] Patruinus probably refers to the fourth canon of Nicea—which requires that a minimum of three bishops be present for an episcopal ordination[46]—and intends thereby to curtail the ordinations performed by Symphosius or Symphosius and Dictinius alone.[47] The conflict with the Galician bishops appears to have been on the minds of those gathered at Toledo from the start.

The remaining twenty judgments are recorded in the indirect *placuit* form.[48] The dominant concern in the meetings over the first three days seems to have been the definition of terms of eligibility for clerical office, a topic discussed in the first four judgments, and then again in the eighth and tenth. In these six judgments, the bishops make particular use of standards of sexual behavior to define the different grades of the hierarchy and to separate the members of the hierarchy, not only from one another and from the mass of the laity, but also from holders of secular office. This advocacy of varying degrees of sexual continence for the ranks of the clergy is distinct from the broad call to asceticism preached by Priscillian and perhaps by such later followers of Priscillian as Dictinius. However, it too represents a response to the influence of ascetic ideals on the Spanish churches and, indeed, can be seen as continuous with the impulse already evidenced at Saragossa to relocate the disciplined authority of the ascetic life at the center rather than on the margins of the ecclesiastical structures. As Samuel Laeuchli comments in reference to an earlier Spanish council, "by setting sexual taboos the synod meant to limn the image of an ascetic clerical leadership."[49]

Most of the judgments regarding eligibility for clerical office are fairly complex, and their wording indicates involved discussion. The first judgment, for example, begins with the statement that deacons are to observe sexual continence "even if they have wives": only those who live chastely are to be appointed to the ministry. The bishops go on to discuss the special case of deacons who had sexual relations with their wives "even before the prohibition was decreed by the Lusitanian bishops" and the similar case of presbyters who had children before the Lusitanian decision, apparently referring to the judgment of an otherwise unknown local synod. They conclude that neither deacons nor presbyters with a history of sexual activity are to be promoted to a higher clerical office.[50] The Toledan bishops did not need to specify punishment beyond the denial of office or promotion.

Another issue on the minds of the bishops at Toledo was the control of the bishop over his clergy, especially presbyters. This issue did not draw the same kind of sustained discussion as did the topic of eligibility for ecclesiastical office, but did reappear at three different points in the course of the meeting. The fifth judgment requires that all clergy attend a daily Eucharist in the church or face possible expulsion by the bishop; the twelfth forbids a member of the clergy to separate voluntarily from his bishop—so long as that bishop is orthodox—and communicate with another bishop; and the twentieth judgment addresses the problem of presbyters who usurp the episcopal right of anointing. The twelfth judgment in particular seems to have the Priscillianist faction in mind and suggests that the Toledan bishops were concerned about members of their own clergy defecting to Priscillianist bishops. This judgment goes on to prohibit any catholics from entering into communion, whether openly or secretly, with excommunicated Christians, a ruling that recalls the concern about the influence of excommunicated supporters of Priscillian expressed in the minutes of the investigation of the Galician bishops.[51]

The bishops were anxious to maintain their authority not only over their clergy but in the community at large. Four of the judgments—the fifth (discussed above), the ninth (discussed below), the thirteenth, and the fourteenth—highlight the liturgy as the focus of the solidarity of the public community gathered around the bishop. Some or all of these may have had the private gatherings of supporters of Priscillian in mind. The thirteenth and fourteenth seem to represent a continuous discussion of the problem posed by those who attend the eucharistic service without partaking of the Eucharist, a practice also denounced at Saragossa.[52] The punishment in the fourteenth judgment is stated in particularly strong terms: "let that one be considered sacrilegious."[53] Also as at Saragossa, the bishops are concerned that their acts of excommunication not be circumvented. This issue is addressed, not only in the twelfth judgment, discussed above, but also in the fifteenth and the related discussions of the sixteenth, in which the bishops warn that those who refuse to follow the command to shun a sinner will also themselves be shunned. Finally, two judgments refer to the relations between clergy and local secular leaders. The tenth judgment acknowledges the right of a patron to grant or deny permission for a dependent to be ordained. The eleventh threatens excommunication to secular leaders who exploit members of the clergy economically.

The remaining seven judgments concern women in one way or another and occur in two clusters: the sixth, seventh, and ninth reflect issues raised relatively early in the meetings, following upon the initial pro-

tracted discussion of eligibility for clerical office. Another series of discussions took place near the end of the meetings, culminating in the sixteenth,
seventeenth, eighteenth, and nineteenth judgments. Anxiety concerning
the roles of women of notable authority and independence of action is the
unifying thread running through the first cluster of judgments regarding
women. The sixth reads as follows:

> Likewise let no maiden of God [*puella dei*] have intimacy with a confessor
> or any layman of strange blood or go to a social gathering alone, except
> where there is a large number of respectable older men or widows, where
> any confessor can respectably take part with the witness of many. More-
> over, the maidens are not to be allowed inside the homes of readers or to
> be seen with them, unless perhaps she is a sister related by blood or of
> the same mother.[54]

The emphasis here, as earlier in the first judgment of the Council of Saragossa, is on the relations between men and women in private gatherings.
Some virgins, designated *puellae*, were evidently in the habit of meeting
with certain Christian men on intimate terms: literally, they had "familiarity" with them, relating to them as if they were members of the same
family or household. These men are described as belonging either to the
laity or to the ambiguous category of "confessors," a rare title, which
seems sometimes to have been applied informally to ascetics.[55] The virgins
were also accustomed to meet with readers, men with special access to the
books of scripture; these meetings commonly took place in the homes of
the readers. Although the readers were members of the lower ranks of the
hierarchy, their authority in such private meetings, like the authority of
the confessors and laymen, would have derived primarily from their ascetic accomplishments or devotion to the study of scripture.[56] In opposing
intimate relationships between virgins and confessors or readers, the bishops at Toledo reinforce a strictly biological definition of family, which ex-
cludes the possibility of intimate relationships between young virgins and
their male friends. Blood and womb define the areas within which men
and women can mingle freely. Christian virgins cannot have "familiarity"
(*familiaritas*) with men of "strange blood" (*sanguinis alieni*) but only with
brothers "of the same blood" (*consanguineus*) and "of the same uterus"
(*uterinus*). Their private interactions with unrelated men are to take place
only under the watchful eyes of older men and women.

 The seventh judgment targets the wives of clergy, who, it is feared,
have "freedom to sin more."[57] The implication may be that these
women—who in the upper ranks, at least, were in theory required to be
continent by virtue of their husbands' vows—might fall back into sexual

relations with their husbands, if not with other men. Whatever the precise nature of the sin feared, the council acted to prevent a transgression by explicitly granting to clerical husbands the right to punish their wives in any way short of death. Specifically, the bishops recommend that sinning wives be imprisoned in their own homes, given only meager rations of food, and denied the companionship of their husbands. There are clear connections here with the foregoing judgment, in which the freedom of ascetic women is likewise restricted and the rights of the family defended. However, the harsh violence directed toward the wives of the clergy reflects their greater potential threat to the honor of the male clergy and their distinctive role in bearing the displaced burden of male shame.

The ninth judgment again reflects concern about gender relations, and here, even more than in the sixth judgment, the competition between the informal authority of ascetics and the official authority of the clergy is clear:

> No professed virgin [*professa*] or widow may in the absence of a bishop or presbyter chant antiphonies in her own home with a confessor or her slave; indeed, the evening prayer may not be read except in church—or, if it is read on an estate, let it be read with a bishop or presbyter or deacon present.[58]

The variation in the terminology designating ascetic women is noteworthy: perhaps by the year 400, distinctions were made between virgins with episcopal consecration (the *devotae*) and virgins who have simply taken a personal vow, by reason either of youth (the *puellae dei*) or choice (the *professae* mentioned here alongside widows). At any rate, the ninth judgment deals with ascetic women who are mistresses of their own homes, in which they hold private devotions along with male companions, who might be either slaves, and therefore legitimate members of the woman's household, or the ambiguous confessors. These private devotions constitute a challenge to the episcopal control of the liturgy. Ideally, the bishops maintain, daily prayers should be read in the church in the presence of a bishop or presbyter.[59] They were not, however, confident of being able to enforce this ideal and concede that prayers might be read on a country estate in the presence of a bishop or presbyter—or even a deacon, they add as a further concession. As in the sixth judgment, no punishment is threatened, suggesting that the bishops' authority over the private activities of ascetic men and women was still somewhat limited.

The second cluster of judgments about women reflect a concern shared by the seventh judgment—namely, that of the clergy for "their" women and "their" honor. The only exception is the seventeenth judgment's ruling about men's relationships with concubines, in which the mild attempt to control male sexual behavior contrasts markedly with the council's severe punishments of female sexual transgressions. The six-teenth judgment punishes virgins (*devotae*) who marry or are otherwise unchaste with ten years' penance; the eighteenth rules that the widow of a bishop, presbyter, or deacon who marries is to remain among the excom-municated until her deathbed; the nineteenth rules that if virgins (*devotae*) who are daughters of a bishop, presbyter, or deacon sin by marrying they are to be shunned by their parents and—unless their husbands die—are to undergo lifelong penance and only be readmitted to communion on their deathbeds. These three judgments, like the seventh judgment and the six judgments discussed above concerning eligibility for clerical office, serve to distinguish the three highest offices by the particularly stringent demands placed on the sexuality not only of the clergy but also of their wives and daughters—whether literal or figurative.[60]

A comparison of the issues that dominate the judgments of the Coun-cil of Toledo with those that had preoccupied the bishops at Saragossa twenty years earlier reveals intriguing continuities and contrasts. In both cases, the bishops sought to promote the authority of their office and the centrality of the episcopally led liturgy for the communal identity of the church. The bishops at Toledo were, however, far more interested than their Saragossan predecessors in articulating the ranks of the clerical hi-erarchy—bishop, presbyter, deacon, subdeacon, reader, doorkeeper—and the relationships among members of that hierarchy. A moderated and hierarchalized sexual asceticism for both the clergy and their wives, wid-ows, and daughters, together with other moral restrictions, was a major means of differentiating that hierarchy. There was also by 400 a height-ened interest in articulating the relationships between officials of the church and local secular leaders.

While the focus was now on competition and differentiation within the ranks of the clergy, the consolidation of all ecclesiastical authority within the hierarchy was not complete. The private gatherings of ascetic Christians, in which men and women mixed with relative freedom and the informal authority of learned or exemplary individuals was acknowl-edged, still aroused particular anxiety. Those who attempted to defend a public model of community and authority and to eliminate competition from rivals whose authority derived primarily from the private sphere insisted on the separation and subordination of women. Women were de-fined by their sexuality, which was strictly controlled by segregating them from nonfamilial men, and was, furthermore, viewed primarily in terms of its consequences for male honor.

Heresy Inquisition at Tarragona

The account of the heresy investigation contained in the letter of Consentius to Augustine brings readers into a very different world, in which "Priscillianism" emerges as a further linguistic abstraction in the heresiological vocabulary, while evidence of any actual continuing positive influence of Priscillian dissolves into "the emptiest mist of suspicion"—to borrow a phrase from one of the participants in the inquisition.[61] Apart from the meddling literary activity of Consentius, the conflict remained local, despite efforts to draw upon the influence of Patroclus of Arles—whose intervention seems to have been ineffective—and Augustine of Hippo—who was as dismayed by the tactics of the accusers as by the supposed heresy of the accused. In the absence of significant external intervention, the Christian communities of the Ebro valley in northeastern Spain were able to rally around their leaders and deflect accusations of heresy, even when those leaders were proven to have compromised themselves by lying publicly about their secret study of unorthodox books.

Consentius, an ascetic living on the Balearic islands off the eastern coast of Spain, had initiated a correspondence with Augustine in the second decade of the fifth century.[62] It was probably in the year 419 that he sent Augustine copies of his works against the Priscillianists, composed at the request of bishop Patroclus of Arles.[63] Accompanying Consentius' anti-Priscillianist writings was a letter in which he explained that while he had not initially intended to bore Augustine with these "inept and rough" works, circumstances had compelled a change of mind. Consentius goes on to relate that he had recently received a visit from Fronto, a fellow ascetic who had been living in a monastery in the city of Tarragona. Fronto had recounted an amazing tale of secret heretics in the Tarragonese province, which Consentius transcribes for Augustine "as I received it from his mouth."[64] Although Fronto had proven their guilt in public investigations at Tarragona, the heretics had not been deposed from the ecclesiastical offices they held; moreover, Fronto himself had been run out of town. He had fled to the sympathetic and influential Bishop Patroclus, who had summoned a council to rectify matters. But Consentius doubted that the Spanish bishops would attend such a council, and he was furthermore concerned because the supporters of the "Priscillianists"—as he identified Fronto's heretics—were using the example of Augustine's own lenient treatment of the Donatists in Africa in order to justify not deposing reformed heretics in Spain. Consentius urged Augustine to write a letter to Patroclus lending support to his call for harsh punishment for the Priscillianists and deposition for their leaders. He also suggested that Augustine might recommend his own books for the training of young heresy hunters and modestly predicted that if such a training were provided, hordes of Priscillianists would be uncovered even in Hippo itself (*in ista praecipue urbe*).[65]

Consentius was not an uninvolved or impartial judge of Fronto's actions against the heretics of Tarragona. It was he who had instructed Fronto in the art of combating heresy. To this end, circa 418, Consentius had sent Fronto a packet of writings that included his anti-Priscillianist works.[66] These works contained practical instructions on how to insinuate oneself into the confidences of a heretic in order to expose heresy. Consentius even composed a discourse written from the point of view of a heretic for use in the undercover investigation of supposed Priscillianists.[67] Augustine, who had read Consentius' works, summarizes the content of this discourse: cautious praise for Dictinius' life; reverent mention of Priscillian; discussion of the divine origin and substance of the soul; and, finally, extravagant admiration for Dictinius' *Libra*.[68] Leaving nothing to chance, Consentius seems to have supplied Fronto with not only a script but also a specific target in the person of Severa, whom Fronto describes to Consentius as the one "whose name you had expressed to me clearly."[69]

Fronto's behavior had come under serious attack in the course of the investigation, and he was anxious to establish legitimacy for his aggressive and duplicitous methods. Invoking the authority of Consentius' writings, he enhanced both his own prestige and that of the author by refusing to surrender the works to the bishops at Tarragona on the grounds that they were not meant for everyone's ears.[70] Fronto insisted that he had understood everything Consentius wrote and followed his recommended method of approaching heretics to the letter.[71] Consentius, for his part, was flattered to have such a receptive disciple and appears to have had no qualms about the controversy provoked by Fronto's use of his writings. But in spite of Fronto's and Consentius' agreement that he had adhered exactly to Consentius' recommended plan, it is at least questionable whether Fronto in fact approached Severa with the prepared script and whether the "heretics" whom he unearthed were actually secret followers of Priscillian. Fronto himself never once invokes the term "Priscillianist," consistently referring more vaguely to "heretics." Nor, as we shall see, do any of his accusations against those whom he identifies as heretics point specifically toward any connection with Priscillian.[72]

Whatever the precise nature of the monk's approach to Severa, she evidently responded positively to his overtures and confided in him some of the activities of the members of her social circle. From her, Fronto learned of Severa's relative Severus, a man "famous for his wealth and power, as well as his scholarship," who was a presbyter in the church of Huesca.[73] According to Severa, Severus possessed three controversial books. Fronto describes the contents of these "cursed" volumes—which he almost certainly had not read—in vague terms: "they contained all kinds of sacrilege" and included "the shameful and sacrilegious knowledge of magic incantations."[74] Severus' possession of these books had been discovered through a remarkable series of events. When Severus was travelling to a fortified family estate, barbarians plundered his baggage, stole the books, and sold them to Sagittius, bishop of the nearby town of Lérida, midway between Tarragona and Huesca. Sagittius, concluding that the books were unorthodox and realizing that they had been taken from Severus, stored two of them away safely in the church archives and forwarded one to Tarragona for the consideration of the metropolitan bishop, Titianus. Titianus, in turn, sent the sample book back to Huesca and recommended that Syagrius, bishop of that town, investigate the orthodoxy of his presbyter Severus. Severus explained that he had inherited the books from his mother, who had recently died, and, not realizing their unorthodoxy, had been taking them out to his castle for a quiet and considered reading when they were stolen. Syagrius believed him, and the matter was laid to rest.[75]

None of this was news. But Severa told Fronto more. First, there were hints that the books did not, after all, come from Severus' mother, with the damaging implication that Severus had acquired them on his own initiative. More explicit and incriminating was Severa's revelation that Severus had in fact persuaded Syagrius and Sagittius to return the books to him quietly, promising certain favors in exchange.[76] Furthermore, Sagittius himself had masked the full extent of the books' unorthodoxy by sending Titianus not the most offensive sample, as he claimed, but rather a book from which he had carefully removed the most unorthodox parts.[77]

Fronto now felt that he had enough evidence to charge both Severa and Severus publicly with heresy.[78] But in attacking Severus, the respected member of a leading family of the region, Fronto, a man of few resources or connections, had bitten off more than he could chew. Severus' supporters charged that Fronto was uncultured and poor, motivated by envy to invent lies about so holy and noble a man as Severus, and the people of Tarragona were sufficiently aroused to threaten him with death. If we can trust his dramatic portrayal of the events, Fronto avoided this immediate disaster only by going on record as agreeing to a sentence of death by stoning if he were unable to prove his charges.[79] Meanwhile, Severus had solicited the support of the powerful Count Asterius, his relative by marriage, claiming that Fronto had attacked their whole family with gross accusations. Asterius arrived on the scene along with his daughter, a woman of great influence. The daughter immediately extended her protection to her kinswoman Severa, who now denied all of Fronto's accusations.[80]

Bishop Titianus had agreed to hear Fronto's charges and had written to Sagittius and Syagrius, requesting them to come to Tarragona with the books in question.[81] However, it was clear that Severus had the strong support, not only of his influential family and the people of Tarragona, but also of the bishops Titianus and Agapius; the latter, whose see is not mentioned, had originally brought the packet of letters and writings from Consentius to Fronto[82] and was still in Tarragona at the time of the heresy investigation. When Count Asterius questioned them, the two bishops repeated that Fronto was a lying detractor who had deceived a defenseless woman, invented false accusations against a presbyter, and finally involved the count's entire illustrious house—including his daughter—in his vicious slander. Upon Fronto's countering that Agapius was not even worthy of reading the documents that Consentius had sent to Fronto under seal, Agapius physically assaulted Fronto in the count's presence.[83]

When Fronto finally succeeded in bringing his story to Asterius' ears, the count was evidently persuaded that he himself was not seriously threatened by Fronto's accusations and that it was neither necessary nor wise for him to intervene directly on Severus' behalf. He withdrew politely, asking for Fronto's blessings in his upcoming campaign against the barbarians and making it clear that his faith was not tainted by any possible heresy on Severus' part. Severus and his supporters were momentarily stunned by the count's unexpected neutrality, but did not cease to campaign actively against Fronto. Indeed, Fronto claimed that at this point he scarcely dared leave the church for fear of his life, and that even in the church he was threatened by a most powerful servant of the count. When that servant subsequently died, Fronto, who interpreted the death as an act of God, was accused of using magic against him.[84]

Meanwhile, Severus was attempting to remove any evidence supporting Fronto's damaging accusations. He sent the monk Ursitio hurrying to fetch two of the books from his castle and return them to Sagittius. Sagittius received them with great relief and set off immediately for Tarragona in order to prove Fronto's accusations false. Armed not only with the apparent evidence of his own possession of the books, but also with his great power and learning, Sagittius swore on the gospels that the books had never left his archives; Severus likewise swore publicly that he had not seen them since they were first taken from him. Fronto was denounced as an envious liar when he persisted in his accusations against them, protesting that Severus must have secretly returned the books to Sagittius.[85]

Fortunately for Fronto, Severus' and Sagittius' attempt to cover up their covert exchanges of books did not ultimately succeed. Before receiving the books from Severus, Sagittius had already taken measures of his own to conceal his return of the books to Severus, and those measures now backfired. Writing to Bishop Syagrius, whom he understood to be in the same predicament of having returned the book now requested by Titianus to Severus, Sagittius had confessed that Severus had the two books that were supposedly in his own keeping as well. He intended to claim, however, that he had meant to send the books to Syagrius—since Syagrius was supposedly undertaking an investigation of Severus—and that it was only by accident that they had been delivered to his presbyter Severus instead.[86] Upon receiving this letter, Syagrius was frightened by the awkward situation in which he now found himself. He initially decided to support Sagittius' lie and thus protect both Sagittius and Severus. But a terrifying dream of future judgment caused him to change his mind. Armed with Sagittius' letter and, furthermore, with a written confession extracted from the monk Ursitio, who had by this point secretly returned the books to Sagittius, Syagrius set out on foot for Tarragona with the intention of exposing Sagittius' and Severus' lies.[87]

According to Fronto, it was on the very day on which he had been judged a false accuser and sentenced to death that Syagrius reached Tarragona. Impressed that one so old—and so rich—had undertaken such a long journey by foot, Fronto approached the quarters where Syagrius was staying and berated him for the lies that would cost Fronto his life. Not anticipating success in obtaining the aged bishop's support, Fronto was astonished when Syagrius immediately confessed to having returned a book secretly to Severus. Still shaken by his dream, Syagrius allowed himself to be persuaded to hand over to Fronto the damaging letter from Sagittius as well as Ursitio's confession.[88]

On the next day, when Fronto was supposedly scheduled to be stoned to death, he allowed his enemies to perjure themselves further before he brandished his proof against Sagittius, who now bore the brunt of Fronto's animosity, perhaps because of his personal attack on him the day before. Unable to defend himself in the face of the written evidence, Sagittius simply left, along with a number of his supporters. Fronto relates that he pursued him and charged him further with having cut out and kept some pages from one of the books. Sagittius initially denied this charge but later was somehow induced to return the pages, which were subsequently read aloud before a horrified crowd. The people pressed for Sagittius' condemnation, but Titianus demurred, offering the explanation that a greater number of bishops were needed to condemn a fellow bishop;[89] Fronto reports that seven, including Sagittius himself, were present.[90]

Eventually it was decided that both the books and the records of the investigation would be burned; no one was to be excommunicated or deposed, much less stoned to death. Fronto was outraged by what he considered a suppression of the truth and the sale of a judgment to the powerful, wealthy, and learned men who were the leaders of the Christian communities in the Ebro valley. As he continued his vocal protests, Bishop Agapius was once again moved to assault Fronto physically—an ill-advised act, which, as in the case of Severus' servant, had fatal consequences for the assailant—and Fronto aroused such general resentment that he was forced to leave town. He travelled first to Arles where he sought and obtained the verbal support of Patroclus; from there he journeyed to visit Consentius.[91]

It is evident from Fronto's narrative that the status of the lay ascetic or monk was somewhat more clearly defined than it had been in Priscillian's day, but also correspondingly diminished. Fronto, who describes himself as the founder of a monastery,[92] is identified by Consentius and by Asterius in Fronto's narrative as a *famulus Christi*, or servant of Christ;[93] Consentius describes himself as a "servant of Christ" as well.[94] Augustine uses a similar phrase, *servus Dei*, in reference to Fronto.[95] Elsewhere in Augustine's writings, this term frequently serves to designate the private asceticism of cultured lay Christians possessing considerable wealth, education, and social status;[96] in this context, the term *servus* invokes a rhetoric of renunciation of power that in fact serves to enhance the authority of the speaker or writer. However, there is little sense of rhetorical paradox in the title *famulus* as it is used in Fronto's narrative. By his own account, Fronto's detractors denounce him as "a worthless man of mean character and an impoverished beggar"; he is repeatedly referred to as a "barking dog," and he himself feels like a "dead flea" when faced with the overwhelming power, wealth, and learning of his opponents.[97] Similarly clear is the inferior position of Ursitio, who is variously described in Fronto's narrative as a monk (*monachus*), as a friend of Severus (*amicus Severi*), as a dependent member of Severus' household (*domesticus*), and finally as "Severus' monk" (*Severi monachus*).[98] He is subject to the will of his clerical and social superiors, being "compelled" by Severus to deliver the codices secretly and then by Syagrius to confess to the same deed.[99] Lay "monks" or "servants of Christ" like Fronto or Ursitio appear, then, clearly subordinate to the higher clergy.

Perhaps responding in part to the exceptional opportunity created by the social and political instability brought on by the Germanic invasions of Spain,[100] Fronto attempted to enhance his personal prestige and authority, first, by standing before the public with accusations of heresy directed against some of the most powerful men and women of the region and, second, by invoking the support and authority of Bishop Patroclus of Arles and of Consentius, a self-proclaimed theologian, who pursued a literary correspondence with such powerful bishops as Patroclus and Augustine. Fronto elaborated and memorialized his heroic role as accuser and his alliance with these influential figures in the dramatic narrative circulated from Arles to Hippo. By identifying Fronto's "heretics" as "Priscillianists" and framing Fronto's narrative in his own self-glorifying prose, the lay ascetic Consentius likewise attempted to enhance his authority, not only by constructing himself as a theologian, but also by placing himself and his own anti-Priscillianist writings at the center of a valiant combat and presenting himself as a peer of such great heresy fighters as the bishops Patroclus and Augustine.

The vigorous attempts of Fronto and Consentius to establish their authority outside the ranks of clerical office were not particularly successful. In Tarragona, Fronto was accused of sorcery and nearly killed, and his opponents retained their positions of power. Consentius himself seems to betray awareness of the need to deflect accusations of heresy through an elaborate—and indeed otherwise somewhat puzzling—protestation of his own aversion to scholarship.[101] And while Patroclus of Arles was happy to make use of both Fronto and Consentius in his own attempts to label Priscillianist heretics in Gaul, Augustine not only doubted the veracity of Fronto's report but also denounced the deceitful methods utilized by Fronto and actively promoted by Consentius. In the end, the "servants of Christ" could not compete with a Christian leadership in which the public authority of ecclesiastical office and the private authority of education, eloquence, or discipline of life had almost completely merged. The presbyter Severus was a man "famous for his wealth and power, as well as his scholarship," and related by marriage to the local potentate Asterius.[102] Severus' bishop, Syagrius, was considered by Fronto to be wealthy and was probably not as simple and credulous as Fronto depicts him in an effort to excuse his support of Severus.[103] Bishop Sagittius was "powerful and learned in higher literature."[104]

This merging of public and private authority in Christian leadership seems to have been accompanied by a lowering of anxieties about gender roles and relations. Such a claim cannot be supported by silence alone, but it is nevertheless noteworthy that in spite of the prominent appearance of a number of women in Fronto's drama—Severa, Severus' mother, Asterius' daughter—overt tensions concerning their roles as women and their relations with men are not evident.[105] Now confined primarily to the circle of their families, women become visible only when the men in their families are highly visible, and all of the women mentioned by Fronto seem to have belonged to the same powerful Tarragonese family.[106] The sole instance in which a woman is described as interacting with a man outside her family is in the relationship between Fronto himself and Severa, who was probably an older woman and perhaps a widow as well.[107] There are slight hints that even this interaction between an ascetic male and an older woman or widow was perceived as somehow improper. Fronto brags about how "Severa, that little woman [*muliercula*] . . . revealed all the secrets of her crimes to me, as if to a heretic," while the bishops charge him with having "craftily deceived an incautious and simple little woman [*incircumspectam ac simplicem mulierculam*]."[108] In both cases, Fronto—or the heretic in whose guise he presents himself—seems to be depicted negatively in the role of the false Christian of 2 Tim. 3.6 who wrongfully enters private households and deceives "little women."

Conclusions

Priscillian was condemned as a Manichaean and magician; Dictinius was charged with membership in the sect of Priscillian; and Severus was labeled a Priscillianist by a secondhand reporter. The increasing abstraction of the language surrounding the figure of Priscillian reflects the progressive simplification of an image that served as a negative counterpart for the evolving identity of a Spanish church that sought to redraw and strengthen its faltering boundaries in a period of dramatic social, political, and cultural change. In the move from "Priscillian" to "sect of Priscillian" and finally to "Priscillianism," one phase in the construction of a heresy was complete. The investigations at Toledo in 400 and at Tarragona circa 418 allow precious glimpses into two moments in the heresiological process and in the accompanying evolution of structures of authority and gender.

In Priscillian's own lifetime, the competition between Priscillian and Hydatius was closely matched: the clearly articulated public authority of ecclesiastical office and the more ambiguous private authority deriving from personal education, eloquence, or asceticism carried almost equal weight in urban contexts dominated by a complex and divided elite class. The social complexity was simplified and the ecclesiastical conflict resolved in favor of Hydatius only by the invocation of the most potent labels available—Manichaeism and sorcery—and the imposition of the most violent instrument of secular power—the emperor's sword.

At Toledo some fifteen years later, the weight had shifted in the balance of authority. While "confessors" and other teachers and ascetics could still provoke some anxiety on the part of the official hierarchy, the threat was no longer acute. The legitimacy of such privately construed authority had been successfully challenged through the condemnation of figures like Priscillian; where it was not challenged outright, it was at least partially harmonized with the authority of office. The scholar and popular leader Dictinius, much like Priscillian before him, was consecrated bishop; unlike Priscillian, he remained successfully, if tenuously, integrated into the ecclesiastical hierarchy.[109] Yet the merging of public and private authority was still incomplete, as is evident from the council's opposition to the consecration of Dictinius and to the other seemingly uncontrolled ordinations of the Galicians. The Toledan bishops suspected, probably rightly, that the authority of their Galician counterparts, however similarly labeled, was nonetheless differently constituted and thereby inherently threatening to their own authority.

Some twenty years later in Tarragona, in the wake of barbarian invasions that left the communities effectively cut off from centralized imperial rule, this merging of public and private authority had progressed still further, reflecting a similar structural simplification or consolidation of the local governing elites. Men like the presbyter Severus and Bishop Sagittius were affirmed and defended as the rightful leaders of their communities on the basis of both ecclesiastical office and personal wealth, influence, and education, and they could moreover anticipate a degree of solidarity with the local general Asterius, to whom Severus was related by marriage. Where the harmony of public and private sources and strategies of authorization was imperfect, it showed up primarily in internal contradictions exemplified most dramatically in the attitude toward books and private study. These contradictions necessitated a degree of compromise and even dissimulation on the part of leaders who were called upon to embody the authority of both the learned scholar and the official guardian of orthodoxy. They also left open the possibility of accusations of heresy like those brought by Fronto. Nevertheless, a layman like Fronto could scarcely compete with the more firmly anchored authority of a leader like Severus, even under exceptional circumstances. The role of the lay ascetic or monk had become more clearly defined, as well as more explicitly subordinate. The "servant of Christ" was no independent leader like Priscillian but belonged now to the retinue of a powerful representative of the official hierarchy. In terms of his strategies of self-authorization, the cultured presbyter Severus was indeed more of a true heir of Priscillian than the monk Fronto. Yet at the same time, the dynamic of alienation in the private construction of authority was now minimized as public and private spheres merged in ecclesiological rhetoric.

Authority deriving from private sphere networks was, then, in large part subsumed by the expanding boundaries of the public sphere. It followed that the space within which women could exert authority and mingle with men grew correspondingly smaller. In Priscillian's lifetime, the women of his circle participated relatively freely in the gatherings of dedicated Christians; celibate women of all ages were granted public respect; Euchrotia and Procula travelled with Priscillian, Instantius, and Salvianus to Rome; and Urbica publicly faced an angry crowd. And at the turn of the century when the Spanish bishops met in council at Toledo, ascetic women, whether professed virgins or widows or the celibate wives of clergy, could still enjoy some degree of authority and freedom to interact with male ascetics.

Yet in the language of the bishops gathered at Toledo, the familial home is the sole locus of even ascetic women's activities, the gatherings envisioned appear smaller and more restricted than those discussed by the bishops at Saragossa, and the bishops' own insistence that women should be defined by and restricted to their family roles grows shriller. It is no longer enough to prohibit women from mingling with "strange" men; the "familiar" is now graphically defined by the exclusive bonds of blood and womb. The sexuality of women, and especially younger women, is not merely represented as troublingly anomalous but presented explicitly as a threat to the honor of fathers and husbands, in terms that not only subordinate even ascetic women to their male relatives but also persistently define women by their family relationships.

At Tarragona some twenty years later, the sphere of women's freedom seems even more fully restricted to the family proper, and concerns about women's roles and relations with men appear correspondingly less urgent, although women do continue to define the boundaries of the acceptable. Only in the case of Severa, probably an older widow, and the monk Fronto is a woman described as interacting with a man outside her family, and allusions to 2 Tim. 3.6 hint that even this might be considered slightly improper. Under the conditions of their virtual restriction to the family, women come into public view primarily when their male relations come into public view. This was the case with Severus' prominent family, which included three women of notable mention: Severus' recently deceased mother, who was believed to have possessed a library containing controversial theological literature; Severa, who was well-informed concerning Severus' dealings and interested in discussions with monks; and Asterius' daughter, who was powerful enough to shelter Severa from Fronto's accusations of heresy.

In the decades of the late fourth and early fifth centuries, the creation of "Priscillianism" accompanied the consolidation of authority in the official hierarchy of the church and the confinement of women within the boundaries of the family or household. The ambiguous territory of social life that had formerly stretched between the household and the imperial political center was now more solidly assigned to the sphere of male activity, while at the same time the male sphere lost much of its sharpness of "public" definition—or, from another perspective, the public acquired a new definition. Classical forms of thought and expression rearranged themselves once again in order to accommodate a fundamental shift in the social and political landscape.

CHAPTER FIVE

"GNOSTIC"

Priscillian Reinterpreted
by Sulpicius Severus and Jerome

While the Spanish churches were establishing "Priscillianism" as a new category of Christian deviance, other Latin-speaking Christians were applying the time-hallowed label of "gnosticism" to Priscillian's movement. Sulpicius Severus and Jerome are the primary representatives of this stream of tradition. Neither author identifies Priscillian or his followers as "Manichaeans" or "Priscillianists." Instead, they invoke the classic heresiological discourse of the second and third centuries, supplying Priscillian with the genealogical credentials and conventional characteristics of an insidious gnostic seducer. Jerome explicitly acknowledges the Irenaean foundations of his portrait, while at the same time going beyond Irenaeus in his use of 2 Tim. 3.6–7 to make gender and sexuality central to his depiction of the Spanish heretic. Severus' dependence on the Christian heresiological tradition is subtler and more complex, and his unnamed sources are more difficult to identify; nevertheless, it is clear that both 2 Tim. 3 and the traditional image of the gnostic heretic strongly influenced Severus' portrait of Priscillian as well.

Since the 1909 publication of E.-Ch. Babut's *Priscillien et le priscillianisme*, Ithacius has been identified as the originator of the gnosticized portrait of Priscillian transmitted by Severus and Jerome. We know through a brief summary by Isidore of Seville that Ithacius composed an *Apology* in which he denounced Priscillian:

> Ithacius, bishop of the Spains, famous in name and eloquence, wrote a
> certain book in apologetic form in which he demonstrates the cursed dog-
> mas of Priscillian, his arts of sorcery, and his disgraceful acts of lechery,
> showing that a certain Mark of Memphis, expert in the magic art, was the
> student of Mani and teacher of Priscillian.[1]

Babut suggests that this *Apology*, which was probably written in the course
of events leading to Ithacius' deposition circa 389,[2] offers a highly fictionalized depiction of Priscillian based directly on Irenaeus' portrait of the
second-century gnostic Mark. Thus, according to Babut, the distorting influence of anti-gnostic heresiology on the portrait of Priscillian was
already established in the tradition by 389, and the parallels between the
accounts of Severus and Jerome arise from their common dependence on
Ithacius' *Apology*.[3]

The brilliant creativity of his source theory, which has long won Babut
adherents,[4] rests on a speculative freedom that also leaves that theory
open to question on a number of points. Isidore in fact makes no mention
of Ithacius' supposed use of Irenaeus and furthermore specifies that Ithacius identified Priscillian not as a gnostic but as a Manichaean. I suggest
that we cannot therefore simply assume, with Babut, that Ithacius' *Apology*
was the source for Severus' and Jerome's parallel depictions of Priscillian
as a *gnostic*. The two authors probably relied in part on prior traditions in
constructing their gnosticized portraits of Priscillian: Filastrius, for example, seems to have associated Priscillian with gnosticism as well as with
Manichaeism at a very early stage in the controversy.[5] However, Severus'
and Jerome's exclusive use of the label of gnosticism and careful avoidance
of any reference to Manichaeism is unprecedented in the extant literary
references to Priscillian.

How, then, does one explain the emergence of these parallel portraits
of the gnostic Priscillian? The answer, I think, is most helpfully sought,
not in hypothetical common sources, but rather in certain commonalities
of context that encouraged Severus and Jerome to utilize the resources of
their Christian tradition in similar ways. Both men met with opposition in
their roles as ascetic scholars, and both struggled to counter that opposition with innovative ecclesiological constructs intended to resolve the conflict between private and public and alienated and accommodating strategies of Christian self-definition. To a certain extent, each succeeded, in part
by linking public authority with an accommodated private authority
through the glorification of the ascetic bishop or cleric, and in part by symbolically distancing bishops from ascetics through the advocation of a
theoretical separation of the spheres of urban church and rural monastery.
The harmonizing of public and private understandings of community and

authority remained, however, incomplete, and ambivalence and inconsistency persisted in Severus' and Jerome's attitudes toward both the official clergy and women. Gender receives particular emphasis as Severus and Jerome each invoke the rhetoric of women's separation and subordination in order to legitimate their distinctive ecclesiologies. At the same time, both struggle with the conflicting experience of women's relative independence and authority in the privatized sphere of ascetic Christianity, and the internal dissonance resulting from each man's ambivalent relationship to the public sphere intensifies his preoccupation with the theme of the separation and subordination of women.

Within this context, the distant figure of the condemned Priscillian—although central to neither man's concerns—once again serves as a lightning rod for tensions over gender and authority. Severus' and Jerome's portraits of Priscillian as a disorderly, traitorous seducer become projections of feared accusations, and as such reveal their particular vulnerability in contemporary ecclesiastical debates: the two authors construct these portraits as pieces of larger strategies to dissociate themselves from similar characterizations. Neither Severus nor Jerome are involved in direct attempts to exclude Priscillian or Priscillian's purported followers from the Christian community. In their works, the archaic label of gnosticism attached to Priscillian functions more subtly not to exclude but to circumscribe and control the role of the ascetic and scholar in the Christian community. At the same time, implied accusations of gnosticism are invoked to control the behavior of women by casting them in the role of unchaste "little women" misled both morally and doctrinally by the gnostic seducer. By exerting control over women's behavior, Severus and Jerome seek to resolve the internal conflict resulting from their contradictory ideals for and experiences of women.

This chapter temporarily disrupts the contextualized narrative account of the heresy of Priscillian, undertaking an initial comparative, chronologically ordered examination of the depictions of Priscillian in the writings of Severus and Jerome. Such an examination illumines both the overlapping contours and the divergent elaborations of Severus' and Jerome's gnosticized portraits of Priscillian, in such a way as to demonstrate their original independence as well as their fundamental compatibility. A brief consideration of the respective careers of Sulpicius Severus and Jerome follows the review of their parallel treatments of Priscillian and returns us to the historical narrative. Both the conflicts the two men experienced and their responses to those conflicts provide a crucial context for interpreting Severus' and Jerome's novel and distinctive portrayals of Priscillian as a gnostic seducer. At the same time, their lives open windows onto the broader ecclesiastical arenas in which issues of gender and authority played themselves out in the west in the late fourth and early fifth centuries.

The Texts and the Question of Influence

Jerome mentions Priscillian briefly in some ten different works written in Palestine between 392 and 415. Severus gives a single, more lengthy account of Priscillian, which serves as the dramatic conclusion to his *Chronicle*, published in Aquitaine between 403 and 406. A careful examination of the two authors' references to Priscillian demonstrates the weaknesses of Babut's source theory and allows the proposal of certain modifications of that theory, while at the same time clarifying the distinctive shape of the portrait of Priscillian as a gnostic seducer. While Severus seems to have been familiar with Ithacius' *Apology*, he apparently does not owe his gnosticized depiction of Priscillian to that work, and it is quite possible that Jerome did not know Ithacius' *Apology* at all. There is furthermore no evidence of any other common source or of direct borrowing between the two authors until sometime between 410 and 415, when Jerome appears to have become familiar with elements of Severus' account. Instead, preexisting and independently established parallels between his own portrait of Priscillian and Severus' portrait facilitated Jerome's assimilation of Severus' material in his final depiction of Priscillian as a gnostic seducer.

Jerome's earliest reference to Priscillian occurs in his biographical encyclopedia *On Famous Men*, written for a Spanish patron in 392 or early 393, some six years after Priscillian's death.[6] The brief chapter devoted to Priscillian is notable for its neutral tone: "Priscillian, bishop of Avila, who at the instigation of Hydatius and Ithacius was slain at Trier by the tyrant Maximus, published many brief works, some of which have reached us."[7] Jerome had probably come into contact with Priscillian's works during his three-year sojourn in Rome (382–84), immediately following Priscillian's own visit to that city. His later writings reveal an awareness of Priscillian's defense of the use of apocryphal scriptures, a theme surfacing in all three of Priscillian's apologetic works and comprising the central focus of the *Book on the Faith and the Apocrypha*. If Jerome had indeed read some of Priscillian's writings by 392, he does not seem to have found them blatantly heretical, since he offers no personal judgment on the issue of Priscillian's orthodoxy and seems confident that such neutrality will please his Spanish addressee.

While he stops short of condemning Priscillian personally, Jerome does report that others accuse Priscillian of the gnostic heresy, offering the further explanation that this is the heresy of Basilides and Mark: "He is still accused by some of the gnostic heresy—that is, of the heresy of Basilides or Mark, concerning whom Irenaeus wrote—while others maintain that he did not think in the way that is claimed."[8] Jerome's language suggests that the explanatory gloss is his own and, despite the claims of Babut, there is no evidence that anyone before him had identified Priscillian with the Alexandrian Basilides or the Mark whose teachings were influential in Gaul.[9] Jerome cites Irenaeus as his authoritative source on the two second-century gnostics, although Irenaeus does not in fact describe Mark as being of the school of Basilides, as Jerome seems to think.[10] Simple geographical proximity may have suggested this connection between Priscillian of Spain and the "Basilidean" Mark of Gaul.[11] Alternatively, Jerome may have known that Ithacius identified a certain Mark of Memphis as Priscillian's teacher. If so, the common name could have suggested the connection between Priscillian and Irenaeus' Mark, while the Egyptian origins of Priscillian's supposed teacher may have led Jerome to identify the Irenaean Mark with Basilides. However, any such hypothesis remains extremely speculative.[12] Regardless of his source or inspiration, Jerome chose at an early date to link Priscillian with the gnostic Mark described by Irenaeus, and this choice proved crucial in shaping the portrait of Priscillian that subsequently emerged from Jerome's pen.

Some seven years later, Jerome mentions the "filthy heresy of Basilides," which has ravaged Spain "like a plague and a sickness."[13] The shift in his attitude toward Priscillian, whom he does not identify by name either here or in his next five allusions to the Spanish heretic, may be owing in part to negative reports received circa 397. The source of these reports was Lucinus, a wealthy Spanish ascetic and student of scripture, who died only two years after initiating a correspondence with Jerome. In a letter written in 399 to Lucinus' widow, Theodora, Jerome praises Lucinus for having upheld the pure faith of the church in the face of the gnostic heresy. He notes that Lucinus rejected the heretics' claim to derive the portentous names of Armazel, Barbelos, Abraxas, Balsamus, and Leosibora from "Hebrew sources."[14] Three of these five names—Armazel, Barbelos, and Balsamus—also occur in Priscillian's denunciation of gnostic interpretations of scripture, and a fourth—Leosibora—is mentioned uncritically in his citation of Job;[15] it is therefore likely that Lucinus knew something of the controversies surrounding Priscillian's use and interpretation of apocryphal scriptures.[16] Jerome may rely on Lucinus, but more probably offers his own interpretation when he remarks scornfully that the heretics invoke such barbarous words in order to mystify and astonish women and other ignorant folk.

The reference to Lucinus' anti-gnostic stance seems intended as an indirect—although hardly subtle—warning to Theodora, and Jerome leans heavily on the theme of women's particular vulnerability to the deceits and seductions of the heretics. As in 392, he identifies the contemporary Spanish "gnosticism" with the gnosticism of the "Basilidean" Mark, again making explicit reference to his source, Irenaeus, whom he inaccurately endows with an apostolic pedigree.

> Irenaeus . . . reports that a certain Mark, descendant of the stock of Basilides the gnostic, first came to Gaul and polluted the Rhône and Garonne regions with his teachings. He especially seduced noblewomen with this error, promising certain mysteries in secret and winning them over with magic arts and the secret pleasure of the body. From there, he crossed the Pyrenees and occupied Spain, and his goal was to approach the houses of the rich, and in them especially the women, who are led by various desires, always learning and never reaching knowledge of truth [2 Tim. 3.6–7].[17]

Irenaeus actually reports only that the Marcosians were active in the district of the Rhône.[18] Jerome either misremembers or, more likely, feels at liberty to extend Mark's activity not only into the Garonne region, home of Priscillian's patron Euchrotia,[19] but even across the Pyrenees into Spain. He furthermore generalizes the role of Mark as a seducer of noble women[20] by capping Irenaeus' account of Mark with a quotation from 2 Tim. 3.6–7, which refers to the false teachers who will come at the end of time and lead women astray.[21] Mark is presented as one of many heretical seducers, and Jerome can use the stereotyped role to create an easy link between Mark and his supposed imitator Priscillian, whose teachings, Jerome implies, threaten to "seduce" the wealthy Theodora. With this letter, most of the crucial elements of Jerome's gnosticized portrait of Priscillian are in place.

In the decade that follows the writing of the letter to Theodora, Jerome's objections to Priscillian and his disciples shift to the topic of the Spanish heretics' invocation of pseudo-Hebrew names drawn from the apocryphal scriptures. A series of five scattered passages dating circa 400 to circa 410 refers scornfully to "the absurdities of the apocrypha,"[22] "Spanish incantations,"[23] "Spanish foolishness,"[24] "Egyptian portents,"[25] and "the portents of Basilides."[26] Jerome's contempt for the amateur Hebrew derivations attributed to Priscillian's followers and his particular sensitivity on the subject of their use of the apocrypha are not surprising in a period in which Jerome was completing his translation of the Hebrew scriptures. During these years, Jerome was particularly eager both to establish his authority as a Hebrew scholar and to defend his preference for the Hebrew text, which not only diverged from the Septuagint at many points but also included fewer books in its canon.[27] With these concerns in mind, he invoked the negative example of the Spanish heretics who misused both Hebrew names and apocryphal scriptures. Here Jerome may have relied not only on Lucinus' account but also on Priscillian's own works. In the preface to his translation of the Pentateuch, completed in 404, he opposes the adherents of "Spanish incantations" who agree with Origen that the New Testament citations of prophecies not contained in the Septuagint constitute a scriptural legitimation for the consultation of the apocrypha[28]—an argument strikingly close to Priscillian's line of reasoning in his *Book on the Faith and the Apocrypha*.[29] In the *Commentaries on Isaiah*, written between 408 and 410, Jerome similarly insists that the canonical Isa. 64.4–5—*not* the apocryphal Apocalypse of Elijah and Ascension of Isaiah,[30] as the followers of "Spanish absurdities" claim—is the source of Paul's paraphrased citation in 1 Cor. 2.9.[31] Finally, Jerome's allusion to the "portents of Basilides" occurs in the context of his objection to Vigilantius' use of 4 Esdras;[32] since 4 Esdras is also an apocryphal work used and defended by Priscillian,[33] this allusion may provide further support for the thesis that Jerome knew Priscillian's third tractate.

As just noted, Jerome's interest in Priscillian during the first decade of the fifth century was driven primarily by an eagerness to denounce an exegete who misused the apocrypha and mishandled Hebrew terms. But during these years Jerome also introduces a new theme—Priscillian's false teachings concerning the soul—and returns to an old theme—Priscillian's supposed forerunner, the gnostic seducer Mark. In a letter responding to twelve exegetical questions posed by a certain Hedibia, Jerome opposes the false views of (1) Pythagoras, Plato, and "their disciples" (presumably the followers of Origen), who teach that souls fall from heaven, and (2) "the heresy of Basilides and Mani and the Spanish foolishness and Egyptian portents."[34] Jerome does not here specify the teaching of Basilides, Mani, and the Hispano-Egyptian heresy; however, in a closely parallel passage written a few years later, he explicitly identifies Mani and Priscillian with the false doctrine of the consubstantiality of human souls and God.[35] His motive in including the unnamed Priscillian among the list of more notorious philosophers and heretics may stem from his awareness of Hedibia's family connections with Euchrotia.[36] As in the letter to Theodora, the reference to Priscillian's heresy appears to represent an indirect warning to a woman whom he perceives as vulnerable to heretical corruption. But Euchrotia, like Priscillian, remains discreetly unnamed. Jerome invokes instead the less controversial figures of Hedibia's esteemed pagan forefathers Patera and Delphidius—Euchrotia's father-in-law and husband respectively: "Your ancestors Patera and Delphidius—of whom the former taught rhetoric at Rome before I was born, [and] the latter made all Gaul famous with his talent in prose and verse while I was still a young man—now, sleeping and silent, justly reproach me for daring to whisper anything to their descendant."[37]

In his *Commentaries on Isaiah*, Jerome returns explicitly to the comparison of Priscillian with the Irenaean Mark:

> And through . . . [arguments in support of the apocrypha], little women of Spain and especially of Lusitania have been deceived, burdened with sins, who are led by various desires, always learning and never reaching the knowledge of truth, so that they accept the portents of Basilides: Balsamus and Thesaurus, as well as Barbelo and Leusibora, and the rest of the names. The apostolic man Irenaeus, bishop of Lyons and martyr, wrote most thoroughly concerning these things, explaining the origins of many heresies, especially the gnostics. Through Mark the Egyptian, they deceived noblewomen, first in the Rhône region of Gaul, then in Spain; the women mixed pleasure with stories and claimed the name of knowledge for their own wantonness.[38]

The parallels between this passage and the letter to Theodora are close, including the citation of 2 Tim. 3.6–7, the list of supposed Priscillianist "portents" or "names," the invocation of the authority of the "apostolic" Irenaeus, the extension of Mark's mission from Gaul into Spain, the account of Mark's sexual and doctrinal corruption of noblewomen, and the avoidance of Priscillian's name. Jerome has also added a few new details. He has inserted the Manichaean *Thesaurus*—in fact, a book, not a title of divinity—into the list of portentous names, hinting at a connection between Priscillian and Mani.[39] Jerome also now identifies Lusitanians as prominent among the "little women" deceived by "Mark," a geographical specification probably intended to provide an unmistakable allusion to the unnamed Priscillian.[40] A third new element is Jerome's identification of Mark as "the Egyptian." The epithet may simply refer to the link between Mark and Basilides, whose Alexandrian provenance was well known. Jerome had already introduced the Egyptian epithet in his letter to Hedibia, in which he refers to the false teachings concerning the soul represented by "the heresy of Basilides and Mani" and those who "follow Spanish incantations and Egyptian portents."[41] But it is also possible that Jerome had in mind the Ithacian tradition, perhaps now mediated through Severus, that Priscillian's forerunner Mark was from Egypt.

As we shift our textual focus from Jerome to Severus, certain stylistic contrasts immediately become evident. Jerome's relatively brief and scattered references to Priscillian often give the impression of having been drafted impulsively, if not carelessly. Severus' portrait of Priscillian, on the other hand, is set in a meticulously crafted narrative, which concludes his *Chronicle.* The well-read Jerome is free with his citation of scriptural passages and quick to state the authority of an ecclesiastical source such as Irenaeus. Severus weaves a subtler text of literary allusions, avoiding direct quotations or explicit references to sources, while at the same time engaging in intimate dialogue with a world of literature more often classical than Christian. Yet, I would argue, heresiological traditions and scriptural texts—above all, 2 Tim. 3—are just as crucial for Severus as they are for Jerome in shaping the portrait of Priscillian.

"There follow the grave and dangerous times of our own age, during which the churches were polluted by an uncustomary evil and all things were thoroughly disturbed," Severus begins his tale of the Priscillianist controversy. "For then for the first time was that infamous heresy of the gnostics detected within Spain: a deadly superstition, shrouded in secret mysteries. The origin of that evil was the Orient and Egypt."[42] Severus here borrows language directly from Tacitus' contemptuous description of Christianity as a "deadly superstition," which erupted not only in Judea, "the origin of the evil," but also in Rome.[43] This allusion functions simultaneously as a simple literary play, a radical expression of denunciation of the Spanish heretics, and a subtle questioning of that very denunciation by its association with the pagan persecution of Christianity.[44] Nor do the allusions end with the invocation of Tacitus: still more layers of meaning are at work in this text. With the reference to "dangerous times," Severus evokes the eschatological context of 2 Tim. 3: "But know this, that in the last days there will come dangerous times."[45] This scriptural passage continues to influence the subsequent presentation of Priscillian and his movement.

Severus moves immediately to qualify his neat identification of the origin of the heresy, acknowledging that "its roots and beginnings [in the Orient and Egypt] are by no means easy to investigate"[46]—a difficulty probably stemming in part from the silence, confusion, or unreliability of Severus' sources. Ithacius' *Apology* must have been among these sources, for Severus goes on to explain that "Mark, who came from Egypt and was born in Memphis, first brought [the heresy] into Spain."[47] Although he passes on the tradition that Mark of Memphis was the originator of Priscillian's heresy, Severus does not follow Ithacius on every point: he makes no mention of Mani, he distances himself from the charges of magic brought against Priscillian, and like Jerome he continues throughout his account to label the adherents of the Spanish movement as "gnostics" or simply "heretics." Nor does he present Mark as Priscillian's immediate teacher. Instead, he identifies the noblewoman Agape and the rhetorician Elpidius as followers of Mark who in turn passed the heresy on to Priscillian. Whether Agape and Elpidius likewise figured in Ithacius' account is unknown. Severus certainly had access to other sources of information about Priscillian, and his subsequent reference to Elpidius[48] seems to place these figures on firmer historical ground than Mark.[49] Whatever his source, it is in keeping with Severus' overall portrait of Priscillian that Priscillian's immediate instructors included a noblewoman and a man of notable education and eloquence.

Unlike Jerome, Severus is not content to make vague references to Spanish gnostics. He introduces Priscillian himself in a passage rich in allusions to Sallust's portrait of the villainous Catiline.[50]

> Priscillian . . . was of noble family, very rich in property, keen, restless, eloquent, learned through much reading, very prompt to discuss and debate: fortunate in his birth, if he had not corrupted his excellent nature with perverse pursuits. In short, you might discern in him many good qualities of mind and body: he was able to make many vigils and to endure hunger and thirst; he had very little desire for possessions and was very frugal in his consumption. But he was likewise extremely vain, and he was more inflated by knowledge of profane things than was appropriate—indeed, it is believed that he also practiced magical arts from his youth.[51]

Severus' allusive style is subtle, consisting in the echo of a single word or phrase, the repetition of a syntactical pattern, or the paraphrase of a familiar passage. Such delicate allusions work together to create—to borrow Jacques Fontaine's metaphor—a "dotted outline" of Sallust's Catiline upon which the portrait of Priscillian is painted.[52] Like Catiline, Priscillian is identified as coming from a noble family and possessing great strength of mind and body, on the one hand, and a nature depraved from youth, on the other.[53] However, there are hints of differences as well as similarities between Catiline and Priscillian. While Severus echoes Sallust's description of Catiline in his report of Priscillian's ability to endure fasts and vigils,[54] he also immediately goes on to emphasize Priscillian's frugality, thereby drawing an implicit contrast with Catiline's notorious greed and love of luxury.[55] By thus comparing Priscillian favorably with Catiline, Severus accentuates an ambivalence already present in Sallust's attitude toward his heroic villain. He emphasizes that ambivalence still further by depicting Priscillian's opponents Hydatius and Ithacius as Catilinian villains even more reprehensible than Priscillian.[56] Out of this complex presentation emerges the following suggestion: Priscillian is a gnostic heretic; however, like Catiline, he possesses not only deplorable vices but also many characteristics worthy of admiration; indeed, he is more admirable than Catiline; and, paradoxically, he is far more virtuous than his opponents among the orthodox bishops.

A second allusion to 2 Tim. 3 fills one break in the dotted outline of the Sallustian portrait of Priscillian. We have seen that Severus stresses that Priscillian, unlike Catiline, was not greedy or desirous of possessions. He goes on to make it clear that Priscilian *was*, however, greedy for knowledge.[57] It was this fatal flaw that, in Severus' view, marked him as a man overly "vain and inflated by knowledge of profane things." Here Severus echoes the description of the self-absorbed individuals who, according to 2 Tim. 3.2–4, will appear in the last times: "greedy, proud, arrogant, blasphemers, . . . traitors, bold, puffed up."[58] Severus goes on to note that the proud Priscillian gave "the appearance of humility in countenance and dress"; his language recalls 2 Tim. 3.5: "they have the appearance of piety while refusing its virtue."[59]

In describing the success of Priscillian's movement, Severus again interweaves Sallustian allusions with allusions to 2 Tim. 3:

> When he entered upon the deadly teaching, he enticed many nobles as well as common people into his company by the authority of his persuasiveness and the art of flattery. In addition, women—desirous of new things, of unstable faith, and by nature curious about everything—flocked to him in masses. Indeed, pretending to an appearance of humility in countenance and dress, he inspired honor and reverence in all people. And now, little by little, the disease of his treachery had pervaded most of Spain; in fact, some of the bishops were perverted, among whom Instantius and Salvianus supported Priscillian not merely by agreement but also with a kind of oath.[60]

Priscillian's very eloquence, like Catiline's, is suspect.[61] Using archaic political terminology reminiscent of republican Rome, Severus notes that Priscillian was able to draw together an alliance of both "the nobles" and "the people" through use of his persuasive powers.[62] Severus describes the shared ascetic vow that joined Priscillian to his supporters as a conspiratorial oath, terminology that again evokes memories of Sallust's *Conspiracy of Catiline*. There are also Sallustian overtones in his observation that Priscillian's supporters included both men and women: Catiline, notorious for his promiscuous sexual relationships,[63] is said to have attracted the support not only of many men of all ranks but even of some women,[64] and Sallust characterizes these noble matrons—epitomized by the figure of Sempronia—as luxury-loving "prostitutes" by whose support Catiline

hoped to win the allegiance of their husbands as well as the slave population of Rome.[65] Sallust elsewhere makes frequent use of the phrase "desirous of new things" to describe the psychological instability of those who
support political rebellion.[66] Severus' delicate allusion to Catiline's female
supporters is thus accomplished not only by his previous, more explicit
allusions to Sallust's text but also by his use of this familiar Sallustian language. The particular phrase "desirous of new things" is not, however,
applied by Sallust to *women* in particular: it is Severus who distinctly genders the stereotypical restless and curious rebel as female.

In emphasizing the women among Priscillian's followers, Severus has
2 Tim. 3.6–7 in mind: "For among them are those who enter into homes
and lead captive little women, burdened with sins, who are led by shifting
desires, always learning and never reaching knowledge of truth."[67] Unlike
Jerome, Severus is unwilling to cast the ascetic Priscillian crudely in the
role of the sexual seducer. However, his allusions to Sallust and 2 Tim. 3
work together to characterize Priscillian as a "seducer" in a more metaphorical sense: treacherous and deceptive, with the appearance of piety,
he works from within the church to lead its most vulnerable—that is, its
most "feminine"—members astray. Here Severus, like Jerome, evokes the
thought world, if not the specific text, of Irenaeus.[68] The second-century
heresiologist was the first to articulate coherently the role of the gnostic
heretic as a peculiarly intimate and paradoxical enemy: an impostor who
plays the role of a true Christian, or an apostate who betrays a faith once
loyally maintained.[69] Like Irenaeus' gnostics, Severus' Priscillian appears
in the roles of both the seducer and the traitor, the one who deceives and
the one who is perverted; his dupes are the simple and women. Severus
returns to the theme of Priscillian's "seduction" of women in two subsequent passages. While distancing himself from malicious rumors regarding Priscillian's sexual relations with Euchrotia and Procula, he nevertheless uses those rumors to construct an image of Priscillian travelling in the
company of a disgraceful band of "wives and even unrelated women." He
again touches on the theme of Priscillian's female followers in his report of
Priscillian's confession to having held "nocturnal gatherings of disgraceful
women."[70]

Severus concludes his narrative with a richly eschatological passage
that evokes the following verses of 2 Tim. 3: "And all who want to live
piously in Christ Jesus will suffer persecution, while the evil ones will
grow worse, erring and sending others into error."[71] He perceives himself
to be living in a time when holy people like his mentor Martin are accused
of heresy, while the evil go unpunished: "only Ithacius was removed from
the episcopacy." Corrupt bishops and their followers have placed the

Christian world in a state of confusion and disgrace with their scandalous quarrels and dissensions. By contrast, "the people of God and every excellent person are held up for abuse and laughter."[72] The question of whether Priscillian might be included among the pious Christians who are persecuted is left tantalizingly open.

Jerome must have read Severus' dazzling narrative by 414 or 415, when he penned his letter to Ctesiphon, a Palestinian supporter of Pelagius, at that point Jerome's primary theological rival. He had also received a visit from the Galician Orosius, who had supplied Jerome with further information concerning the Spanish heresy.[73] In his letter to Ctesiphon, Jerome twice mentions Priscillian, using his name for almost the first time since his initial reference in 392.[74] In the first of the two passages, he identifies "Priscillian in Spain, who shares in Manichaeus' immorality," as Pelagius' forerunner, along with Evagrius and Origen: both Priscillian and Pelagius call their followers to perfection and knowledge, he claims, while masking their true moral depravity:

> [Priscillian's] followers greatly admire [Pelagius], rashly claiming the word of perfection and knowledge for themselves. They shut themselves up alone with little women and sing this to them between intercourse and embraces: "Then the almighty father, Heaven, descends with fruitful showers into the womb of his fertile wife, and the great one, mingled with her great body, nourishes all offspring."[75] Indeed, they also have a share of the gnostic heresy that derives from the impiety of Basilides—whence [the Pelagians] too claim that those who are without knowledge of the law cannot avoid sin. Why do I speak of Priscillian, who was condemned by both the secular sword and the authority of the whole world?[76]

In the second part of this passage, elements of Jerome's earlier presentations of Priscillian recur: he associates Priscillian with the gnostic Basilides and repeats a line he had used in 406 in his work against Vigilantius: "he was condemned by the authority of the whole world."[77] The opening lines, however, seem to betray evidence not only of Jerome's preoccupation with the Pelagian controversy but also of his recent encounters with Orosius, as he both links Priscillian more closely with Mani and recalls the Priscillianists' supposed use of a Manichaean myth. Orosius writes to Augustine that one of the apocryphal books used by the Priscillianists tells of a "prince of wetness" and a "prince of fire."

> For it says that there is a certain virgin light, whom god, when he wants to give rain to humanity, shows to the prince of wetness. The prince of wetness desires to grasp her, and in his excitement he sweats profusely and makes rain; when he is forsaken by her, he produces thunder from his groaning.[78]

Orosius may well have passed this story on to Jerome. Jerome, in turn, apparently transforms it into a Virgilian reference, which, he claims, the followers of Priscillian invoke in order to seduce vulnerable women. Jerome makes no mention of the Manichaean origins or the doctrinal content of the myth, but uses it simply to present Priscillian's followers as worldly and immoral.

In his second reference to Priscillian in the letter to Ctesiphon, Jerome alludes briefly to Priscillian's "Zoroastrian" training; here he is probably inspired by Orosius' report of Priscillian's interest in astrology.[79] The influence of Severus' narrative, however, predominates—not least in the very prominence Jerome gives to the heresy of Priscillian, which he positions as the final and most lengthy entry in a historical review of notorious heretical "couples" beginning with Simon Magus and Helen. This review is ultimately targeted at Pelagius and his female adherents, although they remain unnamed, and is introduced with a paraphrase of 2 Tim. 3.6–7, interwoven with allusions to Eph. 4.4, 2 Tim. 4.3, and Ezek. 13.10–16:

> What do they intend, those miserable little women, burdened with sins, who are carried about by every wind of teaching, always learning and never reaching knowledge of truth; and the others, associates of the little women, with itching ears, ignorant of what they hear or say, who take up the oldest mud as if it were a new concoction—who, as Ezekiel says, smear the wall with unmixed mortar and, when the flood of truth comes upon them, are destroyed?[80]

Here Jerome's generalizing use of 2 Tim. 3.6–7 to implicate all heretics in the crime of sexual immorality is at its most explicit and extreme.[81] Following a litany of five earlier heretical pairs and two more recent examples, Jerome introduces Priscillian:

> In Spain, Agape led Elpidius, the woman led the man, the blind led the blind, into a ditch; and she had as her successor Priscillian, most devoted student of a magus of Zoroaster, who from a magus became bishop. A Gallic woman was connected with him, and she left as heir of another, neighboring heresy a "sister"—not by birth but by name—who ran hither and thither.[82]

In this passage, Jerome makes no mention of either Mark or Basilides but now joins Severus in identifying Agape and Elpidius as Priscillian's immediate teachers. The two fit neatly into his scheme. Mark and his unnamed female adherents, on the other hand, cannot be linked with Priscillian chronologically, at least according to Jerome's earlier accounts, which place Mark either two or three hundred years before his own time; the awkwardness of chronological inconsistencies with Severus' account of *his*

Mark may have further encouraged Jerome to drop Mark from this particular genealogical list.[83] Severus names Agape before Elpidius. Jerome picks up this subtle nuance and here, as nowhere else in his list of heretical couples, he places the woman in the dominant and initiating role. His language draws attention to this anomaly through the threefold repetition of nominative and accusative nouns—"Agape led Elpidius, the woman led the man, the blind led the blind"—and through the identification of Priscillian as the successor not of Agape *and* Elpidius but merely of Agape.[84]

Jerome also now seems to be familiar with rumors concerning immoral relations between Priscillian and a certain "Gallic woman" with whom he pairs Priscillian. He exploits ambiguity by calling to mind a number of possible referents from Severus' account: Euchrotia, Procula, or the other members of the band of women who accompanied Priscillian from Gaul.[85] By leaving the "Gallic woman" unnamed, Jerome also tactfully avoids *explicitly* associating descendants of Delphidius like Hedibia with Priscillian. In addition, he is able to construct a play on the word "Galla," which can indicate either a proper name or a place of origin. This wordplay is sufficiently complex that its meaning is no longer easy to discern. Adhémar D'Alès suggests that Jerome intends to imply a tenuous "sisterly" connection between Euchrotia, a Gallic woman, and the empress Galla, wife of Theodosius the Great, who was not Gallic but *was* named Galla, and who was furthermore associated with the heresy of Arianism; "Galla" (i.e., Arianism) had become a "neighbor" of Priscillianism with the entry of the Goths into Gaul and Spain.[86]

Aside from a brief mention in a lineup of heretics that includes Mani, Evagrius, Jovinian, and the "Syrians," this is Jerome's last reference to Priscillian.[87] In this late treatment of the Spanish heretic, he has abandoned both his interest in Priscillian's use of the apocrypha and his explicit identification of Priscillian with the Irenaean Mark, elements also absent from Severus' account; he has also given new attention to Priscillian's supposed emphasis on human "perfectibility" in the context of the Pelagian controversy. Yet the portrait of Priscillian as a gnostic seducer remains constant from its first introduction in the letter to Theodora of 399 to its final articulation in the letter to Ctesiphon of 414. There are other points of similarity between the accounts of Jerome and Severus—e.g., in the portrayal of Priscillian's worldly learning. But it is the common identification of Priscillian as a seducer of "little women" that facilitates Jerome's assimilation of Severus' material and creates the impression of a strong underlying harmony between the two authors' accounts.

Commonalities of Context

The similar contexts of Severus' and Jerome's lives, and to a lesser extent their reception of the same tradition about Priscillian, interpreted within the framework of a shared heresiological heritage, made their portraits of him profoundly compatible: parallel social and theological pressures nudged the two men toward similar adaptations of their cultural and textual resources. It remains now to examine the conflicts faced by Severus and Jerome as they each attempted to define and defend their authority as ascetics and scholars in the Christian community.

Sulpicius Severus

In 394 or 395, Sulpicius Severus withdrew from public life at the height of a successful rhetorical career.[88] Influenced by the ascetic zeal of Paulinus of Nola, Martin of Tours, and his own mother-in-law, Bassula,[89] Severus divested himself of most of his landed property[90] and determined to dedicate himself wholly to Christ. Within a few years, he had established an ascetic household on a country estate at Primuliacum in southern Aquitaine.[91] Severus may have been living there by the time of his publication of the *Life of Martin* in 396; it was certainly at Primuliacum that he wrote his account of Priscillian in the *Chronicle*, published between 403 and 406, as well as the contemporaneous *Dialogues*.[92]

The evidence for life at Primuliacum is meager, deriving primarily from Paulinus' letters to Severus and secondarily from the fictionalized depiction of Primuliacum in Severus' *Dialogues*. It is difficult to know to what extent the social organization of the community differed from that of a typical country estate—or, in other words, how far Primuliacum had moved along the path toward the more formalized social organization of "cenobitic monasticism." Primuliacum was, in ideal, a community composed entirely of Christian ascetics in which a new spirit of equality reigned. Severus gave up his legal ownership of the property and rejected the social privilege of a luxurious life;[93] Paulinus goes so far as to claim that Severus lived as a fellow slave to his slaves and as a slave to his poorer "brothers."[94] But Paulinus' description of Severus' servant Victor's attention to Paulinus' physical needs contradicts his own rhetoric.[95] In fact, Primuliacum appears to have retained much of the social structure of an aristocratic country estate, and Severus presided over the community with the natural grace of assumed class superiority. His household consisted largely of slaves and other social inferiors, including young boys sent for an education in Christian discipline.[96] In addition, Primuliacum housed frequent visitors, notables of the local ascetic community and travellers from further afield;[97] several of these possessed some clerical rank, and one later source reports that Severus himself was an ordained presbyter.[98]

It is not known whether the community at Primuliacum included women. Neither Severus nor Paulinus explicitly mentions female residents, but if Severus' mother-in-law, Bassula, did not actually live at Primuliacum, she must have resided nearby, and other women may also have belonged to the community.[99] Bassula provided her son-in-law with stenographers,[100] and she was intensely interested in Severus' literary activity,[101] as well as in his building projects at Primuliacum.[102] Paulinus was ready to detect analogies between Severus' partnership with Bassula and his own relationship with his wife and "fellow servant" Therasia, who lived with Paulinus in the ascetic community founded by the couple at Nola.[103]

Even less is known of the daily routine at Primuliacum than of its social structure, but it is fairly certain that no formalized rule was employed. Severus constructed a new basilica and baptistry,[104] but the sources do not indicate whether daily offices were observed communally. If Severus followed Paulinus' recommendation, he and his fellow "monks" were tonsured, dressed in uniform simplicity, and lived on a diet of gruel and beans; however, Paulinus seems to have had reason to fear that this was not always the case.[105]

If the precise regime of Severus' asceticism is unclear, somewhat more is known about the response it elicited from contemporaries. Both Martin and Paulinus had provoked controversy by their zealous championing of asceticism,[106] and Severus likewise encountered serious opposition to his own choice to pursue an ascetic life. The *Life of Martin* was written in order to glorify and defend Martin and his disciples, including Paulinus and Severus himself. Severus had several audiences in mind: addressing the international ascetic community, he set out to prove that Gaul had produced monks as impressive as any in Egypt or the Orient; addressing the traditional Gallic aristocracy, he sought to demonstrate that Christianity could produce sophisticated literature in the tradition of the pagan classics; addressing a largely anti-ascetic Gallic clergy, he argued that it was the ascetic who was the true Christian and bishop. Not surprisingly, Severus' work seems to have intensified the controversy surrounding Martin, who died shortly after its publication. Severus found it necessary to defend the *Life of Martin* in his *Letter to Eusebius* and in the *Dialogues*, in which he answers the criticism of skeptics who claim that his biography includes lies about Martin's miraculous powers.[107] Although its apologetic function is less obvious, Severus' *Chronicle* likewise defends Martin by placing him within the broad context of salvation history. Presenting the ascetic bishop as one of the apostolic and prophetic figures expected to appear—and to be rejected—at the end of time, Severus transforms the opposition to Martin into but another sign of the holy ascetic's power.[108]

Behind these literary defenses of Martin, we catch glimpses of the dispute, or series of disputes, that took place between Severus and the opponents of asceticism in southern Gaul. As early as 396, in concluding the *Life of Martin*, Severus remarks that many of those who criticize Martin, including some bishops, "are barking around me"; he protests that it is an honor to be slandered alongside Martin.[109] Similarly, some seven years later he closes his *Chronicle* with the observation that "the people of God and every excellent person are held up for abuse and laughter," clearly including both Martin and himself in the number of the virtuous persecuted.[110] These vague allusions give way in the *Dialogues* to more specific references to conflict with local bishops and clergy, on whom Severus' resentment now focuses; he complains that, of all the world, only the bishops and clergy of his own region have failed to recognize Martin's virtue and authority.[111]

In the opening passages of the first *Dialogue*, Severus asks the traveller Postumianus pointedly whether Christians in the east "are permitted to live even in the desert"; the clear implication is that local Christians do *not* enjoy the freedom to pursue their chosen way of life. Postumianus responds by asking whether the local bishops are still the same as they were before he left—i.e., actively opposed to asceticism. Not only are those bishops just as hostile as they were before, answers Severus, but one of his former friends has also grown cooler and less constant in his support.[112] Rumblings of a recent worsening of relations between Severus and local ecclesiastical authorities continue throughout the *Dialogues*. Severus' Gallic companion refers to an associate of Severus whose anger has influenced a number of people to turn against Severus. In the same passage, Gallus makes mention of an "ungrateful" freedman who has deserted Severus, seemingly led astray by another (the angry associate?); Severus admits that it is only with great difficulty that he has restrained his own anger against the two.[113] In the third *Dialogue*, Postumianus mentions a notable figure in their neighborhood who, although often wise and judicious, is also quick to take offense and attack both clergy and laity—including, the context suggests, Severus' circle. Finally, the third *Dialogue* closes with an elaborate but enigmatic reference to a recently deceased Pomponius, who appears to have defected from Severus' circle of supporters; he is perhaps to be identified with the freedman mentioned earlier. Severus notes that Pomponius should have listened to Severus or Postumianus and followed the example of Martin rather than "that one whom I do not wish to name"—perhaps the person who led the freedman astray. Some have blamed Severus for Pomponius' unfortunate death at sea, but they should instead examine their own role in the affair, suggests Severus.[114]

Although his references to opposition and dispute are frequent and unmistakable, Severus appears reluctant to discuss the details of the controversies in which he found himself involved. Fortunately, an external source, Jerome's polemical work *Against Vigilantius*, allows reconstruction of some of the issues at stake. The Vigilantius attacked in Jerome's work was a presbyter who carried a letter from Paulinus to Jerome in 395, subsequently returned to the west and accused Jerome of Origenism, and came to Jerome's attention again circa 404 by reason of his opposition to certain ascetic practices in southern Gaul.[115] Vigilantius also appears as the name of a member of Severus' community who carried letters between Severus and Paulinus in 396.[116] If the two Vigilantii are the same—which is quite possible, given the common link with Paulinus and the relative rareness of the name—then it would seem that around 403 a former member of Severus' community began to attack the way of life pursued at Primuliacum.[117] But even if the two Vigilantii are *not* the same, it is probable that the disputes we glimpse in Severus' *Dialogues* and Jerome's *Against Vigilantius* belong to the same context, since both reflect debates over asceticism taking place in the first few years of the fifth century in the Christian communities of southern Gaul.[118]

The practices opposed by Vigilantius, whom Jerome describes contemptuously as a humble innkeeper (*caupo*),[119] can be matched on many points with those advocated and defended by the aristocratic Severus. Severus sought relics for his new basilica at Primuliacum.[120] Vigilantius attacked the veneration of relics and the associated practices of candle-lighting and vigils, urging that the souls of martyrs are not dispersed in bits of bone or ash but gathered under the heavenly altar of God.[121] Severus had devoted much of his *Life of Martin* to the recording of the saint's miracles. Vigilantius questioned the function of miracles within the believing community.[122] Severus, like his friend Paulinus, emphasized the importance of ridding himself of his property in his conversion to the ascetic life.[123] Vigilantius criticized the irresponsible wasting of resources whose income could be managed to support the poor.[124] Severus withdrew to a country estate. Vigilantius called for faithful church attendance and active involvement in the urban communities.[125] In short, Vigilantius opposed the centrifugal dispersal of authority in the shrines of dead martyrs and the persons of aristocrats and ascetics like Severus; in its place, he advocated centripetal focusing of authority, which might be represented by the cathedral, its public liturgy, and its official leaders. If Jerome is right in claiming that he had the support of more than one bishop, Vigilantius' campaign was not without success in southern Gaul.[126] The pro-ascetic presbyters Riparius and Desiderius—the latter perhaps the original recipient of Severus' *Life of Martin*[127]—seem to have felt sufficiently threatened to seek the support of Jerome in faraway Palestine.[128]

Competition between public and private understandings of community and authority is implicit in the attacks of Vigilantius and his anti-ascetic supporters; it is likewise implicit in Severus' defense. In that defense, Severus tacitly accepts the "public" terms of the debate. Invoking the rhetoric of public male and private female spheres, he uses gender to express symbolically the social legitimacy of his own privately centered life. This legitimating function of the gender hierarchy is evident above all in the *Dialogues*, where Severus delivers a set of surprising pronouncements on the necessity for a strict separation and subordination of women. Such a stance is hardly popular, he admits, and he warns his Gallic friend of the dangers of an open endorsement of Jerome's denunciation of intimacies between male and female ascetics.[129] Later, Severus recounts his own sobering experience:

> I chastised a certain wandering and rather elegant widow who lived somewhat wantonly, and likewise a virgin who was clinging somewhat indecently to a certain young man who was dear to me—although I had indeed often heard her rebuking others who did such things. As a result, I aroused such great hatred from all women and the entirety of the monks that both bands undertook sworn wars against me.[130]

Severus declares that he had intended to remain silent from that point on, but his intention is blatantly contradicted by its recounting in a work intended for publication. He furthermore goes to considerable trouble to buttress his position on the separation of men and women with the authority of his hero Martin, framing the above account with three supporting Martinian anecdotes.

The first such anecdote occurs immediately preceding Severus' account of his criticism of the widow and virgin. Severus' friend Gallus relates how an empress, wife of the usurper Maximus, had lavished attention on Martin: following Gospel precedent, she had washed his feet with her tears and wiped them with her hair; like a servant, she had prepared and served him his meals. No woman had ever before touched Martin, claims Gallus, yet he praises the empress for her faith. Upon hearing this tale, Postumianus questions its dangerous implications: might it not seem to legitimate free social intercourse between male ascetics and women? Gallus answers that the circumstances mitigate any suspicions of impropriety: first, Martin was quite old; second, the empress was not a "free widow" or "wanton virgin" but was "living under a husband" and acting under his instructions; third, the empress did not enter into a relationship of equals with Martin, but restricted herself to serving him; and fourth, the event was not repeated. Gallus emphasizes the second and third points with a concise statement of the hierarchy of the genders: "Let a married woman serve, not command you; serve, not recline with you." His presuppositions are clear: a "safe" woman is one who is subordinated to a man through marriage, obedience, and symbolic posture; her subordination implies chastity, whereas a claim to equality implies lack of chastity. Postumianus applauds Gallus' defense of Martin's behavior, but doubts whether he and the other ascetics of his region would ever be sufficiently free of suspicion to be able to observe such fine distinctions in their relations with women.[131] Severus' scripting of the dialogue between Gallus and Postumianus thus defends Martin and the possibility of pure interactions between ascetic men and virtuous women, while at the same time endorsing the general need for a strict separation and subordination of women even in ascetic life.

Severus' account of his own controversial criticism of ascetic women is followed by two paired, complementary tales, which underline the position supported by Severus and only seemingly compromised by the initial story of Martin and the empress. According to the first tale, a hermit and former soldier approached Martin with his desire to live together in spiritual marriage with his former wife, who was now also leading an ascetic life. Martin convinced the monk of the falseness of his desire, demanding to know whether he had ever seen a woman fighting alongside men in the line of battle. Although addressing an ascetic couple, Martin slipped from a military analogy into language appropriate to a traditionally defined marriage relationship:

> Let a woman not enter the camp of men; let the battle line of soldiers remain separate; let the female, dwelling in her own tent, be far away. For it makes an army ridiculous, if a female crowd is mixed with the regiments of men. Let the soldier be in the battle line; let the soldier fight in the plain; let the woman keep herself within the protection of the walls. She also has her own glory, if she preserves her chastity when her husband is absent; this is her first virtue and perfect victory: not to be seen.[132]

Gallus pairs this intended demonstration of Martin's wisdom with the story of a virgin who, in effect, taught Martin the same lesson that he him-

self had taught the soldierly monk. As in the case of his interactions with
the empress, Martin "set aside the rigor of his way of life" and sought to
honor a famed virgin with a visit to her place of withdrawal. Maintaining
a chaste privacy appropriate to her gender as well as her ascetic calling,
the virgin refused to see him. Martin departed in joy, moved by the unusual example of a woman who sheltered herself even from his eyes.
Many women would have thrown themselves at any monk or priest in
their path, notes Gallus, taking the opportunity to chastise more gregarious virgins. And many monks or priests would have labeled the virgin a
heretic in outrage at her seemingly insulting and insubordinate behavior,
he adds still more darkly. But both Martin and the virgin, implies Gallus,
correctly valued and interpreted female privacy as signifying, not disre-
spect and autonomy, but respect for the public social order in which
women are separate from and subordinate to men.[133]

Severus' criticism of the wandering widow and virgin, joined with the
framing Martinian anecdotes, does not merely represent an attack on less
rigorous ascetics. I have suggested that it also constitutes a defense of Severus' own ascetic practice in the face of the opposition of men like Vigilantius and his episcopal supporters.[134] By advocating a strict separation
and subordination of women, Severus struggles to distinguish himself
from the "heretical" ascetics with whom his opponents might identify
him. He combats the hostile public image of the ascetic community as anarchic, as symbolized by the disorderly relations of men and women, with
the alternative image of the ascetic community as carefully ordered according to the classical model of the separation and subordination of the
private female sphere to the public male sphere.[135] While implicitly acknowledging that some might falsely perceive an element of impropriety
or disorder in Martin's own relations with women, Severus uses the example of his hero to endorse the subordination of women to their husbands in particular and to men in general. He casts himself in the role of
one who chastises ascetic women for their disorderly publicity and mingling with men, and then he returns again to the example of Martin in
order to emphasize the ideal of ascetic women's strict separation from men
and their restriction to the private sphere. In this effort to defend his own
ascetic ecclesiology, the classically educated Severus invokes the rhetoric
of public male and private female spheres even in the face of apparent
contradictions with his own social experience: his close relations with Bassula, Paulinus' and Therasia's spiritual partnership, and the acknowledged and approved visits of ascetic women to the holy Martin.[136]

Severus' use of gender relations to express and defend his understanding of Christian community and authority is not only operative in

his *Dialogues* but also surfaces as a minor theme in his account of the Priscillianist controversy in the final passages of the *Chronicle*. In the first book of the *Chronicle*, Severus has set up a conflict between the prophets and kings of Israel that prefigures the conflict in the second book between the prophetic figures of Hilary and Martin and the corrupt bishops of Severus' own time.[137] However, in his concluding account of the Priscillianist controversy, Severus contrasts the prophetic Martin, not only with the worldly bishops who oppose him, but also with "heretical" ascetics like Priscillian, with whom Martin is falsely identified. As we have seen, Severus' Priscillian violates the boundaries that separate and subordinate private to public, female to male, ascetic to bishop. He not only leads simple and ignorant Christians astray by means of his deceptive eloquence but also further disrupts the social order by "seducing" other men's wives and daughters and mingling promiscuously with strange women. He challenges bishops and then lays claim to a false episcopal authority of his own.

By shifting from a simple contrast between Martin and the worldly bishops to a more complex positioning of Martin between the "heretics," on the one hand, and the worldly bishops, on the other, Severus is able to suggest that Martin transcends but *does not eradicate* the distinction between public and private spheres and alienated and accommodating stances toward the world. Martin is unmarried but careful to observe the hierarchy of genders, wise in knowledge of the scriptures yet not puffed up by worldly education, neither subversive of the social order nor corrupted by power. Severus' hero, unlike Priscillian, succeeds in uniting the private authority of the ascetic holy person with the public authority of the episcopal office. And Severus attempts to defend his own role in the Christian community by denouncing and thereby separating himself from the "heretic" Priscillian and associating himself instead with Martin. The gnostic seducer serves effectively as a receptacle for the accusations from which Severus must distance himself, and at the same time provides a fitting counterpart to his attempt to create an acceptable social ideology for the ascetic community and for authority within that community.

Jerome

Jerome, like Sulpicius Severus, came from a relatively wealthy family and was trained in classical literature and rhetoric in preparation for a government career. He had not yet achieved any great worldly success when, circa 370, he turned aside to devote himself to an ascetic life. Ending a temporary sojourn in Trier, Jerome returned to his native Stridon in the company of his friend Bonosus. In the nearby city of Aquileia,[138] Jerome and Bonosus encountered a growing and enthusiastic circle of Christian ascetics. They attached themselves to the ascetic household of the presbyter Chromatius, a household that included Chromatius' mother, sisters, and brother, the deacon Eusebius, as well as the archdeacon Jovinus and Jerome's friend Rufinus.[139] Jerome and Bonosus also formed ties with a broader network of ascetics in Aquileia and nearby towns,[140] and it was probably at Aquileia that Jerome met the wealthy Antiochene presbyter Evagrius.[141]

The restless Jerome did not remain long in Aquileia. By 374, after extensive travel in the east, he had reached Antioch, where he resided for a time in the household of Evagrius. Convinced at this point that anchoritic asceticism represented the holiest form of Christian life, Jerome soon packed up his library and took up residence among the monks of the Syrian desert. Involvement in the bitter theological controversies of the east drove Jerome back to the cities: first to Antioch, then to Constantinople, and finally, in 382, to Rome.[142] His three years in Rome were marked by close and productive relationships with patrons, above all the ascetic Bishop Damasus and the aristocratic widows Marcella and Paula. Although he had been ordained presbyter while in Antioch,[143] Jerome's position in Rome appears to have been based on his reputation as a scholar and his connection with powerful patrons rather than on any official standing as a member of the clergy.[144]

It was at Rome that Jerome must have first learned about Priscillian, who had recently submitted his unsuccessful petition to Damasus. Jerome's impressions of Priscillian at this point were probably mixed, perhaps reflecting Damasus' own ambivalent response; as we have seen, Jerome still hesitated to pass judgment on Priscillian when he wrote *On Famous Men* some ten years later. But it was also at Rome that Jerome became involved in controversies that crystallized the attitudes that ultimately shaped his much later and more vicious characterizations of Priscillian.[145] Although he had the support of the bishop, Jerome's incautious criticisms of the clergy and his uncompromising advocacy of the ascetic life provoked considerable opposition from within the Roman church.[146] In this context, Jerome defended himself from charges of social subversion in part by launching his own attack on undisciplined and promiscuous ascetics. The immediate success of this strategy was limited: after Damasus' death in late 384, Jerome was effectively run out of town, facing official charges of sexual immorality as well as rumors of sorcery and possibly Manichaeism.[147]

If Jerome did not succeed in preserving his informal position of authority in Rome, he nevertheless produced a provocative body of literature and a doctrinal platform for an ascetic elitism that proved extraordinarily influential. Jerome's famous *Letter to Eustochium*, written in Rome in 384, gives forceful expression to his opinions on asceticism and on the closely related issues of gender and authority in the Christian community.[148] As Jerome points out, the letter is not primarily a treatise in praise of female virginity, but rather a set of guidelines for the difficult task of *preserving* female virginity.[149] Again and again, Jerome exhorts the young virgin to guard her chastity by maintaining her privacy. Eustochium is to stay at home, foregoing even visits to the martyrs' tombs.[150] In her virginal sanctity, she should not be exposed to the profane gaze of the public eye. Taking her lesson from the *Song of Songs*, Eustochium should not seek Christ vainly in the streets but should await her "bridegroom" in the privacy of her bedroom. She should avoid the publicity even of a reputation for virtue, taking care that her ascetic accomplishments remain secret. She should refuse all social intercourse with worldly women, choosing her few female companions from among similarly sober-minded ascetics and shunning ostentatious monks, flattering clergy, and even overly gregarious virgins and widows. Proper subordination is a part of the restriction to the private sphere, and Jerome urges the young girl to obey her parents—and also, implicitly, her male mentor, Jerome.[151]

Jerome complements his positive exhortations to Eustochium with negative examples of the paths to be avoided. The letter begins with a caustic description of false or fallen virgins. Spiritual virginity may be lost even by a thought, Jerome warns; but many of the fallen are not only spiritual but literal prostitutes, using drugs to abort their pregnancies and thus maintain the lying semblance of virginity. These false virgins can be recognized by their self-indulgent lives, ostentatious public appearances, and irrepressible sociability. Among the worst offenders are the *agapetae*, women living in spiritual partnership with men who are bound to them by neither blood nor marriage.[152] The male counterparts of the false virgins are found among both ascetics and clergy. Men claiming to be monks drape themselves with chains and proudly exhibit their womanish uncut hair, bare feet, and rough clothing; but like the false teachers of 2 Tim. 3.6–7, they merely offer the appearance of virtue in order to make their way into homes and deceive noble women. Some clergy likewise use their ecclesiastical office to insinuate themselves into the homes—indeed the very bedrooms—of wealthy married women, Jerome warns. Effeminate in appearance and moral character, these men can be recognized by their fastidious dress, perfumed bodies, curled hair, jewelry, and affected gait.[153]

In this series of negative examples offered to the virgin Eustochium, Jerome condemns both men and women who violate the boundaries of public male and private female spheres in order to indulge their "feminine" sexuality. He suggests that sexuality is to be identified not only with female nature but also with heresy, insisting that there can be no true virgins among the heretics: "Virgins such as are said to be among the various heresies and among the followers of the vile Manichaeus must be considered not virgins but prostitutes."[154] This careful opposition of femininity, sexuality, and heresy, on the one hand, and masculinity, chastity, and orthodoxy, on the other, functions rhetorically to control Eustochium's behavior, while encouraging her to be constantly vigilant in protecting her vow. She is not to be accorded the freedom of those women who live without the restraint of either husband or ecclesiastical supervisor.[155]

It is apparent that Jerome's letter to Eustochium functions as a personal defense of his life in Rome as well as a means to advise and control a female ascetic. By his own account, Jerome was frequently surrounded by virgins with whom he enjoyed a relationship of familial intimacy.[156] "I often discussed the divine books with some of them, in so far as I was able. Reading gave rise to constant presence, constant presence created familiarity, and familiarity produced trust."[157] The appropriateness of such familylike relations between ascetic men and women was not universally acknowledged. In a letter in which he presents himself publicly as the aristocratic Eustochium's spiritual advisor, Jerome must, therefore, fend off suspicions of impropriety. He accomplishes this in part by his vehement denunciations of the monks and clergy who "seduce" the women of the Roman nobility. By implied contrast with these deceivers, Jerome suggests that he himself is modest and sober in demeanor, disciplined and austere in his manner of life, and above all respectful of the boundaries that separate male and female and public and private spheres.

Jerome appears curiously unable, however, to augment this negatively inferred self-portrait with an explicit, positive self-presentation. When he offers Eustochium his typology of monastic patterns, he finds no place for men who pursue asceticism in an informal and urban context.[158] Full of praise for both cenobitic and anchoritic lifestyles, he bitterly condemns the urban monks whom he calls "remnuoth": living together in twos or threes without any fixed rule, they are undisciplined, insubordinate, ostentatious, disrespectful of the clergy, and overly fond of socializing with virgins.[159] In this passage, Jerome appears to have accepted the application of the public-private distinction to the community of ascetic Christians, and he vigorously advocates the strict privatization of women in particular and of the ascetic community in general. However, within the terms of the rhetoric of the separation of public and private spheres, his own role with respect to the ecclesiastical hierarchy and to his female associates in Rome is insupportable so long as he fails to clarify his relationship to the clergy and to separate himself from women.

In response to the pressures of public controversy and personal ambivalence, Jerome left Rome and returned to the east. Accompanied by Paula and her daughter Eustochium, he settled in the village of Bethlehem in 386. There he and his companions established two cenobitic communities, one for men, directed by Jerome, and one for women, directed first by Paula and then, after her death in 404, by Eustochium.[160] Jerome had finally found a resting place, and he remained at the Bethlehem monastery until his death in 420, over thirty years later. Although they were influenced by Pachomius' monastic rule, Jerome and Paula did not adhere to it rigidly, instead developing forms of monastic life suited to their circumstances and backgrounds. Paula, for example, seems to have divided her community into groups according to social class, thus echoing the hierarchical structure of the traditional aristocratic household.[161] Jerome himself neglected the Pachomian call to manual labor in favor of more scholarly pursuits. In many respects, he continued to lead the same life, pursuing his ascetic disciplines while remaining active as a scholar, teacher, and theological controversialist, intimately involved with the world around him. The structures of cenobitic monasticism provided a social space in which he could legitimately carry out such activities, relatively safe from charges of sexual immorality or social subversion, in spite of his continued close partnership with Paula and Eustochium and a lengthy conflict with the local bishop, John of Jerusalem.[162] While the separation of women from men within the monastic community must have reduced the scope of authority of such aristocratic patronesses as Paula and Eustochium, the separation of the monastic community from the urban episcopal community seems to have increased Jerome's autonomy. At one point, he and his ally Epiphanius went so far as to argue that a monastery lay outside the jurisdiction of its local bishop.[163]

Having embraced the rural cenobitic life in practice as well as in ideal, by 415 Jerome does not even mention the eccentric urban "remnuoth" in his letter to the aristocratic virgin Demetrias but discusses only the relative merits of the solitary and cenobitic lifestyles. He furthermore warns Demetrias against the dangers of the anchoritic life, which he now perceives to allow a scope of independence inappropriate for most men and for all women.[164] Once again invoking the authority of 2 Tim. 3.6–7,[165] the scriptural passage that also figures so largely in his portrait of Priscillian, Jerome instructs Demetrias to seek the security of communal life and to sub-ordinate herself to the instruction of spiritual advisors.

> It is therefore good to listen to your superiors, to obey those set over you, and, after the rules of the scriptures, to learn the way of life from others, and not to follow the worst teacher, namely, your own audacity. Concerning such women, the apostle says: "they are carried about with every wind of doctrine, ever learning and never able to come to the knowledge of truth."[166]

Jerome's has here reduced his original twofold typology of acceptable ascetic paths to one alternative. He suggests that the cenobitic life alone adequately preserves the social order through the separation and subordination of women to men and—in theory—of ascetics to bishops. In fact, the strict privatization of the ascetic community removed its leaders not only from direct competition with the urban bishops but also from their direct control, thus allowing for the construction of a separate and independent social hierarchy within the monastic community.

The relative stability of Jerome's life at Bethlehem did not preclude his nearly constant involvement in theological disputes, disputes that did not so much displace as continue the controversy over asceticism that had begun for Jerome at Rome. By 393, he found himself embroiled in a long-distance and much-publicized debate with the Italian Jovinian, centering around the question of the superiority of the ascetic over the married life. Once again escaping a controversy over asceticism with his reputation for orthodoxy just barely intact, Jerome continued in subsequent years to defend the notion of a lasting moral hierarchy over against the more egalitarian schemes that he perceived to be at the heart of the theologies of such opponents as the "Origenists" and, later, the followers of Pelagius. Rejecting both the preexistent souls and disembodied resurrection taught by Origen and the Pelagian doctrine of universal human perfectibility, Jerome persistently advocated a theological model that preserved greater continuity between the social distinctions encoded in the fleshly bodies of this life and the rewards to be enjoyed in the life to come.[167]

Throughout the Jovinianist, Origenist, and Pelagian debates, Jerome returned to the topics of gender and sexuality, using these marks of difference both rhetorically as signifiers of the limits of orthodoxy and heresy and theologically as enduring bodily indicators of the heavenly hierarchy. His evolving portrait of Priscillian—however tangential to Jerome's immediate theological concerns—is nevertheless exemplary in this respect. As noted above, Jerome's letter to the Spanish Theodora (c. 399) denounces

Priscillian as a heretic and womanizer in the tradition of Mark the gnostic. Invoking the example of the "little women" of 2 Tim. 3.6–7, Jerome warns the wealthy widow not to be seduced by Priscillian's treacherous followers, but rather to obey chaste and orthodox teachers like himself.[168] The rhetorical manipulation of gender and sexuality in this letter functions on several levels: to distance Jerome from the stereotype of the insubordinate and disorderly urban ascetic teacher; to enable Jerome to assert his hierarchical superiority over rivals among such teachers; and, finally, to persuade and control a woman whose patronage Jerome covets and whose authority of wealth and birth he seems both to admire and to resent. A similar desire to denounce potential rivals and exert control over a distant female correspondent may underlie Jerome's reference to Priscillian in his letter to the Gallic noblewoman Hedibia post 404.[169] The themes of the letter to Theodora are more explicitly echoed circa 410 in his *Commentaries on Isaiah*.[170]

If there are earlier hints that Jerome found Priscillian a peculiarly expressive figure, it was only in the final years of his life, during his conflict with Pelagius, that Jerome made central use of Priscillian in his polemical rhetoric. Probably inspired by Severus but also perhaps impelled by a desire to locate an easily demonized and safely dead western precursor for his new theological rival,[171] Jerome presents Priscillian as the heretical seducer par excellence in his letter to Ctesiphon of 415. Simon Magus, Nicolas, Marcion, Apelles, Montanus, Arius, Donatus—all are notorious for their dubious relations with women, and in this respect all are the forerunners of Priscillian. As the student of Agape and the teacher of "Galla," Priscillian is both seduced and seducer, an insidious magician who leads the women of the church astray, interspersing caresses with murmured phrases of Virgil, while putting on a false front of "perfection." Having painted this portrait of Priscillian, who had long since been executed by the emperor, Jerome hints darkly, "Now also the mystery of iniquity is at work. Both sexes trip each other up."[172] With these words, he points to Pelagius, who is the real target of his denunciation of Priscillian in this letter addressed to a Pelagian supporter.[173]

The portrait of Priscillian is directed not only at Pelagius and his male disciples but also, implicitly, at a powerful family of ascetic women with strong connections to Pelagius. Jerome shuns a direct attack on Demetrias, her mother, or grandmother, whose patronage he hopes to win for himself; he delicately avoids even mentioning Pelagius' name in this passage. Instead, Jerome is content to let the connections he has drawn between female nature, heresy, and sexual promiscuity stand as a gentle warning to those overly independent women, falsely convinced of their capacity for perfection, who might presume to choose their own teachers, and per-haps—like Agape—even to teach themselves. Social intercourse with male teachers like Pelagius may leave women vulnerable to charges of physical unchastity as well as the spiritual faithlessness of heresy, he warns. Weak in mind and will, they risk seduction by false teachers. The solution, as Jerome makes explicitly clear in a letter addressed directly to Demetrias herself,[174] is to stay at home, both physically and intellectually, avoiding the company and influence of all strange men.

Conclusions

Severus and Jerome both characterize Priscillian as a gnostic. This charac-terization appears to derive neither from historically reliable data nor from common dependence on an unreliable source like Ithacius' *Apology*. Rather, Severus' and Jerome's treatments of Priscillian result from their independent utilization of a shared heresiological tradition in the face of similar conflicts experienced in their roles as Christian ascetics and schol-ars. These conflicts are rooted in a clash between two distinct and often contradictory strategies of Christian self-definition that I have called "public" and "private." Both Severus and Jerome attempt to resolve their conflicts by harmonizing the two strategies of communal self-definition. The resulting inconsistencies and ambivalence in their views of gender and authority lend particular depth and complexity to their portrayals of Priscillian as a treacherous gnostic seducer.

Although Jerome was a presbyter and Severus may likewise have been ordained, both derived their authority in the Christian community pri-marily from their reputations as men of education, eloquence, and exem-plary discipline. Like their equally well-educated pagan counterparts, they were at home in a social world structured by hierarchies of class and networks of patronage that were largely indifferent to distinctions of gen-der. However, both men had also been trained for public life, and Severus at least had enjoyed the fruits of a successful rhetorical career, so that even in their more private roles as Christian scholars, neither Severus nor Je-rome altogether abandoned the publicly centered perspective from which elite male identity was almost inevitably defined in antiquity. Moreover, this public perspective likewise shaped the self-understanding of the church's official hierarchy, with which both men were at least tenuously identified. Severus and Jerome thus experienced internal tension as they attempted to assimilate divergent understandings of Christian commu-nity that often entailed conflicting definitions of authority and gender roles. This internal tension was accentuated by external conflicts between Severus and anti-ascetic opponents among the Aquitanian clergy, and between Jerome and the clergy of Rome. In both cases, the ascetic scholars were perceived as subversive of the ecclesiastical order and were suspected of disregard for the authority of bishops and the privacy of women.

Both men responded to these conflicts in part through the shaping of their ascetic lives. In Rome, Jerome attempted to play the role of an independent teacher within the urban community; this experience proved disastrous, and he left the city to establish a cenobitic monastery in the safely distant setting of rural Palestine. As far as we know, Severus withdrew from urban life immediately upon embarking upon his ascetic career; his community at Primuliacum remained more closely modeled on the social structure of a traditional aristocratic household than did the Bethlehem communities led by Jerome and Paula. Through the elaboration of a novel understanding of Christian community, Severus and Jerome responded to conflict discursively as well as socially. Significantly, both men invoked a public rhetoric in order to defend and legitimate their own essentially private or informal authority. They argued first for the separation of the ascetic and urban Christian communities. By privatizing the ascetic community, they removed its leaders from direct competition with the publicly constituted authority of bishops, while implying—without concretizing—the structural subordination of the private ascetic community to the public episcopally led community. Following the example of classical discussions of household economy, they likewise transferred the political model to the private sphere, supporting the separation and subordination of women even in ascetic life; in this argument were the seeds for the reshaping of the male ascetic community as a miniature monastic "city" with its own ranks of official authority.

This proposal that the ascetic community properly possessed a separate but parallel hierarchy led to the establishment of an analogous relationship between the bishop or presbyter and the leader of the monastic community, facilitating their identification in a figure like Severus' exemplary Martin of Tours. While Jerome was more hesitant than Severus to identify the two roles so closely, he too urged clerical friends like Heliodorus and his nephew Nepotianus to buttress their clerical authority with the authority of a life of Christian asceticism.[175] But at the same time that it facilitated such analogies, the strict rhetorical and symbolic separation of monastery and urban congregation also contributed to continuing unclarity about the relative authority of the ascetic leader and the bishop. Severus and Jerome both remain ambivalent in their attitudes toward the clerical hierarchy. Jerome reveres the apostolic authority of ecclesiastical office,[176] and he sides with Bishop Theophilus in his conflict with the Egyptian monks;[177] yet he locates his own authority as ascetic and scholar outside or above the authority of his presbyterial office, and at one point he even denies the right of Bishop John of Jerusalem to dictate in matters concerning his Bethlehem monastery.[178] Severus goes far in exalting Martin's authority as bishop, even dismissing Martin's pre-episcopal life from discussion in his *Dialogues*.[179] Yet the authority that so overwhelms Severus when he is in Martin's presence is not the authority of episcopal office but the authority of the holy saint, and Severus comments that Martin's authority was diminished when he became bishop and when he let himself become involved in episcopal politics.[180] In his critical discussion of Theophilus of Alexandria's opposition to the Origenist monks, Severus remarks that while some might think it wrong for monks to disobey bishops, he finds it worse for bishops to persecute monks.[181]

The application of the public-private model to the ascetic community also produced ambivalence regarding gender roles. There is a large gulf between both Severus' and Jerome's social experiences and their rhetorical emphasis on women's separation and subordination. Jerome vehemently endorses the separation and subordination of women, basing this stance on a traditional misogynistic view of female nature. Yet the intimacy and intensity of this man's relationships with women are virtually unsurpassed in the records of antiquity, and he appears to hold Marcella, Paula, Eustochium, and other female friends in the greatest respect.[182] Nor is it likely that these aristocratic matrons were as humble and compliant as Jerome frequently suggests. While we know less about Severus' interactions with ascetic women, his close relationship with Bassula and his connection with powerful and independent women like Therasia and Melania seem similarly at odds with his stringent rhetoric of women's separation and subordination.

The characterization of Priscillian as a gnostic represents a partial and complex response to the conflicts and ambivalence experienced by Severus and Jerome as they attempt to assimilate public and private understandings of Christian community. First, and most concretely, the use of a second-century heresiological category enables both authors to avoid the more immediately dangerous label of Manichaeism. Severus in particular has good reason to distance himself from labeling strategies that had seriously threatened his master Martin at the time of Priscillian's trial, and that may have threatened Severus as well. Jerome is likewise sensitive to the frequent false identification of orthodox ascetics as Manichaeans,[183] and he himself was accused of Manichaeism,[184] although the seriousness of the charges is unclear.

But even more significant than the avoidance of any reference to Manichaeism is the effectiveness of the label of gnosticism in negatively defining the social role of the orthodox ascetic scholar. In heresiological tradition, the gnostic is a supremely paradoxical figure, simultaneously insider and outsider, Christian and enemy, self and other. The label of gnostic connotes the intimacy of Severus' and Jerome's relation to the figure of Priscillian, who functions as an alter ego of sorts; the label thereby also captures the subtlety of their proposed refinements of authority roles. Severus expresses a grudging admiration for Priscillian and acknowledges a sense of kinship with the learned and aristocratic ascetic of his own portrayal, going so far as to hint that Priscillian might belong to the persecuted remnant of true Christians. Jerome is initially hesitant to condemn Priscillian at all and is subsequently reluctant to name Priscillian in his denunciation of "Spanish gnostics." Typically more volatile and extreme than Severus, he eventually condemns Priscillian explicitly and bitterly and places Priscillian's heresy at the culmination of the entire history of heretical seduction, but he never changes the basic outlines of his portrayal of Priscillian as a man who bears striking resemblance to himself.

The portrait of the gnostic as an insidious seducer serves as a focus of feared accusations and a projection of Severus' and Jerome's own vulnerabilities in the controversies in which they were involved. To this extent, their treatments of Priscillian may be compared with Priscillian's own condemnation of heresies in his *Apology*. Severus' portrait of Priscillian is strongly shaped by an awareness of his own susceptibility to the attacks of opponents like Vigilantius, who perceive him as a threat to the authority of the ecclesial hierarchy and the stability of episcopally led communities. Jerome likewise develops his portrait of Priscillian in the aftermath of charges of illicit sexual relations with Paula brought against him by a jealous and resentful Roman clergy. Both men constructed their portraits of Priscillian in order to dissociate themselves from them. The gnostic seducer is the heretic against whom their particular orthodoxies must be defined. They suggest that the true Christian ascetic and scholar can be distinguished from the heretic by his respect for the authority of bishops and the privacy of women—or, in other words, by his accommodation to the demands of a publicly centered ecclesiology.

The figure of the gnostic seducer is particularly appropriate for the development of a rhetoric for the control of women. Severus and Jerome must both resolve their internal ambivalence regarding the relative freedom and prominence of ascetic women and defend themselves in the face of external accusations of sexual promiscuity and the subversion of gender roles. Both authors use 2 Tim. 3:6–7—a scriptural passage virtually ignored in the second- and third-century debates with the gnostics—in order to emphasize gender and sexuality in their portraits of Priscillian as a gnostic heretic. By condemning Priscillian as one who "enters into homes and captures little women," Severus and Jerome present themselves as defenders of the boundaries of the public male and private female spheres. By evoking the vulnerability of the "little women who are burdened with sins and led by shifting desires, always learning and never reaching knowledge of truth," they deny women's authority and capacity for independence and urge their separation and subordination even within the ascetic community.

CONCLUSIONS

Why do I speak of Priscillian, who has been condemned by the secular sword and by the whole world?

Jerome, *Ep.* 133.3

Deviance is the mirror-image of conventional morality and therefore of existing boundaries.

Nachman Ben Yehuda,
Deviance and Moral Boundaries[1]

A theory of difference, when applied to the proximate "other," is but another way of phrasing a theory of "self."

Jonathan Z. Smith,
"Differential Equations"[2]

The question posed by Jerome at first appears easily answered: for a fourth- or fifth-century Christian, to speak of a Priscillian so universally condemned was to delineate the contours of an acceptable social "self"; to denounce "heresy" was to control the definition of "orthodoxy." But this historical investigation of late-ancient talk about Priscillian has necessarily pressed the issue further: why *this* person, why *this* construction of heresy, why *this* place and time? The goal has been not so much to provide final answers as to complicate and continue the process of inquiry: how, indeed, did late-ancient Christianity come to construct itself around a distinctly and all-too-comfortably patriarchalized and institutionalized conception of orthodoxy? A stance of intentional naivete or even feigned surprise undergirds the posing of such a question, and my interest has been precisely to locate and explore pivotal historical moments in which we may be persuaded to perceive the openness of the historical process—despite the weight of an "unsurprised" historiographic tradition. Late-fourth-century Christianity appears particularly productive of such moments, and the diverse perspectives that collided in the Priscillianist controversy highlight the variety and malleability of contemporary conceptions not only of orthodoxy but also of asceticism, canon, creed, episcopacy, and even maleness and femaleness. In spite of my desire to "reopen" the world of late-ancient Christianity, I have obviously not resisted the temptation of narrative closure: both implicitly and explicitly, this study contrasts the relative fluidity of the late-fourth-century west with the greater stability of the period immediately following, onto which I have projected the crystallizing of a "public" and "accommodating" catholic orthodoxy.

Resistance to the frequently assumed historical inevitability of such a catholic orthodoxy led to the choice of a chronological approach to the Priscillianist controversy, allowing careful delineation of the unfolding of the complex discursive and social processes by which Priscillian was constructed as "other"; the study thereby frequently became entangled in the reconstruction of the controversy's *gesta rerum*, as well as in the analysis of its central social and theological issues. The desire to combat impressions of orthodox inevitability also necessitated a stance of intentional sympathy for Priscillian and the other "losers" in the various interlocking debates. Only by becoming sympathetic, it seemed to me, could we understand that the losers might have been winners, and indeed, that there may not have been any clear winners and losers after all: the process by which religious controversy influences "tradition" is rarely as simple as language of "victory and loss" or even "compromise" implies.

The account began with the local conflict between Priscillian, a learned ascetic exegete, and Hydatius, bishop of Merida. The earliest documented evidence for the conflict is provided by the *Acts of the Council of Saragossa* (380), at which Hydatius' hostility toward Priscillian seems to have been a crucial factor. The conciliar text is marked by an emphasis on the centrality of the episcopally led eucharistic liturgy and the authority of the clerical hierarchy, positioned to resist the centrifugal tug of the "private" ascetic groups in which Priscillian presumably participated. Implicitly invoking the terms of the public discourse of separate male and female spheres, the *Acts* insists that women should remain separate and subordinate within the Christian community and identifies the meetings and eclectic reading habits of small, mixed-sex study groups as both immoral and seditious.

After the council, Priscillian and his associates apparently responded to the attack on their manner of life and of reading with accusations against Hydatius, whom Priscillian's *Tractates* depict as both "schismatic" and "unlearned." Hydatius and his allies charged Priscillian in turn with the dualistic cosmological views, the use of apocryphal texts, and the moral crimes of socially subversive and sexually intemperate Manichaeans and sorcerers. The intensity of the competition between the two parties and their distinctive strategies of Christian self-definition was such that the conflict overflowed the boundaries of the western Spanish communities in which it originated and became entangled with the strands of analogous disputes in such significant urban centers as Bordeaux, Milan, and Rome. The labels of Manichaeism and sorcery ultimately succeeded in defining Priscillian as a threatening outsider and thereby mandating first his departure from the Christian communities of Spain and later his execution in Trier (circa 386). The well-born Euchrotia and three others who had been Priscillian's companions in Christian asceticism were also his companions in death. By seeming to validate the accusations that the authority of a learned teacher derived from illicit sources, the conviction and execution of Priscillian and his associates compromised the legitimacy of privately construed authority per se and thus represented at least a partial, initial triumph for a public and culturally accommodating definition of Christian community.

Controversies and episcopal gatherings at Toledo (400) and Tarragona (circa 418) reflected continuing attempts to limit the scope of private-sphere authority and to subordinate such authority more clearly to the hierarchical structures of a publicly centered community. At both Toledo and Tarragona, the figure of the historical Priscillian was transformed into a symbol of deviance by which subsequent disputes could be negotiated. Like the more exotic labels of Manichaeism and sorcery, the home-grown label of Priscillianism functioned within the Spanish communities to redefine internal opponents as outsiders, and Priscillian's name remained associated with magical practices and secret books, as well as with private, mixed-sex study groups. At Toledo, the council demanded greater respect for episcopal authority and a more careful observance of the separation and subordination of women, while the threat of association with Priscillian was used to force Galician bishops like Symphosius and Dictinius to conform to a more decisively public communal structure.

Almost two decades later at Tarragona, a certain equilibrium was attained through the still greater overlapping of the public and private spheres in Christian communal life, which further diminished the influence of lay teachers and groups. The authority of education, birth, and eloquence was more closely linked than ever with the authority of office in figures like the Huescan presbyter Severus and the Ilerdan bishop Sagittius, and even accusations of heresy or Priscillianism were ineffective in discrediting the standing of these learned and aristocratic ecclesiastics in the communities of the Tarragonese province. The rhetorical manipulation of both class and gender qualified the individual experience of this blurring of the boundaries of public and private: Fronto, possessing neither aristocratic birth nor clerical office, was openly disdained by the leaders of the Tarragonese communities but was nevertheless able to attain a public hearing not only in those communities but also in Arles and on the Balearic islands, where Consentius resided; the well-born Severa, on the other hand, while escaping the consequences of heresy accusations through her family connections, was referred to dismissively as a "little woman" by both parties in the dispute, and she and the other women of Fronto's tale were to some extent confined to family circles.

In western regions outside Spain, the structures and ideals of Christian community evolved along distinct, if not altogether dissimilar, lines. Sulpicius Severus' and Jerome's portraits of Priscillian as a gnostic seducer reflect one such variant evolution. Both Severus and Jerome used the publicly centered rhetoric of public and private to defend their controversial understandings of Christian community. Such a rhetorical strategy enabled the articulation of two distinct domains of public urban and private monastic communities, the latter implicitly subordinated to the former, while at the same time retaining a significant degree of autonomy. Public-private rhetoric also informed Severus' and Jerome's apologetic construction of a monastic social order in which women were separate and subordinate; by this means, the ascetic scholars protected themselves against accusations of anarchic immorality such as those that had eventually defeated Priscillian. But for all the striking prominence of this publicly centered discourse in the rhetoric of Severus and Jerome, their own authority and lifestyle appear to have been linked more closely with the private than the public sphere, and gender does not in fact seem to have been a primary distinction of the social order of ascetic communities that acknowledged the authority of women like Marcella, Paula, Eustochium, Melania, Therasia, and Bassula. By making significant concessions to the public order and its rhetorical traditions, Jerome and Severus succeeded in at least partially preserving a private model of Christian community. However, this strategy produced both theoretical inconsistencies and disjunctions between discourse and social experience, particularly in the area of gender roles and relations. Both men attempted to minimize such inconsistencies and disjunctions by developing a powerful rhetoric for the control of women, which in turn led to the further eroding of the private basis of personal and communal self-definition. The elements of gender and sexuality were emphasized in the elaboration of the content of the gnostic label, an emphasis that functioned not only to narrow the boundaries of legitimate private authority for men but also to enforce greater separation and subordination of women even within monastic communities.

While this study has tended to focus on the social and rhetorical dimensions of the controversy, I have tried not to lose sight of the fact that significant theological issues were also involved and indeed were closely linked to the disputed issues of gender and authority. Unlike Pelagius, Priscillian does not seem to have faced theologians of great stature among his original opponents, and it is in part as a result of this lack that his "heresy" has failed to claim a distinctive place in the history of Christian thought. Traditionally summarily categorized as "Manichaean," Priscillian's thought and the conflict it provoked are more helpfully located in relation to the contemporary controversies surrounding the figures of Evagrius and Pelagius, as Jerome himself recognized. Under debate was a sharp cosmic and anthropological dualism that undergirded an ascetic agenda and a soteriological vision that threatened not only to decenter episcopal authority but finally to relativize all social difference, including distinctions of gender. It was not Jerome but Augustine who was able to articulate a coherent alternative to this powerful late-ancient worldview, simultaneously alienated and optimistic. However often he may be written and rewritten as the "winner"—not least through his own literary efforts—Augustine's complex accommodation to the pressures of a worldly and public model of Christianity is, of course, still hotly contested today.

To "speak of Priscillian" yet again is, I hope, not merely to solidify long-established patterns of western Christian thought by recalling their original moment of closure, but rather to *reopen* questions of body and cosmos, of canon and creed and "textuality" itself, of spiritual leadership, and finally of the constructions of maleness and femaleness that support broader social relations of dominance and submission. In the process, what is sought is not so much a reshaping of orthodoxy, feminist or otherwise, as a new language of difference that would remain open to the vision, and revision, of the "other," and therefore of "self."

NOTES

INTRODUCTION

1. P. Henry, "Why Is Contemporary Scholarship So Enamored of Ancient Heretics?" *Studia Patristica* 17.1 (1982): 123–26.

2. E.g., Patricia Cox Miller, "'Words With an Alien Voice': Gnostics, Scripture, and Canon," *Journal of the American Academy of Religion* 57 (1989): 459–83.

3. For an account of the discovery and its significance, see James M. Robinson, "Introduction," *The Nag Hammadi Library*, 3rd ed. (San Francisco: Harper & Row, 1988), pp. 1–26. While the scholarship devoted to the interpretation of the Nag Hammadi documents is already vast, less attention has been given to the reassessment of the heresiological sources. The most significant work in this area is Alain Le Boulluec, *La Notion d'hérésie dans la littérature grecque, IIᵉ–IIIᵉ siècles* (Paris: Études augustiniennes, 1985). See also the earlier study of Frederik Wisse, "The Nag Hammadi Library and the Heresiologists," *Vigiliae Christianae* 25 (1971): 205–23.

4. Complete lists of possible "Priscillianist" texts, "anti-Priscillianist" texts, and other (generally hostile) sources that may contain references to Priscillian or his movement can be found in Benedikt Vollman, *Studien zum Priszillianismus: Die Forschung, die Quellen, der fünfzehnte Brief Papst Leos des Grossen* (St. Ottilien: EOS Verlag der Erzabtei, 1965), pp. 51–85, and José E. Lopez Pereira, "Prisciliano de Avila y el Priscilianismo desde el siglo IV a nuestros días: Rutas bibliográficas," *Cuadernos Abulenses* 3 (1985): 26–38, 56–77.

5. Sulpicius Severus, *Chron.* 2.46–51.

6. According to Severus' *Chronicle*, many in Spain still honored Priscillian's memory circa 403 (2.51). The minutes of the Council of Toledo (400) record that some of the bishops in Galicia who had formerly honored Priscillian agreed, under

pressure, to conform to the standards of orthodoxy imposed by the council. It is difficult to trace the history of "Priscillianist" Christianity after this point. The chronicler Hydatius remarks upon the confused elections and resulting shameful state of ecclesiastical order in mid-fifth-century Galicia: "deformem ecclesiastici ordinis statum creationibus indiscretis" (*Chron.* pref. 7). The barbarian invasions that began in the second decade of the fifth century were doubtless the primary cause of this confusion. In addition, it appears that Galicia had never had a strong and clearly defined ecclesiastical hierarchy, due both to the relatively late establishment of Christianity in the province and to the particular social organization of fourth-century Galicia; see Alain Tranoy, *La Galice romaine* (Paris: Diffusion de Boccard, 1981), pp. 409–34. Perhaps a distinctive Priscillianist Christianity both contributed to and profited from this chaotic state of affairs. Alternatively, charges of "Priscillianism" may reflect, not the existence of a sect, but simply the need to invoke labels in order to mediate conflicts caused by the disordered or ill-defined social conditions of Galician Christianity. Raymond Van Dam suggests that "in some respects Priscillianism seems to have replaced Manichaeism in Spain and southern Gaul as a homebred idiom of heresy with which people articulated unacceptable aspects of their communities" (*Leadership and Community in Late Antique Gaul* [Berkeley and Los Angeles: University of California Press, 1985], p. 108).

7. The earliest use of the term "Priscillianist" of which I am aware is in the Galician Orosius' *Commonitorium de errore Priscillianistarum et Origenistarum* (414). Orosius is probably the source for Augustine's subsequent use of the term in *Ep.* 36.12 (post 414), *Ep.* 166.3, 7 (415), *Ad Orosium contra Priscillianistas et Origenistas* (415), *De natura et origine animae* 3.7 (419), *Contra mendacium* (420), *Ep.* 237.1–3 (date uncertain), and *De haeresibus* 70 (c. 429). Orosius may also be the source for Consentius' use of the term in *Ep.* 11* to Augustine (419), if Van Dam is right in suggesting that Orosius is the visitor to whom Consentius refers in *Ep.* 12*.9 ("'Sheep in Wolves' Clothing': The Letters of Consentius to Augustine," *Journal of Ecclesiastical History* 37 [1986]: 528–30). The label seems to have become commonplace in mid-fifth-century Galician writings, e.g., the anti-Priscillianist *Regula fidei* falsely attributed to the Council of Toledo I (400), and the *Commonitorium* and *Libellus* submitted by Turribius of Astorga to Leo (preserved in Leo, *Ep.* 15). Orosius, the *Regula fidei*, and Turribius also associate the "Priscillianists" with gnosticism, Manichaeism and astrology, and trinitarian errors; this plurality of heretical associations is taken up in the sixth-century anti-Priscillianist professions of the Galician Councils of Braga I (561) and II (572). As argued in Chapter 5 of this work, Sulpicius Severus and Jerome seem to represent a separate stream of tradition, in which Priscillian is identified simply as a gnostic seducer.

8. The Würzburg tractates were first published by their discoverer Georg Schepss in *CSEL* 18 (1889) and have been reprinted in *PL* suppl. 2 (1961), cols. 1413–83, with additional textual annotations and the retention of the *CSEL* pagination. On the question of authorship, see Henry Chadwick, *Priscillian of Avila: The Occult and the Charismatic in the Early Church* (Oxford: Clarendon Press, 1976), pp. 62–69. Priscillian is not named in the manuscript, but there is broad consensus

based on internal evidence that the tractates stem from his circle. I concur with Chadwick that "it is not unreasonable to think Priscillian himself the principal author of the tractates" (p. 69). Since it is furthermore unnecessary in most cases to distinguish between the views of Priscillian and those of his close associates, I shall henceforth simply refer to Priscillian as the author. Because Priscillian's personal authorship of the first and second tractates is relevant to my argument in Chapter 2, a more careful defense of his authorship of those tractates will be found in that chapter.

9. Van Dam points out the significance of this metaphor in Priscillian's first two tractates: "For Priscillian, life was an *iter*, a road or a journey" (*Leadership and Community*, p. 95).

10. *Tract.* 7, 82.6–7.

11. Priscillian opens his *Liber ad Damasum Episcopum* with a reference to the "road of the creed" (*symboli iter*); later in the same work he recites and explicates that creed at some length (*Tract.* 2, 34.3, 36.13–37.17). The creed is explicitly connected with baptism in the *Liber apologeticus* (*Tract.* 1, 31.28–32.6).

12. *Tract.* 3, passim. See also Virginia Burrus, "Canonical References to Extra-Canonical 'Texts': Priscillian's Defense of the Apocrypha," *Society of Biblical Literature Seminar Papers* (1990): 60–67.

13. Priscillian explicitly denounces the Manichaeans in the first two tractates (*Tract.* 1, 22.13–23.4; *Tract.* 2, 39.8–13).

14. Priscillian's correction of heretical interpretations of creation in the *Tractatus Genesis* appears to be aimed against the Manichaeans, whom he criticizes both for ascribing the creation of the body to the devil and for divinizing material creation; he complains that these heretics fail to understand that the visible world is the finite and temporary creation of the infinite and eternal God (*Tract.* 5, 63.9–64.20). In the same anti-Manichean context, Priscillian remarks that God devised "the nature of what was made" (*facturae naturam*) in such a way that the divisions of temporal existence "would offer a habitation [*habitaculum*] for the human being who labored in the work of Christ"; here he implies that temporal existence has a positive function in God's plan (*Tract.* 5, 64.12–16).

15. In the *Tractatus Exodi*, Priscillian develops the theme that scripture urges Christians to purify the "dwelling place" (*habitaculum*) of the body for divine habitation. Thus, for example, Priscillian interprets the divine injunction to smear the doorposts of the home with the blood of the paschal lamb as a command to make the "doorposts and thresholds of the animated body" (*animati corporis*) suitable for "the entrance of the divine word," noting that our body is the "house of God" (*domus dei*) (*Tract.* 6, 79.10–28).

16. R. P. C. Hanson provides a helpful overview of the often neglected western Nicene party (*The Search for the Christian Doctrine of God: The Arian Controversy, 318–381* [Edinburgh: T. & T. Clark, 1988], pp. 459–556). Henry Chadwick's study of the teachings of the Priscillianist tractates highlights, on the one hand, the extent to which Priscillian's trinitarian thought conforms to that of the western Nicene theologian Hilary of Poitiers and, on the other hand, the comparative lack of anti-

Arian polemic or even anti-Arian awareness in Priscillian's writings (*Priscillian of Avila*, pp. 85–89).

17. The classic statement of this position is A. Hilgenfeld, "Priscillianus und seine neuentdeckten Schriften," *Zeitschrift für wissenschaftliche Theologie* 35 (1892): 1–85. In "Les Origenes du Priscillianisme et l'orthodoxie de Priscillien," *Bulletin d'ancienne littérature et d'archéologie chrétiennes* 2 (1912): 81–95, 161–213, A. Puech presents a more moderate and nuanced argument for Priscillian's doctrinal heresy. A similar position is taken by Adhémar D'Alès, S.J., *Priscillien et l'Espagne chrétienne à la fin du IV* siècle (Paris: Gabriel Beauchesne et ses fils, 1936).

18. Jerome, *Ep.* 133.3.

19. Peter Brown's brief reflections on fifth-century christology suggest the resonance of the late-ancient Christian emphasis on theological transcendence with the experience of autocratic rule (*Power and Persuasion in Late Antiquity: Towards a Christian Empire* [Madison: University of Wisconsin Press, 1992], pp. 152–58). Brown's broader interest in this work lies with power, or rather the control of power, as viewed from the point of view of the upper-class subjects of late Roman emperors; his discussion of the impact of autocracy on elite men and women who could hope only to mitigate the violent effects of absolute imperial power seems to me fruitfully juxtaposed with Elizabeth Clark's recent highlighting of the centrality and theological seriousness of the issues of determinism and freedom raised in the Origenist as well as Pelagian controversies of the late fourth and early fifth centuries (*The Origenist Controversy: The Cultural Construction of an Early Christian Debate* [Princeton: Princeton University Press, 1992]).

20. Georges Duby, "Foreword," *A History of Private Life*, 1: *From Pagan Rome to Byzantium*, ed. Paul Veyne, trans. A. Goldhammer (Cambridge, Mass.: Harvard University Press, 1987), p. viii.

21. Jean Bethke Elshtain, *Public Man, Private Woman: Women in Social and Political Thought* (Princeton: Princeton University Press, 1981), xiv.

22. While "cultural universals" are no longer particularly fashionable in anthropological circles, I am aware that there are many who would find it helpful to approach the public-private distinction as a cross-cultural phenomenon. Particularly revealing of some of the issues here at stake is an early discussion among feminist anthropologists initiated by the groundbreaking essay in which Michelle Zimbalist Rosaldo suggested that the public-private distinction is a universal—although "nonnecessary"—aspect of culture and society ("Woman, Culture, and Society: A Theoretical Overview," in *Woman, Culture, and Society*, ed. Michelle Z. Rosaldo and Louise Lamphere [Stanford: Stanford University Press, 1974], pp. 17–42). In an incisive review article, Rayna Rapp subsequently questioned the value of a universal model to explain historically distinct phenomena ("Review Essay: Anthropology," *Signs* 4 [1979]: 497–510); Rosaldo responded with a follow-up essay in the same journal ("The Use and Abuse of Anthropology: Reflections on Feminism and Cross-Cultural Understanding," *Signs* 5 [1980]: 389–417). The field of political philosophy likewise wrestles with the question of "universals" and "particulars" in its analysis of the public-private distinction, with feminist thinkers

again demonstrating a distinctive commitment to a highly contextualized approach to the history of ideas, while still insisting on a universalized understanding of "patriarchy"; see, e.g., Elshtain, *Public Man, Private Woman*, and Linda J. Nicholson, *Gender and History: The Limits of Social Theory in the Age of the Family* (New York: Columbia University Press, 1986). A more eclectic theoretical approach is represented by the essays in the volume *Public and Private in Social Life*, ed. S. I. Benn and G. F. Gauss (New York: St. Martin's Press, 1983).

23. Aristotle, *Pol.* 1.2.1252b–1253a. The ancient discussion of the separation and interrelation of the public and private spheres spans the disciplines of "politics," "economics" (i.e., household management), and "ethics," but it is most frequently and clearly discussed in the context of household management. David Balch argues persuasively for a high degree of continuity within the tradition, suggesting that ideas of how a household was to be run remained remarkably stable from classical Greece through the hellenistic and Roman periods (*Let Wives Be Submissive: The Domestic Code in 1 Peter* [Chico, Calif.: Scholars Press, 1981], pp. 21–62).

24. Elshtain, *Public Man, Private Woman*, pp. 15–16.

25. Thus Aristotle describes the relationships of the household in terms of political forms of government. While he is content to characterize the relationship of the male head of the household to his children and slaves as monarchical, he has more difficulty describing the relationship of male and female heads of household in political terms and thereby exposes the inadequacy of the political model. He concludes in a somewhat confused fashion that the husband rules his wife, not monarchically—which would imply the fundamental inequality of ruler and ruled—but by a modified constitutional rule—ordinarily shared among equals—which grants the male a permanent, if only nominal, superiority (*Pol.* 1.12.1259b). Aristotle's contemporary Xenophon, on the other hand, is happy to describe the female head of household as a ruler, comparing her to the guardian of a state who oversees the carrying out of its laws, to the commander of a garrison inspecting his guards, to the Athenian Council scrutinizing the cavalry, and to a queen punishing and rewarding her subjects (*Oeconomicus* 9.14–15).

26. The male speaker in Xenophon's dialogue on household management hastens to assure his audience that he maintains a respectable distance from household affairs: "I certainly do not spend my time indoors; for my wife is quite capable of managing the household affairs herself" (*Oeconomicus* 7.3). While Xenophon's view of the female private sphere is relatively benign, other writers perceive it as not only alien but also inherently problematic and uncontrolled. Plato dreams of a utopian society in which the private sphere is not just subordinated but effectively eliminated (Elshtain, *Public Man, Private Woman*, pp. 29–41), while the Athenian dramatists create situations alternately nightmarish and comical in which unruly women transgress the boundaries of the private sphere and thereby threaten to destroy the basis of orderly social existence. Helen Foley argues that whereas a figure like Aeschylus' Clytemnestra might represent a simple inversion of the ideal of the subordinate and private woman, other transgressing females, such as Eurip-

ides' Medea and Aristophanes' Lysistrata, play a more complex role, intruding into the public realm in order to challenge or correct the failure of the male to observe his proper role as member of both household and state. Drama thus reveals an awareness that the essential complementarity and balance of public and private spheres can be threatened by men as well as women, by the demands of the public sphere as well as the private ("The Conception of Women in Athenian Drama," in *Reflections of Women in Antiquity*, ed. H. P. Foley [New York: Gordon & Breach Science Publishers, 1981], pp. 148–62).

27. See the discussion in Karen Torjesen, *When Women Were Priests: Women's Leadership in the Early Church and the Scandal of Their Subordination in the Rise of Christianity* (San Francisco: Harper, 1993), 53–87.

28. As has been recently highlighted and variously interpreted by Paul Veyne, Peter Brown, and Michel Foucault, among others; see the discussion of Averil Cameron, "Redrawing the Map: Early Christian Territory after Foucault," *Journal of Roman Studies* 75 (1986): 266–71.

29. Peter Brown's recent *Power and Persuasion* illumines this space wherein classical rhetoric still had some small but significant room to maneuver.

30. The centering of aristocratic identity and activity on private life in late antiquity has been argued by John Matthews, *Western Aristocracies and the Imperial Court, A.D. 364–425* (Oxford: Clarendon Press, 1975), pp. 9–11.

31. Ibid., pp. 12–17. Note, however, that the decline in the involvement of the traditional senatorial aristocracy in government under Valentinian I was perhaps both less typical for the period and less pronounced than Matthews wants to admit. See, e.g., the discussion of Patrick Wormald, "The Decline of the Western Empire and the Survival of Its Aristocracy," *Journal of Roman Studies* 66 (1976): 217–26.

32. Matthews, *Western Aristocracies*, pp. 17–31.

33. Ibid., p. xi.

34. My own thinking about the various forms and functions of the ancient rhetoric of reluctance to assume the responsibilities of public office and power has been greatly enhanced by the work of Kate Cooper; see, e.g., her "Insinuations of Womanly Influence: An Aspect of the Christianization of the Roman Aristocracy," *Journal of Roman Studies* 82 (1992): 150–64.

35. Priscillian, *Tract.* 1, 4.8–11, 5.2–4.

36. Ibid., 33.9–13.

37. This is the purpose of the *Liber ad Damasum Episcopum* (*Tract.* 2), probably composed slightly later than the *Liber apologeticus* (*Tract.* 1).

38. Peter Brown, "Sorcery, Demons, and the Rise of Christianity from Late Antiquity into the Middle Ages," in *Witchcraft Confessions and Accusations*, ed. Mary Douglas (London: Tavistock Publications, 1970), pp. 17–45, quotation at p. 22.

39. Cf. Brown, ibid., pp. 24–25, and *Power and Persuasion*, pp. 41–47.

40. Brown, "Sorcery, Demons, and the Rise of Christianity," p. 20.

41. Ibid., p. 21.

42. Ibid.

43. For example, Brown's discussion of fourth-century sorcery accusations hints at the "resentments and anomalous power on the edge of the court" emanating from those frustrated aristocrats for whom "the days of a 'senatorial opposition' . . . were gone forever" (ibid., p. 23).

44. Here again the work of Raymond Van Dam's *Leadership and Community in Late Antique Gaul* is particularly helpful in demonstrating the remarkable consistency of the roles of local leaders in the late-ancient west.

45. Brown, *Power and Persuasion*, p. 62.

46. Ibid., p. 63.

47. On the real and symbolic functions of the role of the philosopher in late-ancient political life, see most recently ibid., pp. 61–70. See also Garth Fowden, "The Pagan Holy Man in Late Antique Society," *Journal of Hellenic Studies* 102 (1982): 33–59, and, more recently, Robert Kirschner, "The Vocation of Holiness in Late Antiquity," *Vigiliae Christianae* 38 (1984): 105–24.

48. For the last, see Prudentius, *Praef.* 16–35.

49. Elizabeth Clark notes that "in many respects, the patristic assertion that ascetic women were 'virile' is based on an accurate representation of the concrete conditions of their lives, conditions that resembled the men's" ("Ascetic Renunciation and Feminine Advancement: A Paradox of Late Ancient Christianity," in *Ascetic Piety and Women's Faith: Essays on Late Ancient Christianity* [Lewiston, N.Y.: Edwin Mellen Press, 1986], p. 180; see also Clark, *Jerome, Chrysostom, and Friends: Essays and Translations* [Lewiston, N.Y.: Edwin Mellen Press, 1979], pp. 15, 19, 55–56). Kerstin Aspegren's posthumously published study of the ancient theme of virile femininity, tracked across eight centuries and across polytheistic, Jewish, and Christian sources, hints at the significance and complex function of this gendered paradox in ancient Mediterranean thought (*The Male Woman: A Feminine Ideal in the Early Church*, ed. René Kieffer, Acta Universitatis Upsaliensis, Uppsala Women's Studies [Uppsala, 1990]).

50. Prior to the discovery of the Nag Hammadi documents, Walter Bauer had already challenged what he labeled a "Eusebian" view of heresies as deviations or perversions of a prior orthodox tradition, arguing instead that what we identify as "orthodoxy" was simply one of a number of simultaneously coexisting forms of early Christianity, a form that did not begin to dominate until the end of the second century (*Orthodoxy and Heresy in Earliest Christianity*, English trans. of 2d German ed., ed. R. Kraft and G. Krodel [Philadelphia: Fortress Press, 1971]). It is Alain Le Boulluec, working in the post–Nag Hammadi era, who has carried Bauer's critique further: whereas Bauer continued to use the terms "orthodoxy" and "heresy" in a somewhat conventional, although perhaps ironical, manner, Le Boulluec explores the foundations of the concepts of "orthodoxy" and "heresy," locating their birth not in Eusebius but in the earlier anti-gnostic works of Justin and Irenaeus and arguing that the very conception of "orthodoxy" was simultaneous with and dependent upon the negative conception of "heresy" (*Notion d'hérésie*).

51. See the careful discussion of Le Boulluec, *Notion d'hérésie*, 1: 39–91.

52. Ibid., pp. 157–86.

53. Virginia Burrus, "The Heretical Woman as Symbol in Alexander, Athanasius, Epiphanius, and Jerome," *Harvard Theological Review* 84 (1991): 229–48.

54. Hanson, *Search for the Christian Doctrine of God*, pp. 329–34.

55. Ibid., pp. 508–16, 519–26.

56. Jerome, *Dialogus contra Luciferianos* 1.

57. Hanson, *Search for the Christian Doctrine of God*, pp. 335–38.

58. *Collectio Avellana* 2.43–45.

59. Matthews highlights the distinctive "orthodoxy" of Theodosius and many of his court and explores "the possible contribution of their native environment to the formation of the Christian piety which they expressed so distinctively in distant parts of the Roman world" (*Western Aristocracies*, p. 145; see also pp. 100, 121–44, 146–72). Matthews further emphasizes the similarities between the "pious soldiers" Theodosius and Magnus Maximus, noting that Maximus was "almost in every respect the double of Theodosius himself—and as events immediately proved, his equal in hostility to heresy" (p. 165) and raising the possibility that "Maximus' suppression of Priscillianism was, in part at least, a calculated attempt to attract Theodosius' support for his regime, as the regime of a compatriot [they were both Spaniards] and fellow Catholic with a shared interest in the elimination of heresy" (p. 170).

60. Priscillian is not only adamantly "orthodox" in his self-understanding but also presents himself as bearing witness under persecution. In the *Liber apologeticus*, he opens by noting that the bishops' attack provides him the opportunity to win great glory, since his faith, "when struck by diabolical detraction" will be "proven more where it is attacked" (*Tract.* 1, 3.3–6). Galician Priscillianists honored Priscillian as a martyr after his death.

61. Anne-Marie Palmer, *Prudentius on the Martyrs* (Oxford: Clarendon Press, 1989), p. 3. In the preface to his collected poems, Prudentius first of all exhorts his soul to "fight against heresies and expound the catholic faith" (*Praef.* 39).

62. I concentrate here only on those works that have most strongly influenced my approach. For a comprehensive bibliography and history of scholarship, see Vollman, *Studien*, and the update in "Priscillianus," in *Paulys Realenzyklopädie der classischen Altertumswissenschaft*, suppl. 14 (Munich, 1974), cols. 485–559; Lopez Pereira's "Prisciliano de Avila" further updates the bibliography to 1985.

63. E.-Ch. Babut, *Priscillien et le priscillianisme* (Paris: Librairie Honoré Champion, 1909), pp. 60–78.

64. Ibid., p. 73.

65. Ibid., pp. 79–96.

66. See, e.g., Puech's incisive critique ("Les Origenes du Priscillianisme," pp. 82–95).

67. Willy Schatz, "Studien zur Geschichte und Vorstellungswelt des frühen abendländischen Mönchtums" (diss., Freiburg i. Br., 1957), pp. 98–259.

68. Schatz (ibid., p. 217) comments on the relative superficiality of Babut's interpretation: "Auf der anderen Seite hat man den Zusammenstoss mit dem spa-

nischen Episkopat einfach allgemein als einen Gipfelpunkt jener anti-asketischen Welle fassen wollen, die das Vordringen der asketischen Bewegung und die Bestrengungen zur Verwirklichung des Ideals der Virginität im Abendland im letzten Viertel des 4. Jahrhunderts auslösten; man glaubte, gerade in ihm einen Beweis für die Heftigkeit der Reaktion sehen zu dürfen. Zwar wird ein Zusammenhang mit dieser umfassenderen anti-asketischen Strömung nicht bestritten werden können; trotz der entgegenstehenden, scheinbar einheitlichen Opposition darf aber die Verschiedenheit der einzelnen asketischen Erscheinungen des Abendlands nicht übersehen werden. Ein Erklärungsversuch nach der Art des obigen bleibt daher auch zu sehr an der Oberfläche der Dinge; er berücsichtigt weder die Eigenart der priscillianistischen Gemeinschaft, noch stösst er zu den tieferliegenden Motiven der Gegenseite vor."

69. Ibid., p. 228. Although he is primarily interested in western monasticism, parallels between eastern and western ascetic movements are important to Schatz's argument. He aligns the eastern "sects" of the Messalians, Eustathians, and "apotaktites" with the Priscillianists on the basis of a shared ascetic worldview as well as a common estrangement from mainstream ecclesiastical institutions (ibid., p. 228).

70. Ibid., p. 228 n. 1.

71. Ibid., p. 229. Here Schatz rightly modifies the interpretation of Babut, who suggests that Priscillian and his associates were explicitly and consciously in opposition to official authority.

72. Ibid., p. 254.

73. Ibid., pp. 254–55.

74. Rudolf Lorenz criticizes Schatz on this point, arguing that Priscillian's movement has no place in the evolution from early Christian asceticism to monasticism, but instead represents a separate and unorthodox tradition: "Das spanische Mönchtum wuchs neben Priszillian heran" ("Die Anfänge des abendländischen Mönchtums im 4. Jahrhundert," *Zeitschrift für Kirchengeschichte* 77 [1966]: 23). But Lorenz's inability to fit Priscillian's movement into any category of "orthodox" asceticism appears to be owing not so much to the deviant nature of Priscillian's movement as to the limits of a relatively simple typology for describing the diversity of fourth-century ascetic practices.

75. Schatz, *Studien*, pp. 127ff.

76. Note that Weber actually distinguishes among three ideal types of authority: rational or legal, traditional, and charismatic; see Talcott Parsons' analysis and translation in Max Weber, *The Theory of Social and Economic Organization* (New York: Oxford University Press, 1947), pp. 56–66, 324–63. The rational or legal authority of office corresponds closely to what I term "public-sphere authority," and indeed Weber himself suggests that the theoretical distinction between public and private spheres is typical of rational or legal authority (Parsons, p. 58), much as I argue that the rhetoric of public and private is essentially a "public" discourse. However, my "private-sphere authority" meshes less easily with the Weberian categories and may be closer to "traditional" than to the "charismatic" authority

emphasized by Schatz. Although fourth-century Christians, especially in the east, proved ready to acknowledge the revolutionary "charismatic" authority of ascetic figures like Antony, one of the elements that distinguishes fourth-century western Christianity is the novel and significant presence of men and women who could lay claim to the "traditional" authority of aristocratic birth and/or culture. Elizabeth Clark provides an illuminating analysis of the social position of late-fourth-century ascetic women in terms of Weber's category of "traditional" authority ("Authority and Humility: A Conflict of Values in Fourth-Century Female Monasticism," in *Ascetic Piety and Women's Faith: Essays on Late Ancient Christianity* [Lewiston, N.Y.: Edwin Mellen Press, 1986], pp. 209–28).

77. Vollman, *Studien*, pp. 40–42.

78. Vollman, "Priscillianus," cols. 485–559.

79. Abilio Barbero de Aguilera, "El priscilianismo: ¿Herejía o movimiento social?" *Cuadernos de historia de España* 37–38 (1963): 5–41, esp. 16–25.

80. See, e.g., Van Dam's concise critique of Barbero de Aguilera's use of the rural-urban distinction (*Leadership*, pp. 90–91).

81. Chadwick, *Priscillian of Avila*, pp. vii, 51–56, 54–55, 74, 82–84, 97.

82. Ibid., p. 99.

83. Ibid., pp. 70–100, 111–233.

84. See, e.g., Chadwick's discussion of the Saragossan council's prohibition of going barefoot and of Ithacius' charge that Priscillian took part in some sort of magical ritual (ibid., pp. 17–20, 51–56).

85. Chadwick's first chapter, which deals with events through the synod of Bordeaux, is entitled "The Sorcerer's Apprentice" (ibid., pp. 1–56).

86. Ibid., pp. 57–110.

87. Van Dam, *Leadership*, p. 92.

88. Ibid., pp. 64–69, 78–87.

89. Van Dam suggests that both the spread of the conflict beyond community boundaries and the fact that Priscillian was eventually killed point to the "failure" of the "mechanism" of accusations of Manichaeism (ibid., p. 104).

90. Ibid., pp. 70, 92–106.

91. Ibid., pp. 70–74.

92. Ibid., pp. 74–76. Quotation from p. 75.

CHAPTER 1. "A STRANGE MAN"

1. Priscillian, *Tract.* 2, 34.19–35.5.

2. Supporting the interpretation of the term *electi Deo* as holders of clerical office, see E.-Ch. Babut, *Priscillien*, pp. 92–96, and José María Ramos y Loscertales, *Prisciliano: Gesta rerum* (Universidad de Salamanca, 1952), pp. 11–14. Note that Babut and his followers frequently highlight such language in the *Letter to Damasus* without sufficiently acknowledging its rhetorical function to uphold the legitimacy of the episcopacy of Priscillian and his supporters; they thereby falsely exaggerate the degree to which Priscillian and his circle actively sought clerical office.

3. Severus, *Chron.* 2.46.

4. Cf. the suggestion of Manuel C. Díaz y Díaz that *ex vicino* indicates an ideological rather than geographical closeness—i.e., Hyginus was a "rigorist" like Priscillian ("L'Expansion du christianisme et les tensions épiscopales dans la Péninsule Ibérique," *Miscellanea Historiae Ecclesiasticae* 6, Congrès de Varsovie 1 [1983]: 89).

5. Jerome, *De viris inlustribus* 123; cf. *Priscillian, Tract.* 1, 3.9.

6. Severus, *Chron.* 2.46.

7. Note that the reliability of Severus' identification of Hydatius as the chief provoker of the dissensions may be slightly compromised by his own intense dislike of Hydatius and his ally Ithacius based on their later activities in Gaul. Severus constructs an even more condemning portrait of Priscillian's opponents than of Priscillian. See Jacques Fontaine on the nuanced allusion to Sallust's Catiline in Severus' portraits of Priscillian, Hydatius, and Ithacius ("L'Affaire Priscillien ou l'ère des nouveaux Catilina: Observations sur le 'sallustianisme' de Sulpice Sévère," in *Classica et Iberica: A Festschrift in Honor of the Rev. Joseph M.-F. Marique, S.J.*, ed. P. T. Brannan, S.J. [Worcester, Mass: Institute for Early Christian Iberian Studies, 1975], pp. 355–92). See Ralph W. Mathisen on the disputes in Severus' own day that biased him so strongly against Ithacius and Hydatius (*Ecclesiastical Factionalism and Religious Controversy in Fifth-Century Gaul* [Washington, D.C.: Catholic University of America Press, 1989], pp. 11–26).

8. Severus, *Chron.* 2.46.

9. Ibid. 2.47.

10. Puech, "Origines du priscillianisme," p. 209, and Ramos y Loscertales, *Prisciliano*, p. 44.

11. Jacques Fontaine, "Société et culture chrétiennes sur l'aire circumpyrénéenne au siècle de Théodose," *Bulletin de littérature ecclésiastique* 75 (1974): 241–82. I see no evidence, however, of Priscillian's influence having spread into Aquitaine at this point, in agreement with Puech ("Origines du priscillianisme," pp. 81–95), and against Babut (*Priscillien*, pp. 79–91). Babut goes so far as to suggest possible Aquitanian origins for Priscillian's movement by positing the leadership of the rhetorician Attius Tiro Delphidius, whom he identifies with the Elpidius referred to by Severus.

12. *Acts of the Council of Saragossa* (hereafter *ACS*), ll. 18–20; line numbers correspond to the critical edition of Felix Rodríguez, "Concilio I de Zaragoza: Texto crítico," in *Primero Concilio Caesaraugustano: MDC aniversario* (Zaragoza, 1981), pp. 9–25.

13. Chadwick, *Priscillian of Avila*, p. 13. Babut's proposal that the Aquitanians head the list because of their status as foreign guests is less convincing (*Priscillien*, p. 5). Both Jerome (*De viris inlustribus* 108) and Sulpicius Severus (*Chron.* 2.44) speak highly of Phoebadius as a steadfast opponent of the Arians, and Phoebadius' name stands first in the episcopal list of the letter of the Synod of Valence (374).

14. Delphinus' later hostile reception of Priscillian and his Bordeaux "converts" is discussed in Chapter 3 below. Note, however, that Delphinus remained

on friendly terms with the aristocratic Paulinus, later of Nola, who converted to an ascetic life some years after the outbreak of the Priscillianist controversy; five letters in the extant correspondence of the ascetic Paulinus are addressed to Delphinus (*Epp.* 10, 14, 19, 20, and 35).

15. Chadwick, *Priscillian of Avila*, pp. 12–13, 20–21.

16. Priscillian, *Tract.* 2, 40.1–27.

17. *Exemplar professionum habitarum in concilio Toletano contra sectam Priscilliani aera ccccxxxviii*, (hereafter *Exemplar*), ll. 71–72. Line numbers correspond to the critical edition in Chadwick, *Priscillian of Avila*, pp. 234–39. If Symposius did indeed leave the Saragossan council after one day, were the eight judgments promulgated by the council, to which his name is affixed, formulated on that first day, or were some or all formulated in his absence?

18. See Jerome, *Ep.* 69.2, and Chadwick, *Priscillian of Avila*, pp. 12–13.

19. Benedikt Vollman considers it probable that Hydatius presided over the council ("Priscillianus," col. 500).

20. Sulpicius Severus' account implies that some among Priscillian's circle had already been excommunicated before the council, presumably by Hydatius, but that the excommunication had not been recognized by Hyginus. The council's fifth judgment against dissenting bishops was then applied retroactively to excommunicate Hyginus; see *Chron.* 2.47. This latter point appears unlikely, and Babut suggests that the Severan text be amended to read *commonefaceret* instead of *communione faceret*, indicating that Hyginus was formally warned by the council rather than excommunicated (*Priscillien*, p. 138 n. 2). Another possibility is that Sulpicius Severus has collapsed the time frame in which events occurred and falsely attributed Hyginus' subsequent excommunication on the basis of the council's fifth judgment to the council itself.

21. Severus, *Chron.* 2.47.

22. Priscillian, *Tract.* 2, 35.19–21.

23. Ibid., 35.24–36.6.

24. E.g., Priscillian *Can. Ep. Pauli* 35, 44, 47.

25. E.g., Priscillian, *Tract.* 4, 58.13–20.

26. Ramos y Loscertales, *Prisciliano*, p. 47, and Chadwick, *Priscillian of Avila*, p. 23.

27. Priscillian, *Tract.* 2, 42.11–12.

28. Ibid. 3, 51.10–12.

29. Ibid. 2, 41.21–23.

30. Ibid., 35.15–19; see also 35.21–22; 39.20–21; 40.7–8; 42.19–21.

31. Ibid., 35.22–24. It is unclear whether this letter of Damasus was addressed to the council itself; if so, Damasus' later refusal to intervene in the controversy seems more surprising.

32. *Exemplar*, ll. 70–71.

33. Severus, *Chron.* 2.47.

34. This solution, which assumes that both Priscillian and Severus are telling at least partial truths, is supported by Vollman ("Priscillianus," col. 502), based in

part on the argument of Ramos y Loscertales (*Prisciliano*, pp. 55–62), and more recently by María Victoria Escribano Paño ("Sobre la pretendida condena nominal dictada por el Concilio de Caesaraugusta del año 380," *Primero Concilio Caesaraugustano: MDC aniversario* [Zaragoza, 1981], pp. 123–33). Cf. Babut's dismissal of Severus' evidence as deriving from the lies of Ithacius (*Priscillien*, pp. 39–41). Chadwick offers an alternative harmonizing interpretation: he suggests that while the formal *sententiae* of the council did not condemn the Priscillianists by name, there may have been minutes that included attacks on named individuals and gave rise to rumors that they had in fact been officially condemned; these rumors may be reflected in Priscillian's vehemence in denial as well as in the later accounts of Sulpicius Severus and the acts of the Council of Toledo (*Priscillian of Avila*, pp. 27–28).

35. *Exemplum sententiarum episcoporum concilii Cesaragustani, quarto Nonas Octbrs* (*ACS*, ll. 16–17). The document as it has been transmitted also includes the epigraph "Concilium Cesaragustanum XII episcoporum," along with summaries of the judgments, which are provided as a table of contents at the beginning of the *Acts* and reappear as headings for each decision. It can be deduced from the form of the other conciliar documents included in the *Hispana* that the epigraph was added to the *Acts of the Council of Saragossa* by the author of the *Hispana*; the summaries appear to have been part of the source that the author of the *Hispana* used, but were clearly added sometime after the original drafting of the conciliar acts and can therefore also be disregarded in the present consideration (Gonzalo Martínez Díez, *La colección canónica hispana*, 1: *Estudio* [Madrid, 1966], pp. 247–53, and Rodríguez, "Concilio I de Zaragoza," p. 11). The text that provided the source for the compiler of the *Hispana* did not include the year, with the result that the compiler was unable to place the *Acts* in proper chronological order (Rodríguez, "Concilio I de Zaragoza," pp. 10–11, and Martínez Díez, *Colección canónica hispana*, 1: 293). Perhaps the names of the consuls, by which the year would have been identified, were dropped in a period when this method of dating was no longer used or understood. One derivative family of manuscripts of the *Hispana* (Paris B.N. lat. 3.846, s.ix; Paris B.N. lat. 1.455, s.x med.; see Martínez Díez, *Colección canónica hispana*, 1: 14, 205) seems to include a date of 418 of the Spanish era, i.e., 380 C.E.; on this, see Babut, *Priscillien*, pp. 244–48. Since this date of 380 accords well with the known dates of other events of the controversy, it is generally accepted without question. There is no independent manuscript evidence witnessing to the form of the text before it was incorporated into the *Hispana* circa 633–36. A summary of the council's eight judgments contained in the *Spanish Epitome*, compiled in Spain between 598 and 610, does, however, provide independent verification of the number and basic content of the judgments recorded in the acts (*El epítome hispánico: Una colección canónica española del siglo VII*, ed. Gonzalo Martínez Díez [Comillas: Universidad Pontifica, 1961], p. 179).

36. Hamilton Hess, *The Canons of the Council of Sardica, A.D. 343* (Oxford: Clarendon Press, 1958), p. 35. In addition to the Saragossan acts, examples of such "stenographic records" include the *Canons of the Council of Sardica*, with which

Hess is primarily concerned, various series of African canons from the second half of the fourth and beginning of the fifth centuries, and the acts of a Roman synod under Pope Hilary in 465 (p. 25).

37. Hess, *Canons of the Council of Sardica*, pp. 28–29.

38. Ibid., p. 26.

39. Note that the emphasis that Hess and others have placed on the importance of the Senate as a model for Christian synods has been questioned by Philip Amidon, who suggests that while the Roman Senate and Christian synods did indeed stand "in the same procedural tradition," this tradition was so widely diffused in the practices of councils and assemblies that "it had lost any specific identification with the Senate of Rome" ("The Procedure of St. Cyprian's Synods," *Vigiliae Christianae* 37 [1983]: 328–39, 339).

40. Hess, *Canons of the Council of Sardica*, pp. 30, 32.

41. Ibid., pp. 36–38.

42. At the conclusion of the *Acts of the Council of Carthage* (390), the bishops give a blanket statement of approval for all of their judgments, without, however, reciting these judgments at length: "Genedius episcopus dixit: Omnia ergo quae a vestro coetu gloriosissimo statuta sunt, placet ab omnibus custodiri? Ab universis episcopis dictum est: Placet, placet, ut custodiantur ab omnibus." The *Anti-Priscillianist Professions* from the Council of Toledo (400) culminate with the reading of more lengthy minutes, but there is no episcopal acclamation at all (*Exemplar*, ll. 69–154). I am not aware of any direct formal parallels to the *Acts of the Council of Saragossa*, a document centered entirely on the reading of the minutes and including a statement of episcopal acclamation after the reading of each judgment. Note further that the acclamations following the first two judgments include the only statement of penalty in those judgments; this indicates that the acclamation is more than a mere ratification of the minutes.

43. Samuel Laeuchli, *Power and Sexuality. The Emergence of Canon Law at the Synod of Elvira* (Philadelphia: Temple University Press, 1972), 10–55.

44. *ACS*, can. 1, ll. 24–29.

45. Laeuchli, *Power and Sexuality*, pp. 19–21. This general rule holds true for all eight of the Saragossan judgments, although in several cases the naming of the person is indefinite or ambiguous.

46. Note that Laeuchli discusses analogous interjections of emotional justifications into the judgments of the Council of Elvira (ibid., pp. 23–26). The phrase *virorum alienorum* is sometimes taken to refer to men alien to the catholic church, i.e., "heretical" or "Priscillianist" men. So Roger Gryson: "According to the historical context, the 'foreign men' referred to in this canon are the Priscillianists" (*The Ministry of Women in the Early Church*, trans. J. Laporte and M. L. Hall [Collegeville, Minn.: Liturgical Press, 1976], p. 101). Others find it more probable that the phrase refers to men alien to a woman's family (Ramos y Loscertales, *Priscilliano*, pp. 49–50, and Chadwick, *Priscillian of Avila*, p. 14). Vollman assumes with greater specificity that the phrase refers to men other than a woman's husband, which allows him to conclude that ascetically inclined married women are the tar-

get of the judgment: "Ich lese aus dem virorum alienorum heraus, dass es sich um verheiratete Frauen handelte, die in ihren Familien lebten, aber asketisch bzw. theologisch interessiert waren" ("Priscillianus," col. 547; so also Díaz y Díaz, "A propósito del Concilio de Zaragoza de 380 y su canon VI," in *Primero Concilio Caesaraugustano: MDC aniversario* [Zaragoza, 1981], p. 226 n. 3 and p. 227). While Vollman's conclusion seems unwarranted, it is unnecessary to eliminate either of the two options of "nonfamilial" and "heretical," since both meanings seem to be exploited by the council's rhetoric and indeed one reinforces the other, not least through the invocation of a shared sexual imagery.

47. Note that there is a textual variant that replaces the initial *vel* with *nec*, in which case the second clause is a further prohibition rather than a concession, and the point is that women are not to meet in any study groups, whether mixed-sex or segregated. This reading occurs in only one of fourteen significant manuscripts; the reading *vel* is therefore to be preferred. See Rodríguez, "Concilio I de Zaragoza," p. 18.

48. Manuel C. Díaz y Díaz has pointed out that the phrase "reading and meetings" is one of several instances of the redactor's use of hendiadys, a figure of speech in which a single complex idea—in this case, meetings at which the reading of scripture took place—is expressed by means of two words connected by a conjunction—reading and meetings ("A propósito del Concilio de Zaragoza," pp. 228–29). Díaz y Díaz also notes that such rhetorical devices have tended to obscure the canons' meanings for later readers (p. 226 n. 3). For example, the author of the index and section headings that accompany the judgments in the *Hispana* collection has simplifed the text of the first canon to read simply *coetibus* instead of *lectione et coetibus*. This abridgement intends to clarify but actually distorts the sense of the canon, which refers more specifically to meetings of Christians at which scripture was read. More recent interpretations similarly generalize the meaning of "meetings" by treating "reading" and "meetings" as two separate items. For example, Ramos y Loscertales notes that while meetings for the purpose of reading and instruction are emphasized, the decision may also refer to other types of meetings, such as prayer meetings, or even possibly the practice of ascetic men and women living together as celibate couples (*Prisciliano*, pp. 49–50).

49. Priscillian, *Tract.* 3, 52.25–53.2, 53.15–18.

50. Note, however, that some scholars seem to interpret this second clause as describing a practice observed by the groups being censured. Babut assumes that it refers to an activity of the Priscillianist ascetics: "Les religieux, en effet, les hommes et les femmes tantôt réunis, tantôt séparés, s'assemblaient entre eux pour lire et expliquer les livres saints" (*Priscillien et le priscillianisme*, p. 83). Ramos y Loscertales likewise assumes that both practices—meeting together and meeting separately—were followed by the Priscillianists. Combining the evidence of the judgments of the Council of Saragossa with Priscillian's reference to a distinction between those who forsake the world and those who are not able to accomplish such a total renunciation (*Tract.* 2, 36.1–6), he suggests that there were three different modes of instruction of the female followers of Priscillian: the individual in-

struction by an ascetic man of a widow or virgin living in ascetic seclusion in her own home; the direction by an ascetic man of a group of ascetic women living in community; and, finally, group study sessions of women following a less rigorous ascetic lifestyle, which were taught by other women (*Prisciliano*, pp. 49–50, 109–10). Ramos y Loscertales is followed in this highly speculative reconstruction of Priscillianist women's organization and instruction by J. M. Blazquez, "Prisciliano, introductor del ascetismo en Hispaña," in *Primero Concilio Caesaraugustano: MDC aniversario* (Zaragoza, 1981), p. 81. Curiously, none of these scholars invokes the variant textual reading of *nec* to support interpretations implying that not only the first but also the second clause of the first Saragossan judgment is prohibitive in import.

51. Laeuchli notes that only 5 percent of the judgments of the Council of Elvira invoke scriptural justification; he finds no correlation between the importance of the canon and the use of scriptural justification (*Power and Sexuality*, p. 25). In the case of the Council of Saragossa, however, it is interesting to note that the only two judgments invoking scriptural justification—can. 1 and can. 7—both reflect the bishops' uneasiness with the role of lay teachers in the Christian community.

52. This use of the masculine form *futuros* in the final sentence creates a possible ambiguity. Opposition to male (and possibly female) teachers will come out directly in the sixth judgment, although in less passionate form. Are the women targeted in the first judgment because they are the primary source of outrage? Or is the first judgment indirectly targeted at the male teachers as well, while appearing to focus on a group who can be accused with less risk?

53. Cf. Laeuchli's discussion of analogous threats of punishment in the judgments of the Council of Elvira (*Power and Sexuality*, pp. 38–41).

54. In contrast, penance seems to be required in can. 6, for example, while perpetual exclusion from the community is specified in can. 3 and can. 4.

55. *ACS*, can. 2, ll. 32–39. Díaz y Díaz briefly discusses the textual difficulties associated with the use of the phrase *de quadragesimarum die* (here translated "during Lent") where one might expect *quadragesimae diebus* ("A propósito del Concilio de Zaragoza," p. 226).

56. Difficulties arise above all in determining the relationship of the parts of the judgment to one another. My own tendency is to assume that the parts of the judgment are somehow interconnected. But it is also possible to view Sunday fasting, Lenten withdrawal, and rural asceticism, for example, as three separate and unrelated ascetic practices prohibited within one judgment. Retirement on a rural estate is a form of ascetic lifestyle particularly well attested in Spain and Gaul, as well as elsewhere. See Jacques Fontaine, "El ascetismo, ¿manzana de discordia entre latifundistas y obispos en la Tarraconense?" in *Primero Concilio Caesaraugustano: MDC aniversario* (Zaragoza, 1981), pp. 201–6; "Société et culture chrétiennes"; and "Valeurs antiques et valeurs chrétiennes dans la spiritualité des grands propriétaires terriens à la fin du IVe siècle occidental," in *Epektasis: Mélanges patristiques offerts au Cardinal Jean Daniélou*, ed. J. Fontaine and Ch. Kannengiesser (Beauchesne, 1972), pp. 571–95.

57. Díaz y Díaz notes that the use of the word *suspicionibus*, or "opinions," is surprising if the reference is to the previously mentioned practices of fasting or ascetic withdrawal, as it seems to be, rather than to a doctrinal matter ("A propósito del Concilio de Zaragoza," pp. 226–27). Some prefer to translate *suspicionibus* as "suspicions," understood in the sense of "activities provoking suspicion" (e.g., Vollman, "Priscillianus," col. 547). Ramos y Loscertales suggests in a rather complicated argument that the term refers exclusively to the practice of secluding oneself during Lent; he sees in the phrase *qui in his suspicionibus perseverant* a concession that changes an apparent prohibition into mere limitation: those who persist in living a retired life must still attend church every day during Lent and follow the example and precepts of their priests (*Prisciliano*, pp. 52–53).

58. The phrase *causa temporis aut persuasionis aut supprestitionis* consists of a series of conjectural explanations for the Sunday fast, each including an innuendo more damaging than the last, but all of them strikingly vague. Díaz y Díaz calls attention to this arrangement of terms in a gradated series, which he takes as a sign of a careful reworking of the language of the canon at some stage ("A propósito del Concilio de Zaragoza," pp. 229–80). *Tempus* is the vaguest of all and may refer to the day Sunday, or to the season of Lent, or even to the eschaton. *Persuasio* may be interpreted to mean either "belief," with connotations of falsehood or self-delusion, or "at the persuasion of others," implying an external source of delusion. Ramos y Loscertales follows the latter interpretation, suggesting that here as elsewhere in the second decision, authority is a key issue: the problem is influence of others outside the episcopal hierarchy (*Prisciliano*, p. 53). Marie Odile Greffe likewise translates *persuasionis* as "under the influence of another" ("Etude sur le canon II du premier Concile," in *Primero Concilio Caesaraugustano: MDC aniversario* [Zaragoza, 1981], p. 163). The term *superstitio* has still stronger and more disturbing connotations of unorthodoxy or membership in an illegal religious sect like Manichaeism, whose adherents were known to fast on Sundays.

59. Greffe relates the two practices of Sunday fasting and Lenten withdrawal directly, suggesting that the members of the group withdrew during Lent precisely in order to observe Sunday fasts and other ascetic disciplines ("Etude sur le canon II," p. 163). This seems to me a possible but not a necessary explanation of how the two practices come to be denounced in the same canon, since their conjunction could also be explained by the fact that one targeted group observed both practices. Ramos y Loscertales believes Priscillian advocated a Sunday fast all year (*Prisciliano*, p. 108).

60. *Ep.* 36.28. Cf. Jerome's protest, addressed to the Spaniard Lucinus, that Sunday fasting is not Manichaean (*Ep.* 71.6). Of course, Sunday fasting has strong social as well as doctrinal implications. Vollman ("Priscillianus," col. 547), and Greffe ("Etude sur le canon II," pp. 165–66) call attention to the parallel with the Eustathians, who were condemned by the Council of Gangra not only for fasting on Sunday but also for eating on fast days observed by the rest of the church; here the emphasis seems to be not on the doctrinal implications of the practice but on the problematic refusal to conform to the dominant communal eating patterns.

61. The choice of the word *conventus* was probably dictated by both its ascetic and pejorative connotations; like the term *superstitio, conventus* could invoke an image of secret and seditious meetings (see Fontaine, "El ascetismo," pp. 202–3). *Conventus* is also the term used in Priscillian's purported confession to convening nocturnal meetings of shameful women (Severus, *Chron.* 2.50).

62. As with the first judgment, there is some question as to how the adjective *alienus* should be understood. Greffe considers the possible interpretations of "foreign" (e.g., Gallic), "pagan," and simply "other," in the sense of "houses where the Christians are not in the habit of meeting for the regular liturgical assemblies"; she favors this final interpretation ("Etude sur le canon II," pp. 171–72). Díaz y Díaz goes so far as to suggest that the term is unintelligible in its present context and attributes the text's incoherence to successive stages of redaction ("A propósito del Concilio de Zaragoza," p. 227). But here, as in the first judgment, the term quite likely distinguishes between family members (including slaves and freed persons and other dependents of a household as well as those related by birth or marriage) and those who are not part of the household. Fontaine suggests that the intent may be to allow for gatherings among the inhabitants of an estate, who might even constitute a permanently settled religious community, while prohibiting those who live outside the estate to participate ("El ascetismo," p. 204).

63. See especially *Tract.* 4, 58.6–20.

64. *ACS*, can. 3, ll. 42–44.

65. Manuel Sotomayor offers a recent and clear discussion of the various interpretations proposed by scholars ("El canon 3 del Concilio de Zaragoza del 380," in *Primero Concilio Caesaraugustano: MDC aniversario* [Zaragoza, 1981], pp. 177–87).

66. Ibid., pp. 184–87. Although Sotomayor stresses that the motivations of those who abstain cannot be known with certainty, Vollman suggests that groups like the Priscillianists may have abstained from communion with Christians whom they considered "impure" ("Priscillianus," cols. 547–48). Vollman here leaves open the possibility, dismissed by Ramos y Loscertales (*Prisciliano*, p. 55), that this decision is directed against the Priscillianists. Cf. Priscillian's remarks on the necessary purity of the priest who administers the sacrament of the Eucharist: "Quia corpus ac sanguinem Christi, quod est magnum pietatis sacramentum, manifestatum in carne, justificatum in spiritu, si quis indigne sumpserit, corporis ipsius sanginisque sit reus" (*Can. Ep. Pauli* 42).

67. *ACS*, can. 4, ll. 47–53.

68. A three-week period of fasting and prayer before Christmas or Epiphany is mentioned in a fragment attributed to Hilary of Poitiers and in letters attributed to the Galician Bachiarius (Chadwick, *Priscillian of Avila*, pp. 14–17). See also Luis García Iglesias, "Sobre el canon IV del Primer Concilio de Zaragoza," in *Primero Concilio Caesaraugustano: MDC aniversario* (Zaragoza, 1981), pp. 189–99.

69. Chadwick, *Priscillian of Avila*, p. 17.

70. Augustine, *Conf.* 9.6.

71. Priscillian, *Tract.* 1, 23.22–24.6.

72. Chadwick, *Priscillian of Avila*, pp. 18–20.

73. It is more likely that any perceived connection between Priscillian's ascetic practices and magic was fabricated by Ithacius than that it was due to any actual participation by Priscillian in magical rituals, as Chadwick suggests (ibid., pp. 18–20). Even Sulpicius Severus is sceptical about the basis of the charges of magic (*Chron.* 2.46). Ramos y Loscertales takes a moderating stance, suggesting that Priscillian did indeed study magic out of a general intellectual curiosity in his pre-Christian youth, but never actually practiced it (*Prisciliano*, pp. 74–75, 95, 101–2).

74. Cf. Ramos y Loscertales's attempt to provide some sort of rational justification for the discrepancy by suggesting that the group targeted in the fourth judgment is different from the group targeted in the second, and that the bishops have less concern about whether they will be able to impose their authority on the former group (ibid., p. 54).

75. *ACS*, can. 5, ll. 55–60.

76. A more precise assessment of the intent of the judgment depends upon the interpretation of the phrase *per disciplinam aut sententiam*. I follow the looser interpretation of Díaz y Díaz, who suggests that the phrase signifies something fairly general like "through disciplinary judgment" ("A propósito del Concilio de Zaragoza," p. 229). According to Ramos y Loscertales, however, the elements of *disciplina* and *sententia* are distinct, with *sententia* referring to a condemnation for heresy, which requires the following of a formal procedure of accusation, interrogation, trial, and sentencing, and *disciplina* to a disciplinary excommunication, which requires no such formal procedure; in this view, the fifth judgment intends to enforce universal episcopal compliance both with a formal condemnation of heresy and with a disciplinary excommunication, whether issued by a bishop independently, by a bishop in enforcement of the conciliar decisions, or by the council itself (*Prisciliano*, pp. 55–61). Ramos y Loscertales further suggests that Hydatius had excommunicated Instantius, Salvianus, Priscillian, and Elpidius before the council; that this excommunication was not accepted by the four or by Hyginus and some other bishops who received them in communion; and that in effort to strengthen the authority of the metropolitan bishop, the council supported his excommunication of the four by issuing its own disciplinary excommunication of the Lusitanian "rebels" and then by formulating the fifth judgment to force bishops to comply with both Hydatius' original excommunication and with the council's excommunication (*Prisciliano*, pp. 31–36, 59–61). It is not necessary, however, to assume with Ramos y Loscertales that the fifth judgment refers to either of these undocumented excommunications, since it could equally well refer to excommunications anticipated as a consequence of the enforcement of the council's judgments (Vollman, "Priscillianus," col. 502).

77. Cf. Elvira (309) can. 5, Arles (314) can. 17, Nicea (325) can. 5, Antioch (341) can. 6, Sardica (343) can. 13. See also Domingo Ramos-Lissón, "Estudio sobre el canon V del I Concilio de Caesaraugusta (380)," in *Primero Concilio Caesaraugustano: MDC aniversario* (Zaragoza, 1981), p. 223.

78. Severus, *Chron.* 2.47.

79. *ACS*, can. 6, ll. 63–68. There are a number of grammatical peculiarities in the language of this judgment. These may be attributable to the interpolation of marginal comments, as Díaz y Díaz suggests ("A propósito del Concilio de Zaragoza," pp. 230–32). Alternatively, they may reflect the text's close adherence to the verbal patterns of an original, complex discussion.

80. Díaz y Díaz points out that a correct interpretation of the phrase "on account of presumed luxury and vanity" (*propter luxum vanitatemque praesumptam*) requires acknowledging not only the use of the rhetorical device of hendiadys (the breaking up of a single complex idea into a series), but also the allusion to Eccles. 6:9: "melius est videre quod cupias, quam desiderare quod nescias, sed et hoc vanitas est et praesumptio spiritus" ("A próposito del Concilio de Zaragoza," p. 231 n. 8 and p. 234). That is to say, the monks view the bishops' enjoyment of the goods of the world as vanity or "emptiness"; yet their "presumption" is itself "vanity," the bishops counter. Contrast the ascetic interpretation given to the same scriptural passage by Priscilllian: "nobis omnia quae sub sole sum vana sunt et praesumptio perversi spiritus, scientes eum cum mundo esse periturum" (*Tract.* 1, 16.11–13).

81. *ACS*, can. 7, ll. 70–73.

82. Whether women would have been included among those recognized as "teachers" in the Spanish communities is difficult to determine. The council's first judgment reflects at least a tentative willingness to present women as the teachers of other women in order to seclude them from "strange men"; this evidence of course cuts both ways, as does the broader evidence for the masculinization of the teaching role in the fourth century. Susanna Elm's provocative study of Evagrius Ponticus' monastic rules for women and men is intriguing in this regard, insofar as it suggests that Evagrius is attempting to distinguish between the male ascetic goal of becoming a *gnostikos* of God, and therefore a teacher, and the female ascetic goal of "bodily" union with Christ, in which neither *gnosis* nor teaching plays a role ("Evagrius Ponticus' *Sententiae ad Virginem*," Dumbarton Oaks Papers 45 [1991] 97–120). Elm herself notes, however, that Evagrius addresses his clearest articulation of his doctrine of *gnosis* to Melania, a female ascetic, and that exceptional ascetic women could be addressed as "teachers." In addition, one might question whether the broader ascetic corpus does not provide many instances in which the gender boundaries delineated by Elm's reading of Evagrius are blurred, not only by "gnostic" women, but also by men for whom homoerotic imagery continues to play a large role in the articulation of the spiritual goal of union with God.

83. Prohibitive judgments that fail to specify a punishment generally reflect either extreme confidence on the part of the bishops, who have no fear of noncompliance, or extreme ambivalence and the desire to avoid confrontation on a ruling that might prove difficult to enforce (Leuchli, *Power and Sexuality*, pp. 33–38).

84. Priscillian, *Can. Ep. Pauli* 39.

85. Antonino Gonzáles Blanco surveys the role of teachers in the ancient church, rightly concluding that the seventh judgment presupposes a social context

in which teaching authority is not centralized ("El canon 7 del Concilio de Zaragoza (380) y sus implicationes sociales," in *Primero Concilio Caesaraugustana: MDC aniversario* [Zaragoza, 1981], pp. 237–53).

86. *ACS*, can. 8, ll. 75–78.

87. Only a few years later, however, a Roman synod addressing Gallic bishops was careful to distinguish the two classes of virgins (Siricius, *Ad gallos episcopos* 1.3–4). There were two Aquitanian bishops at the council of Saragossa, but whether they or any other Gallic bishops shared the Roman view at this point is unknown. The Synod of Valence (374), at which Phoebadius was also present, made no distinction between veiled and unveiled virgins when prescribing penance for a dedicated virgin's transgression of her vow.

88. Jerome did not object to the practice of Roman parents' dedicating their daughters to virginity at their birth, whereas Ambrose insisted that the vow should be voluntarily taken by the girl whenever she became spiritually mature (which might be as early as the onset of puberty at twelve), and the Council of Hippo in 393, followed by other African councils, set a minimum age of twenty-five for a virgin's consecretion. If it had in fact enforced the high minimum age requirement of forty, the Council of Saragossa would drastically have reduced the number of virgins wearing the veil. Following Keith Hopkins, "On the Probable Age Structure of the Roman Population," *Population Studies* 20 (1966): 245–64, I calculate that assuming life expectancy for women at birth were thirty years and the patterns established in the U.N. model life tables applied, if women vowed virginity and "took the veil" at puberty (between the ages of ten and fourteen) and the number of new virgins each year were constant from 310 to 380, the bishops' ruling would have reduced the number of veiled virgins by more than 60 percent. If, on the other hand, the number of women vowing virginity doubled in the decade from 370 to 380, the reduction would be still greater, roughly 70 percent.

89. The right of consecration implies an acknowledged liturgical role for the bishop. The earliest evidence of a liturgical ceremony of dedication is Ambrose's description of his sister's consecration by Pope Liberius in the basilica of St. Peter on Epiphany in the year 353 (*De virginibus* 3.1.1); note, however, that Ambrose here makes no mention of veiling but only of donning a somber monastic habit. René Metz gives a thorough treatment of the consecration of virgins in late-fourth-century Rome in *La Consécration des vierges dans l'église romaine* (Paris: Presses universitaires de France, 1954), pp. 95–138. Metz admits that there is no clear evidence of ceremonies of episcopal consecration of virgins in fourth- and fifth-century Gaul: "nous n'avons pour la Gaule aucun texte de cette époque qui exige effectivement du consecrateur des vierges le caractère épiscopal" ("La Consécration des vierges en Gaule, des origines à l'apparation des livres liturgiques," *Revue de droit canonique* 6 [1956]: 328). He nevertheless thinks such episcopal ceremonies commonly took place in Gaul as in Rome, citing as his primary support the letter traditionally attributed to Sulpicius Severus: "quasi sanctiores puriores que hostiae pro voluntatis suae meritis a Sancto Spiritu eliguntur, et per summam sacerdotem Dei offeruntur altario" (*Ep.* 2 *Ad Claudiam sororem de virginitate* 1). The phrase

"high priest" could, however, refer as easily to Christ as to the bishop, given the metaphorical character of the passage; note also the emphasis on the "merits of [the virgins'] will" rather than episcopal consecration; finally, the letter to which Metz refers is not securely tied to Gaul (see, e.g., B. R. Rees, *The Letters of Pelagius and His Followers* [Woodbridge, Suffolk: Boydell Press, 1991], p. 71). On Gallic virgins more generally, see also Metz, "Les Vierges chrétiennes en Gaule au IVe siècle," in *Saint Martin et son temps*, Studia Anselmiana 46 (Rome: Herder, 1961), pp. 109–32.

90. See Tertullian, *De virginibus velandis*.

91. Consider, e.g., the abovementioned letter attributed traditionally to Sulpicius Severus: "Nam et Christi sponsas virgines dicere ecclesiastica nobis permittit auctoritas, dum sponsarum modo eas Domino consecrat et velat, ostendens eas vel maxime habituras spirituale connubium quae subterfugerint carnale consortium" (*Ep. 2 Ad Claudiam sororem de virginitate* 1). Raymond d'Izarnay argues for a very close correlation between the fourth-century Christian marriage rite, *velatio conjugalis*, and the ritual veiling of virgins as practiced by Ambrose in Milan in the late fourth century ("Marriage et consécration virginale au IVe siècle," *Vie spirituelle*, suppl. 24 [1953]: 92–118).

92. Compare the costume of ancient Roman priestesses: the *flaminica Dialis* wore a red bridal veil, and the Vestal Virgins dressed their hair like brides. On the crucial function of this "liminal" dress in defining the priestesses' power, see Mary Beard, "The Sexual Status of Vestal Virgins," *Journal of Roman Studies* 70 (1980): 12–27, and N. Boels, "Le Statut religieux de la flaminica Dialis," *Revue des études latines* 51 (1973): 77–100.

93. I tend to assume that the women themselves, as well as the bishops, would have experienced the ruling as an attempt to reverse their social and spiritual elevation as perpetual virgins—itself a liminal reversal of their "normal" status as women. Note however the important critique of Carolyn Walker Bynum, who cautions that "liminality" may itself be an androcentric category and highlights the element of continuity—rather than reversal or elevation—in medieval women's appropriations of the polysemic symbol of the "bride of Christ," for example ("Women's Stories, Women's Symbols: A Critique of Victor Turner's Theory of Liminality," in *Anthropology and the Study of Religion*, ed. R. L. Moor and F. E. Reynolds [Chicago: CSSR, 1984], pp. 105–25). Susanna Elm, who cites Bynum's work, brings a slightly different perspective to bear on the theme of female "continuity," noting that Evagrius Ponticus views ascetic women as differing from their male counterparts in that they do not progress spiritually in this life but achieve mystical union with Christ only in the moment of their deaths ("Evagrius Ponticus' *Sententiae ad virginem*," pp. 111–14). Certainly, a similar tendency in the view of ascetic women can be documented for the late-fourth-century west, e.g., in the attention given to the highly eroticized deaths—rather than the lives—of the virgin martyrs so extravagantly praised by men like Ambrose of Milan or the Spaniard Prudentius. Here, however, we are clearly still in the realm, not of women's self-understanding, but of alternative androcentric readings of women's ascetic "liminality."

94. Sotomayor notes concern about the "weaknesses of virgins" in fourth-century Spain in the following episcopal documents: Elvira (c. 300) can. 13, Siricius' letter to Himerius of Tarragona (385), and Toledo (400) can. 6 ("Sobre el canon VIII del Concilio de Zaragoza del 380," in *Primero Concilio Caesaraugustano: MDC aniversario* [Zaragoza, 1981], p. 261).

95. Aristotle (*Historia animalium* 7.5.585a) and Pliny the Elder (*Historia naturalis* 7.14.61) regard forty as the average age of menopause; Soranus (*Gynaeciorum* 1, 4.20) puts it between forty and fifty; and Oribasius (*Eclogae medicamentorum* 142) opts for fifty (D. Amundsen and C. J. Diers, "The Age of Menopause in Classical Greece and Rome," *Human Biology* 42 [1970]: 79–86).

96. Once past menopause, a woman was no longer perceived as desirous, desirable, or even fully female. Jerome remarks that a postmenopausal woman "ceases to be a woman and is freed from the curse of God" (mulier esse desiit, a Dei maledictione fit libera), i.e., she no longer desires or is subjected to her husband (*Adversus Helvidium* 20). Thus the postmenopausal woman is transformed, not only physically and socially, but also theologically, being returned to her prelapsarian state.

97. Peter Brown, *The Body and Society: Men, Women, and Sexual Renunciation in Early Christianity* (New York: Columbia University Press, 1988), pp. 260–61.

98. Elizabeth Castelli emphasizes the extent to which early Christianity "adopted the reigning idea of women's sexuality as token of exchange and reinforced it by investing it with theological significance" ("Virginity and Its Meaning for Women's Sexuality in Early Christianity," *Journal of Feminist Studies in Religion* 2 [1986]: 86).

99. Consider especially Prudentius' spectacular portraits of the virgin martyrs Eulalia and Agnes (*Peristephanon* 3, 14). See also Patricia Cox Miller's nuanced treatment of Jerome's deeply ambivalent response to the young virgin Eustochium's sexuality in "The Blazing Body: Ascetic Desire in Jerome's Letter to Eustochium," *Journal of Early Christian Studies* 1 (1993): 21–45.

100. Laeuchli, *Power and Sexuality*, p. 4.

101. Peter Brown, "Pelagius and His Supporters: Aims and Environment," *Journal of Theological Studies*, n.s., 19 (1968): 98, uses the metaphor of centrifugal force to describe Pelagianism's tendency "to scatter, to form a pattern of little groups, each striving to be an *élite*, each anxious to rise above their neighbours and rivals."

CHAPTER 2. "MANICHAEAN"

1. On the date of Priscillian's trial and execution, see Chadwick, *Priscillian of Avila*, pp. 132–38. The dating of these events has traditionally hinged on the date of Ambrose's second mission to Trier, which took place during the closing phases of the trial (Ambrose, *Ep.* 24). Chadwick surveys scholarly arguments for dating Ambrose's second mission anytime from the spring of 384 to the spring of 387 (pp. 135–36 n. 3); he himself suggests the summer of 386 as the most probable date

for Ambrose's second mission, noting that 385 is also a possibility (p. 137). More recently, A. R. Birley has reopened the question, suggesting that Sulpicius Severus' *Life of Martin* provides evidence that Priscillian's trial did not begin before 386; he further argues that Ambrose's second mission, and therefore the end of Priscillian's trial, can most plausibly be dated to 387 ("Magnus Maximus and the Persecution of Heresy," *Bulletin of the John Rylands University Library* 66 [1983–84]: 29–33). Finally, the work of Daniel Williams further supports dating Ambrose's second mission, and therefore the trial of Priscillian, to the period after Easter of 386 ("The Ecclesiastical Politics of Ambrose of Milan: His Two Embassies to Trier" [paper delivered to the North American Patristic Society, May 1994]; see also Daniel H. Williams, *Ambrose of Milan and the End of the Nicene-Arian Conflicts* [Oxford University Press, forthcoming], chs. 7 and 8).

2. Severus' depiction of the controversy in political rather than theological terms is influenced not only by his choice of genre and rhetorical strategy but also by contemporary ecclesiastical politics and personal circumstances. Fontaine offers a brilliant treatment of Severus' relation to the models of classical historiography, focusing particularly on his use of Sallust's portrait of Catiline to create a condemning depiction of both Priscillian and his opponents as political conspirators ("L'Affaire Priscillien," pp. 355–92). On the factionalism of the fifth-century ecclesiastical politics of Gaul, see Mathisen, *Ecclesiastical Factionalism*.

3. Van Dam, *Leadership*, p. 95.

4. Priscillian, *Liber ad Damasum episcopum* = *Tract.* 2, 34–43.

5. Priscillian, *Liber apologeticus* = *Tract.* 1, 3–33; id., *Liber de fide et de apocryphis* = *Tract.* 3, 44–56.

6. Priscillian, *Tract.* 3, 51.8–9; id., *Tract.* 1, 10.24, 24.8, 26.2, 27.27, 33.12–13.

7. Severus, *Chron.* 2.48.

8. The letter's account of the conflict at Merida presents a potential problem for the argument for Priscillian's authorship, since it refers from a distinctly episcopal point of view to events that almost certainly took place before Priscillian's ordination. Thus D. G. Morin proposes that Instantius was in fact the author of the second tractate ("Pro Instantio: Contre l'attribution à Priscillien des opuscula du manuscrit de Würzburg," *Revue bénédictine* 30 [1913]: 167–72). Josef Martin refutes Morin's arguments and supports the traditional attribution of the letter to Priscillian ("Priscillianus oder Instantius?" *Historisches Jahrbuch* 47 (1927): 237–51), and in more recent years, Ramos y Loscertales (*Prisciliano*, pp. 112–17) and Chadwick (*Priscillian of Avila*, pp. 31–32, 69), among others, have likewise deemed Priscillian the most probable author of the *Letter to Damasus*; Vollman considers Priscillian's authorship possible, if not probable ("Priscillianus," cols. 556–57). In further support of Priscillian's authorship of the second tractate, I argue that it is precisely the account of the conflict at Merida in the *Letter to Damasus* that most closely reflects Priscillian's concerns and point of view; the episcopal voice with which he recounts the events is part of his overall effort to buttress the authority of his own episcopacy (see also Ramos y Loscertales, *Prisciliano*, pp. 64–70).

9. Severus, an ascetic who was himself vulnerable to charges of Manichaeism,

makes no mention of Manichaeism in his account of the Priscillianist controversy, referring obliquely to "heresy" or "gnosticism" instead (*Chron.* 2.46–51)

10. Priscillian, *Tract.* 2, 39.17–18. Compare Priscillian's account of the events leading up to the Council of Saragossa; there, too, he portrays his supporters as living peaceably when disputes suddenly arose from without (ibid., 34.19–35.7).

11. Ibid., 39.18–23.

12. Ibid., 39.23–28. Cf. Priscillian's opinion on the necessity for moral purity in the bishop: "Quia episcopus inreprehensibilis esse debeat" (*Can. Ep. Pauli* 45).

13. Priscillian, *Tract.* 2, 35.5–7.

14. A letter of Siricius of Rome suggests that the issue of clerical celibacy and specifically the begetting of children by bishops, presbyters, and deacons, was being hotly debated in Spain circa 385 (*Ep.* 1 *Ad Himerium Episcopum Tarraconensem*). Although the Roman bishop's letter makes no explicit mention of the Priscillianists, it is possible that the debate over clerical celibacy was in fact an aspect of the Priscillianist controversy. Chadwick speculates that "if Himerius of Tarraco's letter to Rome is understood to refer even obliquely to the Priscillianist affair, then the charge can be expected to be that Hydatius had cohabited with his wife or even that she had secretly produced an infant, such evidence of conjugal acts being felt to be unsuitable in a bishop." He goes on to suggest that moral delicacy motivated Priscillian's silence: "The nature of the charge Priscillian cannot bring himself to mention" (*Priscillian of Avila*, p. 31). This latter suggestion is not convincing, given both the importance of this charge for Priscillian's defense and the overall sophistication of Priscillian's rhetoric in this letter. The fact that Priscillian fails to specify the charges brought against Hydatius surely indicates that it was not in his interest to do so.

15. Priscillian, *Tract.* 2, 43.6–7.

16. Ibid., 40.1.

17. Chadwick suggests that the two Lusitanian bishops were simply performing their duty in intervening in the conflict: "the responsibility for judgement necessarily lay in the hands of the other bishops of Lusitania" (*Priscillian of Avila*, p. 31). But other Lusitanian bishops were apparently able to remain silent and uninvolved, and I find it difficult not to see Instantius' and Salvianus' intervention as remarkably assertive, if not outright aggressive.

18. Priscillian, *Tract.* 2, 40.1–8.

19. Ibid., 40.5.

20. Vollman suggests rather that it was Hydatius' bias or prejudice that illegitimated his authority in this matter ("Priscillianus," col. 503). He calls attention to a parallel passage in Severus' text—*si ipsi suspecti habantur* (Severus, *Chron.* 2.49)—which he interprets to indicate that the bishops at the Council of Bordeaux should have referred the matter to other bishops, rather than to the emperor, "if they themselves were considered suspicious."

21. Priscillian, *Tract.* 2, 40.7–8.

22. Ibid., 40.10–13.

23. Puech suggests that Hydatius was not far from wrong if he sensed that

there was a conspiracy against his episcopacy ("Les Origines du Priscillianisme," p. 183). Chadwick likewise considers it probable that Instantius and Salvianus were attempting to depose Hydatius and consecrate a successor, perhaps Priscillian himself (*Priscillian of Avila*, p. 31–33).

24. Priscillian, *Tract.* 2, 40.11–21.

25. Ibid., 40.21–27.

26. This is also the view of Vollman ("Priscillianus," col. 503). Babut sees Priscillian as originally part of the Meridan laity, but places his elevation to the episcopacy before the events at Merida (*Priscillien*, p. 85). Ramos y Loscertales differs; he makes a sharp distinction between the opposition to Hydatius in Merida—which in his view was only among the clergy—and in the congregations of Instantius and Salvianus—which in his view was dominated by certain lay people, among whom was the itinerant teacher Priscillian (*Prisciliano*, pp. 64, 115–16).

27. Priscillian, *Tract.* 2, 42.21–23.

28. Severus, *Chron.* 2.47.

29. Priscillian, *Tract.* 2, 40.27–41.2.

30. It would not have been the first time in Meridan history that a bishop had been deposed by a group of moral rigorists. Cyprian writes in 257 to the Meridan deacon and laity who had deposed and replaced a bishop whose behavior during persecution compromised his moral purity; maintaining that a people have the right not only to choose worthy bishops but also to separate themselves from sinful bishops, Cyprian supports the Meridan deposition in the face of opposition from Stephen of Rome (*Ep.* 67).

31. Severus, *Chron.* 2.47.

32. Severus accuses Hydatius and Ithacius of rash behavior in appealing to the civil authorities: "sed parum sanis consiliis saeculares judices adeunt" (*Chron.* 2.47). He is still more disapproving of the Spanish bishops' collaboration with the civil trial at Trier that resulted in the execution of Priscillian and several of his followers (*Chron.* 2.49–51).

33. Contemporary laws promulgated in the west include *Codex Theodosianus* 16.5.3 (372), 16.5.4 (376–380), 16.5.5 (379). An anti-Manichean law issued in Rome in 389—later than the Spanish controversy itself but predating the composition of Severus' *Chronicle*—echoes Severus' statement that the heretics were expelled, not only from their churches or cities, but from the whole world (Severus, *Chron.* 2.47; *Codex Theodosianus* 16.5.19).

34. Priscillian, *Tract.* 2, 41.2–3.

35. Severus, *Chron.* 2.48.

36. Vollman finds it most likely that Hydatius sought simply to have standing laws against Manichaeans and other heretics enforced, e.g., *Codex Theodosianus* 16.5.3, 5, 7, 9 ("Priscillianus," col. 504). Aline Rousselle offers a more detailed interpretation of the processes followed in securing Priscillian's exile, attempting to harmonize the evidence of Priscillian's *Letter to Damasus*, Severus' *Chronicle*, and contemporary sources for secular and ecclesiastical law. She suggests that Hydatius requested that the local administration expel Priscillian and his associates

from their churches as heretics immediately after the Council of Saragossa; they refused, probably because no one had actually been condemned by name at the council. Next, suppressing Priscillian's name, Hydatius appealed to the emperor for a more general ruling against heretics; his appeal may have been responsible for the issuance by Gratian of *Codex Theodosianus* 16.5.4 (commonly dated 376–80). Subsequently, the civil authorities in Spain decided to apply the rescript to expel Priscillian and his followers, who were at this point designated "pseudo-bishops and Manichaeans" ("Quelques aspects politiques de l'affaire priscillianiste," *Revue des études anciennes* 83 [1981]: 86–87). Note that Rousselle's identification of *Codex Theodosianus* 16.5.4 as (at least indirectly) anti-Priscillianist in origin is questionable; while scholars have traditionally identified this as a piece of anti-Arian legislation betraying the influence of Ambrose on Gratian, Gunther Gottlieb has persuasively argued that it is instead to be read as anti-Donatist in intention (*Ambrosius von Mailand und Kaiser Gratian* [Göttingen: Vandenhoeck & Ruprecht, 1973], pp. 63–68).

37. It has often been assumed that Hydatius' apparent role in the process was based on his authority as the "metropolitan" bishop of Lusitania, under whose jurisdiction the sees of Instantius, Salvianus, and Priscillian probably fell. The events of the Priscillianist controversy do not, however, indicate that such authority was consistently acknowledged. Manuel C. Díaz y Díaz notes, "On a l'habitude de parler de diocèses et de provinces qui dépendraient des sièges épiscopaux ou métropolitains, ce qui s'accorde avec la situation générale dans la deuxième moitié du iv*ᵉ* siècle. Mais . . . il me semble difficile de prouver que la notion même de territoire ait une certaine consistence pendant le iv*ᵉ* siècle dans la Péninsule" ("L'Expansion du christianisme," p. 92). See also the summary remarks of Jean Gaudemet in regard to the institution of the authority of the metropolitan bishop in Spain: "L'organisation métropolitaine y fut tardive. . . . Le métropolitain et la nécessité de son concours aux élections épiscopales n'apparaissent qu'au cours du v*ᵉ* siècle" (*L'Église dans l'Empire romain (iv*ᵉ*–v*ᵉ* siècles* [Paris: Sirey, 1955], pp. 387–88).

38. Priscillian, *Tract.* 2, 41.3–5.

39. Ibid., 41.7–13.

40. Severus, *Chron.* 2.47.

41. Priscillian, *Tract.* 2, 41.10–11; Severus, *Chron.* 2.48.

42. Priscillian, *Tract.* 2, 36.13–39.16, 41.21–42.12

43. Ibid. 3, 44–56.

44. E.g., ibid. 2, 35.15–19, 35.21–22, 39.20–21, 40.7–8, 42.19–21.

45. Ibid., 35.23–24.

46. Ibid. 1, 3–33.

47. Puech suggests that it is not merely difficult but impossible ("Les Origines du Priscillianisme," p. 185).

48. Martin argues against Morin ("Pro Instantio," pp. 153–72) that the first tractate was composed by Priscillian in the period before the Council of Saragossa, without being written specifically for that council ("Priscillianus oder Instantius," pp. 237–51). More recently, Chadwick has supported the theory that the *Apology*

was written by Priscillian as a layperson in the period before the Council of Sara-gossa, although he understands the document to have been addressed to the coun-cil itself (*Priscillian of Avila*, pp. 47–51).

49. Babut argues that the *Apology* represents the profession of the Meridan laity—with Priscillian as ghostwriter—referred to in the *Letter to Damasus* (*Priscil-lien*, pp. 143–46). Ramos y Loscertales differs with Babut on a number of points of interpretation of the Meridan conflict but agrees that the period between the coun-cils of Saragossa and Bordeaux, and specifically the period immediately following the conflict at Merida, is the most likely setting for the *Apology*; he further suggests that the confident tone of the work makes a date immediately after Priscillian's ordination probable (*Prisciliano*, pp. 112–17).

50. Morin, following J. Dierich ("Die Quellen zur Geschichte Priscillians" [diss., Breslau, 1897], pp. 35–40), argues that the *Apology* was directed to the Coun-cil of Bordeaux and furthermore proposes that Instantius was the author of the tractate ("Pro Instantio," pp. 153–72). Among the supporters of Morin's theory is D'Alès (*Priscillien et l'Espagne chrétienne*). More recently, Vollman has judged it likely that the *Apology* was written either during the period between Gratian's re-script and its appeal or in preparation for the Council of Bordeaux; he, however, considers episcopal authorship highly improbable and suggests that the tractate was composed by a lay follower of Priscillian ("Priscillianus," col. 558).

51. The *Apology* is sufficiently different in style and tone from the *Letter to Damasus* that some scholars have found it difficult to attribute the two to the same author. Vollman notes, "Ich halte für ausgemacht, dass Tr. I nicht von P[riscil-lianus] stammt, für höchst wahrscheinlich, dass Tr. I und II nicht den gleichen Ver-fasser haben und für wahrscheinlich, dass der Verfasser [des Tr. I] ein Laie, oder besser, ein nichtbischöflicher Kleriker ist" ("Priscillianus," cols. 557–58). Never-theless, there are good reasons to attribute the *Apology*, as well as the *Letter to Damasus*, to Priscillian, and the differences between the two works can be attrib-uted to differences in audience and circumstance of composition rather than di-verse authorship. Note that Vollman's conviction that Priscillian is not the author of the *Apology* rests primarily on his dating of the *Apology* to a period after Priscil-lian's episcopal ordination; I suggest that this dating is faulty, however, and that the document was most likely composed by Priscillian before his ordination.

52. Priscillian, *Tract.* 2, 43.10.

53. Ibid. 1, 4.8–11.

54. Severus, *Chron.* 2.46.

55. Priscillian, *Tract.* 1, 4.11–5.4 ; 6.10–11; 5.6–8; 4.2–4; 3.12–4.8. Cf. the clos-ing lines of Priscillian's preface to the *Can. Ep. Pauli*, in which he protests that he has "faithfully made the content of the scriptures open, being the enemy of no one."

56. *Tract.* 1, 3.6–7 (cf. 1, 14.5 and 33.7); 4.2; 6.14–17.

57. Ibid., 5.10; cf. 3, 49.8.

58. Chadwick suggests that the "Binionite" heresy was coined by Priscillian in response to accusations that he was a "Unionite," pointing out that the term "Unionita" is applied to Sabellius by a work falsely attributed to Jerome (*Indiculus*

de haeresibus), which may be based on the *Apology* of Ithacius (*Priscillian of Avila*, p. 87). However, there is in fact no evidence that Priscillian's unitive theology was an issue in the controversies of his lifetime. In 400, trinitarian issues were implicitly raised in the demand of the Council of Toledo that the Galicians Symphosius and Comasius condemn Priscillian's statement that the Son is *innascibilis* (*Exemplar*, ll. 27–37, 52–58). It was not until the second decade of the fifth century that Orosius explicitly charged Priscillian with trinitarian errors: "Trinitatem autem solo verbo loquebatur, nam unionem absque ulla exsistentia aut proprietate adserens sublato 'et' patrem filium spiritum sanctum hunc esse unum Christum docebat" (*Commonitorium de errore Priscillianistarum et Origenistarum* 2). Several mid-fifth-century documents that also stem from Galicia associate Priscillianism with the failure to distinguish adequately between the persons of the Trinity and consequently with the claims that either God suffered or the man Jesus did not suffer. But Abilio Barbero de Aguilera argues that the anti-Priscillianist *Regula fidei* falsely attributed to the Council of Toledo (400) is in fact a mid-fifth-century revision of a fourth-century document reflecting the trinitarian concerns of an earlier, pre-Priscillianist era; the redacted *Regula fidei* in turn shaped the anti-Priscillianist *Commonitorium* and *Libellus* that Turibius of Astorga addressed to Leo of Rome (preserved only in Leo, *Ep.* 15) and the anti-Priscillianist chapters of the Council of Braga (561) ("El priscilianismo: ¿Herejía o movimiento social?" 25–41).

59. Priscillian, *Tract.* 1, 6.19–7.26.

60. See, e.g., the *Longer Latin Formula of Abjuration*, chs. 2, 6, 7, and 8 (Alfred Adam, *Texte zum Manichäismus* [Berlin: Walter de Gruyter, 1954], pp. 90–93).

61. A letter of Siricius of Rome refers to controversy in Spain over the rebaptism of heretics (*Ep.* 1 *Ad Himerium Episcopum Tarraconensem* 2 [385]), and Priscillian's strong emphasis on baptism and his general "rigorist" stance make it at least plausible that he was one of those who denied the validity of heretical baptism.

62. Contrast the view of Chadwick, who seems to assume that all errors denounced by Priscillian reflect accusations against him: "The nature of the heresies disowned . . . makes it evident that the Priscillianists are accused of a Patripassian doctrine of God, a docetic Christology, Manichaeism, studies in heretical apocrypha, and nocturnal orgies, whether magical or sexual" (*Priscillian of Avila*, p. 47; see also pp. 90–91).

63. Priscillian, *Tract.* 1, 7.23–8.4.

64. Chadwick suggests that the *Physiologus* "supplies an almost exact illustration of the doctrine which Priscillian so elaborately disowns." In this work, scriptural animals are interpreted as symbols of God, Christ, and the Spirit, as well as of the ascetic conflict with temptation. To Chadwick, it seems likely that the Priscillianists studied and admired such a work; their "elaborate disowning," then, responds only to malicious caricatures of the work, not to the work itself (*Priscillian of Avila*, pp. 92–94). Alternatively, Priscillian might genuinely have disagreed with those parts of the *Physiologus* that interpret animals positively. However, without any firm date for the *Physiologus*, the suggestion of any possible Priscillianist use of or opposition to the work remains extremely speculative.

65. Priscillian, *Tract.* 1, 13.14–16.

66. Ibid., 9.15–19.

67. Ibid., 12.21–23.

68. Ibid., 12.19–21; cf. 1, 13.23, and 3, 47.25 and 51.13.

69. Ibid. 1, 8.16–17; cf. 28.8.

70. Ibid. 1, 9.25–27; cf. 1, 19.22, 6, 69.10–11 and 80.1–2, 8, 87.7–10.

71. Ibid. 1, 9.27–10.1.

72. In his *Liber de fide et de apocryphis*, Priscillian explicitly opposes Hydatius' demand that all apocryphal literature be condemned, citing the divine command to "search the scriptures" (*Tract.* 3, 51.8–13). Cf. the parallel invocation of John 5.39 in *Tract.* 3, 47.25.

73. Priscillian, *Tract.* 1, 15.1–6 (cf. Pss. 80.13 and 91.13); 1, 18.7–8 (cf. Rev. 13.1).

74. Nag Hammadi Codex II 1, pp. 10, 11, 24; English trans., F. Wisse, in *Nag Hammadi Library*, pp. 110, 111, 118. We know that the *Apocryphon of John* circulated in various versions; both a long and a short version are extant in Coptic translations of Greek originals, and Irenaeus seems to have known a work similar to, but not identical with any of, these versions (F. Wisse, "Introduction to the Apocryphon of John," in *The Nag Hammadi Library in English*, 3d ed., ed. J. M. Robinson [San Francisco: Harper & Row, 1988], pp. 104–5). That Latin translations may have circulated is not out of the question, especially if they were used by the Manichaeans as well.

75. Priscillian, *Tract.* 1, 10.24; 13.20–21.

76. Ibid., 14.5–14.

77. Ibid., 16.9–26.

78. *Commonitorium de errore Priscillianistarum et Origenistarum* 2. It is not certain whether the fragment of Priscillian's letter is authentic, whether Orosius quotes it fairly in context, or whether the system outlined in the fragment and in Orosius' supplementary description would have been considered particularly reprehensible by most of Priscillian's Christian contemporaries (Chadwick, *Priscillian of Avila*, pp. 191–202).

79. E. R. Dodds describes late-antique cosmology with an emphasis on its most dualistic articulations (*Pagan and Christian in an Age of Anxiety* [New York: Norton, 1965], pp. 5–7). See also Jean Pépin's discussion of more positive ancient religious attitudes toward the cosmos ("Cosmic Piety," in *Classical Mediterranean Spirituality*, ed. A. H. Armstrong [New York: Crossroad, 1986], pp. 408–35).

80. Priscillian, *Tract.* 1, 16.13. Cf. the more explicit references to Ecclus. 17.31 in 1, 23.1–2, and 5, 64.1.

81. Ibid. 6, 78.22–24.

82. Anti-astrological polemics in the Greek church commonly took the form both of questioning the validity of astrology per se and of proclaiming that Christ has freed humanity from the domination of the heavenly powers. See Utto Riedinger, *Der heilige Schrift im Kampf der griechischen Kirche gegen die Astrologie von Origenes bis Johannes von Damaskos* (Innsbruck: Universitätsverlag, 1956). Chadwick suggests that the second argument—which concedes a limited validity to the as-

trological science—was less common in the west, in which context Priscillian's language may have appeared more radical (*Priscillian of Avila*, pp. 200–201). However, the very proliferation of Christian anti-astrological arguments in the west in the last quarter of the fourth century indicates that many Christians did not fully reject astrological speculations; see, e.g., David Hunter's discussion of the context of Ambrosiaster's late-fourth-century *De fato* ("Ambrosiaster, Astral Fatalism, and the Prehistory of the Pelagian Controversy" [paper delivered at the North American Patristic Society Conference, 1990]).

83. Priscillian, *Tract.* 1, 17.29–18.9.

84. Ibid., 18.28.

85. Nag Hammadi Codex II 1, p. 24; trans. Wisse, in *Nag Hammadi Library*, pp. 118–19.

86. See Samuel N. C. Lieu, *Manichaeism in the Later Roman Empire and Medieval China: A Historical Survey* (Manchester: Manchester University Press, 1985), pp. 16–17.

87. Priscillian, *Tract.* 1, 18.29–22.12.

88. This argument is developed at length in ibid. 3, 44–56.

89. Ibid. 1, 22.10–12.

90. Ibid., 30.14 and 17. Cf. 3, 46.22–26.

91. Ibid. 3, 56.6–7.

92. Ibid., 46.28–47.1.

93. Ibid. 1, 22.13–23.4.

94. Chadwick remarks that "it is even possible that the wretched man wrote his own death-warrant by these two fierce anti-Manichaean sentences" (*Priscillian of Avila*, p. 97).

95. Priscillian, *Tract.* 2, 41.16–17; id., *Can. Ep. Pauli* 46.

96. E.g., *Codex Theodosianus* 9.16.1 (319–20), 9.16.4 (357), 9.16.5 (357; 356), 9.16.7 (364), 9.16.8 (370; 373). Hermann Funke gives an overview of anti-magical legislation under the fourth-century Christian emperors, concluding that it did not deviate significantly from pre-Christian legislation ("Majestäts- und Magieprozesse bei Ammianus Marcellinus," *Jahrbuch für Antike und Christentum* 10 [1967]: 146–51).

97. Priscillian, *Tract.* 2, 39.8–10.

98. Ibid. 1, 23.4–21.

99. Ibid. 1, 23.22–24.5.

100. Ibid., 24.1–3.

101. Ibid., 24.10–11.

102. Chadwick, *Priscillian of Avila*, pp. 51–52.

103. Ibid., p. 54–55.

104. Priscillian, *Tract.* 1, 25.25–26.12.

105. Severus, *Chron.* 2.50.

106. Priscillian, *Tract.* 1, 24.13–14.

107. Chadwick, *Priscillian of Avila*, p. 55.

108. Priscillian, *Tract.* 1, 23.1–2; cf. 5, 64.1, 1, 16.13, and 6, 78.22–24.

109. Ibid. 1, 24.3.

110. Ibid., 28.15–16; 28.24–26.

111. Ibid., 29.13–15; 30.13–15; 31.21–24.

112. On this last point, see Peter Brown's classic study, *The Making of Late Antiquity* (Cambridge, Mass.: Harvard University Press, 1978).

113. Rebecca Lyman notes of the cosmological issues implicit in the Arian controversy that there, too, "the primary theological issue was . . . transcendence and the alienation of material existence" (*Christology and Cosmology: Models of Divine Activity in Origen, Eusebius, and Athanasius* [Oxford: Clarendon Press, 1993], p. 139).

114. Clark, *Origenist Controversy*, p. 245.

115. Ibid., pp. 4, 9.

116. Note that the seeming paradox of a "cosmology" expressed in "uncosmological" terms results in part from a certain slippage in my own application of the terminology of "cosmology," which in common theological usage may refer either more narrowly to an account of the creation and/or the structure of the universe or more broadly to a religious "worldview" or a basic theological "model" articulated within the context of a "worldview" (see, e.g., *Cosmology and Theology*, ed. D. Tracy and N. Lash, Concilium 166 [New York: Seabury Press, 1983], p. vii, and Lyman, *Christology and Cosmology*, pp. 3–6). Such slippage is, however, legitimate where it is the case that a particular theological worldview or model is implicit in a particular view of creation, and vice versa; thus, Rebecca Lyman argues that ancient Christian cosmology should not be marginalized as "philosophical" or, worse yet, "heretical," but that "a more helpful course is to consider early cosmology as the theological model that reveals basic assumptions about the nature and relation of God and humanity" (*Christology and Cosmology*, p. 5). In the case of Priscillian, as we shall see, to speak of the human being is to speak implicitly of the cosmos, which is in turn to address the broader issue of the relationship of the material and the divine, of the human person and God, of creation and redemption.

117. Clark, *Origenist Controversy*, p. 246.

118. Clark is explicit about her interest in the intersection of "theory (theology) and praxis (liturgical and ascetic practice)" (ibid., p. 4). Her discussion of eucharistic dimensions of the anthropomorphite controversy is particularly illumining (pp. 50, 63–66, 105–16, 156–57); she also firmly grounds the anti-Origenism of Epiphanius, Theophilus, and Jerome in late-fourth- and early-fifth-century debates over asceticism, marriage, and reproduction (pp. 94–100, 113–51).

119. Priscillian, *Tract.* 5, 63.23–25); cf. 6, 73.9–10, 7, 83.24–84.1.

120. Ibid. 5, 63.17–23.

121. Ibid., 63.25–27.

122. Ibid., 64.83–86.

123. Ibid. 6, 73.3–13.

124. Ibid., 93.3–12.

125. Cf. ibid. 5, 65.27–66.3.

126. Ibid. 6, 73.3–18.

127. For this language I am indebted to Patricia Cox Miller, who adapts Jean Vernant's analysis of archaic Greek constructions of the human body and applies it to the Christian desert literature, suggesting that these pre- and postclassical periods have in common both "a comparative standard for perceiving human identity" and the "use of the image of a divine, 'dazzling' body as the privileged signifying ground of that 'dim' human identity" ("Desert Asceticism and 'The Body from Nowhere,' " *Journal of Early Christian Studies* 2 [1994]: 137–53, 140).

128. Priscillian, *Tract.* 7, 82.7–84.17.

129. Miller explicitly distinguishes the anthropological assumptions of the desert literature from "the Platonic, and later Cartesian, dichotomous model of human composition that splits the person into a positive soul or mind housed in a negative body construed as a prison or mechanistic object in space" ("Desert Asceticism," p. 140). Cf. Brown's parallel suggestion that late-ancient thought was marked, not so much by a sharpened dichotomy of soul and body, as by a sense of the distance separating the "soul" and the "true soul" or heavenly genius (*Making of Late Antiquity*, pp. 68–69).

130. Priscillian, *Tract.* 5, 67.12–18.

131. For an "Origenist" view of the soteriological function of scripture, see, e.g., Priscillian's discussion of scripture's threefold operation in ibid. 6, 70.7–71.3. Chadwick speculates that Priscillian would have absorbed Origen's doctrine of scripture via Hilary, although Origen's use of the Pauline trichotomy as an exegetical principle is not found in the extant works of Hilary (*Priscillian of Avila*, p. 71 n. 1). Mark Vessey provides a nuanced discussion of the convergence of understandings of Christian reading and writing in the works of Hilary, on the one hand, and the Priscillianist tractates and Pauline canons, on the other, attributing such convergence not only to the direct influence of Hilary's writings on Priscillianist circles, but also to a shared Christian literary heritage fed by both Alexandrian traditions of "ascetical gnosis" and "a shared background of western ideas of Bible-study and Christian utterance" ("Ideas of Christian Writing in Late Roman Gaul" [D. Phil. thesis, Oxford University, 1988], pp. 11–34).

132. Priscillian, *Tract.* 3, 44.3–5; 45.23–24; 51.7–15; 56.6–7.

133. Priscillian, *Can. Ep. Pauli*, prol. Mark Vessey has pointed out to me that the Pauline canons seem to represent an interesting precursor to the western genre of monastic "rules"; their literary form, which mediates between *scriptura* and *regula*, thus appears to offer a parallel expression of the tractates' conviction that a true reading of scripture is inevitably productive of an ascetic "orthodoxy."

134. Van Dam here has Martin of Tours in mind, but his point is more generally applicable (*Leadership*, p. 61).

135. Priscillian, *Tract.* 4, 58.6–9.

136. Severus, *Chron.* 2.46, 47; cf. Jerome, *Ep.* 133.4.

137. Priscillian, *Tract.* 1, 3.9; Jerome, *De viris inlustribus* 123; Severus, *Chron.* 2.51.

138. Priscillian, *Tract.* 1, 3.9.

139. The Spanish poet Latronianus may already have been among Priscillian's supporters at this point; see Severus, *Chron.* 2.51, and Jerome, *De viris inlustribus* 122.

CHAPTER 3. "SORCERER"

1. Severus, *Chron.* 2.48. Jacques Fontaine argues that the western routes connecting Spain and Aquitaine were used by Priscillian and Paulinus, among other well-known figures of the period; Priscillian probably progressed through the valleys of the Adour and the Garonne as he made his way north toward Bordeaux ("Société et culture chrétiennes," pp. 251–54).

2. Severus, *Chron.* 2.48. There is no direct evidence that the exiled bishops visited Agen or even intended to do so. However, we know that the group passed through Eauze, which does not lie on the shortest path between the far western passes and Bordeaux; one possible explanation for the choice of route is an original intention to visit Agen as well as Bordeaux. Note that Rousselle suggests that the exiled bishops may have sought more than a letter of support from Delphinus: observing that the rulings of the Council of Antioch (341) dictated that a larger council must consider the appeal of a bishop deposed by a local synod before the matter could be brought before the emperor (can. 12), she proposes that Priscillian sought out the bishop of Bordeaux because he had the authority to convene a pan-Gallic council to consider rescinding the judgments of the Council of Saragossa, which (in Rousselle's opinion) had led to the deposition of Priscillian and his companions ("Quelques aspects politiques," p. 87). Rousselle seems to me to overestimate both the degree of hierarchalization among western bishops and the extent to which the rulings of an eastern council would have been either known or honored in the west.

3. That Priscillian already had followers in Aquitaine has frequently been suggested, based on the presence of Delphinus and Phoebodius at the Council of Saragossa, as well as on Filastrius' early knowledge of "abstinents" in both Spain and Gaul. Babut has been the strongest proponent of this theory, going so far as to suggest possible Aquitanian origins for Priscillian's movement by positing the leadership of Attius Tiro Delphidius, whom he identifies with the Elpidius referred to by Severus (*Priscillien*, pp. 79–91); Puech refutes Babut on these points ("Les Origenes du priscillianisme," pp. 81–95). More recently, Jacques Fontaine has emphasized the cultural unity of the areas north and south of the Pyrenees and suggested that Priscillian's route through precisely those portions of Gaul where the sees of the Aquitanian bishops who attended the Council of Saragossa were located indicates that those were areas where Priscillianism was strong *before* the council ("Société et culture chrétiennes," p. 254). However, Fontaine's emphasis on the close connections between Aquitaine and Spain makes it possible to view these two separate instances of close communication between Spanish and Aquitanian

Christians as less directly related. Alternatively, the connection may be even more direct than he posits, as I have suggested by proposing that Priscillian intended to visit the Aquitanian bishops present at Saragossa in order to obtain letters substantiating his claim not to have been condemned by the Council of Saragossa. Finally, the close unity between Gaul and Spain was not just the cultural unity of a literary elite, which is Fontaine's primary focus, but also a unity in the sphere of ecclesiastical politics. Priscillian's journey to Aquitaine is one of several instances of Spanish Christians appealing to neighboring Gallic bishops for support, especially when they found themselves representing a minority position at home: in this controversy, we find Hydatius drawing upon the support of Delphinus and Phoebadius by inviting them to the Council at Saragossa, Priscillian appealing to Delphinus and other Aquitanian bishops following his exile from Spain, and Ithacius later finding powerful support from the bishop of Trier when he faces strong opposition in Spain.

4. Severus, *Chron.* 2.48.

5. Ibid. Severus makes no mention of Delphidius, but Pacatus identifies Euchrotia as the widow of a famous poet (*Pan.* 29) and Ausonius seems to have her in mind when he refers to the "punishment" (*poena*) of the wife of Attius Tiro Delphidius (*Prof.* 5); Prosper, writing some forty or more years later, but certainly relying on earlier Aquitanian sources, explicitly refers to Euchrotia as the wife of Delphidius the rhetorician (*Chron.* 1187). It is probable that Delphidius died not long before Priscillian's visit, since Ausonius congratulates him for a timely death, through which he escaped knowledge either of his wife's execution or his daughter's "mistake" (*error*); see A. D. Booth, "Notes on Ausonius' *Professores*," *Phoenix* 32 (1978): 238–39.

6. Prosper, *Chron.* 1187. The earliest edition of Prosper's *Chronicle*, which included the entries about Priscillian and his followers, is dated to 433 in Theodore Mommsen, ed., *Chronica Minora Saec. IV, V, VI, VII*, vol. 9 of *Monumenta Germaniae Historica: Auctorum Antiquissimorum*, p. 345. Prosper's information about Priscillian generally parallels Severus' account, and most of it probably derives either from Severus or from a closely related Aquitanian source: the reports of the Council of Bordeaux and of the trial and executions at Trier (*Chron.* 1187, *an.* 385) remain close to Severus' text in language and content, and the report of the excommunication of Ithacius and Ursacius (*Chron.* 1193, *an.* 389) is also consistent with his account, although Severus does not mention Ursacius; Babut suggests that Ursacius is to be identified with Hydatius (*Priscillien*, pp. 36–37 n. 1). However, the report of the establishment of the Priscillianist heresy "from the dogma of Manichaeans and gnostics" seems to derive from Filastrius via Augustine, although Prosper adds the mistaken note that Priscillian was a Galician bishop (*Chron.* 1171, *an.* 379). And the particular passage in which Urbica is mentioned is unparalleled in Severus or any other known source. The reference to "obstinacy in impiety," which reflects classical Roman rather than specifically Christian language, may suggest that Prosper's information derived from the pagan or nominally Christian aristocratic circles of late-fourth-century Gaul exemplified by a figure like Ausonius. Note that

Ausonius was not only familiar with Urbica herself (as argued below) but also accused Paulinus, whom he may have suspected of having Priscillianist leanings, of "impiety" (Paulinus, *Ep.* 31.83–84).

7. R. P. H. Green, "Prosopographical Notes on the Family and Friends of Ausonius," *Bulletin of the Institute of Classical Studies* 25 (1978): 22.

8. Priscillian probably arrived in Bordeaux in 381. If, as Green suggests, Ausonius' *Parentalia* was largely complete early in the 380s, Pomponia Urbica's husband, Julianus Censor, who is commemorated in *Par.* 22, was probably already dead by 381 ("Prosopographical Notes," p. 22). Green suggests that the commemoration of Pomponia Urbica in *Par.* 30 was a later addition made sometime before publication between 386 and 388; Prosper's account, if the identification is accepted, makes it likely that she died in the events surrounding the council of Bordeaux circa 384. Her widowhood would thus have lasted several years. As we shall see, Ausonius' emphasis on its extreme brevity may result from his embarrassment at the manner of her death and his attempt to present her as a faithful wife rushing to reunite with her husband in death.

9. Ausonius, *Par.* 30.3–6.

10. Jerome uses both figures as examples of the virtue of married women (*Adversus Jovinianum* 1.49). In the allusion to Tanaquil as the possessor of a "virtue rare among women" (*rara inter feminas virtus*), he may be relying on Seneca's lost treatise on marriage (F. Haase, ed., *L. Annaei Senecae Opera* [Teubner, 1853], 3: 433). Silius Italicus likewise represents Tanaquil as an exemplary female figure, describing her as "of chaste mind" (*castae mentis*), as well as gifted in prophecy (13.818–820). Livy gives the fullest account of Tanaquil's unique career (1.34–35, 39, 41), and Juvenal presents Tanaquil in unambiguously negative terms (6.566). Theano, identified sometimes as the disciple, sometimes as the wife of Pythagoras, is presented by Diogenes Laertius as a paragon of wifely virtue, advising other women to clothe themselves in shame before all men but their husbands and defining shame as "that through which I am called a woman" (8.43). Female philosophers were generally viewed with some ambivalence; see, for example, the stories told of Hipparchia in Diogenes Laertius 6.96–98.

11. Green, "Prosopographical Notes," p. 22. Green also compares the allusion to Theano here with the allusions to Pythagoras and Bellerophon in Ausonius' *Ep.* 24 to Paulinus, noting that Ausonius was perfectly capable of using such allusions in a complex and/or polemical manner.

12. Dennis Trout argues persuasively that Ausonius' references to Tanaquil (*Ep.* 28.31) and Bellerophon (*Ep.* 29.72) reflect his suspicions that Therasia and Paulinus may have become involved with the Priscillianist movement during their sojourn in Spain. These suspicions were not based on any real knowledge of Paulinus' and Therasia's situation in Spain and were emphatically rejected by Paulinus (*Ep.*31.189–92) (Trout, "Secular Renunciation and Social Action: Paulinus of Nola and Late Roman Society" [diss., Duke University, 1989], pp. 144–70).

13. Green refers to Pomponia Urbica's "penchant for martyrdom" ("Prosopographical Notes," p. 22).

14. Ausonius, *Par.* 30.7–10.

15. Severus, *Chron.* 2.48.

16. *ACS*, can. 1.

17. Severus, *Chron.* 2.48.

18. Ausonius, *Prof.* 5.37.

19. *ACS*, can. 8.

20. Note that Delphinus does not appear to have objected to the ascetic conversion of the wealthy and aristocratic Therasia several years later. The fact that she, like Euchrotia, was a mature woman, may have facilitated his acceptance. Still more significant, Therasia's husband Paulinus was still living and had joined his wife in her ascetic lifestyle. Delphinus could not afford to alienate such a powerful man, and Paulinus' writings provide evidence that he and Delphinus remained on friendly terms following Paulinus' conversion and move away from Bordeaux (*Epp.* 10, 14, 19, 20, and 35 are addressed to Delphinus).

21. Peter Brown notes that the majority of well-born young women vowing virginity seem to have been the daughters of widows; had they still been alive, their fathers would have opposed their vows to do so (*Body and Society*, p. 344).

22. Chadwick speculates that if Euchrotia were a recent widow, "her motives could have included a quest for consolation by making pilgrimage to the shrines of the apostles and martyrs of Rome" (*Priscillian of Avila*, p. 37). For a discussion of pilgrimage in this period, see Gustave Bardy, "Pèlerinages à Rome vers la fin du IVe siècle," *Analecta Bollandiana* 67 (1949): 224–35, and Hagith Sivan, "Who Was Egeria? Piety and Pilgrimage in the Age of Gratian," *Harvard Theological Review* 81 (1988): 59–72.

23. See Babut, *Priscillien*, p. 153.

24. Severus, *Chron.* 2.48. Mathisen, *Ecclesiastical Factionalism* , pp. 14–18, provides a helpful analysis of the fifth-century conflicts that shaped Severus' perspective. Fontaine, "L'Affaire Priscillien," pp. 368–69, highlights Severus' subtle preference for the Priscillianists over the Ithacians. The latter were identified with the "Felicians," who tended to be Gallic isolationists in ecclesiastical terms but were not averse to seeking political patronage to further their cause, whereas their opponents, among whom Severus was numbered, were willing to appeal to Italian ecclesiastical authority but opposed the intervention of secular patrons.

25. Note that Chadwick follows Severus in placing the Roman visit first; his position seems to require dating the *Letter of Damasus*—with its reference to the Priscillianists' petitioning of the quaestor—to the period *after* the visit to Rome and the subsequent stay in Milan (*Priscillian of Avila*, p. 40).

26. Priscillian, *Tract.* 2, 41.13–16. It should be noted that the letter does initially seem to imply that the group immediately set out for Rome; however, in light of what follows, this should be understood primarily as part of a strategy to flatter Damasus: "eclesias nostras commendavimus deo, quarum communicatorias ad te epistulas detulimus totius cleri et plebis suscribtione transmissas, et ad te qui potuimus venientes voluimus quidem absentes supplicare" (*Tract.* 2, 41.7–11).

27. Severus, *Chron.* 2.49, and Chadwick, *Priscillian of Avila*, p. 40 n. 3. Proculus

Gregorius was *praefectus annonae* in 377, and *praefectus praetorio Galliarum* in 383, before Gratian's death; Symmachus, *Ep.* 3.19, indicates that Gregory was at court in 379 or 380, at which point he most likely held the office of *quaestor sacri palatini* (A. H. M. Jones, J. R. Martindale, and J. Morris, *The Prosopography of the Later Roman Empire*, vol. 1 [1971], p. 526; Matthews, *Western Aristocracies*, p. 71–72). Although tenure in such offices was typically quite short, Gregory could easily have held the palace quaestorship for as long as two or three years, which would include the period in which Priscillian must have visited Milan (on tenure in office, see A. H. M. Jones, *The Later Roman Empire: A Social, Economic, and Administrative Survey, 284–602* [Oxford: Basil Blackwell, 1964], 1: 381).

28. Priscillian, *Tract.* 2, 41.2–3. It is the context of this passage that suggests the connection with the issuing of the rescript: immediately preceding the mention of Ambrose is a an account of Hydatius' attempt to procure a rescript, and immediately following it is the report of his use of the rescript that was brought back to him.

29. Severus, *Chron.* 2.48. Since Severus does not mention the first stop in Milan, his mention of Ambrose's hostility is necessarily in conjunction with the second stop. Ambrose's *Epp.* 24.12 and 26.3 refer disapprovingly to episcopal participation in the civil trial and execution of certain "heretics" or "criminals," but Ambrose does not mention Priscillian's name or refer to any earlier involvement in Priscillian's case.

30. See the defense of this "traditional" dating by Pierre Nautin, "Les Premières Relations d'Ambroise avec l'empereur Gratien: Le *De fide* (livres I et II)," in *Ambroise de Milan: XVIe centenaire de son élection épiscopale*, ed. Yves-Marie Duval (Paris: Études augustiniennes, 1974), pp. 229–44, 231–35. Nautin here challenges the suggestion of Gunther Gottlieb that the document should be dated instead to the late spring or summer of 380 (*Ambrosius von Mailand und Kaiser Gratian* [Göttingen: Vandenhoek & Ruprecht, 1973], p. 50). For our purposes the exact dating of the document is not crucial. Note that while Gottlieb has demonstrated that Gratian followed his father's relatively evenhanded religious policies as late as 380, he continues the scholarly tradition of presenting the post-380 Gratian as a religiously naive youth seeking refuge in the theological wisdom of the Milanese bishop. Nautin rightly challenges this view, arguing that both Gratian's religious policy and Ambrose's response to Gratian suggest that the young emperor was theologically and politically astute in his handling of the conflict between the Nicene and Homoian parties (pp. 238–44).

31. While Nautin emphasizes the opposition of the Illyrican bishops, Daniel Williams suggests that the local opposition of the Homoian party was the more pressing factor (*Ambrose of Milan*, ch. 5).

32. *Cupio valde* (PL 16.913–14). Again, note that Gottlieb dates Gratian's letter more than a year later, to the summer of 380 (*Ambrosius von Mailand*, p. 50).

33. Building on the work of Nautin, Daniel Williams provides an important discussion of the context of these final books, emphasizing that they were composed not at the formal request of the emperor but rather in response to both local and extralocal Homoian attacks (*Ambrose of Milan*, ch. 5).

34. Ambrose, *De fide* 2.141–43; 3.1–2.

35. See Williams, *Ambrose of Milan*, ch. 4.

36. Ambrose, however, is remarkably reticent concerning Julian Valens, who is mentioned only in *Ep*. 10, in which Ambrose on behalf of the Council of Aquileia requests Valens' exile, and *Ep*. 11, which refers to Valens in connection with Ursinus, whose exile is also requested.

37. Our only direct reference either to the "sequestering" or "return" of the basilica is Ambrose, *De spir. sanc.* 1.1.19–20. Note that two recent reconstructions of this first Milanese conflict over a basilica are at odds: Harry O. Maier suggests that the Homoians never gained access to the basilica ("Private Space as the Social Context of Arianism in Ambrose's Milan," *Journal of Theological Studies*, n.s., 45 [1994]: 72–93], while Daniel H. Williams argues that they did ("Ambrose, Emperors and Homoians in Milan: The First Conflict over a Basilica," in *Arianism after Arius: Essays on the Development of the Fourth-Century Trinitarian Conflicts*, ed. Michel R. Barnes and Daniel H. Williams [Edinburgh: T. & T. Clark, 1993], pp. 127–46, 137–39).

38. Maier has fruitfully applied the public-private distinction to the analysis of the Milanese conflict, pointing first to the privileged claim to authority inherent in the occupation of public space and the resulting intensity of the "battle" to control that space, and, second, to the fluid adaptability of Christian movements that were privatized following upon their "defeat" ("Private Space"). Note that Maier has challenged the widespread assumption that the Homoians had one or two of their own basilicas during Ambrose's episcopacy; if he is right, the Homoian attempts to acquire basilical space may become still more significant for our understanding of the issues at stake in the conflict. Where Maier's use of the public-private distinction is not in complete harmony with mine is in his tendency to accept somewhat uncritically both the rhetorical polarization of public and private and the negative valorization of the private sphere; while clearly a "battle" of some sort was being waged over public space in Milan, the terms of that "battle" continue to be defined by Ambrose, so that I might, for example, question whether the Homoians themselves always experienced their private location negatively as a "defeat." On the late-ancient privatization of heresy more generally, see Harry O. Maier, "Religious Dissent, Heresy and Households in Late Antiquity," *Vigiliae Christianae*, forthcoming.

39. Richard Krautheimer has demonstrated the value of the topographical approach for the study of the architectural construction of a public Milanese orthodoxy (*Three Christian Capitals: Topography and Politics* [Berkeley and Los Angeles: University of California Press, 1983], pp. 68–92). Maier refines the approach by attempting to construct a complementary "map" of privatized heterodox movements in Milan ("Private Space"). While Krautheimer's treatment of Ambrosian Milan highlights Ambrose's construction of Milan as an episcopally centered "Christian capital" in direct competition with Constantinople's imperially centered capital, Maier calls attention to the conflict *within* the Milanese "capital," articulated spacially in the division of public and private meeting places.

40. Paulinus of Milan, *Vita Ambrosii* 13; cf. Augustine, *Conf.* 9.7, and Robert

Taft, *The Liturgy of the Hours in East and West* (Collegeville, Minn.: Liturgical Press, 1986), pp. 141–43, 174–76.

41. I emphasize this point in my "Ascesis, Authority, and Text: *The Acts of the Council of Saragossa*," *Semeia* 58 (1992): 95–108.

42. Maier, "Private Space," p. 93.

43. Ambrose, *De spir. sanc.* 1.1.19–20.

44. In a review of Roger Gryson's critical edition of the "Arian Scholia" (*Scolies ariennes sur le concile d'Aquilée* [Sources chrétiennes 267; Paris: Éd. du Cerf, 1980]), Yves-Marie Duval has emphasized the competitive motive behind Theodosius' decision to call a general eastern council at Constantinople in the same year in which Gratian's general council at Aquileia had been scheduled by agreement of the two emperors; this unexpected development provided an opening for Ambrose, who offered Gratian the possibility of continuing with his plans for a council while yet recasting it in such a way that the council would not be in direct—and unsuccessful—competition with Constantinople ("La Présentation arienne du concile d'Aquilée de 381," *Revue d'histoire ecclésiastique* 76 [1981]: 317–31, 327–28). Neil McLynn adds that "it is unlikely . . . that Gratian foresaw the effect that the revised arrangements would have upon the conduct of the council" ("The 'Apology' of Palladius: Nature and Purpose," *Journal of Theological Studies*, n.s., 42 [1991]: 52–76, 71).

45. Palladius' *Apology* is preserved in the "Arian Scholia" published by Gryson, *Scolies ariennes*, pp. 264–74.

46. The history of continued conflict between pro-Nicene and anti-Nicene factions in Milan, culminating in the struggle over the basilica in 386, is well known. McLynn has recently emphasized the significant threat represented by the opposition of Palladius even after the Council of Aquileia ("'Apology' of Palladius," pp. 70–76).

47. The Council of Saragossa, which met in October of 380, provides the absolute *terminus a quo* for the dating of the rescript, but a period of some months must have elapsed, during which both the conflict at Merida and Priscillian's ordination occurred; in addition, Priscillian's mention of Ambrose in relation to the rescript suggests a date when Gratian was either in Milan or in close touch with Ambrose, e.g., March 381 or the months following (on Gratian's whereabouts during this period, see Otto Seek, *Regesten der Kaiser und Päpste für die Jahre 311 bis 476 n. Chr.* [Stuttgart: J. B. Metzlersche Verlagsbuchhandlung, 1919], p. 256). The death of Gratian in August 383 provides the absolute *terminus ad quem* for both the rescript and Priscillian's visit to Italy, but again chronological "space" must be allowed for Priscillian's return to Spain, Volventius' summoning of Ithacius, Ithacius' flight, Gregory's intervention and report to Gratian, and Macedonius' engineering of the transfer of the case to Spain; this makes it unlikely that Priscillian's visit to Milan could have taken place later than 382.

48. Mathisen emphasizes the close connections between Ambrose and Gallic bishops (*Ecclesiastical Factionalism*, p. 11); note that Ambrose' *Ep.* 87 is addressed to Phoebadius and Delphinus.

49. Babut dates Filastrius's *Diversarum hereseon liber* to 383 and places great emphasis on the significance of his testimony to the geographical spread of Priscillianism (*Priscillien*, pp. 6–8, 79–83). Puech challenges Babut's use of Filastrius' text, noting that the document cannot safely be dated with greater precision than 375–92 and rightly stressing its unreliability as a source of information about Priscillian's movement ("Les Origines du priscillianisme," pp. 84–89). Filastrius, remains a useful source about impressions of Priscillian at a relatively early stage in the controversy, however; if—as most would agree—the text does refer to the Priscillianists, it probably dates to the period between the first emergence of conflict and Priscillian's execution—that is, between 380 and 386 or 387.

50. Filastrius, *Diversarum hereseon liber* 61, 84. Filastrius' language suggests that his report of the dualistic teaching of the "abstinents" is simply inferred from their ascetic practice (see Babut, *Priscillien*, p. 7). The identification of these ascetics with gnostics and Manichaeans may also be based on such an inference; however, given the probable content of Hydatius' communication to Ambrose, Filastrius could easily have known of the specific charge of Manichaeism.

51. It is unclear whether Ambrose's asceticism was a further point of significant vulnerability—as well as strength—at this early date. Some years later, the "anti-ascetic" Jovinian seems to have accused Ambrose of Manichaeism, and Ambrose neatly turned the charge back on his accuser; see David G. Hunter's analysis of Ambrose, *Ep.* 42 to Siricius ("Resistance to the Virginal Ideal in Late-Fourth-Century Rome: The Case of Jovinian," *Theological Studies* 48 [1987]: 51–53). If controversy over Ambrose's asceticism was already in the air in the early 380s, this would have made him still more cautious about any association with Priscillian. However, the conflict with the Homoians seems clearly the more significant context for interpreting Ambrose's response to Priscillian, while Ambrose's own ascetic agenda in many respects aligns him more closely with Priscillian's opponents than with Priscillian.

52. Ambrose, *Ep.* 20.17–18.

53. Priscillian, *Tract.* 2, 34.10–11, 35.21–24, 41.8–10, 41.16–17, 42.24–43.7. On preference for ecclesiastical judgment, cf. *Can. Ep. Pauli* 46.

54. Severus, *Chron.* 2.48.

55. Jerome, *De viris inlustribus* 121.

56. This is not certain, since Jerome's rhetorical context provides him with another possible motive for his neutral presentation of Priscillian. Jerome's *De viris inlustribus* was written at the request of Nummius Aemilianus Dexter, a powerful figure at Theodosius' court in the mid 380s, and Matthews points out that in order to please his Spanish patron, Jerome seems to have included references, not only to Dexter's father, Bishop Pacianus of Barcelona, but also to Priscillian, Tiberianus, and Latronianus. Obviously, for this strategy to be effective, Jerome would have to assume that, at least in Dexter's eyes, the reputations of Priscillian, Tiberianus, and Latronianus were not entirely negative (*Western Aristocracies*, pp. 133–34, 167–68; see now Stefan Rebenich, *Hieronymus und sein Kreis: Prosopographische und sozialgeschichtliche Untersuchungen* [Stuttgart: Franz Steiner Verlag, 1992], pp. 213–15).

57. Charles Pietri, *Roma Christiana* (Rome: École française, 1976), pp. 423–27, and Maier, "Topography of Heresy and Dissent."

58. Note that the Roman "schism" is more complicated than the Milanese, not least because the Roman factions cannot be neatly aligned with "pro-Nicene" and "anti-Nicene" positions: although Liberius was exiled for his strong pro-Nicene commitments, he was also later bitterly maligned as a compromiser and traitor to the Nicene cause; nor does Felix seem to have had an "Arian" theological orientation, in spite of the fact that he was the preferred choice of the emperor Constantius (see the helpful account of Pietri, *Roma Christiana*, 1: 237–68). Harry Maier has recently highlighted the private-sphere location of many out-of-favor factions or "protest movements": just as Liberius' supporters were probably driven into private meeting places during Felix' episcopacy, so Felix's supporters seem to have occupied the private sphere when driven out of the basilicas following Liberius' return ("The Topography of Heresy and Dissent in Late-Fourth-Century Rome," *Historia* [forthcoming]). That the Damasan-Ursinian factions stand in some sort of important historical continuity with the Liberian-Felician factions is clear, and Maier places particular emphasis on this connection in order to demonstrate the "private" persistence of the Felician faction. However, as Pietri notes, while "le conflit qui oppose Ursinus à Damase pour la succession de Libère prolonge une ancienne querelle," it was also doubtless fuelled by "nouvelles oppositions," stemming in his opinion from resistance to the effects of the conversion of the aristocracy (*Roma Christiana*, 1: 407–8). I would add that while Ursinus struggled to define himself as the legitimate successor to Liberius in part by casting Damasus as a "Felician," Damasus certainly would not have represented himself that way by 366, and we have only his opponents' word that his supporters were identical with those who had supported Felix.

59. "Et hoc gloriae vestrae" (*PL* 13.575–84); Ambrose, *Ep.* 11.

60. Charles Pietri provides an overview of the disorderly state of ecclesiastical politics in Italy in the 370s, during which not only Damasus but also Ambrose found himself embroiled in conflict with Ursinus; with the help of the emperor, Damasus was able to restore order and reestablish Rome's prominence among the Italian churches, but in the 380s, Milan emerged as a formidable rival to Roman supremacy in Italy (*Roma Christiana*, 1: 729–54).

61. A hostile *libellus* circulated shortly after Ursinus' ejection from Rome in 368 claims that Damasus was so much esteemed by the matrons of the city that he was called *matronarum auriscalpius* ("tickler of matronly ears") (*Collectio Avellana* 1.9); as André Hoepffner notes, "elle établit que Damase fréquentait avec assiduité les dames de la bonne société romaine et qu'il y était un hôte choyé" ("Les Deux Procès du Pape Damase," *Revue des études anciennes* 50 [1948]: 296). Hoepffner argues for the reliability of the testimony of the *Liber Pontificalis*, which records that Damasus was accused of adultery but cleared by a synod of bishops (*Liber Pontificalis: Damasus* 3); he further suggests that this synod is to be identified with the Council of Rome of 378 ("Deux Procès," pp. 289–304). That same council had also petitioned Gratian to recognize the right of bishops to be tried only by a council of

their fellow bishops (*Ep.* "Et hoc gloriae vestrae" 3 and 10). Priscillian may therefore have had good reason to hope that Damasus would support his own request for a hearing from an episcopal council.

62. Cf. Maier, "Topography of Heresy and Dissent."

63. See Gratian's rescript, *Collectio Avellana* 13. Bishop Damasus' imperial support is particularly emphasized by Pietri, *Roma Christiana*, 1: 414–31.

64. Pietri, *Roma Christiana*, 1: 461–68. Note that Krautheimer, *Three Christian Capitals*, pp. 94–105, adds another church to the list of those projects initiated by Damasus: the sumptuous basilica at the site of Paul's grave.

65. Note that John Baldovin has recently challenged the dating of the "systemization" of the Roman stational liturgy to the episcopacy of Damasus, without however denying that significant enhancement of stational "practices" probably took place under Damasus' leadership (*The Urban Character of Christian Worship: The Origins, Development, and Meaning of Stational Liturgy* [Rome: Pont. Institutum Studiorum Orientalium, 1987], pp. 119, 147–51).

66. Pietri provides a critical review of the sources for the chain of events immediately following Liberius' death (*Roma Christiana*, 1: 408–12), largely following the chronological and geographical reconstruction of Adolf Lippold ("Ursinus und Damasus," *Historia* 14 [1965]: 105–28). The terminology of "first" and "second" Christian establishments is Pietri's.

67. Krautheimer, *Three Christian Capitals*, pp. 12–20.

68. In attributing the building of St. Paul's Outside the Walls to the initiative of Damasus, Krautheimer associates Damasus with a new "classical tenor" in architectural style "which looks back to the Hadrianic and Augustan past of Rome" (ibid., p. 104).

69. Severus, *Chron.* 2.48.

70. Severus suggests that both bribery and persuasion played a role in the Spaniards' success (*Chron.* 2.48). Persuasion was not out of the question: recall that Priscillian claims that the *quaestor* found their requests fair (*Tract.* 2, 41.15). Macedonius and Ambrose do not seem to have been on friendly terms; see Paulinus, *Vita Ambrosii* 37. Rousselle suggests that Gratian was probably absent from Milan at the time of Priscillian's visit and, as was customary, had delegated greater powers to his *magister officiorum* during his absence ("Quelques aspects politiques," pp. 88–89). This may not be a necessary condition for Macedonius' interference.

71. The "legislative incoherence" of this rescript of Macedonius has an interesting parallel in a report of the urban prefect Symmachus to Valentinian II, dated 384 and indicating that Macedonius had on at least one other occasion been responsible for the issuing of a rescript that conflicted with previous imperial directives. Certain members of the salt-workers' guild had been exempted from their duties, but the guild was demanding that those exempted be forced to return to service, on the grounds that it was otherwise unable to fulfill its obligations; the exempted workers countered by citing "a divine directive" and were found to be "protected by the support of Macedonius." Symmachus comments carefully that only direct action of the emperor could untangle the knot of conflicting imperial

rescripts, some of which had been "extracted unfairly"—a disapproving reference to Macedonius' initiative (*Rel.* 44.1). Note that Macedonius' behavior can hardly have been unique. Such incoherencies in imperial policy should probably not be attributed solely either to the deficient characters of a few individuals or to the lags and gaps in communication that inevitably plagued a highly centralized government ruling so wide a geographical area; inconsistency also had its positive function, responding to the need for a certain flexibility of policy within the context of the patronage system undergirding imperial governance.

72. Severus, *Chron.* 2.48.

73. Barbero de Aguilera goes so far as to suggest that support for Priscillian came primarily from rural areas whose native inhabitants resisted the new alliance of Roman and episcopal authority in a time of social and economic crisis ("El priscilianismo: ¿Herejía o movimiento social?" pp. 16–25); he has more recently been followed in this interpretation by Narciso Santos Yanguas, "Movimientos sociales en la España del Bajo Imperio," *Hispania* 40 (1980): 237–69. There are serious problems with the argument, at least as it is applied to the early stages of the Priscillianist controversy, in which the primary context was clearly urban; see Van Dam, *Leadership*, pp. 90–91. Nevertheless, there may be some truth in the suggestion that there was local resentment of Hydatius' invocation of the authority of the imperial court to expel leaders with popular support in their own communities.

74. Rousselle speculates, perhaps unnecessarily, that this was accomplished at the request of Priscillian's patron Macedonius ("Quelques aspects politiques," p. 90).

75. Severus, *Chron.* 2.49.

76. Ibid.

77. See Maximus, *Epistula ad Siricium papam.* Birley argues against the view that Maximus in this letter is responding to Siricius' criticism of his handling of the Priscillianist affair. Birley suggests, rather, that Maximus replies to a more general question about the catholic faith and spontaneously offers his handling of Priscillian as proof of his outstanding orthodoxy ("Magnus Maximus and the Persecution of Heresy," pp. 36–37). If this interpretation is accurate, it further confirms the impression that Maximus viewed the Priscillianist controversy as a chance to demonstrate his own zeal for orthodoxy.

78. Severus, *Chron.* 2.49.

79. Klaus Girardet, "Trier 385: Der Prozess gegen die Priscillianer," *Chiron* 4 (1974): 587–89.

80. Severus, *Chron.* 2.49.

81. Girardet, "Trier 385," pp. 593–94. Rousselle offers the innovative suggestion that Priscillian's appeal was directed not at Maximus but at the court of Valentinian II at Milan ("Quelques aspects politiques," p. 93).

82. Severus reports disapprovingly: "Priscillianus . . . ad principem provocavit; permissumque id nostrorum inconstantia, qui aut sententiam in refragantem ferre debuerat, aut si ipsi suspecti habebantur, aliis episcopis audentiam reservare, non causam imperatori de tam manifestis criminibus permittere" (*Chron.* 2.49).

83. Prosper, *Chron.* 1187.

84. The tendency to view Priscillian's trial and execution as a foreshadowing of later medieval developments exaggerates the impression that the events surrounding Priscillian's death were out of place or are inexplicable in their late-fourth-century setting. The comment of Peter Stockmeier is representative: "Der Blutspruch von Trier leitet eine Entwicklung in der Geschichte der Kirche ein, die in Religionskriegen und Inquisition endet" ("Das Schwert im Dienste der Kirche: Zur Hinrichtung Priszillians in Trier," in *Festschrift für Alois Thomas* [Trier: Selbstverlag des Bistumsarchivs, 1967], p. 428).

85. Priscillian, *Tract.* 2, 41.16–17; id., *Can. Ep. Pauli* 46; id., *Tract.* 1, 22.14–19.

86. Severus, *Chron.* 2.50.

87. Severus, *Dial.* 3.11. Note that here, as elsewhere, Severus avoids any mention of the term "Manichaean"; nevertheless, this was almost certainly the label invoked by Ithacius. Manichaeans were frequently identified by their fasting, paleness, and dress. Jerome, for example, describes the suspicions of certain Christian women in Rome with regard to their ascetic sisters: "quam viderint pallentem atque tristem, miseram et Manichaeam vocant: et consequenter: tali enim proposito jejunium haeresis est" (*Ep.* 22.13).

88. Priscillian, *Tract.* 1, 23.22–24.3; Severus, *Chron.* 2.46.

89. Ibid. 2.48.

90. Priscillian's anonymous Roman contemporary "Ambrosiaster" describes the Manichaeans' supposedly duplicitous and immoral behavior as follows: "None are as troublesome, as treacherous, as deceitful as these very ones who are known to cultivate one idea and to confess something else, to bear one notion inwardly and to claim something else in public. For they defend purity and live shamelessly by their own supporting law. . . . They find women who want to hear something on account of its new appearance, and through what is pleasing they recommend to them what is foul and unlawful" (*Commentaria in epistulam ad Timotheum secundam* 3.6–7). An early work of Augustine's, written around 388 in Rome, highlights more specifically the purported Manichaean use of contraception: "Is it not you who consider begetting children, by which souls are bound in flesh, a more serious sin than copulation? Is it not you who used to advise us to observe, as much as possible, the time after menstruation when a woman is most ready for conception and to refrain from copulation at that time, so that the soul would not be entangled in flesh?" (*De moribus Manichaeorum* 18.65). According to M. K. Hopkins, abortion and contraception were not consistently distinguished in ancient thought, nor could many of the recommended methods have been effective, with the possible exception of the use of certain vaginal suppositories ("Contraception in the Roman Empire," *Comparative Studies in Society and History* 8 [1965]: 124–51). More recently, John Riddle has argued for widespread knowledge, particularly among women, of the effective use of herbal contraceptives as well as early-stage herbal abortifacients; he also traces a growing reticence on the part of late-ancient male physicians to prescribe abortifacients, reflected in the common mistranslations of Hippocrates to the effect that to assist in abortion is a violation

of the physician's oath (*Contraception and Abortion from the Ancient World to the Renaissance* [Cambridge, Mass.: Harvard University Press, 1992]). From the point of view of late-ancient Christian authors, who clearly shared these negative views of abortion, contraception and abortion remain closely linked precisely through their association with duplicitous sexual behavior, especially on the part of women, as the texts collected in the study of Michael Gorman indicate (*Abortion and the Early Church* [New York: Paulist Press, 1982], pp. 63–73).

91. Both Severus and Prosper refer to Ithacius' deposition: Severus, *Chron.* 2.51; Prosper, *Chron.* 1193, *an.* 389.

92. Isidore, *De viris illustribus* 14.

93. Severus, *Chron.* 2.50.

94. Ibid.

95. Ambrose, *Ep.* 24.12. Cf. Ambrose's (later?) expressions of disapproval of those bishops who accused criminals in the context of public trials, some actively calling for the sword, others merely approving such "bloody triumphs of bishops" (*cruentos sacerdotum triumphos*) (*Ep.* 26.3).

96. Severus. *Chron.* 2.50–51. The simplest explanation seems to me to be that Ithacius withdrew at the same time that Maximus did, and that the trial also officially became a sorcery trial at that point, rather than a personal consideration by the emperor of the charge of Manichaeism. Severus' account, however, leaves some confusion as to the sequence of events: as Girardet notes, his report of Ithacius' withdrawal seems to be added out of order, as a further elaboration of the events already narrated ("Trier 385," p. 600).

97. Severus, *Chron.* 2.50.

98. The Council of Elvira (309) had also ruled against women's attendance of vigils, on the grounds of suspected immorality: "Placuit prohiberi ne foeminae in coemeterio pervigilent, eo quod saepe sub obtentu orationis latenter scelera committunt" (can. 35). On magic and vigils, cf. *Codex Theodosianus* 9.16.7.

99. Chadwick, *Priscillian of Avila*, pp. 18, 140. It is highly unlikely that Priscillian actually prayed completely naked. "I have looked in vain for historical accounts of practices of nakedness," Margaret R. Miles comments in reference to late ancient Christian asceticism (*Carnal Knowing* [Boston: Beacon Press, 1989], p. 63).

100. Maximus Augustus, *Epistola ad Siricium papam* 4.

101. Augustine, *De natura boni* 47.

102. Severus, *Chron.* 2.50–51. Jerome records a similar list of those initially condemned, substituting the name "Julianus" for "Armenius" (*De viris inlustribus* 122).

103. Pacatus, *Pan.* 29.

104. Ausonius, *Prof.* 5.35–38.

CHAPTER 4. "PRISCILLIANIST"

1. Severus, *Chron.* 2.51; Hydatius, *Chron.* 16, *an.* 387.

2. "In fact, in some respects Priscillianism seems to have replaced Manichae-

ism in Spain and southern Gaul as a homebred idiom of heresy with which people articulated unacceptable aspects of their communities" (Van Dam, *Leadership*, p. 108).

3. E.g., Braga I (561).

4. The term *Priscillianistae* appears in five anti-heretical laws of the *Codex Theodosianus*; of these, two were issued in the west and appear to refer to the Spanish sect (16.5.40, 16.5.43), while three were issued in the east and appear to refer to the followers of the Montanist prophet Priscilla (16.5.48, 16.5.59, 16.5.65) (cf. Jones, *Later Roman Empire*, 3: 323–324 n. 33).

5. E.g., Augustine, *De haeresibus* 70 (c. 429). Augustine may get the term from the Galician Orosius, whose *Commonitorium de errore Priscillianistarum et Origenistarum* (414) represents the earliest extant use of the vocabulary of "Priscillianism" of which I am aware. See Introduction, n. 7, above.

6. E.g., Henry Chadwick, *Priscillian of Avila*, pp. 174–76, 181–85, and id., "The New Letters of St. Augustine," *Journal of Theological Studies*, n.s., 34 (1983): 434–36.

7. These include (1) the *Transcript of the Professions Held in the Council of Toledo against the Sect of Priscillian* (hereafter *Exemplar*) (critical edition by Henry Chadwick, *Priscillian of Avila*, pp. 234–39), and (2) the *Acts of the Council of Toledo* (400) (hereafter *ACT*). There is also a third document traditionally attached to the first Council of Toledo, a rule of faith with accompanying anathemas; this document occurs in both longer and shorter recensions. It is now generally acknowledged that neither of these versions of the *Regula fidei* was originally promulgated by the Council of Toledo. The shorter recension appears unrelated to Priscillianism and probably dates back to the period before the outbreak of the Priscillianist controversy. The longer recension is clearly an anti-Priscillianist work but appears to be considerably later than the first Council of Toledo; it has been suggested that it is the mid-fifth-century work of the Galician bishop Pastor (Barbero de Aguilera, "El priscilianismo: ¿Herejía o movimiento social?" pp. 25–36).

8. *Ep.* 11* (*CSEL* 88 [1981], pp. 51–70). This letter is part of a collection recently discovered by Johannes Divjak, including twenty-six new letters of Augustine and three of his correspondents.

9. *ACT*, preface.

10. Augustine (*Contra mendacium* 5), Leo (*Ep.* 15.16.1), and Hydatius (*Chron.* 32, *an.* 400), also seem familiar with this portion of the council's minutes.

11. On the manuscript tradition, see Chadwick, *Priscillian of Avila*, pp. 179–81, 234.

12. *ACT*, ll. 1–9. It is almost universally assumed that Symphosius was bishop of the Galician capital Astorga, but as Van Dam points out, "his see is nowhere explicitly stated" (*Leadership*, p. 109 n. 100).

13. *Exemplar*, ll. 3–43.

14. *Exemplar*, ll. 44–154.

15. *Exemplar*, ll. 70–74.

16. *Exemplar*, ll. 74–94.

17. *Exemplar*, ll. 82–84, 90–103. The openings filled by Symphosius' ordinations may have resulted in part from the spread of Christianity into the Galician

countryside and the corresponding emergence of new rural episcopacies. Alain Tranoy highlights the importance of the emergence of the *villae* and the reoccupation of the *castra* in fourth-century Galicia and notes that these social developments must have favored the proliferation of rural Christian communities (*La Galice Romaine*, pp. 409–434, and "Contexto histórico del priscilianismo en Galicia en los siglos IV y V," in *Prisciliano y el priscilianismo* [Oviedo: Cuadernos del norte, 1982], pp. 78–79). It is unclear whether Dictinius was co-bishop of Astorga alongside his father Symphosius or ordained by Symphosius to lead one of the rural communities in the vicinity of Astorga.

18. *Exemplar*, ll. 84–90.

19. See Chadwick, *Priscillian of Avila*, p. 152 n. 3.

20. *Exemplar*, ll. 78–81.

21. *Exemplar*, ll. 25, 30, 31, 32–33, 37, 58, 59–60, 65–66.

22. *Exemplar*, ll. 15–16.

23. *Exemplar*, ll. 11–14, 17; 20; 87. Cf. Augustine, *Contra mendacium* 5.

24. Dictinius cites Matthew 16.19 (*Exemplar*, ll. 12–13), and Galatians 1.8–9 (*Exemplar*, ll. 63–64); the latter passage is twice cited by Priscillian, once in an important statement on canon and orthodoxy (*Tract.* 1, 7.11–13 and 30.11–20).

25. *Exemplar*, ll. 25–26, 65–66.

26. *Exemplar*, ll. 61–63. Cf. Comasius's statements (*Exemplar*, ll. 38–43, 49–50).

27. Priscillian, *Tract.* 6, 74.13. As Chadwick points out, Priscillian's use of the term *innascibilis* to emphasize the paradox of the birth of the unbegettable appears neither technical nor unorthodox (*Priscillian of Avila*, pp. 88–89).

28. *Exemplar*, ll. 27–30.

29. *Exemplar*, ll. 34, 51.

30. *Exemplar*, ll. 137–44. Innocent of Rome eventually responded to the Council of Toledo and supported its reinstatement of Symphosius and Dictinius (*Ep.* 3).

31. *Exemplar*, ll. 108–35.

32. *Exemplar*, ll. 147–54.

33. Hydatius, *Chron.* 32, *an.* 400.

34. This seems to be the sense of the following passage: "[Symphosius] nullis libris apocryphis aut novis scientiis quas Priscillianus composuerat involutum; Dictinium epistolis aliquantis pene lapsum" (*Exemplar*, ll. 84–85).

35. *Exemplar*, ll. 18–23, 86.

36. Augustine, *Contra mendacium* 5. Augustine is our sole informant, and he probably knew the *Libra* only through the distorted lens of Consentius' anti-Priscillianist writings; Consentius, a monk on the Balearic islands, may in turn have derived his information from the Galician Orosius (Van Dam, "Sheep in Wolves' Clothing," pp. 528–30).

37. Augustine clearly attributes the defense of lying to Dictinius' *Libra* (*Contra mendacium* 35). The reliability of Augustine's report is compromised both by his source—Consentius—and by the close conformity of the reported content of Dictinius' work with Augustine's own stereotype of Manichaeans, with whom he categorized the Priscillianists. On the other hand, Augustine's refutation of Dictinius'

position in *Contra mendacium* 26–34 consists of a fairly detailed discussion of scriptural passages cited as precedents for dissimulation, and both the level of detail and the scriptural emphasis suggest that Augustine may after all have had more than a simple caricature of Dictinius' position before him (see Anne-Marie la Bonnardière, "Du nouveau sur le priscillianisme (*Epist.* 11*)," in *Les Lettres de saint Augustin découvertes par Johannes Divjak* [Paris: Études augustiniennes, 1983], pp. 207–8, 212–13). In the end, we know too little about Dictinius' work to claim it as evidence for the existence of a secret or elitist sect of Priscillian in Galicia either before or after the Council of Toledo; cf. the discussion of Chadwick, *Priscillian of Avila*, pp. 155–56.

38. Leo, *Ep.* 15.16.1.

39. Hydatius remarks upon the confused elections and resulting shameful state of ecclesiastical order in Galicia: "deformem ecclesiastici ordinis statum creationibus indiscretis" (*Chron.* pref. 7). Although he is apparently referring primarily to the disruption resulting from the barbarian invasions of Galicia, it appears that Galicia had no strong or clearly defined ecclesiastical hierarchy even before the invasions (Tranoy, *La Galice romaine*, pp. 409–34).

40. *Exemplar*, ll. 147–52.

41. As noted above, the Toledan bishops command that the churches from which their "brother Ortygius" had been driven away be returned to him (*Exemplar*, ll. 153–54); the Galician chronicler Hydatius, who was familiar with the *Acts of the Council of Toledo*, further identifies Ortygius as a "bishop who had been ordained at Celenis, but was driven away by the powerful Priscillianist factions for his catholic faith and banished" (*Chron.* 32, *an.* 400). Chadwick suggests that Exuperantius of Celenis, who sat among the bishops at Toledo, was a former Priscillianist who had replaced Ortygius but managed to dissociate himself from the Priscillianists before the council (*Priscillian of Avila*, pp. 157, 171). Tranoy proposes alternatively that Ortygius was bishop of a small rural community in the neighborhood of Exuperantius' see of Celenis, noting that Hydatius states merely that Ortygius was "ordained at Celenis" and may thereby imply not that he was bishop of Celenis but that he was under the jurisdiction of the bishop of Celenis (*Hydace: Chronique*, vol. 2 [Paris: Éditions du Cerf, 1974], p. 30). Tranoy's proposal avoids the need to hypothesize that the Exuperantius who sat with the bishops at Toledo was a reformed Priscillianist; it now also has the support of his analysis of Galician social structure (*La Galice romaine*, pp. 409–34, and "Contexto histórico del priscilianismo en Galicia," pp. 78–79). One might compare the case of Astorga, where there also seem to have been at least two bishops, Symphosius and Dictinius, in or around a single city.

42. Here the parallels with the use of the figure of Arius at the Council of Aquileia (381) are intriguing.

43. *Exemplar*, ll. 3–4.

44. *Concilium Toletanum Primum. Decem et novem episcoporum actum Arcadii et Honorii temporibus sub die VII. Iduum Septembrium, Stilicone consule era CCCCXXXV.* Cf. *Exemplar*, l. 44.

45. *ACT*, preface. Patruinus' see is identified by Innocent (*Ep.* 3.8).

46. Nicea I (325), can. 4. In light of Symphosius' ordination of Dictinius as co-bishop in Astorga and of the apparent existence of two bishops in Celenis, it is possible that Patruinus also had in mind a more obscure ruling in which the Nicene bishops instruct that former Novatianists who have been ordained to clerical office are to retain that office unless a situation results in which there are two bishops of one city; in that case, the former Novatianist bishop might be demoted to the rank of presbyter or "country bishop" (can. 8). With this ruling, the Nicene council (and perhaps also the Toledan council) supports a more urban and hierarchical ecclesiastical structure than seems to have been common among either the Novatianist or Galician Christians.

47. Innocent indicates that the Galicians may not, however, have been the only ones failing to observe the Nicene canons in respect to episcopal ordinations. He reprimands two bishops of unspecified sees for their irregular ordinations following the Council of Toledo; at least one of these—Minicius—seems to have been from the Tarragonese province, since he ordained a bishop in Gerona, in the far east of that province (*Ep.* 3.5).

48. Hess, *Canons of the Council of Sardica*, pp. 36–38.

49. Laeuchli, *Power and Sexuality*, p. 88. As Roger Gryson points out, the Council of Elvira (309) to which Laeuchli refers was somewhat precocious in this respect, and it was not until the late fourth century that the issue of clerical celibacy began to be seriously debated in Spain (*Les Origines du célibat ecclésiastique du premier au septième siècle* [Gembloux: Éditions J. Duculot, 1970], pp. 180–82); indeed, Gryson considers it likely that can. 33 of the Council of Elvira, which requires that bishops, presbyters, and deacons observe sexual continence, is a late-fourth-century addition to the council's original rulings ("Dix ans de recherches sur les origines du célibat ecclésiastique," *Revue theologique de Louvain* 11 [1980]: 160–64).

50. *ACT*, can. 1.

51. *Exemplar*, ll. 149–52.

52. See Sotomayor, "El canon 3," pp. 183–87.

53. *ACT*, can. 14.

54. *ACT*, can. 6.

55. D. B. Botte, O.S.B., cites two other instances in which this term seems to indicate an ascetic: the title of a lost work by Macrobius the Donatist—*Ad confessores et virgines*—and Jerome's use of *confessio* to indicate a religious vow (Botte, "Confessor," *Archivum Latinitatis Medii Aevi* 16 [1942]: 137–48).

56. The office of reader appears to have been established relatively early in Spain: the *Passio S. Fructuosi, Augurii et Eulogii*, which records the martydom of the bishop of Tarragona in 258, refers to a reader named Augustalis. See Alexandre Faivre, *Naissance d'une hiérarchie: Les Premières Étapes du cursus clérical* (Paris: Éditions Beauchesne, 1977), pp. 269–70.

57. *ACT*, can. 7.

58. *ACT*, can. 9.

59. Relatively little is known of the development of the *lucernarium* and other daily prayers from practices of private devotion to "cathedral" or "monastic offices." Egeria, a contemporary ascetic from Spain or Gaul, was familiar with the *lucernarium*, perhaps in a monastic context (*Peregrinatio Egeriae* 24). The bishops at

Toledo appear to be establishing or protecting an episcopally led evening liturgy by opposing private devotions, at least in a nonmonastic context.

60. The *devota*, in contrast to the *professa* mentioned in the ninth decision, is probably a virgin consecrated by the bishop. This hypothesis is supported by the council's particular concern with the sexual purity of *devotae*, who by episcopal consecration might be seen as "daughters" of the church or the bishop, and whose sexual purity was therefore closely associated with the honor of the higher clergy.

61. Consentius to Augustine, *Ep.* 11*.9.2.

62. In *Ep.* 12* Consentius indicates he first wrote Augustine in about 415 (Van Dam, "Sheep in Wolves' Clothing," p. 528). Lack of scholarly consensus as to whether the Consentius of *Ep.* 11* and *Ep.* 12* (both probably written in 419) is to be identified with the Consentii of *Epp.* 119 and 120 or *Ep.* 205 makes the extent and length of their correspondence debatable. Jules Wankenne supports the identification of the authors of *Epp.* 11*, 12*, and 119 ("Le Correspondance de Consentius avec saint Augustin," in *Les Lettres de saint Augustin découvertes par Johannes Divjak* [Paris: Études augustiniennes, 1983], pp. 225–42), while Van Dam is skeptical of such identification ("Sheep in Wolves' Clothing," pp. 532–35); more recently, Carol Quillen has reaffirmed the theory of a single Consentius as author of *Epp.* 119, 11*, and 12* ("Consentius as a Reader of Augustine's *Confessions*," *Revue des études augustiniennes* 37 [1991]: 87–109, 87 n. 2).

63. For the dating of the letter and events reported therein, see Van Dam, "Sheep in Wolves' Clothing," pp. 517–18. In 417, Patroclus was involved in intense struggles to support the newly asserted metropolitan rights of Arles. In the course of his struggles with the bishop of Marseilles, at least one of his opponents was accused of Priscillianism, a circumstance almost certainly related to Patroclus' interest in encouraging the proliferation of anti-Priscillianist literature. See Zosimus, *Ep.* 4.3; Van Dam, "Sheep in Wolves' Clothing," pp. 529–30; and Mathisen, *Ecclesiastical Factionalism*, pp. 48–60.

64. *Ep.* 11*.1.1–3, 24.1. Consentius seems aware that the story might seem so amazing as not to be believable, and he assures Augustine: "de historiae veritate nulla cunctatio sit" (*Ep.* 11*.24.2). Augustine appears to have retained certain doubts, pointing out to Consentius that Fronto's professed enthusiasm for lying might compromise the reliability of his tale (*Contra mendacium* 4). M. Moreaux highlights similarities between Fronto's narrative and the hagiographical romances of the martyrological tradition and suggests that Fronto's account has at the very least been extensively embellished by Consentius ("Lecture de la Lettre 11* de Consentius à Augustin: Un Pastiche hagiographique?" in *Les lettres de saint Augustin découvertes par Johannes Divjak* [Paris: Études augustiniennes, 1983], pp. 215–22). I am less inclined to doubt the basic reliability of Fronto's account and would furthermore attribute any embellishing of the tale to Fronto himself, since there is evidence of a certain discrepancy between Consentius' framing of the story and the story itself, above all in Consentius' consistent use of the label "Priscillianist," which appears nowhere in Fronto's account. It is possible that Fronto had already put the account into writing before he reported it to Consentius; or perhaps Consentius actually had it transcribed by stenographers.

65. *Ep.* 11*.21–27. If Consentius really intends to refer to Hippo with the

phrase *in ista praecipue urbe* (27.3), his reliability as a witness to the spread of Priscillianism in the early fifth century is seriously compromised indeed.

66. *Ep.* 11*.2.1.

67. *Ep.* 11*.1.4–5.

68. *Contra mendacium* 6. See La Bonnardière, "Du nouveau sur le priscillianisme," pp. 206–7.

69. *Ep.* 11*.2.2. It is puzzling that Consentius was able to identify Severa by name. Perhaps he knew her from a former sojourn in Tarragona or relied on reports from Fronto or some other correspondent. Or perhaps it was merely Consentius' generic description of heretics or Priscillianists that appeared to Fronto to point clearly to Severa.

70. *Ep.* 11*.10.3–10.

71. *Ep.* 11*.2.2.

72. Van Dam emphasizes this lack of evidence confirming the identification of Fronto's "heretics" as "Priscillianists" ("Sheep in Wolves' Clothing," pp. 515, 523). Other scholars have accepted Consentius' assessment of the Tarragonese "heresy," e.g., Henry Chadwick ("New Letters of St. Augustine," pp. 434–36), Manuel Díaz y Díaz ("Consencio y los priscilianistas," in *Prisciliano y el priscilianismo* [Oviedo: Cuadernos del norte, 1982], pp. 71–76), W. H. C. Frend ("The Divjak Letters: New Light on St. Augustine's Problems, 416–428," *Journal of Ecclesiastical History* 34 [1983]: 510–11), and La Bonnardière ("Du nouveau sur le priscillianisme," pp. 211–12).

73. *Ep.* 11*.2.3; 3.1.

74. *Ep.* 11*.2.5; 2.7.

75. *Ep.* 11*.2.4–3.2.

76. *Ep.* 11*.2.3; 3.3.

77. *Ep.* 11*.2.7. Fronto suggests that Sagittius was motiviated by a desire to keep the "sweet poisons" of the books, which "insanely pleased him." But perhaps it was, rather, either personal loyalty to Severus or—on a more cynical interpretation—the perceived opportunity for blackmail that led Sagittius to send Titianus some, but not all, of the books.

78. *Ep.* 11*.4.1.

79. *Ep.* 11*.5–6.

80. *Ep.* 11*.7.2–3; 4.3. Count Asterius is also known to us from Hydatius: "Vandali, Suevorum obsidione dimissa instante Asterio Hispaniarum comite" (*Chron.* 74, *an.* 420).

81. *Ep.* 11*.7.1.

82. *Ep.* 11*.2.1.

83. *Ep.* 11*.9.2–11.1.

84. *Ep.* 11*.11.8; 12.2–13.10.

85. *Ep.* 11*.15.1; 16.

86. *Ep.* 11*.14.3–4. Presumably, Sagittius' story also somehow explained Severus' possession of the book supposedly in Syagrius' keeping. Fronto appears to be covering up certain aspects of Syagrius' involvement, since Syagrius had ulti-

mately assisted Fronto. Although Sagittius and Syagrius both initially supported Severus, Fronto attributes this to heresy only in Sagittius' case, attributing Syagrius' actions to too much kindness and simplicity. Likewise, Fronto never explicitly states that Ursitio secretly restored the books to Syagrius as well as Sagittius or that the lie proposed by Sagittius would have protected Syagrius as well as Sagittius and Severus, although both seem likely.

87. *Ep.* 11*.15.2–3.

88. *Ep.* 11*.17.1–19.1.

89. *Ep.* 11*.19.2–20.2.

90. *Ep.* 11*.21.2.

91. *Ep.* 11*.21–23.

92. *Ep.* 11*.2.1. Fronto makes no mention of other members of his community, and Chadwick suggests that Fronto's *monasterium* may have been a mere hermit's cell ("New Letters of St. Augustine," p. 435). Van Dam is less sceptical, pointing out that monasteries are known to have existed at Tarragona ("Sheep in Wolves' Clothing," p. 515 n. 3).

93. *Ep.* 11*.1.2, 12.2.

94. *Ep.* 12*.2.3; cf. 12*.14.3.

95. *Contra mendacium* 4.

96. Peter Brown, *Augustine of Hippo* (Berkeley and Los Angeles: University of California Press, 1967), pp. 132–37, and L. J. van der Lof, "The Threefold Meaning of Servi Dei in the Writings of Saint Augustine," *Augustinian Studies* 12 (1981): 43–59.

97. *Ep.* 11*.5.1; 13.1; 7.3.

98. *Ep.* 11*.14.2, 15.1, 15.3, 18.3, 19.3.

99. *Ep.* 11*.14.2, 15.3.

100. Van Dam, "Sheep in Wolves' Clothing," p. 525.

101. *Ep.* 12*.14.1. This rhetorical stance is discussed by Quillen in the context of Consentius' response to "the power which is attributed . . . to reading itself" in Augustine's *Confessions* ("Consentius as a Reader of Augustine's *Confessions*," 91).

102. *Ep.* 11*.2.3, 4.3, 11.8.

103. *Ep.* 11*.17.5; 3.2.

104. *Ep.* 11*.16.3.

105. Fronto may have insulted Asterius' "very powerful" daughter, but both the reliability and the content of this claim are uncertain; see *Ep.* 11*.7.2, 9.2.

106. Roland Delmaire, "Contribution des nouvelles lettres de saint Augustin à la prosopographie du Bas-Empire Romain (*PLRE*)," *Les Lettres de saint Augustin découvertes par Johannes Divjak* (Paris: Études augustiniennes, 1983), pp. 83, 86, and Van Dam, "Sheep in Wolves' Clothing," p. 519.

107. Severa is at least not likely to have been extremely young, since Asterius' daughter—herself no longer a child—is identified as Severa's granddaughter or niece: "[Severa] ad neptis suae Asterii comitis filiae potentissimae feminae auxilium convolaret" (*Ep.* 11*.4.3).

108. *Ep.* 11*.3.3, 9.2.

109. The bishops of the Baetican and Carthaginian provinces in Spain originally protested the reacceptance of the reformed Dictinius by the Council of Toledo. However, Innocent of Rome supported his reinstatement (*Ep.* 3.2–4), and Augustine still considered Dictinius a Catholic, corrected of his error (*Contra mendacium* 5).

CHAPTER 5. "GNOSTIC"

1. Isidore of Seville, *De viris illustribus* 15. Cf. Severus' note that Ithacius initially defended the appropriateness of his participation in the criminal lawsuit (perhaps in part by arguing for the seriousness of Priscillian's crime?), but later shifted his strategy and accused the allies who had advised his course of action (*Chron.* 2.51).

2. Prosper, *Chron.* 1193; Severus, *Chron.* 2.51.

3. Babut, *Priscillien*, pp. 33–56.

4. Babut's source theory has been most recently endorsed by Chadwick, *Priscillian of Avila*, pp. 22, 152, 201.

5. Filastrius, *Diversarum hereseon liber* 84. This dual association of Priscillian's movement with gnosticism and Manichaeism may be because of the strict ascetic practices attributed to both heresies, as to Priscillian's movement, and to Priscillian's use of apocryphal writings deriving from both gnostic and Manichaean circles. Although fourth-century texts do not explicitly refer to the Manichaeans as "gnostics," some link between Manichaeism and gnosticism was commonly acknowledged. Fourth-century writers draw upon the heritage of anti-gnostic polemics in their denunciations of the Manichaeans, who are deemed guilty of similar "errors" of christology and cosmology. The influential *Acta Archelai* hints at parallels between the life of Mani and the life of the first "gnostic," Simon Magus (Samuel N. C. Lieu, "Some Themes in Later Roman Anti-Manichaean Polemics: I," *Bulletin of the John Rylands University Library of Manchester* 68 [1985–86]: 446), and Cyril of Jerusalem, relying in part on the *Acta Archelai*, explicitly describes Mani as the successor of the "gnostics" refuted by Irenaeus: Simon Magus, Cerinthus, Menander, Carpocrates, the Ebionites, Marcion, Basilides, and Valentinus (*Catecheses* 6.14–33).

6. For the dating of Jerome's works, I have generally followed Ferdinand Cavallera, *Saint Jérôme: Sa vie et son oeuvre* (Louvain: "Specilegium Sacrum Lovaniense" Bureaux, 1922), vol. 2.

7. Jerome, *De viris inlustribus* 121.

8. Ibid.

9. As noted above, Babut proposes that Ithacius had already linked Priscillian with the Irenaean Mark (*Priscillien*, pp. 37, 45–56). Ithacius had likewise identified this Mark as a disciple of Mani; Babut suggests, therefore, that Jerome, or perhaps an intermediary source like Lucinus, had "corrected" Ithacius' hypothetical error of chronology by omitting mention of Mani.

10. Irenaeus seems rather to imply that Marcus is of the school of Valentinus (*Adversus haereses* 1.13.1); he clearly does *not* associate him with the school of Basilides (described in 1.24.3–7). Parallels that might have led Jerome to make this connection include Irenaeus' description of the licentious habits of the followers of Basilides and of their use of magic (1.24.5), practices likewise attributed to Mark (1.13). There are a number of other inaccuracies in Jerome's account of Irenaeus. Babut and his followers have viewed this as support for the theory that the Irenaean allusion derives from Ithacius, the implication being that so careful a scholar as Jerome would never have made such errors, while Ithacius is easily believed to have done so (e.g., Babut, *Priscillien*, p. 33 n. 1, and Chadwick, *Priscillian of Avila*, p. 22). It would not, however, have been entirely out of character for Jerome to have introduced either careless inaccuracies or willful misinterpretations into his citation of a source.

11. Whether Irenaeus in fact means that Mark was *himself* active in the Rhône district is irrelevant; Jerome clearly understands *Adversus haereses* 1.13.7 to imply a Gallic sphere of activity for the gnostic Mark.

12. The question that drives such speculations is: Are there two Marks or one in the tradition surrounding Priscillian? Babut judges it highly improbable that there could be more than one and likewise suggests that this one Mark is identical with the gnostic Mark described by Irenaeus; his connection with Priscillian is thus purely fictional (*Priscillien*, pp. 33–56). Babut's solution requires attributing the Irenaean connection to Ithacius and making both Jerome and Sulpicius Severus dependent on Ithacius. Puech, although originally supporting a theory of two Marks ("*Priscilliani quod superest*, ed. G. Schepss, 1889," *Journal des savants* [1891]: 112), later concedes that one fictional, Irenaean-based Mark is, if by no means certain, at least the simplest solution ("Les Origines du priscillianisme," p. 163), and most scholarship in this century has followed Babut's theory of one Mark. However, given the tenuous nature of the evidence, it is necessary to acknowledge the possibility that two different Marks may in fact have made their way into the tradition surrounding Priscillian, and also to keep in mind that only Jerome's Mark is explicitly identified with the Irenaean tradition. V. C. de Clercq argues for the existence of a fourth-century Manichaean Mark who was active in Cordoba in the years 325–40 ("Ossius of Cordova and the Origins of Priscillianism," *Studia Patristica* 1 [1957]: 601–6).

13. Jerome, *Ep.* 75.3.

14. Ibid.

15. Priscillian, *Tract.* 1, 29.13–15 and 11.18–19.

16. Jerome probably derived the fifth name from Irenaeus, who attributes the title "Abraxas" to the chief of the Basilidean heavens (*Adversus haereses* 1.24.7). As to the role of Lucinus as a source for Jerome, note that Babut suggests that Lucinus may have derived his knowledge of Priscillian from Ithacius' *Apology*, and thus may have served as the transmitter of the Ithacian tradition to Jerome (*Priscillien*, p. 37 n. 1). I consider it likely that Lucinus had sources more reliable and closer to home than Ithacius' *Apology*, which was probably published in Gaul: Lucinus was,

according to the address of Jerome's *Ep.* 71, a native of Baetica, likewise the home of Hyginus, first an accuser and later a supporter of Priscillian (Severus, *Chron.* 2.46), and of Tiberianus, also among Priscillian's supporters (Jerome, *De viris inlustribus* 123).

17. Jerome, *Ep.* 75.3.

18. Irenaeus, *Adversus haereses* 1.13.7.

19. Severus' account suggests that Euchrotia's estate was in the vicinity of Bordeaux, situated at the mouth of the Garonne River (*Chron.* 2.48).

20. Irenaeus, *Adversus haereses* 1.13.1–7.

21. Irenaeus may already allude to this passage when he states that Mark's disciples deceived and defiled many "little women" (*Adversus haereses* 1.13.6); however, unlike Jerome, he does not exploit the full implications of 2 Tim. 3.6–7, nor does he show any interest in creating a close association of women and heresy elsewhere in his work. See my "Hierarchalization and Genderization of Leadership in the Writings of Irenaeus," *Studia Patristica* 21 (1989): 42–48.

22. Jerome, *Praefatio in Pentateuchum* (398) and *Commentarii in Isaiam* 17.64.4–5 (408–9).

23. Jerome, *Praefatio in Pentateuchum* and *Ep.* 120.10 (407).

24. Jerome, *Commentarius in Amos* 1.3 (406).

25. Jerome, *Ep.* 120.10.

26. Jerome, *Contra Vigilantium* 6 (406); *Commentarii in Isaiam* 17.64.4–5.

27. For Jerome's restriction of the canon, see *Praefatio in libros Samuel et Malachim*; *Praefatio in libros Salomonis*; and J. N. D. Kelly, *Jerome: His Life, Writings, and Controversies* (London: Duckworth, 1975), pp. 160–61.

28. Jerome, *Praefatio in Pentateuchum*: "Maximeque quae evangelistarum et apostolorum auctoritas promulgavit [Origenes]: in quibus multa de veteri Testamento legimus, quae in nostris codicibus non habentur; ut est illud." (There follow five examples of New Testament citations of authoritative words: Matt. 2.15 and 23; John 19.37 and 7.38; and 1 Cor. 2.9.) "Interrogemus ergo eos, ubi haec scripta sint: et cum dicere non potuerint, de libris Hebraicis proferamus." (There follow the Hebrew sources for the New Testament citations: Hos. 11.1; Isa. 11.1, Zech. 12.10; Prov. 18.4; Isa. 64.4.) "Quod multi ignorantes, apocryphorum deliramenta sectantur; et Iberas naenias libris authenticis praeferunt."

29. Priscillian actually uses one of the New Testament examples cited by Jerome—Matt. 2.15—as proof that not all prophecy is contained in the canonical scriptures (*Tract.* 3, 48.3–7).

30. A work with which Priscillian was familiar (*Tract.* 3, 47.18–20).

31. Jerome, *Commentarii in Isaiam* 17.64.4–5. 1 Cor. 2.9 was also one of the texts cited by Jerome in the *Praefatio in Pentateuchum*.

32. Jerome, *Contra Vigilantium* 6.

33. Priscillian, *Tract.* 3, 52.10–24.

34. Jerome, *Ep.* 120.10.

35. In a letter addressed to Marcellinus, an imperial commissioner in Carthage, and his wife Anapsychia, Jerome responds to a question about the origin of

the soul, repeating his opposition to the teachings of Pythagoras, Plato, and Origen, on the one hand, and the Stoics, Manichaeus, and "the Spanish heresy of Priscillian," on the other, and specifying that the common heresy of the Stoics, Manichaeus, and Priscillian consists in the teaching that human souls are a part of the substance of God (*Ep.* 126 [411]). Jerome gives no indication of the source of his knowledge of Priscillian's doctrine. He may have simply inferred it based on a stereotype of gnosticism. However, the transcript of the anti-Priscillianist professions from the Council of Toledo (400) accuse Priscillian's "follower" Dictinius of teaching that the soul was part of God (*Exemplar*, ll. 15–16), and it is possible that Jerome already knew of this charge by the time he wrote *Epp.* 120 (407) and 126 (411). In 414, Jerome was to meet the Galician Orosius, who must have informed him at that point of Priscillian's supposed heretical teachings concerning the soul (cf. Orosius, *Commonitorium de errore Priscillianistarum et Origenistarum* 2).

36. Jerome clearly knew of Euchrotia's connection with Priscillian as early as 392, when he lists Felicissimus, Julianus, and Euchrotia as those executed alongside Priscillian at Trier (*De viris inlustribus* 122). He does not, however, identify Euchrotia as the wife of Delphidius.

37. Jerome, *Ep.* 120, preface.

38. Jerome, *Commentarii in Isaiam* 17.64.4–5.

39. Jerome had first inserted this "name" into the catalogue a few years earlier (*Contra Vigilantium* 6 [406]). He had also grouped Priscillian's doctrine of the soul with the Manichaean doctrine (*Ep.* 120.10 [407]).

40. In the *Letter to Theodora*, the link between Priscillian and Mark is secured by the placement of the story of Mark in the context of the praise of Lucinus' zeal in fighting the Spanish heresy in his own time. In the *Commentaries on Isaiah*, it is the reference to Lusitania that clearly points to a connection between Mark and Priscillian. Priscillian's episcopal see of Avila may have been considered part of Lusitania, and his disputes with the Lusitanian bishops Hydatius and Ithacius were familiar to Jerome (*De viris inlustribus* 121).

41. Jerome, *Ep.* 120.10.

42. Severus, *Chron.* 2.46.

43. Tacitus, *Ann.* 15.44.5.

44. Jacques Fontaine, "L'Affaire Priscillien," pp. 359–61.

45. "Hoc autem scito, quod in novissimis diebus instabunt tempora periculosa" (2 Tim. 3.1 [Vulgate]). G. K. van Andel points out this scriptural reference and provides a careful discussion of Severus' eschatology in *The Christian Concept of History in the Chronicle of Sulpicius Severus* (Amsterdam: Adolf M. Hakkert, 1976), pp. 99, 117–38.

46. Severus, *Chron.* 2.46.

47. Ibid. As noted, Babut was an early proponent of the theory that Ithacius' *Apology* was Severus' major source on Priscillian (*Priscillien*, pp. 33–44).

48. Severus, *Chron.* 2.47.

49. Most scholars reject the highly speculative suggestions of Babut that Elpidius and Agape are the Christian names of Delphidius and Euchrotia, or, alter-

natively, that they are names derived from Irenaeus' description of the gnostic aeons (*Priscillien*, pp. 49–52); see, e.g., the response of Puech, "Les Origines du Priscillianisme," pp. 89–95.

50. A number of scholars have commented on the parallels between Severus' portrait of Priscillian and Sallust's portrait of Catiline; see, e.g., the recent interpretations of Fontaine ("L'Affair Priscillien," pp. 362–65), and van Andel (*Sulpicius Severus*, pp. 72–74).

51. Severus, *Chron.* 2.46.

52. Fontaine, "L'Affaire Priscillien," p. 362.

53. Cf. Sallust: "L. Catilina, nobili genere natus, fuit magna vi et animi et corporis sed ingenio malo pravoque" (*Cat.* 5.1).

54. Cf. Sallust: "Corpus patiens inediae, algoris, vigiliae supra quam credibile est" (*Cat.* 5.3).

55. Cf. Sallust: "Alieni appentens, sui profusus, ardens in cupiditatibus. . . . Vastus animus immoderata, incredibilia, nimis alta semper cupiebat. . . . Lubido maxuma invaserat rei publicae capiendae" (*Cat.* 5.4–6). See also Fontaine, "L'Affaire Priscillien," p. 364.

56. Fontaine, "L'Affaire Priscillien," pp. 368–71.

57. Severus describes Priscillian as "habendi minime cupidus" but "plus justo inflatior profanarum rerum scientia"; his female followers are "novarum rerum cupidae . . . et ad omnia curioso ingenio" (*Chron.*2.46). The contrast then, is between the desire or greed for possessions, on the one hand, and curiosity, or the desire or greed for knowledge, on the other. Priscillian and his followers are guilty of the latter.

58. 2 Tim. 3.2–4 (Vulgate): "et erunt homines se ipsos amantes, cupidi, elati, superbi, blasphemi, parentibus inoboedientes, ingrati, scelesti, sine affectione, sine pace, criminatores, incontinentes, inmites, sine benignitate, proditores, protervi, tumidi, voluptatium amatores magis quam Dei."

59. *Chron.* 2.46: "quippe humilitatis speciem ore et habitu praetendens." Cf. 2 Tim. 3.5 (Vulgate): "habentes speciem quidem pietatis virtutem autem eius abnegantes."

60. Severus, *Chron.* 2.46.

61. Cf. Sallust: "satis eloquentiae, sapientiae parum" (*Cat.* 5.5).

62. Fontaine, "L'Affair Priscillien," p. 365, and van Andel, *Sulpicius Severus*, p. 74.

63. Sallust, *Cat.* 15.

64. Ibid. 24.3: "Ea tempestate plurimos cuiusque generis homines adscivisse sibi dicitur, mulieres etiam aliquot."

65. Ibid. 24.3–4, 25.

66. E.g., Sallust, *Cat.* 28.4; *Jug.* 19.1; *Cat.* 48.1; *Jug.* 66.2; *Cat.* 57.1; *Cat.* 37.1; *Jug.* 46.3; *Jug.* 66.2. Fontaine, "L'Affaire Priscillien," p. 367.

67. 2 Tim. 3.6–7 (Vulgate): "Ex his enim sunt qui penetrant domos et captivas ducunt mulierculas oneratas peccatis quae ducuntur variis desideriis semper discentes et numquam ad scientiam veritatis pervenientes."

68. I have been unable to detect specific allusions to Irenaeus or any other nonscriptural heresiological text; but whatever the specific sources of influence may be, it seems clear that Severus was familiar with the terms of what had become standard Christian heresiological discourse.

69. Le Boulluec demonstrates that Irenaeus modifies Justin's heresiological scheme in such a way as to accentuate the "heresiological paradox" of otherness and identity (*La Notion d'hérésie*, 1: 157–86).

70. Severus, *Chron.* 2.48, 50.

71. 2 Tim. 3.12–13 (Vulgate): "Et omnes qui volunt pie vivere in Christo Jesu persecutionem patientur, mali autem homines et seductores proficient in peius, errantes et in errorem mittentes."

72. Severus, *Chron.* 2.50, 51.

73. Augustine's *Ep.* 166, addressed to Jerome in 414 or 415, functions in part as a letter of introduction for Orosius. Orosius' depiction of Priscillian and his movement is contained in his *Commonitorium de errore Priscillianistarum et Origenistarum*, addressed to Augustine shortly before this date.

74. The exception is *Ep.* 126, where Jerome appears to be quoting his correspondent when he names Priscillian.

75. Virgil, *Georgics* 2.325–27.

76. Jerome, *Ep.* 133.3.

77. Note that Jerome with this phrase clearly "corrects" his first reference to Priscillian, in which he states that only some people thought him heretical (*De viris inlustribus* 121).

78. Orosius, *Commonitorium de errore Priscillianistarum et Origenistarum* 2.

79. Ibid.

80. Jerome, *Ep.* 133.4.

81. Cf. the following reference to 2 Tim. 3.6–7: "Nulla enim heresis nisi propter gulam ventremque construitur, ut seducat mulierculas oneratas peccatis semper discentes et numquam ad scientiam veritatis pervenientes." (Jerome, *Commentarius in Hieremiam* 1.57 [415–20]).

82. Jerome *Ep.* 133.4.

83. Severus' Mark is Priscillian's "grandparent" in false teaching, whereas Jerome's Mark is a figure of the distant past, living either two or three hundred years before Priscillian.

84. I follow D'Alès in taking Agape as the subject of *"habuit"* (*Priscillien et l'Espagne chrétienne*, p. 177).

85. There has been much discussion of the identity of "Galla," revolving around the interpretation of the phrase *non gente sed nomine*; see D'Alès, *Priscillien et l'Espagne chrétienne*, pp. 174–88, and Ferdinand Cavallera, "Galla non gente sed nomine," *Bulletin de littérature ecclésiastique* 38 (1937): 186–90. Most recent scholarship has followed Cavallera, interpreting the phrase in relation to "Galla," which seems to imply that Galla is the name of a person and not the designation of native country and therefore precludes an identification with Euchrotia or Procula; see, e.g., Chadwick, *Priscillian of Avila*, p. 38. The grammatical sense of the text is, how-

ever, ambiguous. Given the fact that Jerome knew of Euchrotia and her execution alongside Priscillian, and now also seems to know Severus' narrative, I think it is far more likely that the reference is in fact to Euchrotia or Procula or the other women of Priscillian's Gallic entourage, and I would therefore interpret the phrase *non gente sed nomine* to modify not "Galla" but *germanem*, and to signify either that she was named Galla, but was not Gallic, or that she was Euchrotia's or Procula's sister in some metaphorical sense.

86. D'Alès, *Priscillien et l'Espagne chrétienne*, pp. 177–82. Note that this identification of the empress Galla as an Arian is controversial. Daughter of the notorious Arian Justina, Galla may have renounced her Arian loyalties in the course of the negotiations of her marriage to the fervently orthodox Theodosius in 387, as Steward I. Oost suggests (*Galla Placidia Augusta* [Chicago: University of Chicago Press, 1968], p. 48). Whether such a hypothetical conversion to orthodoxy would have precluded her continuing association with Arianism in the mind of a writer like Jerome is another question.

87. Jerome, *Dialogus contra Pelagianos*, prol. 1.

88. According to Paulinus, Severus was in his prime as a rhetorician: "Tu, frater dilectissime, ad Dominum miraculo maiore conversus es, quia aetate florentior, laudibus abundantior, oneribus patrimonii levior, substantia facultatum non egentior et in ipso adhuc mundi theatro id est fori celebritate diversans et facundi nominis palmam tenens, repentino inpetu discussisti servile peccati iugum et letalia carnis et sanguinis vincula rupisti" (*Ep.* 5.5).

89. Severus' friendship with Paulinus predated Paulinus' and Therasia's conversions circa 393 (Paulinus, *Ep.* 11.5), and both Severus and the broader Aquitanian public associated Severus' slightly later conversion with that of Paulinus (Paulinus, *Ep.* 1.4). Severus began to visit Martin in 393 or 394, perhaps at the urging of Paulinus, whose cataracts Martin had healed (Severus, *Vita* 19; see also *Vita* 25). Severus later honored both Martin and Paulinus with portraits and inscriptions in the baptistry erected at Primuliacum (Paulinus, *Ep.* 32.2–4). A third major influence on Severus was Bassula, who may have converted to asceticism at around the same time as her son-in-law. Paulinus refers to Bassula as Severus' spiritual parent (*Ep.* 5.6,19; cf. the designation of Bassula as *parens venerabilis* in the adscription to Severus' *Ep.* 3).

90. Severus seems to have given up both his paternal inheritance and the property acquired through his prestigious marriage into a consular family; on Severus' rejection of his patrimony, see Paulinus, *Epp.* 1.1 and 5.6, and on his marriage, *Ep.* 5.5.

91. On the location of Primuliacum, see Claire Stancliffe, *St. Martin and His Hagiographer: History and Miracle in Sulpicius Severus* (Oxford: Clarendon Press, 1983), p. 30 n. 3.

92. See ibid., pp. 80–81, on the dating of the *Chronicle* and *Dialogues*.

93. Even Severus' property at Primuliacum was transferred to the legal ownership of the church: "te contra adhuc infelicem et in luto faecis infernae adhaerentem ingemiscas, quod vel unum, ut scripsisti, praediolum non vendidisse vi-

dearis, cum ipsum quoque aeque ut venditum a tuo iure praesenti alienaveris" (Paulinus, *Ep.* 24.1).

94. Paulinus, *Epp.* 24.3 and 27.3.

95. Paulinus, *Ep.* 23.3–10.

96. Paulinus, *Epp.* 24.3 and 27.3; cf. *Carm.* 24.715.

97. Severus indicates that the company gathered at Primuliacum on one occasion included a Gallic disciple of Martin, the traveller Postumianus, the presbyter Refrigerius, the presbyter Evagrius, Aper, Sabbatius, Agricola, the presbyter Aetherius, the deacon Calupio, the subdeacon Amator, and the presbyter Aurelius; all are identified loosely as "monks" (*Dial.* 1.1, 1.14 and 2.1). Paulinus also mentions a Postumianus (*Epp.*16.1 and 27.1–2), and he addresses *Epp.* 38, 39, and 44 to Aper; these may be identical with the Postumianus and Aper mentioned in the *Dialogues.*

98. Gennadius, *De viris inlustribus* 19.

99. Severus implies that Bassula's sojourn at Trier at the time of Martin's death in 397 was anomalous; she is "far from her native country," and her absence is causing her "son" in Toulouse (or in Primuliacum in the area around Toulouse?) much grief: "Ego enim Tolosae positus, tu Treveris constituta et tam longe a patria filio inquietante divulsa" (*Ep.* 3.3). See *Sulpice Sévère: Vie de Saint Martin*, ed. Jacques Fontaine, vol. 3 (Paris: Éditions du Cerf, 1969), pp. 1279–81.

100. Severus, *Ep.* 3.2. Cf. Paulinus' reference to Bassula's generosity: "socrum sanctam omni liberaliorem parente" (*Ep.* 5.6). Fontaine suggests that this generosity may have gone well beyond providing Severus with stenographers: "Qui sait même si ce n'est pas à sa 'générosité' que Sulpice a dû non seulement les tachygraphes d'élite qu'elle a mis à sa disposition, mais encore les ressources qui lui ont permis de faire vivre la communauté ascétique de Primuliacum?" (*Sulpice Sévère: Vie de Saint Martin*, 3: 1267–68).

101. Bassula seems to have promoted Severus' Martinian writings vigorously. Severus was perhaps only half joking when he charged his mother-in-law with sending spies to steal his private or unfinished manuscripts (*Ep.* 3.2–3).

102. Therasia sent Bassula a piece of the cross brought back from Palestine by Melania circa 403; Paulinus explains that the gift—to be enshrined in the new basilica at Primuliacum—is intended for both Severus and Bassula, who share a common religious calling and—evidently—a common interest in the building project at Primuliacum (*Ep.* 31.1).

103. Paulinus passes on greetings to Severus from his own partner Therasia and begs Severus to greet his "holy mother" in Paulinus' name (*Ep.* 5.19).

104. Paulinus, *Epp.* 31.1 and 32.1.

105. Paulinus criticizes Severus' courier on the basis of his worldly clothing, ruddy complexion, and unshaven head, accusing him of being no real monk (*Epp.* 17.1 and 22.1). In contrast, he praises the monk-courier Victor and takes the opportunity of giving Severus a long discourse on the advantages of simple diet and a shaven head (*Ep.* 23); one has the impression he suspects Severus of not taking these disciplines seriously enough. Cf. Paulinus' response to Severus' claim that

his own austerities fall short of Paulinus' and his ironic expression of concern that Paulinus has made himself so poor that he cannot afford to entertain visitors (*Ep.* 11.12–13). Regarding Paulinus' dietary recommendations, Peter Dreyer notes that "vegetarians in antiquity might have had fava beans (although the Pythagoreans banned them), lentils, chickpeas, of course, and various field peas, but beans as we now commonly know them—*Phaseolus vulgaris* in its many varieties—are New World plants and could not have been available. Conceivably, western Manichaeans and early Christian ascetics also had Mung and Urd beans to eat if these plants had by then reached the Near East and Europe from India. But absent *Phaseolus vulgaris* and other New World species (no potatoes, tomatoes, or sweet peppers), the diets of Severus and his ilk must have been austere indeed; malnutrition may have been widespread among them, one imagines—perhaps in part the cause of the pallor of the Manichaeans" (personal communication).

106. Paulinus outraged the traditional Gallo-Roman aristocracy (Ausonius, *Epp.* 27, 28, and 29, and Paulinus, *Ep.* 1.4–7) and provoked the envy of the clergy of Rome (Paulinus, *Ep.* 5.13). Martin was threatened with the label of Manichaeism because of his support for Priscillian and the Spanish ascetics (Severus, *Chron.* 2.50; *Dial.* 3.11–13). Afterwards, Martin determined to have no further dealings with other bishops (*Dial.* 3.13). Nevertheless, he continued to meet with opposition even within his own monastery and episcopal see. The monk and presbyter Brictio, who succeeded Martin as bishop of Tours, accused him of impurity on the basis of his years as a solider, and he further denied the legitimacy of the miracles and visions that constituted the basis of Martin's unusual authority (*Dial.* 3.15). As was perhaps also the case with the aristocratic Paulinus in Rome, the ill-defined and uncontrolled source of Martin's authority as ascetic and miracle-worker seems to have been perceived as a challenge to the more clearly defined official authority of his fellow bishops and clergy.

107. Severus, *Ep.* 1, *Dial.* 1.26.

108. See Van Andel, *Sulpicius Severus*, pp. 139–42.

109. Severus, *Vita* 27.

110. Severus, *Chron.* 2.51.

111. Severus, *Dial.* 1.26.

112. Ibid. 1.2.

113. Ibid. 1.12.

114. Ibid. 3.16, 18.

115. Jerome, *Ep.* 58.11; *Ep.* 61; *Ep.* 109; *Contra Vigilantium*.

116. Paulinus, *Ep.* 5.11.

117. This somewhat controversial position has been most recently and carefully argued by Stancliffe, *St. Martin*, pp. 297–311. Elizabeth Clark, who accepts Stancliffe's argument, suggests that Rufinus may have played a crucial role in turning Vigilantius against the ascetic position represented by men like Jerome, Paulinus, and Sulpicius Severus (*Origenist Controversy*, p. 36). Stefan Rebenich, who rejects the identification of the two Vigilantii (*Hieronymus und sein Kreis*, pp. 249–51), nevertheless addresses the question of the "conversion" of the Vigilantius who began as the client of the ascetic Paulinus and ended as the anti-ascetic controver-

sialist opposed by Jerome, suggesting the importance not of the eastern Origenist controversy but rather of the local Gallic situation (pp. 247–49, 258).

118. The exact location of the church in which Vigilantius served as presbyter is unknown, but it must have been in the vicinity of St. Bertrand-de-Comminges (in which diocese Vigilantius' native Calugirris was located) and Toulouse (home of the deacon Sisinnius, who delivered the letter of the presbyters Riparius and Desiderius along with the works of Vigilantius) (*Contra Vigilantium* 1, 3). Gennadius reports that the Gallic Vigilantius was head of the church of Barcelona (*De viris illustribus* 36); if Gennadius is right, he probably refers to a later period of Vigilantius' life, since Jerome clearly describes controversies taking place not in Spain but in Gaul.

119. Jerome, *Contra Vigilantium* 1.

120. Paulinus, *Ep.* 31.1.

121. Jerome, *Ep.* 109, *Contra Vigilantium* 4–9. It is tempting to see in the reference to the heavenly altar of Apoc. 6.9–11, embedded in a passage that also contains the striking image of the throne of God, an allusion to the episcopal cathedral and altar as earthly reflections of the heavenly archetype.

122. Jerome, *Contra Vigilantium* 10.

123. E.g., Paulinus, *Epp.* 1.1, 5.6, and 24.1–4.

124. Jerome, *Contra Vigilantium* 14.

125. Ibid. 15.

126. Ibid. 2.

127. Severus, *Vita*, pref.

128. Jerome, *Contra Vigilantium* 3.

129. Severus, *Dial.* 1.9.

130. Ibid. 2.8.

131. Ibid. 2.6–2.8.

132. Ibid. 2.12.

133. Ibid.

134. Stancliffe suggests that Jerome provides an indirect link between Severus' discussion of gender and his debate with Vigilantius. Severus attempts to placate an unfriendly Jerome through his explicit affirmation of Jerome's controversial criticism of free relations between male and female ascetics or male clergy and female ascetics; the context for Jerome's presumed coolness toward Severus is primarily the dispute over Origen between Jerome and Rufinus (the latter a friend of Paulinus)—and now also between Jerome and Vigilantius—and secondarily Jerome's reservations about the purity of a Gallic asceticism exemplified by a former solider (*St. Martin*, pp. 297–312). Stancliffe also points out that the laxer "traditional ascetics," or *continentes*, are the more immediate target of Severus' criticism of male-female relations (*St. Martin*, pp. 272–73, 311). I am here proposing still another audience for Severus' remarks regarding the separation of male and female ascetics: Vigilantius and his episcopal supporters. Severus' anti-ascetic opposition may well have constituted his *primary* intended audience for the discussion of gender.

135. It is not clear whether Vigilantius also used gender to symbolize the dis-

ordered state of the ascetic community. In *Contra Vigilantium* 9, the argument against vigils on the basis of sexual promiscuity seems more likely to have been introduced by Jerome.

136. Severus, *Dial.* 2.12.

137. Van Andel, *Sulpicius Severus*, pp. 55–116.

138. Stridon was apparently located near the western border of Dalmatia, within easy striking distance of Aquileia (Kelly, *Jerome*, pp. 3–5).

139. Jerome, *Ep.* 7, *Chron. an.* 374; Rufinus, *Apologia contra Hieronymum* 1.4; and Kelly, *Jerome*, pp. 31–33.

140. These include the deacon Julian, the subdeacon Niceas, the monk Chrysogonus, the elderly scholar Paul of Concordia, a group of virgins in Emona, the monk Antony of Emona, and the presbyter Heliodorus, to whom Jerome's *Epp.* 6, 8, 9, 10, 11, 13, and 14 are addressed respectively.

141. Kelly, *Jerome*, p. 33.

142. Ibid., pp. 38–79.

143. Jerome, *Liber contra Joannem Hierosolymitanum* 41. If Jerome's rhetoric can be trusted, he accepted ordination grudgingly, probably as a sign of support for Bishop Paulinus in his struggle against other Antiochene factions; see Kelly, *Jerome*, p. 58.

144. See now Stefan Rebenich's careful account of Jerome's Roman "network" (*Hieronymus und Sein Kreis*, pp. 141–80).

145. Note that by highlighting the significance of these early conflicts at Rome for Jerome's shift in attitude not only toward Priscillian but also toward broader issues of community, authority, and gender, I diverge somewhat from traditions of scholarship that would place more emphasis on the later Origenist controversy in explaining changes in Jerome's positions. Willy Schatz, focusing specifically on Jerome's depictions of Priscillian, locates the crucial moment of transition from a spiritual or charismatic model of authority to an institutional model of authority in Jerome's decision to support Theophilus rather than the "Origenist" monks of Egypt (*Studien*, pp. 224–28). Peter Brown, surveying Jerome's views of bodies and sexuality, links Jerome's changes in attitudes toward gender with his abandonment of Origen's highly spiritualized anthropology, which seems to have entailed equality of mature, well-educated minds, whether male or female (*Body and Society*, pp. 368–83).

146. That the writings attributed to "Ambrosiaster" reflect the viewpoint of the Roman clergy who opposed Jerome's teachings is persuasively argued by David G. Hunter in "*On the Sin of Adam and Eve*: A Little-Known Defense of Marriage and Childbearing by Ambrosiaster," *Harvard Theological Review* 82 (1989): 283–99; and "The Paradise of Patriarchy: Ambrosiaster on Woman as (Not) God's Image," *Journal of Theological Studies*, n.s., 43 (1992): 447–69.

147. In a letter to his friend Asella, Jerome highlights accusations of sexual immorality regarding his relations with Paula and likewise refers to rumors that he deceives by means of "Satanic arts" (*Ep.* 45.2). In the same letter, he goes on to report that he has been called *maleficus* and identifies himself defiantly as the ser-

vant of Christ, who was labeled *magus*, and the follower of the apostle who was called *seductor* (*Ep.* 45.5). Cf. Jerome, *Apologia* 3.21, and Kelly, *Jerome*, pp. 111–15. While Jerome does not explicitly acknowledge charges of Manichaeism, it is not unlikely that he would have been threatened with such a label at this point. In his *Letter to Eustochium*, he notes that many Roman Christians equate fasting and a pale and mournful demeanor with Manichaeism (*Ep.* 22.13); cf. his comment that some have attacked him on the basis of his appearance and manner (*Ep.* 45.2). Some years later, Jovinian in Rome accused Jerome of upholding Manichaean positions (Jerome, *Ep.* 48.2–3 and *Adv. Jov.* 1.3 and 5, and David Hunter, "Resistance to the Virginal Ideal," p. 50).

148. This letter was known to Severus, who refers to it approvingly in *Dial.* 1.8–9.

149. Jerome, *Ep.* 22.23.

150. Ibid. 17. Cf. Jerome's condoning of Asella's visits to the martyrs' shrines on the grounds that she maintained her privacy to such an extent that even when she appeared in public she was unnoticed (*Ep.* 24.4).

151. Jerome, *Ep.* 22.16–17, 23, 25–29.

152. Ibid. 5–6, 13–14; cf. ibid. 26, 27, and 29.

153. Ibid. 28.

154. Ibid. 38.

155. Ibid. 16.

156. Elizabeth Clark points out several instances of Jerome's use of familial language to describe relationships between ascetics: "He accepts Marcella's mother Albina as his own [*Ep.* 32.2]; he calls himself Blaesilla's 'father in the spirit, her guardian in affection' [*Ep.* 39.2]; all Christians are his children [*Ep.* 79.1]; and he urges Christian ascetics to view each other as foster-fathers, brothers, and so forth, depending on their age in relation to each other [*Ep.* 117.11]" (*Jerome, Chrysostom, and Friends: Essays and Translations* [New York: Edwin Mellen Press, 1979], pp. 54–55). Clark rightly highlights the radicality of language that establishes a "new" Christian family based on the dissolution of traditional family relationships. However, I am suggesting that such language can also be seen as less radical and more simply reflective of the private-sphere orientation of the Christian community within which Jerome operated in Rome. Aristocratic women's patronage of learned men as mentors or teachers was not an utter novelty (see, e.g., Peter Brown, "Pelagius and His Supporters," p. 97). The relationships between ascetic women and their male teachers appeared radical and shocking primarily when viewed through the lens of a publicly defined church.

157. Jerome, *Ep.* 45.2.

158. Cf. Jerome's negative contrast of the hustle and bustle of worldly Rome with the peace of the countryside, which is so conducive to the ascetic life; he recognizes one exception to this general rule in the *senatus matronarum*, or the private gatherings of ascetic Christian *women* in Rome (*Ep.* 43.3). But again, there is no place for *male* ascetics in the city.

159. Jerome, *Ep.* 22.34–36.

160. Kelly, *Jerome*, pp. 129–40.

161. Jerome, *Ep.* 108.20.

162. Kelly, *Jerome*, pp. 195–209.

163. See Jerome's translation of Epiphanius' letter to John (*Ep.* 51.1–2). On the other hand, Jerome took the side of Bishop Theophilus of Alexandria in his quarrel with the monks of Egypt.

164. Jerome, *Ep.* 130.17.

165. Here and elsewhere, Jerome conflates this text with Ephesians 4.4.

166. Jerome, *Ep.* 130.17.

167. Elizabeth Clark has not only highlighted the importance of the moral or ascetic hierarchy for Jerome but also demonstrated the remarkable persistence of Jerome's concern with this issue from his debate with Jovinian through his participation in the Origenist and Pelagian debates (*Origenist Controversy*, pp. 121–51, 221–27).

168. Jerome, *Ep.* 75.3.

169. Jerome, *Ep.* 120.10.

170. Jerome, *Commentarii in Isaiam* 17.64.4–5.

171. While Clark has persuasively demonstrated the continuity in Jerome's construction of the Origenist and Pelagian debates (*Origenist Controversy*, pp. 221–27), "Origenism" was in the late fourth century a heresy less easily personified than "Priscillianism." Origenism's eponymous "founder" was historically remoter, and the continued popularity of his exegetical works made his "heretical" identity more ambiguous; Evagrius Ponticus, also mentioned in Jerome's initial lineup of Pelagian forerunners in the letter to Ctesiphon (*Ep.* 133.3), might have been a convenient stand-in, and indeed he does stand at the center of Clark's own construction of "Origenism" (see pp. 50–84), but she points out that it was only very late in the Origenist controversy that Jerome seems to have "discovered" Evagrius (pp. 122, 146–47). In addition, Priscillian's western origins may have made him an appealing figure for the role of immediate "perfectionist" forerunner in a heretical Pelagian succession.

172. Jerome, *Ep.* 133.4.

173. Cf. Alberto Ferreiro's argument in "Sexual Depravity, Doctrinal Error, and Character Assassination in the Fourth Century: Jerome against the Priscillianists," *Studia Patristica* 28 (1993) 29–38, that the list is intended "to hurl a devastating blow against the Priscillianist sect" (p. 33) or "to develop a typological critique of Priscillian" (p. 37).

174. Jerome, *Ep.* 130.19.

175. Jerome, *Ep.* 52.

176. Jerome, e.g., *Ep.* 14.8.

177. As noted above, Willy Schatz argues that Jerome's decision to support Bishop Theophilus in the Egyptian disputes is closely linked with the shift in his attitude toward Priscillian as representative of a charismatic ascetic spirituality (*Studien*, pp. 224–28).

178. Jerome, *Ep.* 51.1–2.

179. Severus, *Dial.* 1.27.

180. Severus, *Vita* 25; *Dial.* 2.4 and 3.13.

181. Severus, *Dial.* 1.7.

182. Jerome's deep friendships with women have been widely celebrated in recent scholarship; see, e.g., Clark, *Jerome, Chrysostom, and Friends,* pp. 35–106, and Rosemary Rader, *Breaking Boundaries: Male/Female Friendship in Early Christian Communities* (New York: Paulist Press, 1983), pp. 99–110.

183. Jerome, *Ep.* 22.13.

184. Jerome, *Ep.* 48.2–3; *Adversus Jovinianum* 1.3 and 5.

CONCLUSIONS

1. Nachman Ben Yehuda, *Deviance and Moral Boundaries* (Chicago: University of Chicago Press, 1985), p. 20.

2. Jonathan Z. Smith, "Differential Equations: On Constructing the 'Other' " (Thirteenth Annual University Lecture in Religion, Arizona State University, 1992), p. 14.

SELECTED BIBLIOGRAPHY

ANCIENT SOURCES

For consistency and ease of access, I have used J. P. Migne's *Patrologia Latina* (hereafter *PL*) for the citations of ancient texts. In some cases I have also listed critical editions found in the *Corpus Scriptorum Ecclesiasticorum Latinorum* (*CSEL*), *Sources chrétiennes* (*SC*), or elsewhere. English translations (hereafter ET) have been cited when available in the Nicene and Post-Nicene Fathers series (hereafter NPNF) or elsewhere; all translations that appear in the course of this study are, however, my own.

Acta Concilii Caesaraugustani. *PL* 84 (1850), 315–18. Critical ed.: Felix Rodríguez, "Concilio I de Zaragoza: Texto crítico," in *Primero Concilio Caesaraugustano: MDC aniversario*, 9–25. Zaragoza, 1981.

Acta Concilii Toletani I. *PL* 84 (1850), 327–34. Critical ed. of *Exemplar professionum habitarum in concilio Toletano contra sectam Priscilliani aera ccccxxxviii* in Henry Chadwick, *Priscillian of Avila: The Occult and the Charismatic in the Early Church*, 234–39. Oxford: Clarendon Press, 1976.

Ambrose. *De fide*. *PL* 16 (1845), 523–698. Critical ed: O. Faller, *CSEL* 78 (1962). ET: H. De Romestin, NPNF, ser. 2, vol. 10 (1896), pp. 199–314.

———. *De spiritu sancto*. *PL* 16 (1845), 697–816. Critical ed.: O. Faller, *CSEL* 79 (1964). ET: H. De Romestin, NPNF, ser. 2, vol. 10 (1896), pp. 91–158.

———. *Epistulae*. *PL* 16 (1845), 875–1286. Critical ed.: O. Faller and M. Zelzer, *CSEL* 82, pts. 1–3 (1968–90). ET: M. M. Beyenka, *Saint Ambrose: Letters*. Fathers of the Church 26. New York: Fathers of the Church, 1954. Note that I have followed the *PL*'s traditional Maurist enumeration of Ambrose's letters.

Augustine. *Ad Consentium contra mendacium. PL* 40 (1845), 517–48. ET: H. Browne, NPNF, ser. 1, vol. 3 (1887), pp. 481–500.

———. *Ad Orosium contra Priscillianistas et Origenistas. PL* 42 (1845), 669–78.

———. *De haeresibus* 70. *PL* 42 (1845), 44.

Ausonius. *Commemoratio professorum Burdigalensium* V: *Attius Tiro Delphidus, rhetor. PL* 19 (1846), 853. ET: H. G. Evelyn White, *Ausonius*, 1: 105–7. Loeb Classical Library. London: W. Heinemann, 1919.

———. *Epistulae. PL* 19 (1846), 927–35. ET: H. G. Evelyn White, *Ausonius*, 2: 81–119. Loeb Classical Library. London: W. Heinemann, 1919. Note that I have followed White's numbering of Ausonius' letters, which diverges from that used in *PL*.

———. *Parentalia* 30. *PL* 19 (1846), 850. ET: H. G. Evelyn White, *Ausonius*, 1: 95. Loeb Classical Library. London: W. Heinemann, 1919.

Collectio Avellana. CSEL 35 (1895).

Consentius. *Epistulae* 11*, 12* *Ad Augustinum. CSEL* 88 (1981), 51–70, 70–80.

Filastrius. *Diversarum hereseon liber* 61, 84. *PL* 12 (1845), 1175–76, 1196–97.

Hydatius. *Chronicon. PL* 51 (1846), 870–890. Critical ed.: Alain Tranoy, *Hydace: Chronique. SC* 218–19. Paris: Éditions du Cerf, 1974.

Jerome. *Commentarii in Isaiam* 17.64. *PL* 24 (1845), 622–23.

———. *Commentarius in Amos* 1.3. *PL* 25 (1845), 1018.

———. *Contra Vigilantium. PL* 23 (1845), 353–68. ET: W. H. Fremantle, NPNF, ser. 2, vol. 6 (1893), pp. 417–23.

———. *De viris inlustribus* 121–23. *PL* 23 (1845), 750–51. ET: E. C. Richardson, NPNF, ser. 2, vol. 3 (1892), p. 383.

———. *Epistulae. PL* 22 (1845), 235–1182. ET: W. H. Fremantle, NPNF, ser. 2, vol. 6 (1893), pp. 1–295.

———. *Praefatio in Pentateuchum. PL* 28 (1845), 147–52.

Magnus Maximus. *Epistula ad Siricium papam. PL* 13 (1845), 589–92.

Orosius. *Commonitorium de errore Priscillianistarum et Origenistarum. CSEL* 18 (1889), 149–57. *PL* 31 (1846), 1211–16.

Pacatus. *Panegyricus Theodosio Augusto Dictus. PL* 13 (1845), 477–522. ET: C. E. V. Nixon, *Pacatus: Panegyric to the Emperor Theodosius.* Liverpool University Press, 1987.

Paulinus. *Epistolae. PL* 61 (1847), 153–420. ET: P. G. Walsh, *Letters of St. Paulinus of Nola.* Ancient Christian Writers 35–36. London: Longman's, Green, 1966.

Priscillian. *Canones Epistularum Pauli Apostoli. CSEL* 18 (1889), 107–47. *PL* suppl. 2B (1961), 1391–1413.

———. *Tractatus* 1–11. *CSEL* 18 (1889), 1–106. *PL* suppl. 2B (1961), 1413–83.

Prosper Aquitanus. *Chronicon. PL* 51 (1846), 535–606. Critical ed.: Theodore Mommsen, *Chronica Minora Saec. IV. V. VI. VII,* 1: 341–449. Berlin: Weidmann, 1892.

Sulpicius Severus. *Chronicorum libri duo. PL* 20 (1845), 95–160. ET: A. Roberts. NPNF, vol. 11 (1894), pp. 71–122.

———. *Dialogi*. PL 20 (1845), 183–222. ET: A. Roberts, NPNF, ser. 2, vol. 11 (1894), pp. 24–54.

———. *Epistulae* 1–3. PL 20 (1845), 175–84. ET: A. Roberts, NPNF, ser. 2, vol. 11 (1894), pp. 18–23.

———. *Vita Martini*. PL 20 (1845), 159–76. Critical ed.: Jacques Fontaine. *Sulpice Sévère: Vie de Saint Martin*. SC 133–35. Paris: Éditions du Cerf, 1967–69. ET: A. Roberts, NPNF, ser. 2, vol. 11 (1894), pp. 3–17.

MODERN STUDIES

Arias, Luis. "El priscilianismo en san Agustín." *Augustinus* 25 (1980): 71–82.

Babut, E.-Ch. *Priscillien et le priscillianisme*. Paris: Librairie Honoré Champion, 1909.

Barbero de Aguilera, Abilio. "El priscilianismo: ¿Herejía o movimiento social?" *Cuadernos de historia de España* 37–38 (1963): 5–41.

Bardy, Gustave. "Pèlerinages à Rome vers la fin du IVe siècle." *Analecta Bollandiana* 67 (1949): 224–35.

———. "Priscillien." *Dictionaire de théologie catholique* 13.1 (1950): 391–400.

———. "Vigilantius." *Dictionaire de théologie catholique* 15.2 (1950): 2992–94.

Benn, S. I., and Gauss, G. F. *Public and Private in Social Life*. New York: St. Martin's Press, 1983.

Ben Yehuda, Nachman. *Deviance and Moral Boundaries*. Chicago: University of Chicago Press, 1985.

Birley, A. R. "Magnus Maximus and the Persecution of Heresy." *Bulletin of the John Rylands University Library* 66 (1983–84): 13–43.

Blazquez Martínez, J. M. "Prisciliano: Estado de la cuestion." In *Prisciliano y el Priscilianismo*, 47–52. Oviedo: Cuadernos del norte, 1982.

———. "Prisciliano, introductor del ascetismo en Gallaecia." In *Primera reunión gallega de estudios clásicos*, 210–36. Santiago de Compostela: Secretariado de Publicaciones de la Universidad de Santiago, 1981.

———. "Prisciliano, introductor del ascetismo en Hispania." In *Primero Concilio Caesaraugustano: MDC aniversario*, 65–121. Zaragoza, 1981.

Booth, A. D. "Notes on Ausonius' *Professores*." *Phoenix* 32 (1978): 235–49.

Botte, D. B., O.S.B. "Confessor." *Archivum Latinitatis Medii Aevi* 16 (1942) 137–48.

Brown, Peter. "Aspects of the Christianization of the Roman Aristocracy." *Journal of Roman Studies* 51 (1961): 1–11.

———. *The Body and Society: Men, Women, and Sexual Renunciation in Early Christianity*. New York: Columbia University Press, 1988.

———. "Pelagius and His Supporters: Aims and Environment." *Journal of Theological Studies*, n.s., 19 (1968): 93–114.

———. *Power and Persuasion in Late Antiquity: Towards a Christian Empire*. Madison: University of Wisconsin Press, 1992.

———. "Sorcery, Demons, and the Rise of Christianity from Late Antiquity into the Middle Ages." In *Witchcraft Confessions and Accusations*, ed. Mary Douglas, 17–45. London: Tavistock Publications, 1970.

Burrus, Virginia. "Ascesis, Authority, and Text: *The Acts of the Council of Saragossa.*" *Semeia* 58 (1992): 95–108.

———. "Canonical References to Extra-Canonical 'Texts': Priscillian's Defense of the Apocrypha." *Society of Biblical Literature Seminar Papers*, 1990: 60–67.

———. "The Heretical Woman as Symbol in Alexander, Athanasius, Epiphanius, and Jerome." *Harvard Theological Review* 84 (1991): 229–48.

Castelli, Elizabeth. "Virginity and Its Meaning for Women's Sexuality in Early Christianity." *Journal of Feminist Studies in Religion* 2 (1986): 61–88.

Cavallera, Ferdinand. "Galla non gente sed nomine." *Bulletin de littérature ecclesiastique* 38 (1937): 186–90.

———. *Saint Jérôme: Sa vie et son oeuvre*. Louvain: "Specilegium Sacrum Lovaniense" Bureaux, 1922.

Chadwick, Henry. "The New Letters of St. Augustine." *Journal of Theological Studies*, n.s., 34 (1983): 425–52.

———. "Priscillien." *Dictionaire de spiritualité* 12.2 (1986): 2353–69.

———. *Priscillian of Avila: The Occult and the Charismatic in the Early Church*. Oxford: Clarendon Press, 1976.

Clark, Elizabeth A. *Ascetic Piety and Women's Faith: Essays on Late Ancient Christianity*. Lewiston, N.Y.: Edwin Mellen Press, 1986.

———. *Jerome, Chrysostom, and Friends: Essays and Translations*. Lewiston, N.Y.: Edwin Mellen Press, 1979.

———. *The Origenist Controversy: The Cultural Construction of an Early Christian Debate*. Princeton: Princeton University Press, 1992.

Cooper, Kate. "Insinuations of Womanly Influence: An Aspect of the Christianization of the Roman Aristocracy." *Journal of Roman Studies* 82 (1992): 150–64.

D'Alès, Adhémar, S.J. *Priscillien et l'Espagne chrétienne à la fin du IVe siècle*. Paris: Gabriel Beauchesne et ses Fils, 1936.

De Clercq, V. C. "Ossius of Cordova and the Origins of Priscillianism." *Studia Patristica* 1 (1957): 601–6.

Delmaire, Roland. "Contribution des nouvelles lettres de saint Augustin à la prosopographie du Bas-Empire Romain (*PLRE*)." In *Les Lettres de saint Augustin découvertes par Johannes Divjak*, pp. 83–86. Paris: Études augustiniennes, 1983.

Díaz y Díaz, Manuel C. "A propósito del Concilio de Zaragoza de 380 y su canon VI." In *Primero Concilio Caesaraugustano: MDC aniversario*, 225–35. Zaragoza, 1981.

———. "Consencio y los priscilianistas." In *Prisciliano y el Priscilianismo*, 71–76. Oviedo: Cuadernos del norte, 1982.

———. "L'Expansion du christianisme et les tensions épiscopales dans la Péninsule ibérique." *Miscellanea Historiae Ecclesiasticae* 6, Congrès de Varsovie 1 (1983): 84–94.

D'Izarnay, Raymond. "Marriage et consécration virginale au IVe siècle." *Vie spiri-tuelle*, suppl. 24 (1953): 92–118.

Dudden, F. Homes. *The Life and Times of St. Ambrose*. Oxford: Clarendon Press, 1935.

Duval, Yves-Marie. "Pélage est-il le censeur inconnu de l'Adversus Iovinianum a Rome en 393? ou: Du 'Portrait-Robot' de l'hérétique chez s. Jérôme." *Revue d'histoire ecclésiastique* 75 (1980): 524–57.

Elshtain, Jean Bethke. *Public Man, Private Woman: Women in Social and Political Thought*. Princeton: Princeton University Press, 1981.

Escribano Paño, María Victoria. "Sobre la pretendida condena nominal dictada por el Concilio de Caesaraugusta del año 380." In *Primero Concilio Caesarau-gustano: MDC aniversario*, 123–33. Zaragoza, 1981.

Faivre, Alexandre. *Naissance d'une hiérarchie: Les Premières Étapes du cursus clérical*. Paris: Éditions Beauchesne, 1977.

Fatas, Guillermo. "Caesaraugusta christiana." In *Primero Concilio Caesaraugustano: MDC aniversario*, 135–60. Zaragoza, 1981.

Ferreiro, Alberto. "Sexual Depravity, Doctrinal Error, and Character Assassination in the Fourth Century: Jerome against the Priscillianists." *Studia Patristica* 28 (1993): 29–38.

Fontaine, Jacques. "L'Affaire Priscillien ou l'ère des nouveaux Catilina: Observa-tions sur le 'sallustianisme' de Sulpice Sévère." In *Classica et Iberica: A Fest-schrift in Honor of the Rev. Joseph M.-F. Marique, S.J.*, ed. P. T. Brannan, S.J., 355–92. Worcester, Mass.: Institute for Early Christian Iberian Studies, 1975.

———. "El ascetismo, ¿manzana de discordia entre latifundistas y obispos en la Tarraconense?" In *Primero Concilio Caesaraugustano: MDC aniversario*, 201–6. Zaragoza, 1981.

———. "Panorama espiritual del occidente peninsular en los siglos IV° y V^o: Por una nueva problemática del priscilianismo." In *Primera reunión gallega de es-tudios clásicos*, 185–209. Santiago de Compostela: Secretariado de publica-tiones de la Universidad de Santiago, 1981.

———. "Société et culture chrétiennes sur l'aire circumpyrénéenne au siècle de Théodose." *Bulletin de littérature ecclésiastique* 75 (1974): 241–82.

———. "Valeurs antiques et valeurs chrétiennes dans la spiritualité des grands propriétaires terriens à la fin du IVe siècle occidental." In *Epektasis: Mélanges patristiques offerts au Cardinal Jean Daniélou*, ed. J. Fontaine and Ch. Kannen-giesser, 571–95. Beauchesne, 1972.

Frend, W. H. C. "The Divjak Letters: New Light on St. Augustine's Problems, 416–428." *Journal of Ecclesiastical History* 34 (1983): 497–512.

Funke, Hermann. "Majestäts- und Magieprozesse bei Ammianus Marcellinus." *Jahrbuch für Antike und Christentum* 10 (1967): 145–75.

García Iglesias, Luis. "Sobre el canon IV del Primer Concilio de Zaragoza." In *Pri-mero Concilio Caesaraugustano: MDC aniversario*, 189–99. Zaragoza, 1981.

García Moreno, Luis A. "España e el imperio en epoca teodosiana." In *Primero Concilio Caesaraugustano: MDC aniversario*, 27–63. Zaragoza, 1981.

Gaudemet, Jean. *L'Église dans l'Empire Romain (ive-ve siècles)*. Paris: Sirey, 1955.

Girardet, Klaus. "Trier 385: Der Prozess gegen die Priscillianer." *Chiron* 4 (1974): 577–608.

Gonzáles Blanco, Antonino. "El canon 7 del Concilio de Zaragoza (380) y sus implicationes sociales." In *Primero Concilio Caesaraugustano: MDC aniversario*, 237–53. Zaragoza, 1981.

Goosen, A. B. J. M. "Algunas observaciones sobre la neumatologia de Priciliano." In *Primera reunión gallega de estudios clásicos*, 237–42. Santiago de Compostela: Secretariado de Publicaciones de la Universidad de Santiago, 1981.

Gottlieb, Gunther. *Ambrosius von Mailand und Kaiser Gratian*. Göttingen: Vandenhoeck & Ruprecht, 1973.

Green, R. P. H. "Prosopographical Notes on the Family and Friends of Ausonius." *Bulletin of the Institute of Classical Studies* 25 (1978): 19–27.

Greffe, Marie Odile. "Etude sur le canon II du premier Concile." In *Primero Concilio Caesaraugustano: MDC aniversario*, 161–75. Zaragoza, 1981.

Gryson, Roger. "Dix ans de recherches sur les origines du célibat ecclésiastique." *Revue theologique de Louvain* 11 (1980): 157–85.

———. *Les Origines du célibat ecclésiastique du premier au septième siècle*. Gembloux: Éditions J. Duculot, 1970.

Hanson, R. P. C. *The Search for the Christian Doctrine of God: The Arian Controversy, 318–381*. Edinburgh: T. & T. Clark, 1988.

Hess, Hamilton. *The Canons of the Council of Sardica, A.D. 343*. Oxford: Clarendon Press, 1958.

Hickey, Anne Ewing. *Women of the Roman Aristocracy as Christian Monastics*. Ann Arbor, Mich.: UMI Research Press, 1987.

Henry, P. "Why Is Contemporary Scholarship So Enamored of Ancient Heretics?" *Studia Patristica* 17.1 (1982): 123–26.

Hilgenfeld, A. "Priscillianus und seine neuentdeckten Schriften," *Zeitschrift für wissenschaftliche Theologie* 35 (1892): 1–85.

Hoepffner, André. "Les Deux Procès du Pape Damase." *Revue des études anciennes* 50 (1948): 288–304.

Hopkins, M. K. "Social Mobility in the Later Roman Empire: The Evidence of Ausonius." *Bulletin of the Institute of Classical Studies, University of London* 25 (1978): 19–27.

Hunter, David G. "Ambrosiaster, Astral Fatalism and the Prehistory of the Pelagian Controversy." Paper delivered to the North American Patristics Society, Chicago, 1990.

———. *"On the Sin of Adam and Eve*: A Little-Known Defense of Marriage and Childbearing by Ambrosiaster." *Harvard Theological Review* 82 (1989): 283–99.

———. "The Paradise of Patriarchy: Ambrosiaster on Woman as (Not) God's Image." *Journal of Theological Studies*, n.s., 43 (1992): 447–69.

———. "Resistance to the Virginal Ideal in Late-Fourth-Century Rome: The Case of Jovinian." *Theological Studies* 48 (1987): 45–64.

Jones, A. H. M. *The Later Roman Empire: A Social, Economic, and Administrative Survey, 284–602.* Oxford: Basil Blackwell, 1964.

Kelly, J. N. D. *Jerome: His Life, Writings, and Controversies.* London: Duckworth, 1975.

Krautheimer, Richard. *Three Christian Capitals: Topography and Politics.* Berkeley and Los Angeles: University of California Press, 1983.

La Bonnardière, Anne-Marie. "Du nouveau sur le priscillianisme (Epist. 11*)." In *Les Lettres de saint Augustin découvertes par Johannes Divjak,* 205–14. Paris: Études augustiniennes, 1983.

Laeuchli, Samuel. *Power and Sexuality: The Emergence of Canon Law at the Synod of Elvira.* Philadelphia: Temple University Press, 1972.

Le Boulluec, Alain. *La Notion d'hérésie dans la littérature grecque IIe–IIIe siècles.* Paris: Études augustiniennes, 1985.

Lienhard, Joseph T. *Paulinus of Nola and Early Western Monasticism.* Cologne: Peter Hanstein Verlag, 1977.

Lieu, Samuel N. C. *Manichaeism in the Later Roman Empire and Medieval China: A Historical Survey.* Manchester: Manchester University Press, 1985.

Linaje, Antonio. "Prisciliano y los orígenes monásticos hispanos." In *Prisciliano y el Priscilianismo,* 88–99. Oviedo: Cuadernos del norte, 1982.

Lippold, Adolf. "Ursinus und Damasus." *Historia* 14 (1965): 105–28.

Lopez Pereira, José E. "Prisciliano de Avila y el Priscilianismo desde el siglo IV a nuestros días: Rutas bibliográficas." *Cuadernos Abulenses* 3 (1985): 13–77.

Lorenz, Rudolf. "Die Anfänge des abendländischen Mönchtums im 4. Jahrhundert." *Zeitschrift für Kirchengeschichte* 77 (1966): 1–61.

Maier, Harry O. "Private Space as the Social Context of Arianism in Ambrose's Milan." *Journal of Theological Studies,* n.s., 45 (1994): 72–93.

———. "Religious Dissent, Heresy and Households in Late Antiquity." *Vigiliae Christianae.* Forthcoming.

———. "The Topography of Heresy and Dissent in Late-Fourth-Century Rome." *Historia.* Forthcoming.

Markus, Robert. *The End of Ancient Christianity.* Cambridge: Cambridge University Press, 1990.

———. "The Problem of Self-Definition: From Sect to Church." In *Jewish and Christian Self-Definition,* ed. E. P. Sanders, 1: 1–15. London: SCM Press, 1980.

Martin, Josef. "Priscillianus oder Instantius?" *Historisches Jahrbuch* 47 (1927): 237–51.

Martínez Díez, Gonzalo. *La colección canónica hispana.* Madrid, 1966.

Mathisen, Ralph W. *Ecclesiastical Factionalism and Religious Controversy in Fifth-Century Gaul.* Washington, D.C.: Catholic University of America Press, 1989.

Matthews, John. *Western Aristocracies and the Imperial Court, A.D. 364–425.* Oxford: Clarendon Press, 1975.

McClure, Judith. "Handbooks against Heresy in the West, from the Late Fourth to the Late Sixth Centuries." *Journal of Theological Studies,* n.s., 30 (1979): 186–97.

Metz, René. *La Consécration des vierges dans l'église romaine.* Paris: Presses universitaires de France, 1954.

———. "La Consécration des vierges en Gaule, des origines à l'apparation des livres liturgiques." *Revue de droit canonique* 6 (1956): 321–39.

———. "Les Vierges chrétiennes en Gaule au IVe siècle." In *Saint Martin et son temps,* 109–32. Studia Anselmiana 46. Rome: Herder, 1961.

Miller, Patricia Cox. "The Blazing Body: Ascetic Desire in Jerome's Letter to Eustochium." *Journal of Early Christian Studies* 1 (1993): 21–45.

———. "Desert Asceticism and 'The Body from Nowhere.'" *Journal of Early Christian Studies* 2 (1994): 137–53.

———. "'Words With an Alien Voice': Gnostics, Scripture, and Canon." *Journal of the American Academy of Religion* 57 (1989): 459–83.

Moreaux, Madeleine. "Lecture de la Lettre 11* de Consentius à Augustin: Un Pastiche hagiographique?" In *Les Lettres de saint Augustin découvertes par Johannes Divjak,* 215–23. Paris: Études augustiniennes, 1983.

Morin, D. G. "Pro Instantio: Contre l'attribution à Priscillien des opuscula du manuscrit de Würzburg." *Revue bénédictine* 30 (1913): 153–73.

Nautin, Pierre. "Les Premières Relations d'Ambroise avec l'empereur Gratien: Le *De fide* (livres I et II)." In *Ambroise de Milan: XVIe Centenaire de son élection épiscopale,* ed. Yves-Marie Duval, 229–44. Paris: Études augustiniennes, 1974.

Pietri, Charles. *Roma Christiana.* Rome: École française, 1976.

Primera reunión gallega de estudios clásicos. Santiago de Compostela: Secretariado de publicationes de la Universidad de Santiago, 1981.

Primero Concilio Caesaraugustano: MDC aniversario. Zaragoza, 1981.

Prisciliano y el Priscilianismo. Oviedo: Cuadernos del norte, 1982.

Puech, A. "Les Origenes du Priscillianisme et l'orthodoxie de Priscillien." *Bulletin d'ancienne littérature et d'archéologie chrétiennes* 2 (1912): 81–95, 161–213.

Quillen, Carol E. "Consentius as a Reader of Augustine's Confessions." *Revue des études augustiniennes* 37 (1991): 87–109.

Rader, Rosemary. *Breaking Boundaries: Male/Female Friendship in Early Christian Communities.* New York: Paulist Press, 1983.

Ramos-Lissón, Domingo. "Estudio sobre el canon V del I Concilio de Caesaraugusta (380)." In *Primero Concilio Caesaraugustano: MDC aniversario,* 207–24. Zaragoza, 1981.

Ramos y Loscertales, José María. *Prisciliano: Gesta rerum.* Universidad de Salamanca, 1952.

Rebenich, Stefan. *Hieronymus und sein Kreis: Prosopographische und sozialgeschichtliche Untersuchungen.* Stuttgart: Franz Steiner Verlag, 1992.

Robles, Laureano. "San Agustín y la cuestión priscilianista sobre el origen del alma: Correspondencia con autores españoles." *Augustinus* 25 (1980): 51–69.

Rosaldo, Michelle Zimbalist. "Woman, Culture, and Society: A Theoretical Overview." In *Woman, Culture, and Society,* ed. Michelle Zimbalist Rosaldo and Louise Lamphere, 17–42. Stanford: Stanford University Press, 1974.

Rousseau, Philip. *Ascetics, Authority, and the Church in the Age of Jerome and Cassian.* Oxford: Oxford University Press, 1978.

Rousselle, Aline. "Quelques aspects politiques de l'affaire priscillianiste." *Revue des études anciennes* 83 (1981): 85–96.

Sáinz Rodríguez, Pedro. "Estado actual de la cuestión priscilianista." *Anuario de estudios medievales* 1 (1964): 653–57.

Santos Yanguas, Narciso. "Movimientos sociales en la España del Bajo Imperio." *Hispania* 40 (1980): 237–69.

Schatz, Willy. "Studien zur Geschichte und Vorstellungswelt des frühen abendländischen Mönchtums." Diss., Freiburg i. Br., 1957.

Sivan, Hagith. "Who Was Egeria? Piety and Pilgrimage in the Age of Gratian." *Harvard Theological Review* 81 (1988): 59–72.

Smith, Jonathan Z. "Differential Equations: On Constructing the 'Other.'" Thirteenth Annual University Lecture in Religion, Arizona State University, March 5, 1992.

Sotomayor, Manuel. "El canon 3 del Concilio de Zaragoza del 380." In *Primero Concilio Caesaraugustano: MDC aniversario,* 177–87. Zaragoza, 1981.

———. "Sobre el canon VIII del Concilio de Zaragoza del 380." In *Primero Concilio Caesaraugustano: MDC aniversario,* 255–71. Zaragoza, 1981.

Stancliffe, Claire. *St. Martin and His Hagiographer: History and Miracle in Sulpicius Severus.* Oxford: Clarendon Press, 1983.

Stockmeier, Peter. "Das Schwert im Dienste der Kirche: Zur Hinrichtung Priszillians in Trier." In *Festschrift für Alois Thomas,* 415–28. Trier: Selbstverlag des Bistumsarchivs, 1967.

Tranoy, Alain. "Contexto histórico del priscilianismo en Galicia en los siglos IV y V." In *Prisciliano y el priscilianismo,* 77–81. Oviedo: Cuadernos del norte, 1982.

———. *La Galice Romaine.* Paris: Diffusion de Boccard, 1981.

Trout, Dennis. "Secular Renunciation and Social Action: Paulinus of Nola and Late Roman Society." Diss., Duke University, 1989.

Van Andel, G. K. *The Christian Concept of History in the Chronicle of Sulpicius Severus.* Amsterdam: Adolf M. Hakkert, 1976.

Van Dam, Raymond. *Leadership and Community in Late Antique Gaul.* Berkeley and Los Angeles: University of California Press, 1985.

———. "'Sheep in Wolves' Clothing': The Letters of Consentius to Augustine." *Journal of Ecclesiastical History* 37 (1986): 515–35.

Vessey, Mark. "Ideas of Christian Writing in Late Roman Gaul." D. Phil. thesis, Oxford University, 1988.

Veyne, Paul, ed. *A History of Private Life,* vol. 1: *From Pagan Rome to Byzantium.* Trans. A. Goldhammer. Cambridge, Mass.: Harvard University Press, 1987.

Vollman, Benedikt. "Priscillianus." In *Paulys Realenzyklopädie der classischen Altertumswissenschaft,* suppl. 14, cols. 485–559. Munich, 1974.

———. *Studien zum Priszillianismus: Die Forschung, die Quellen, der fünfzehnte Brief Papst Leos des Grossen.* St. Ottilien: EOS Verlag der Erzabtei, 1965.

Wankenne, Jules. "Le Correspondance de Consentius avec saint Augustin." In *Les Lettres de saint Augustin découvertes par Johannes Divjak*, 225–42. Paris: Études augustiniennes, 1983.

Wiesen, David S. *St. Jerome as a Satirist: A Study in Christian Latin Thought and Letters*. Ithaca, N.Y.: Cornell University Press, 1964.

Williams, Daniel H. "Ambrose, Emperors and Homoians in Milan: The First Conflict over a Basilica." In *Arianism after Arius: Essays on the Development of the Fourth-Century Trinitarian Conflicts*, ed. Michel R. Barnes and Daniel H. Williams, 127–46. Edinburgh: T. R. T. Clark, 1993.

———. *Ambrose of Milan and the End of the Nicene-Arian Conflicts*. Oxford: Oxford University Press, forthcoming.

Yarbrough, Anne. "Christianization in the Fourth Century: The Example of Roman Women." *Church History* 45 (1976): 149–65.

INDEX

Compositor: G & S Typesetters, Inc.
Text: 10/13 Palatino
Display: Palatino
Printer: Thomson-Shore, Inc.
Binder: Thomson-Shore, Inc.